CAMBRIDGE STUDIES IN
ANGLO-SAXON ENGLAND

11

ARCHBISHOP THEODORE

CAMBRIDGE STUDIES IN
ANGLO-SAXON ENGLAND

GENERAL EDITORS

SIMON KEYNES

MICHAEL LAPIDGE

ASSISTANT EDITOR: ANDY ORCHARD

Editors' preface

Cambridge Studies in Anglo-Saxon England is a series of scholarly texts and monographs intended to advance our knowledge of all aspects of the field of Anglo-Saxon studies. The scope of the series, like that of *Anglo-Saxon England*, its periodical counterpart, embraces original scholarship in various disciplines: literary, historical, archaeological, philological, art historical, palaeographical, architectural, liturgical and numismatic. It is the intention of the editors to encourage the publication of original scholarship which advances our understanding of the field through interdisciplinary approaches.

Volumes published

ARCHBISHOP THEODORE

COMMEMORATIVE STUDIES ON HIS
LIFE AND INFLUENCE

EDITED BY

MICHAEL LAPIDGE

Elrington and Bosworth Professor of Anglo-Saxon
University of Cambridge

CAMBRIDGE
UNIVERSITY PRESS

Published by the Press Syndicate of the University of Cambridge
The Pitt Building, Trumpington Street, Cambridge CB2 1RP
40 West 20th Street, New York, NY 10011-4211, USA
10 Stamford Road, Oakleigh, Melbourne 3166, Australia

© Cambridge University Press 1995

First published 1995

Printed in Great Britain at the University Press, Cambridge

A catalogue record for this book is available from the British Library

Library of Congress cataloguing in publication data

Archbishop Theodore: Commemorative studies on his life and
influence / edited by Michael Lapidge.
p.   cm. – (Cambridge Studies in Anglo-Saxon England; 11)
Includes bibliographical references and index.
ISBN 0 521 48077 9 (hardback)
1. Theodore of Canterbury, Saint, 602–690.
2. Christian saints – England – Biography.
3. England – Church history – 449-1066.
I. Lapidge, Michael. II. Series.
BR754.T44A73   1995
270.2′092–dc20
[B] 94-23021 CIP

ISBN 0 521 48077 9 (hardback)

Contents

Contents

Preface

On 19 September 1990 fell the 1300th anniversary of the death of Theodore of Tarsus, archbishop of Canterbury (668–90). The years immediately preceding 1990 had seen the organization of scholarly conferences to celebrate the anniversaries of various other Anglo-Saxon churchmen – for example, Æthelwold, Cuthbert and Dunstan – but, with the exception of two commemorative lectures arranged by the Dean of Canterbury, the Very Reverend John Simpson, and delivered at Canterbury in September 1990 (by Sr Benedicta Ward and myself), the anniversary of Archbishop Theodore seemed destined to pass unnoticed by the scholarly world. Yet it seemed to myself and to several Cambridge colleagues that so important an anniversary should be commemorated in some way, even if the resources needed for mounting a full-scale conference were lacking. We decided instead to hold a small symposium dedicated to the life and works of Archbishop Theodore, at which a small group of invited speakers would have the opportunity to discuss matters relevant to Theodore, but at which (for logistical reasons) no audience other than the speakers themselves would be present. The symposium took place in Cambridge on 18–19 September 1990 and included the following members (in alphabetical order): Martin Brett, Sebastian Brock, Henry Chadwick, Thomas Charles-Edwards, David Dumville, Christopher Hohler, Simon Keynes, Michael Lapidge, Patrizia Lendinara, Richard Marsden, Patrick McGurk, Thomas Noble, J. D. Pheifer and Jane Stevenson. I should like to express my gratitude to the British Academy for a small grant which helped to defray the costs of transportation for speakers from overseas, to Christopher Brooke for intervening helpfully on our behalf at a crucial moment, and above all to David Dumville for unstinting help in organizing the symposium itself.

The articles contained in the present volume are largely the record of the proceedings of the symposium. It very quickly became clear from discussion at the symposium that a wholly new – indeed revolutionary – awareness was emerging of the role which Theodore had played in transmitting Greek learning to the Latin West, and in the establishment of higher education in Anglo-Saxon England. The foundations of this new awareness were twofold: the demonstration that the vast body of scholarship preserved in the so-called 'Leiden Family' of glossaries had its origin in the school of Theodore and Hadrian at Canterbury; and the imminent publication of the biblical commentaries to the Pentateuch and gospels which were similarly produced in that school. Together these previously untapped sources revealed an extraordinary range of learning in Greek and Latin patristic literature, as well as expertise in scholarly disciplines otherwise scarcely known in the Latin West at that time, such as Roman civil law, medicine, rhetoric and metrology, among others. Evaluation (and assimilation) of the information contained in these sources provided the opportunity for revaluation and fresh exploration of a number of related subjects which could now be seen to bear directly on our understanding of Theodore's legacy, and members of the symposium duly addressed these relevant subjects: thus the symposium included discussion of Theodore's possible Syriac background (Brock); his early training in Constantinople in light of seventh-century Byzantine culture (Lapidge); the imperial and ecclesiastical politics of seventh-century Rome (Noble), in particular the monothelete controversy (Chadwick); the importation of Mediterranean books into Theodore's England (Dumville); the impact of eastern liturgical practices in early Anglo-Saxon England (Hohler); and the known Latin works attributable to Theodore, such as his *Iudicia* (Charles-Edwards) and octosyllabic verse (Lapidge), which merited fresh consideration in light of Greek tradition. The immense task of sorting the impossibly tangled network of (largely unpublished) glossaries which constitute the 'Leiden Family' received fresh attention (Pheifer), which led in turn to a new estimation of the importance of the Canterbury school for our knowledge of the text of the Vulgate Bible (Marsden, McGurk) and the corpora of canon law (Brett) which were available in seventh-century England. Scholarly awareness of the exegetical method employed in the Canterbury biblical commentaries led to the exciting possibility that an unusual Latin exegetical text, the *Laterculus Malalianus*, could with great plausibility be attributed to the pen of Theodore himself (Stevenson).

The members of the symposium were, however, fully aware that this sudden explosion of new information concerning Archbishop Theodore was yet but a beginning, and that an immense amount of work remains (indeed has scarcely begun). No single scholar, or group of scholars, could hope to control the range of expertise demanded by Theodore's intellectual legacy, and in preparing the articles for publication – which has been a lengthy process, given the technical difficulties posed by much of the material – the members of the original symposium thought it appropriate to invite contributions from other scholars working in fields germane to our understanding of Theodore's career. Thus Guglielmo Cavallo, an outstanding authority on early Byzantine manuscripts and libraries, kindly agreed to contribute a discussion of the Mediterranean background to Theodore's early studies, and Carmela Vircillo Franklin, who has done pioneering work on the Latin hagiography of St Anastasius, undertook to reconsider the transmission of the Greek and Latin *passiones* of St Anastasius with the career of Theodore in mind; her reconsiderations, prompted by Jane Stevenson's analysis of the technique of translation seen in the *Laterculus Malalianus*, led to the wholly new hypothesis that Theodore was himself the author of the earliest Latin translation of the Greek *Passio S. Anastasii*.

It will be clear from the above summary that the study of Archbishop Theodore is moving on to a new plane, and that our scholarly perception of the achievements of seventh-century Canterbury will be wholly transformed. But it must be stressed that the story is still far from complete, and that an overall assessment of those achievements must await the outcome of various work in progress. Publication of Jane Stevenson's edition of the *Laterculus Malalianus* is imminent (in the series CSASE), as is Carmela Vircillo Franklin's edition of the Latin *Passio S. Anastasii*. In the present volume Joe Pheifer has mapped out the relationships between the most important members of the 'Leiden-Family' glossaries; but since nearly all of these glossaries are unpublished, a final assessment of the biblical scholarship of Theodore's Canterbury school must await their detailed analysis and publication. Various other texts relevant to Theodore's interests will merit fresh attention as well. New editions of the various redactions of Theodore's *Iudicia* would help to illuminate his knowledge of legislative literature (much of it in Greek), as Thomas Charles-Edwards has shown, and the implications of Martin Brett's study of Theodore's knowledge of canon law are that an edition of Cologne,

Dombibliothek, 213, would help to clarify the study of canon law in early England. A new edition and source-study of Bede's *Martyrologium* would provide new evidence for the Anglo-Saxons' knowledge of the cults of those unusual eastern saints to which Christopher Hohler has here drawn attention. The list of scholarly desiderata is a long one, therefore, and it may be many years before Theodore's impact on Anglo-Saxon England can be fully assessed. But enough is known, or has recently come to light, for us to affirm that the twenty-one years which this influential Greek scholar spent in England were one of the most extraordinary moments in the history of the English church and people. It will be a suitable commemoration if the present collection of essays serves to awaken further interest in his life and work.

MICHAEL LAPIDGE

Abbreviations

AB	*Analecta Bollandiana*
Acta SS	*Acta Sanctorum*, ed. J. Bolland *et al.* (Antwerp and Brussels, 1643–)
AH	*Analecta Hymnica Medii Aevi*, ed. C. Blume and G. M. Dreves, 55 vols. (Leipzig, 1886–1922)
AHR	*American Historical Review*
ASE	*Anglo-Saxon England*
ASNSL	*Archiv für das Studium der neueren Sprachen und Literaturen*
Bede, *HE*	Bede, *Historia ecclesiastica* (ed. B. Colgrave and R. A. B. Mynors, *Bede's Ecclesiastical History of the English People* (Oxford, 1969; rev. ed. 1992))
BHG	*Bibliotheca Hagiographica Graeca*, ed. F. Halkin, 3rd ed., 3 vols. (Brussels, 1957)
BHL	*Bibliotheca Hagiographica Latina*, ed. Bollandists, 2 vols. (Brussels, 1899–1901), with *Supplementum* by H. Fros (Brussels, 1986)
BHO	*Bibliotheca Hagiographica Orientalis*, ed. Bollandists (Brussels, 1910)
Biblical Commentaries, ed. Bischoff and Lapidge	*Biblical Commentaries from the Canterbury School of Theodore and Hadrian*, ed. B. Bischoff and M. Lapidge, CSASE 10 (Cambridge, 1994)
Bibliotheca Sanctorum	*Bibliotheca Sanctorum*, ed. E. Josi, A. Palazzini and A. Piolanti, 13 vols. (Rome, 1961–70)
BZ	*Byzantinische Zeitschrift*
CCSG	Corpus Christianorum Series Graeca (Turnhout)

CCSL	Corpus Christianorum Series Latina (Turnhout)
CGL	*Corpus Glossariorum Latinorum*, ed. G. Goetz, 7 vols. (Leipzig, 1888–1923)
CLA	E. A. Lowe, *Codices Latini Antiquiores*, 11 vols. and suppl. (Oxford, 1934–71; 2nd ed. of vol. II, 1972)
CLitLA	K. Gamber, *Codices Liturgici Latini Antiquiores*, 2nd ed. (Fribourg, 1968)
CMCS	*Cambridge Medieval Celtic Studies*
CPG	*Clavis Patrum Graecorum*, ed. M. Geerard *et al.*, 5 vols. (Turnhout, 1974–87)
CPL	*Clavis Patrum Latinorum*, ed. E. Dekkers and A. Gaar, 2nd ed. (Steenbrugge, 1961)
CSASE	Cambridge Studies in Anglo-Saxon England (Cambridge)
CSCO	Corpus Scriptorum Christianorum Orientalium (Louvain)
CSEL	Corpus Scriptorum Ecclesiasticorum Latinorum (Vienna)
DACL	*Dictionnaire d'archéologie chrétienne et de liturgie*, ed. F. Cabrol and H. Leclercq, 15 vols. in 30 (Paris, 1907–53)
EEMF	Early English Manuscripts in Facsimile (Copenhagen)
EvII	the second series of gospel glosses contained in Milan, Biblioteca Ambrosiana, M. 79 sup., ed. Bischoff and Lapidge, *Biblical Commentaries*, pp. 396–423
GCS	Die griechischen-christlichen Schriftsteller der ersten drei Jahrhunderte (Leipzig, 1897–1941; Berlin, 1954–)
HBS	Henry Bradshaw Society Publications
ICL	D. Schaller and E. Könsgen, *Initia Carminum Latinorum saeculo undecimo Antiquiorum* (Göttingen, 1977)
JTS	*Journal of Theological Studies*
LXX	the Septuagint translation of the Old Testament, ed. A. Rahlfs, *Septuaginta*, 2 vols. (Stuttgart, 1935)
Mansi, *Concilia*	*Sacrorum Conciliorum Nova et Amplissima Collectio*, ed. J. D. Mansi, 31 vols. (Florence, 1759–98)

MGH	Monumenta Germaniae Historica
Auct. Antiq.	Auctores Antiquissimi
Ep.	Epistolae (in quarto)
PLAC	Poetae Latini Aevi Carolini
SRG	Scriptores rerum Germanicarum
SRM	Scriptores rerum Merovingicarum
MS	*Mediaeval Studies*
ODB	*Oxford Dictionary of Byzantium*, ed. A. P. Kazhdan, 3 vols. (Oxford, 1991)
PentI	the first series of Pentateuch glosses contained in Milan, Biblioteca Ambrosiana, M. 79 sup., ed. Bischoff and Lapidge, *Biblical Commentaries*, pp. 298–385
PG	Patrologia Graeca, ed. J.-P. Migne, 162 vols. (Paris, 1857–66)
PL	Patrologia Latina, ed. J.-P. Migne, 221 vols. (Paris, 1844–64)
PO	Patrologia Orientalis, ed. R. Graffin, F. Nau *et al.* (Paris and Freiburg, 1907–66; Turnhout, 1968–)
RB	*Revue Bénédictine*
SettSpol	*Settimane di studio del Centro italiano di studi sull'alto medioevo* (Spoleto)
SM	*Studi medievali*
ZRG	*Zeitschrift der Savigny Stiftung für Rechtsgeschichte*, kanonistische Abteilung

1

The career of Archbishop Theodore

MICHAEL LAPIDGE

Until quite recently, our knowledge of the career of Archbishop Theodore has depended almost entirely on the information conveyed by Bede in his *Historia ecclesiastica*, which may be summarized as follows: Theodore died on 19 September 690, aged 88 (*HE* V.8), and hence was born in 602; according to Bede he was a native of Tarsus in Cilicia, was well instructed in secular and Christian literature both Greek and Latin (*HE* IV.1) and was latterly living as a monk in Rome when he came to the attention of Pope Vitalian (657–72), through the recommendation of Hadrian, then abbot of a monastery near Naples but subsequently to become Theodore's companion during his English appointment; and after being consecrated archbishop of Canterbury in Rome on 26 March 668, Theodore arrived in England a year later, on 27 May 669, then aged 67, to begin his twenty-two-year archbishopric, a period described by Bede as the happiest since the English first came to Britain.[1] From even this brief summary it is clear that, although Bede was well informed on the circumstances of Theodore's appointment, he knew virtually nothing about his previous career. However, the recent publication of the biblical commentaries which originated in Theodore's Canterbury school provides new information which makes possible a fresh understanding of the earlier phases of Theodore's career.[2]

---

[1] *HE* IV.1 (ed. Colgrave and Mynors, p. 334): 'neque umquam prorsus, ex quo Brittaniam petierunt Angli, feliciora fuere tempora'.

[2] For a reconstruction of Theodore's career in light of all evidence now available, see *Biblical Commentaries*, ed. Bischoff and Lapidge, pp. 5–81; the present essay represents an abbreviated version of that discussion, to which reference should be made on all points of bibliographical detail.

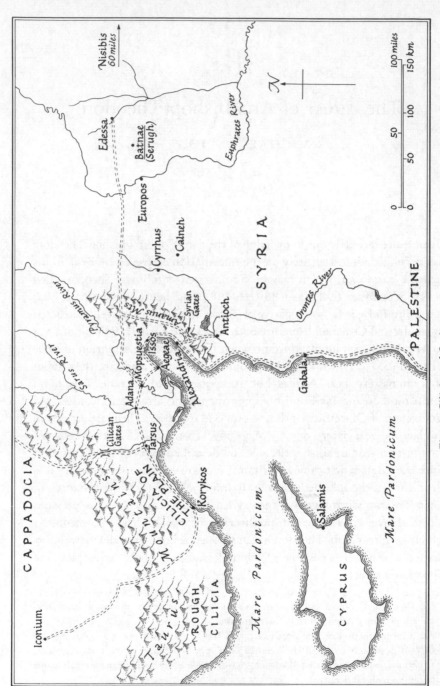

Fig. 1 Cilicia and Syria

TARSUS, ANTIOCH AND SYRIA

As we learn from Bede, Theodore was born in Tarsus in 602. Tarsus was one of the principal cities of the Greek-speaking diocese of Cilicia (see fig. 1),[3] but although it had achieved considerable prominence in imperial times, little is known of Tarsus in late antiquity, especially during the period from the fifth century to the seventh.[4] We know from various sources of building works undertaken there during the reigns of Justinian (527–65) and his successors;[5] but unfortunately Tarsus itself lies buried some twenty feet beneath the modern Turkish city of Gözlü Kule, and it is consequently impossible to form any visual impression of the Christian city.[6] More important for the present discussion is the fact that no late antique source mentions any school in Tarsus. A native of Tarsus interested in the pursuit of higher education would have been obliged to turn elsewhere, therefore. The largest city near to Tarsus was Antioch (modern Antakya), some 100 miles distant by way of the Roman coastal road which linked the two sites; and since Tarsus was part of the patriarchate of Antioch,[7] it is a reasonable assumption – though it cannot be proved outright – that the young Theodore will have gone to Antioch in pursuit of his scholarly career.

Antioch, by contrast with a provincial city such as Tarsus, was one of the great cities of the Roman empire.[8] We know something of its

---

[3] See F. Hild, *Tabula Imperii Byzantini V: Kilikien und Isaurien*, Österreichische Akademie der Wissenschaften, phil.-hist. Klasse, Denkschriften 215 (Vienna, 1990), 428–39.

[4] The fullest account is still that by V. Schulze, *Altchristliche Städte und Landschaften*, 3 vols. in 4 (Gütersloh, 1922–30) II.2, 266–90.

[5] See Hild, *Tabula Imperii Byzantini V*, pls. 378–80 (a bridge built by Justinian which is still standing).

[6] There were extensive excavations at Gözlü Kule during the 1930s (published as *Excavations at Gözlü Kule, Tarsus*, ed. H. Goldman, 3 vols. in 6 (Princeton, NJ, 1950–63)); but these were conducted at the periphery of the ancient city, and recovered nothing of relevance to Christian Tarsus.

[7] See R. Devreesse, *Le Patriarcat d'Antioche depuis la paix de l'église jusqu'à la conquête arabe* (Paris, 1945), pp. 151–3.

[8] The fullest account of Antioch is G. Downey, *A History of Antioch in Syria from Seleucus to the Arab Conquest* (Princeton, NJ, 1961); see also Schulze, *Altchristliche Städte* III (devoted entirely to Antioch).

appearance both from archaeological excavation[9] and from the detailed descriptions of a number of its natives, including Libanius and Ammianus Marcellinus in the fourth century, and John Malalas in the later sixth. Antioch's situation at the western gateway, as it were, of the network of trade routes which stretched inland to Syria and Persia and beyond to India and China, meant that it was always a large and wealthy city, and may have had a population of half a million in late antiquity. Antioch at that time was renowned above all for its schools. In the later fourth century the famous rhetor Libanius maintained a school in Antioch, and from the vast corpus of his correspondence we know of the activities and achievements of his numerous students.[10] These students included some who were Christian, and it is probable that Libanius taught two of the most important Christian exegetes of the patristic period, namely John Chrysostom (d. 407)[11] and Theodore of Mopsuestia (d. 428).[12] However, John and Theodore were both subsequently associated with the Antiochene school of Diodore, later bishop of Tarsus (d. *c.* 394).[13] In their biblical studies, Diodore and his followers practised a type of exegesis which is appropriately described as 'literal': in contrast with Alexandrine exegetes such as Origen, who were interested above all in extracting allegorical or symbolic meaning from the biblical text, the Antiochenes attempted to elucidate the exact sense of the text by repair to techniques which we would today describe as 'philological'.[14] That is to say, the Antiochene exegetical method lay in the careful comparison of variant versions of the transmitted biblical text (in Hebrew and Greek) and in consultation of relevant ancillary aids (such as ancient etymological lexica) and disciplines, such as

---

9 See *Antioch on the Orontes*, ed. G. W. Elderkin, R. Stillwell *et al.*, 5 vols. in 6 (Princeton, NJ, 1934–72). On the churches of Antioch, see (briefly) R. Krautheimer, *Early Christian and Byzantine Architecture*, 4th ed. rev. S. Curcic (Harmondsworth, 1986), pp. 75–8.

10 See P. Petit, *Les Etudiants de Libanius* (Paris, n.d. [1956?]), pp. 17–40 and *passim*, as well as D. S. Wallace-Hadrill, *Christian Antioch: a Study of Early Christian Thought in the East* (Cambridge, 1982).

11 A clear introduction to John Chrysostom is given by F. M. Young, *From Nicaea to Chalcedon. A Guide to the Literature and its Background* (London, 1983), pp. 143–59.

12 See esp. R. Devreesse, *Essai sur Théodore de Mopsueste*, Studi e testi 141 (Vatican City, 1948), and Young, *From Nicaea to Chalcedon*, pp. 199–213.

13 Young, *ibid.*, pp. 191–9.

14 On Antiochene exegesis, see the excellent study by C. Schäublin, *Untersuchungen zu Methode und Herkunft der antiochenischen Exegese*, Theophaneia 23 (Cologne and Bonn, 1974), and the brief discussion (with bibliography) in *Biblical Commentaries*, ed. Bischoff and Lapidge, pp. 243–5.

philosophy, rhetoric and medicine. This approach is seen not only in the surviving exegetical fragments of Diodore and the numerous biblical commentaries on both Testaments by Theodore of Mopsuestia, but also throughout the huge corpus of homiletic and exegetical writing of John Chrysostom. The same 'philological' approach is to be seen in later adherents of the Antiochene school, such as Theodoret of Cyrrhus (d. 466),[15] Severian of Gabala (d. *c.* 408)[16] and the scholarly layman who is known as Cosmas Indicopleustes.[17]

The first point relevant to our reconstruction of Theodore's early career is the fact that the Canterbury biblical commentaries are wholly Antiochene in orientation.[18] They reveal a persistent concern with explaining the literal sense of scripture: the nature of the flora, fauna, minerals and precious stones mentioned in the Bible; Hebrew customs; the topography of the Holy Land; the appurtenances of everyday life as described in the Bible. The Vulgate (Latin) text is frequently elucidated by reference to the earlier Septuagint (Greek) version. Problematic expressions in the biblical text are approached by frequent appeals to etymology, whether in Syriac, Greek or Latin. The ancillary disciplines of philosophy, rhetoric and medicine are often the sources of explanations. Furthermore, Antiochene exegetes are frequently cited as authorities for the interpretation of individual passages. John Chrysostom, for example, is cited by name seven times in the Canterbury biblical commentaries.[19] Cosmas Indicopleustes is quoted verbatim under the title *Christianus historiographus.*[20] Although they are not named, the writings of Theodoret of Cyrrhus and Severian of Gabala were very probably drawn upon in the Canterbury commentaries, as also, possibly, were writings of Theodore of Mopsuestia.[21] On the evidence of the Canterbury biblical commentaries, then, there can be no

---

[15] See Young, *From Nicaea to Chalcedon*, pp. 265–89, as well as G. W. Ashby, *Theodoret of Cyrrhus as Exegete of the Old Testament* (Grahamstown, 1972), pp. 17–55.

[16] See J. Zellinger, *Die Genesishomilien des Bischofs Severian von Gabala*, Alttestamentliche Abhandlungen 7.1 (Münster, 1916).

[17] See W. Wolska, *La Topographie chrétienne de Cosmas Indicopleustès: théologie et science au VIe siècle* (Paris, 1962), pp. 40–61, and Devreesse, *Essai sur Théodore de Mopsueste*, pp. 273–4.

[18] *Biblical Commentaries*, ed. Bischoff and Lapidge, pp. 245–9.

[19] PentI 28 and 44; Gn-Ex-EvIa 22; EvII 3, 41, 87 and 97. See discussion by Bischoff and Lapidge, *Biblical Commentaries*, pp. 214–16.

[20] PentI 91; see *Biblical Commentaries*, ed. Bischoff and Lapidge, pp. 208–11.

[21] *Ibid.*, pp. 222–4.

doubt that Archbishop Theodore was thoroughly trained in Antiochene exegesis. It is not possible to affirm that such training could have been received at Antioch and nowhere else, for the writings of the great Antiochene exegetes were known throughout the Greek world; furthermore, many of these writings were available in Syriac (see below, pp. 36–48). However, we should recall that Tarsus lay within the patriarchate of Antioch and that Antioch was the nearest large city to Tarsus. Although there was a distance of two centuries' time between the florescence of the Antiochene exegetical school in the late fourth and early fifth centuries, and the early seventh century, when the young Theodore was pursuing his biblical studies, there is nevertheless sufficient evidence to indicate that schools were still flourishing in Antioch in the late sixth and early seventh centuries: John Malalas (d. 578) composed his *Chronographia* there, probably in the 570s;[22] Evagrius Scholasticus (d. *c.* 594) composed his *Historia ecclesiastica* there in the 590s;[23] and in the early decades of the seventh century John of Antioch produced a world chronicle (based partly on that of John Malalas) which extended from Adam to AD 610.[24] There is no doubt, therefore, that there were active schools and scholars in Antioch during the period of Theodore's youth; and given the Antiochene orientation of the Canterbury biblical commentaries, it is a reasonable hypothesis that he received some part of his early training there.

At the time of Theodore's (presumed) sojourn in Antioch, Syria was a thoroughly bilingual country in which both Greek and Syriac were spoken.[25] Many of the church fathers mentioned in previous paragraphs were bilingual: Theodore of Mopsuestia and Theodoret of Cyrrhus were native speakers of Greek who knew Syriac,[26] for example, and John Malalas was a native speaker of Syriac who learned to write in Greek.[27] And just as there was a rich Syrian tradition of patristic literature in

[22] See B. Croke, 'Malalas, the Man and his Work', in *Studies in John Malalas*, ed. E. Jeffreys, B. Croke and R. Scott, Byzantina Australiensia 6 (Sydney, 1990), 1–25.

[23] P. Allen, *Evagrius Scholasticus the Church Historian*, Spicilegium Sacrum Lovaniense, Etudes et documents 41 (Louvain, 1981).

[24] H. Hunger, *Die hochsprachliche profane Literatur der Byzantiner*, 2 vols. (Munich, 1978) I, 326–8.

[25] See G. Haddad, *Aspects of Social Life in Antioch in the Hellenistic-Roman Period* (New York, n.d. [1952?]), pp. 104–21.

[26] For Theodore of Mopsuestia, see L. Pirot, *L'Oeuvre exégétique de Théodore de Mopsueste* (Rome, 1913), pp. 95–6; for Theodoret, see Young, *From Nicaea to Chalcedon*, p. 267.

[27] Croke, 'Malalas, the Man and his Work', p. 3.

Greek, so there was a rich tradition in Syriac, as Sebastian Brock demonstrates in a subsequent chapter (below, pp. 48–9). And whereas the focal point of Greek Christianity in Syria was Antioch, so that of Syriac Christianity was Edessa (modern Sanliurfa in southeastern Turkey), which lies on a fertile plain some 150 miles inland from Antioch, across the Euphrates river.[28] Like Antioch, Edessa was situated on important eastern trade routes; also like Antioch, it was a wealthy city full of lavish churches, which are known both from excavation and from written sources.[29] Many of the most important Syriac church fathers lived in Edessa. In particular, Ephrem the Syrian (d. 373), perhaps the greatest of all Syriac exegetes, spent much of his life in Edessa.[30] Although scholarly tradition at Edessa underwent various vicissitudes, it is clear that an important school still existed there in the time of Theodore's youth, for the renowned exegete Jacob of Edessa (*c.* 640–708) was active there in the generation after Theodore.[31] The point is worth stressing, for in the Canterbury biblical commentaries we find an observation concerning Edessa which appears to record a first-hand experience. With regard to the 'cucumbers and melons' mentioned in Numbers XI.5, the explanation is given that large cucumbers are called *pepones*, and that in the city of Edessa they grow so large that a camel could scarcely carry two of them:

cucumeres et pepones unum sunt, sed tamen cucumeres dicuntur pepones cum magni fiunt; ac saepe in uno pepone fiunt .xxx. librae. In Edissia ciuitate fiunt ut uix potest duo portare unus camelus.

(PentI 413)

cucumbers and melons are the same thing, but cucumbers are called *pepones* when they grow large, and often one *pepon* will weigh thirty pounds. In the city of Edessa they grow so large that a camel can scarcely carry two of them.[32]

---

[28] See, in general, J. B. Segal, *Edessa, 'the Blessed City'* (Oxford, 1970).

[29] See A. Baumstark, 'Vorjustinianische kirchliche Bauten in Edessa', *Oriens Christianus* 4 (1904), 164–83; A.-M. Schneider, 'Die Kathedrale von Edessa', *Oriens Christianus* 36 (1941), 161–7; and A. Palmer and L. Rodley, 'The Inauguration Anthem of Hagia Sophia in Edessa', *Byzantine and Modern Greek Studies* 12 (1989), 117–69.

[30] The best general introduction is S. Brock, *The Luminous Eye: the Spiritual World Vision of St Ephrem* (Rome, 1985); see also Brock's discussion below, p. 40.

[31] On scholarly tradition at Edessa, see E. R. Hayes, *L'Ecole d'Edesse* (Paris, 1930); on Jacob, see A. Baumstark, *Geschichte der syrischen Literatur* (Bonn, 1922), pp. 248–56, and discussion by Brock, below, p. 49.

[32] *Biblical Commentaries*, ed. Bischoff and Lapidge, pp. 374–5, with discussion at p. 35.

We can scarcely recover the reasons which led the young Theodore to
Edessa; but it is interesting to note that the Canterbury biblical commentaries reflect an awareness of Syriac language and patristic literature.[33] At
three points in the commentaries, biblical expressions are explained in
terms of Syriac etymology (EvII 58, 70 and 72). Ephrem the Syrian is once
quoted by name (EvII 29), even though the quotation in question comes
not directly from Ephrem's original Syriac but from an intermediary Greek
translation. On other occasions, however, explanations in the Canterbury
biblical commentaries have striking parallels in Ephrem's *Commentary on
Genesis*, a work which is not known to have been translated into Greek, as
well as in the Syriac *Book of the Cave of Treasures*, a sixth-century exegetical
compilation. None of this need imply that Theodore had a profound
knowledge of Syriac and its patristic literature; but in light of the
above-quoted remark concerning Edessa, there is no need to doubt that he
had travelled in Syria, both to Antioch and to Edessa, and that he had
some knowledge not only of Antiochene biblical exegesis but also perhaps
an awareness of Syriac exegesis. By carrying such awareness to far-distant
England, as he was later to do, Theodore imported perspectives and
experiences which were unique to the western world in the seventh
century.

THE PERSIAN AND ARAB INVASIONS OF SYRIA

The period of Theodore's study in Syria, which probably fell during the
second or third decade of the seventh century, witnessed violent political
upheavals which have left their mark on the Near East down to the present
day.[34] Theodore can scarcely have been unaffected by them. At this time
the Byzantine empire was under assault on all fronts, and the fact that
Emperor Heraclius (610–41) was occupied fully by Avar/Slav invaders to
the north enabled the Persian king Chosroes II (590–628) to invade Syria
and Palestine from the south-east. Because the Byzantine armies were
engaged on other frontiers, Chosroes II was able to conquer Antioch in 613

---

[33] See detailed discussion *ibid.*, pp. 233–40.

[34] For the historical circumstances, see in general G. Ostrogorsky, *Geschichte des byzantinischen Staates*, 3rd ed. (Munich, 1973), pp. 73–103; J. Herrin, *The Formation of
Christendom* (London, 1989), pp. 186–204 (the Persians) and 211–13 (Islam); and J. F.
Haldon, *Byzantium in the Seventh Century: the Transformation of a Culture* (Cambridge,
1990), pp. 41–53.

and Damascus and Jerusalem in the following year. (The conquest of
Jerusalem led to the capture of one of the most precious – and symbolic –
relics in Christendom, the remnant of the True Cross.) Shortly after taking
Antioch, the Persian armies moved northwards and occupied Tarsus;
further advance was only halted by the nearly impenetrable Taurus Mountains which loom behind Tarsus. At the time Tarsus was captured the
young Theodore will have been 11 or 12 years old. The Persian occupation
of Syria will therefore have formed the background to his childhood and
earliest phases of schooling. It is thus interesting to find several observations on Persian culture in the Canterbury biblical commentaries.[35] Thus
at one point (PentI 206) it is said that the Persians, like the Byzantine
Greeks, kept as eunuchs only those who had been castrated; elsewhere, at
PentI 303, the 'cups' (*scyphos*) mentioned in Exodus XXV.31 are explained
as being 'not round like a saucer, but long and angular; the Persians still
use them for drinking at feasts'. The Persians did indeed use long,
horn-shaped vessels similar to Greek *rhyta*;[36] but the interesting question
is when and in what circumstances the young Theodore was able to observe
Persians drinking at a feast.

The Persian assault on Syria and Palestine was a problem which *inter alia*
occupied Heraclius for many years; but after a series of exhausting campaigns, the Byzantine army finally defeated the Persians at Nineveh in 627
(Chosroes II was murdered by his own men the following year) and
succeeded in recovering the relic of the True Cross. But the long and
exhausting campaigns left the Byzantine army unprepared for the Arab
threat which arose suddenly in the 630s; by the same token, the Persian
occupation had left the cities of Syria and Palestine without the fully
functioning municipal defences which had been in effect before the Persian
invasions.[37] The Arabs had hitherto existed as a loose confederation of
nomadic tribes, whose characteristic form of warfare was the viking-style
raid; but through the efforts of Muhammad (d. 632) they began to achieve
some religious and political cohesion; and this, in combination with the
strategies of a succession of brilliant military commanders and the weakened defences of Syria and Palestine, allowed an astonishingly rapid

[35] See *Biblical Commentaries*, ed. Bischoff and Lapidge, pp. 8–9.
[36] *Ibid.*, p. 478 (comm. to PentI 303).
[37] See esp. W. E. Kaegi, *Byzantium and the Early Islamic Conquests* (Cambridge, 1992),
pp. 47–51 and *passim*, and F. M. Donner, *The Early Islamic Conquests* (Princeton, NJ,
1981), pp. 91–155.

expansion of Arab strength, with the result that the Arabs won a number of important battles there in 633–4. The decisive battle took place at Yarmuk (east of the Sea of Galilee) in 636, when the Arab armies comprehensively defeated a massive Byzantine army (said to have numbered 100,000).[38] Following this defeat, Heraclius in effect abandoned Syria and Palestine to the Arabs: Jerusalem and Antioch were taken in 637, and Tarsus soon after (once again the Taurus Mountains halted further advance towards Constantinople). One result of the Arab conquest was that large numbers of Palestinian and Syrian monks fled as refugees from the Arab occupation: to North Africa, to Sicily and Italy, and to Constantinople. Christian writers from these areas, such as Sophronius, the patriarch of Jerusalem who had the sad office of relinquishing that city to the Arabs, describe vividly the terror which the Arabs inspired among the natives of those regions.[39] The experience of such terror may possibly lie behind an acerbic comment in the Canterbury biblical commentaries concerning the 'Saracens' or Arabs:[40]

sic fuit genus eius Saracenis, numquam cum omnibus pacem habentes sed semper contra aliquos certantes.

(PentI 104)

thus Ishmael's race was that of the Saracens, a race which is never at peace with anyone, but is always at war with someone.

We later find Theodore at Constantinople (see below), and it is a reasonable assumption that he fled at this point as a refugee from the invading Arab armies – if he had not fled earlier from the Persian occupation of Syria. The absolute *terminus ante quem* for his departure from his homeland may reasonably be given as 637, when he will have been 35 years old.

---

[38] See the comprehensive discussion by Kaegi, *Byzantium and the Early Islamic Conquests*, pp. 112–46.

[39] See D. J. Constantelos, 'The Moslem Conquests of the Near East as revealed in the Greek Sources of the Seventh and Eighth Centuries', *Byzantion* 42 (1972), 325–57; on the reaction of Sophronius, see esp. p. 332.

[40] *Biblical Commentaries*, ed. Bischoff and Lapidge, pp. 324–5 (with comm. at pp. 455–6). On early western perceptions of the Arab expansion, see the excellent study by E. Rotter, *Abendland und Sarazenen. Das okzidentale Araberbild und seine Entstehung im Frühmittelalter* (Berlin and New York, 1986), who does not (understandably) make reference to the Canterbury biblical commentaries, the evidence of which predates all of the western sources discussed by him.

CONSTANTINOPLE

From the time of its foundation by the emperor Constantine in the early fourth century AD, Constantinople rivalled Rome in importance (see fig. 2).[41] This importance was reflected in the magnificence of its public building-works – palaces, basilicas, aqueducts, cisterns, walls, streets, fora – and its churches.[42] Some of its most magnificent churches – especially Hagia Sophia, H. Eirene and H. Sergius and Bacchus – were built in the sixth century by Justinian (527–65) and are still to be seen in present-day Istanbul.[43] A powerful impression of this magnificence can be gained by standing in the interior of Hagia Sophia, surely one of the most stunning sights in the world. Although modern Istanbul is a teeming, crowded city, it is still possible to form an impression of the layout of the city as it was in Justinian's day (and as it was in the early seventh century): from Hagia Sophia, for example, the principal artery of the city (then called the Mese, now the Divan Golu) leads towards the city walls and the Golden Gate. Following this artery one passes the great Basilica Cistern (now the Yerebatan Sarayi) on the left, and shortly thereafter Constantine's great 'Porphyry Column' (now called the Çemberlitas or 'Burnt Column') on the right.[44] This column originally stood in the centre of the Forum of Constantine, of which nothing remains but the column itself, but which must once have created an impression similar to that of Bernini's colonnades surrounding St Peter's square in Rome. The Porphyry Column originally had a shrine at its base,[45] and in this shrine were

---

[41] The principal study is G. Dagron, *Naissance d'une capitale: Constantinople et ses institutions de 330 à 451*, 2nd ed. (Paris, 1984); see also the more concise studies by R. Krautheimer, *Three Christian Capitals: Topography and Politics* (Berkeley, CA, 1983), pp. 41–67; and C. Mango, *Le Développement urbain de Constantinople (IVe-VIIe siècles)* (Paris, 1985), pp. 23–36.

[42] An excellent topographical guide is W. Müller-Wiener, *Bildlexikon zur Topographie Istanbuls* (Tübingen, 1977).

[43] The churches of Constantinople are discussed and illustrated by T. F. Mathews, *The Byzantine Churches of Istanbul: a Photographic Survey* (University Park, PA, 1976). For Hagia Sophia, see also R. Mainstone, *Hagia Sophia: Architecture, Structure and Liturgy of Justinian's Great Church* (London, 1988).

[44] The principal discussions of the 'Porphyry Column' are by Cyril Mango, *Studies on Constantinople* (Aldershot, 1993), nos. II (pp. 306–13) and III-IV.

[45] See the reconstruction of the shrine by Mango, *Studies on Constantinople*, no. IV.

11

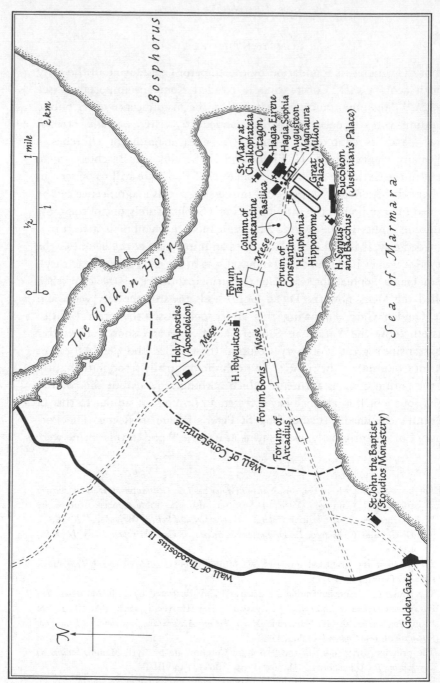

Fig. 2   Constantinople in the seventh century

housed various famous relics:[46] the axe with which Noah built the Ark, for example, or the 'Twelve Baskets' (*Dodekathronon*) in which the left-over loaves and fishes from Christ's miraculous feeding of the five thousand had been collected (the 'Twelve Baskets' were found near the Sea of Galilee by the dowager empress Helena, Constantine's mother, and subsequently brought to Constantinople). We know that Theodore, the future archbishop of Canterbury, had seen these 'Twelve Baskets' with his own eyes, for at one point the Canterbury biblical commentaries record the following information (with reference to John VI.13):[47]

.xii. cophinos de palmatis factos Theodorus se uidisse testatur in Constantinopolim ob memoriam obseruatos ab Elina regina portatos.

Theodore reports that in Constantinople he saw the Twelve Baskets woven from palm-branches and preserved as relics, which had been brought there by the empress Helena.

There is no doubt, then, that at some (early) point in his career Theodore had gone to Constantinople, perhaps as a refugee from Persian or Arab invasions of Syria and Cilicia. The young Theodore was a scholar; and we may reasonably assume that his principal interest in Constantinople was its schools and university. This is not to exclude the possibility that he had studied in other eastern Mediterranean schools as well; as Guglielmo Cavallo has shown (below, pp. 54–67), various other cities in Syria, Palestine and Egypt could have offered opportunities for advanced study to a promising young scholar such as Theodore. But we know that he travelled at some point to Constantinople, and it is therefore essential to explore the opportunities for advanced study which were available there in the early seventh century.

It is possible that Constantinople never rivalled other great schools of late antiquity, such as Antioch, Gaza, Beirut or Alexandria; however, the early seventh century witnessed a remarkable florescence of learning in the imperial city, inspired by the patronage of the emperor Heraclius (610–41) and Sergius, the patriarch of Constantinople (610–38).[48] In the

---

[46] See G. P. Majeska, *Russian Travellers to Constantinople in the Fourteenth and Fifteenth Centuries*, Dumbarton Oaks Studies 19 (Washington, DC, 1984), 260–3.

[47] *Biblical Commentaries*, ed. Bischoff and Lapidge, p. 549; on the 'Twelve Baskets', see pp. 550–2.

[48] See P. Lemerle, *Le Premier Humanisme byzantin: Notes et remarques sur l'enseignement et culture à Byzance des origines au Xe siècle* (Paris, 1971), pp. 77–88 (trans. H. Lindsay and A. Moffatt, *Byzantine Humanism: the First Phase* (Canberra, 1986), pp. 84–98).

early seventh century, perhaps *c.* 610, the young Theophylact Simocatta had come from Alexandria to Constantinople in pursuit of legal education; in the preface to his *Universal History*, he acknowledges (obliquely but unambiguously) the patronage of both Heraclius and Sergius.[49] In addition to his *Universal History*, Theophylact composed a number of writings of a rhetorical nature on philosophical and scientific subjects, which in sum are a useful index to the scholarly concerns then in vogue at Constantinople. At approximately the same time, the poet George of Pisidia (d. 631/4) composed a number of panegyrical poems in honour of Heraclius as well as a lengthy verse *Hexaemeron*, in which he shows familiarity with the technical vocabulary of scientific disciplines such as cosmology, medicine and astronomy.[50] George became patriarchal *referendarius* or nuncio to Heraclius; he will thus have enjoyed the patronage both of the emperor and Patriarch Sergius, and it is interesting that his prose encomium to St Anastasius Magundat – a saint who figured importantly in the career of Archbishop Theodore, as we shall see – contains an oblique but unambiguous reference to the patronage of Sergius.[51] Sergius was also the patron of the anonymous author of the so-called *Chronicon Paschale* (a world history extending to AD 630 and based largely on that of John Malalas), who was apparently a member of the clergy of Hagia Sophia, the seat of the patriarch of Constantinople.[52]

An important focal point of intellectual life in Constantinople was the university.[53] There is reliable evidence that Emperor Theodosius II (408–50) endowed a substantial number of chairs at the university in subjects such as grammar, rhetoric, law and philosophy; and although no

[49] *The History of Theophylact Simocatta*, trans. M. and M. Whitby (Oxford, 1986), p. 4; cf. discussion of Theophylact's career on pp. xiii-xvii.
[50] See the useful introduction by J. D. C. Frendo, 'The Poetic Achievement of George of Pisidia', in *Maistor. Classical, Byzantine and Renaissance Studies for Robert Browning*, ed. A. Moffatt (Canberra, 1984), pp. 159–87, as well as A. Pertusi, *Giorgio di Pisidia, Poemi: I. Panegirici epici* (Ettal, 1959), pp. 11–76.
[51] See A. Pertusi, 'L'encomio di S. Anastasio martire persiano', *AB* 76 (1958), 5–63, at 13–14.
[52] *Chronicon Paschale 284–628 AD*, trans. M. and M. Whitby (Liverpool, 1989); on the author, see pp. ix-xiv.
[53] See F. Fuchs, *Die höheren Schulen von Konstantinopel im Mittelalter*, Byzantinisches Archiv 8 (Leipzig and Berlin, 1926), 1–17; L. Bréhier, 'Notes sur l'histoire de l'enseignement supérieur à Constantinople', *Byzantion* 3 (1926), 73–94 and 4 (1927–8), 13–28; and esp. Lemerle, *Le Premier Humanisme byzantin*, pp. 63–88 (trans. Lindsay and Moffatt, pp. 66–98).

comparable evidence exists for the seventh century, there is no need to doubt that the university continued to function, at least during the reign of Heraclius. The university was located in the Imperial Basilica (opposite Hagia Sophia, on the Mese), and it was here that lectures took place; adjacent to the Basilica was the Octagon, where the university's professors were housed, and close nearby was the great public library.[54] From various sources we know that grammar and rhetoric continued to be taught at Constantinople through the Dark Ages. Instruction in jurisprudence was apparently available through the seventh century.[55] Medicine had long been taught at Constantinople (Aetius of Amida and Alexander of Tralles both taught there in the sixth century), and during the reign of Heraclius the distinguished physician Theophilus 'Protospatharius', who is known as the author of a work on the structure of the human body as well as of minor treatises on excrement and urine, gave lectures there on medical set-texts such as the *Aphorisms* of Hippocrates.[56] Finally, it is clear from Theophylact Simocatta that both Heraclius and Sergius were patrons of the study of philosophy (which embraced the natural sciences and medicine, as well as philosophy in the modern sense).[57]

The study of many of these disciplines is epitomized in the career of the great polymath, Stephen of Alexandria (*c.* 550–*c.* 635).[58] Although he was perhaps of Athenian origin, Stephen's early career was spent at Alexandria, in the school of Olympiodorus (d. 565) and his successors.[59]

---

[54] On the location of the university, see R. Janin, *Constantinople byzantine*, 2nd ed. (Paris, 1964), pp. 157–62; R. Guilland, *Etudes de topographie de Constantinople byzantine*, 2 vols. (Berlin and Amsterdam, 1969) II, 3–13; and P. Speck, *Die Kaiserliche Universität von Konstantinopel*, Byzantinisches Archiv 14 (Munich, 1974), 92–107 (who treats the evidence sceptically). On the library, see N. G. Wilson, 'The Libraries of the Byzantine World', *Greek, Roman and Byzantine Studies* 8 (1967), 53–80, at 54–62.

[55] Haldon, *Byzantium in the Seventh Century*, pp. 272–3.

[56] The complex evidence for the study of medicine in Constantinople is summarized in *Biblical Commentaries*, ed. Bischoff and Lapidge, pp. 249–55; see also J. M. Duffy, 'Byzantine Medicine in the Sixth and Seventh Centuries: Aspects of Teaching and Practice', *Dumbarton Oaks Papers* 38 (1984), 21–7.

[57] See *The History of Theophylact Simocatta*, trans. Whitby and Whitby, pp. 3–5.

[58] The indispensable study of Stephen is W. Wolska, 'Stéphanos d'Athènes et Stéphanos d'Alexandrie. Essai d'identification et de biographie', *Revue des études byzantines* 47 (1989), 5–89.

[59] On Stephen's contributions to philosophy, see R. Vancourt, *Les Derniers Commentateurs alexandrins d'Aristote: l'école d'Olympiodore, Etienne d'Alexandrie* (Lille, 1941), pp. 26–38,

The school was famous for its work on Plato and especially Aristotle, and we have from Stephen commentaries on various works of Aristotle, including *De interpretatione* and bk III of *De anima* (he is also known to have composed commentaries on several other works of Aristotle, but these have not been preserved). Stephen was also renowned for his work in the field of medicine: John Moschus and Sophronius, future patriarch of Jerusalem, heard Stephen lecturing on medicine in Alexandria sometime between 581 and 584,[60] and a number of *scholia* or lecture notes on various set-texts of the medical curriculum, such as Hippocrates's *Aphorisms* and Galen's *Therapeutica, ad Glauconem*, have been transmitted in his name.[61] He is also known to have written treatises on astronomy, astrology, horoscopy and ecclesiastical computus.[62] The essential point is that Heraclius invited Stephen from Alexandria to Constantinople soon after 610; in Constantinople he assumed the title 'universal teacher' (οἰκουμενικὸς διδάσκαλος) and gave lectures there, presumably at the university.[63] He was evidently teaching there some years later, for a dating clause in his treatise on astronomy refers to the 'ninth year of the reign of Heraclius' (= AD 619/620).[64] We do not know the precise year in which he died, but we know that Patriarch Sergius, who himself died in 638, expended considerable energy in trying to find a successor to Stephen.[65]

It is clear, therefore, that the vigorous patronage of Heraclius and Sergius attracted to Constantinople some of the finest scholars in the Greek-speaking world. Stephen and Theophylact Simocatta came there from Alexandria. Sophronius, future patriarch of Jerusalem, and his

and L. G. Westerink, *Anonymous Prolegomena to Platonic Philosophy* (Amsterdam, 1962), pp. xxiv–xxv.

[60] See Wolska, 'Stéphanos d'Athènes et Stéphanos d'Alexandrie', pp. 47–59.

[61] *Stephanus of Athens. Commentary on Hippocrates' Aphorisms*, ed. L. G. Westerink, 2 vols. (Berlin, 1985–92); *Stephanus the Philosopher. A Commentary on the Prognostica of Hippocrates*, ed. J. M. Duffy (Berlin, 1983); and *Apolloni Citiensis, Palladii, Theophili, Meletii, Damasci, Ioannis et aliorum Scholia in Hippocratem et Galenum*, ed. F. R. Dietz, 2 vols. (Königsberg, 1834) I, 51–232 (Stephen's *scholia* on Galen's *Therapeutica*).

[62] H. Usener, *De Stephano Alexandrino Commentatio altera* (Bonn, 1880) [Stephen's treatise on astronomy, including discussion of the method of calculating Easter]; *idem*, *Stephani Alexandrini quod fertur Opusculum apotelesmaticum* (Bonn, 1879–80) [Stephen's treatise on astrology and horoscopy].

[63] On the title, see Lemerle, *Le Premier Humanisme byzantin*, pp. 85–8 (trans. Lindsay and Moffatt, pp. 93–8).

[64] Usener, *De Stephano Alexandrino Commentatio altera*, pp. 6–7 and 15 (text).

[65] See *Biblical Commentaries*, ed. Bischoff and Lapidge, pp. 58–9.

companion John Moschus, came to Constantinople sometime in the early 630s, as has been conclusively demonstrated only recently.[66] It is possible, too, that Maximus the Confessor (*c.* 580–662), a protégé of Sophronius and one of the greatest Greek church fathers, studied at Constantinople before setting off for Africa and eventually for Rome.[67] There is, in short, abundant evidence for intellectual activity at Constantinople during the reign of Heraclius. Did Theodore of Tarsus, future archbishop of Canterbury, participate in this activity?

We have incontrovertible evidence of Theodore's presence in Constantinople, and the entire complexion of scholarly interests articulated in the Canterbury biblical commentaries implies that he did indeed study there.[68] We have noted that Theophylact Simocatta, who had been trained in rhetoric in Alexandria, went to Constantinople to study law and composed treatises on philosophy and natural science. The poems of George of Pisidia reveal knowledge of philosophy, astronomy and medicine. The anonymous author of the *Chronicon Paschale* was expert in ecclesiastical computus (as was Maximus the Confessor, who also had considerable familiarity with philosophy and medicine). Stephen of Alexandria was expert in philosophy, medicine, ecclesiastical computus, astronomy, astrology, horoscopy and medicine. Theodore of Tarsus shared with these men this community of interests. His English pupil Aldhelm states in a letter to Abbot Hadrian that he had studied Roman civil law at Theodore's school at Canterbury,[69] and both Theodore's *Iudicia* and the Canterbury biblical commentaries show expertise in the legal terminology used in the Justinianic *Corpus iuris ciuilis*, a fact which can best be explained by supposing that Theodore received some training in jurisprudence at Constantinople.[70] To judge from the evidence of the Canter-

---

[66] By E. Follieri, 'Dove e quando morì Giovanni Mosco?', *Rivista di studi bizantini e neoellenici* ns 25 (1988), 3–39.

[67] His sojourn at Constantinople depends on the evidence of the Greek life of Maximus (*BHG*, no. 1234), and is contradicted by that of a recently discovered Syriac life (S. Brock, 'An Early Syriac Life of Maximus the Confessor', *AB* 91 (1973), 299–346). Opinions vary on the reliability of the Greek life for the earliest phases of Maximus's life: see below, pp. 50 and 91, n. 9.

[68] The evidence is set out in *Biblical Commentaries*, ed. Bischoff and Lapidge, pp. 60–4.

[69] *Aldhelmi Opera*, ed. R. Ehwald, MGH, Auct. Antiq. 15 (Berlin, 1919), 476 (*Epist.* i); trans. M. Lapidge and M. Herren, *Aldhelm: the Prose Works* (Cambridge, 1979), p. 152.

[70] See *Biblical Commentaries*, ed. Bischoff and Lapidge, p. 61.

bury biblical commentaries (as well as that of the 'Leiden-Family glossaries', on which see below), Theodore was familiar with Greek rhetorical terminology, which once again implies some training in that subject. Bede reports (*HE* IV.2) that Theodore gave instruction in astronomy and ecclesiastical computus at Canterbury; and Aldhelm, who (unlike Bede) had studied there, confirms the report and adds that he had also acquired some knowledge of astrology (*astrologicae artis peritia*) and the use of the horoscope (*perplexa oroscopi computatio*).[71] Stephen of Alexandria had expertise in – and had published treatises on – all these subjects. An even closer link between Stephen and Theodore is demonstrated by their knowledge of Greek medicine.[72] Stephen evidently lectured on the introductory texts of the medical curriculum, such as the *Aphorisms* and *Prognostica* of Hippocrates, and the *Therapeutica, ad Glauconem* of Galen, for we have in his name *scholia* or lecture notes on those texts, as we have seen. It is a reasonable assumption that Theodore attended such lectures, for the Canterbury biblical commentaries contain extended discussion of the various kinds of fever (EvII 15), a subject treated in Galen's *Therapeutica* and explained in detail in Stephen's *scholia* on that work. A discussion of lunacy in EvII 43, in which the brain is said to increase and diminish with the waxing and waning of the moon, has a precise parallel in Stephen's *scholia* on the *Prognostica* of Hippocrates, but not (as far as I have been able to discover) in any other Greek medical source. Finally, the Canterbury biblical commentaries show familiarity with the technical vocabulary of Greek philosophy.[73] For example, in discussing the creation of the world in the early chapters of Genesis, the Canterbury commentaries several times render the Latin word *firmamentum* ('firmament') by the Greek word *aplanes* (ἀπλανής), a cosmological term used by Plato and Aristotle, rather than by the word *stereoma* (στερέωμα), which is used in the Septuagint and by virtually all Greek church fathers (PentI 17, 26 and 27). At another point (PentI 16) the commentaries give a detailed exposition of the eight *accessus* or διδασκαλικά according to which philosophical texts were to be analysed, a method of analysis which originated in the Alexandrian school of Olympiodorus, but subsequently penetrated many genres of Greek literature. They are applied, for

---

[71] *Aldhelmi Opera*, ed. Ehwald, p. 476 (*Epist*. i); trans. Lapidge and Herren, *Aldhelm: the Prose Works*, p. 152.

[72] *Biblical Commentaries*, ed. Bischoff and Lapidge, pp. 253–5.

[73] *Ibid*., pp. 63 and 255–9.

example, by Stephen of Alexandria in his *scholia* on the medical writings of Hippocrates and Galen. In short, the familiarity with all these subjects revealed in the Canterbury biblical commentaries indicates convincingly that the young Theodore took advantage of his stay in Constantinople to pursue his studies in the subjects which were then particularly in vogue. It is even possible that he attended the lectures of Stephen of Alexandria, or that he knew personally Theophylact Simocatta, George of Pisidia and the other scholars (such as the anonymous author of the *Chronicon Paschale*) who were then in Constantinople; but such suggestions take us into the realm of conjecture.

ROME

The next documented stage in Theodore's career took place in Rome. We do not know why or when he went to Rome. Our principal information concerning his Roman sojourn derives from Bede (*HE* IV.1), who notes simply that he was living in Rome as a monk (*ipso tempore Romae monachus*) when he came to the attention of Pope Vitalian, probably in late 667. Bede adds that Theodore was tonsured, 'like St Paul, in the manner of oriental monks', which apparently means that his head was totally shaved.[74] Before he could be consecrated, Theodore had to let his hair grow out, so that he could be properly tonsured in the western, 'Petrine', manner, with the hair in the shape of a crown. The important point, however, is that Theodore was living in Rome in the 660s in the manner of an oriental monk. The clear implication is that he was a member of one of the well-attested communities of oriental monks then present in Rome. It is appropriate to attempt to identify the community in question.

From various written sources we know of four such communities of oriental monks in seventh-century Rome:[75] a monastery of Armenian monks known as *Renatus* (location unknown); one of Nestorian (that is,

---

[74] *Ibid.*, p. 65 and n. 285.

[75] The indispensable study of these communities is J.-M. Sansterre, *Les Moines grecs et orientaux à Rome aux époques byzantine et carolingienne (milieu du VIe s. – fin du IXe s.)*, 2 vols., Académie Royale de Belgique, Mémoires de la classe des lettres, Collection in octavo 2nd ser. 86 (Brussels, 1983); but see also F. Antonelli, 'I primi monasteri di monaci orientali in Roma', *Rivista di archeologia cristiana* 5 (1928), 105–21, and A. Michel, 'Die griechischen Klostersiedlungen zu Rom bis zur Mitte des 11. Jahrhunderts', *Ostkirchliche Studien* 1 (1952), 32–45.

the 'Church of the East') monks known as *Boetiana* (location unknown); one apparently housing Palestinian monks known as St Saba, named after the fifth-century founder of one of the great Palestinian monasteries in the vicinity of Jerusalem and partially preserved in the present church of S. Saba on the Aventine; and finally, a community of Cilician monks housed outside the city walls to the south of Rome at a site known as *ad aquas Salvias*, but better known as the monastery of St Anastasius, in honour of Anastasius Magundat who was martyred by the Persians in 628, and who was the community's patron saint.

Of these four possibilities, it is unlikely that our Theodore belonged to a community of either Armenian or Nestorian monks. The community of Palestinian monks at St Saba cannot be ruled out entirely, in view of Theodore's possible links with Sophronius and Maximus the Confessor (see below). But the likeliest possibility is the community of Cilician monks located *ad aquas Salvias*.[76] Theodore himself was a Cilician by origin, as Bede tells us. The possibility would seem to be confirmed by the fact that the *Passio S. Anastasii* had been transmitted to England by the late seventh century, since Bede himself produced a revision of this work which, in his opinion, had been badly translated from the Greek ('librum uitae et passionis sancti Anastasii male de Greco translatum'),[77] and Theodore would seem an obvious agent of transmission, either of the Greek original or of the poor Latin translation which Bede subsequently undertook to revise. Building on this hypothesis, Carmela Vircillo Franklin has assembled various evidence to show that it may have been Theodore himself who produced the first Latin translation of the Greek text, probably in the form of a literal, interlinear gloss on it (see below, pp. 191–203). This suggestion helps to explain Bede's severe opinion of the Latin translation (one wonders whether he would have tempered his remarks had he realized that the probable author of the Latin translation was Archbishop Theodore, whom he venerated unreservedly). The important point, however, is that Theodore's involvement with the *Passio S.*

---

[76] On the monastery *ad aquas Salvias*, see G. Ferrari, *Early Roman Monasteries* (Vatican City, 1957), pp. 33–48; U. Broccoli, *L'abbazia delle Tre Fontane. Fasi paleocristiane e altomedievali del complesso 'ad aquas Salvias'* (Rome, 1980); and Sansterre, *Les Moines grecs et orientaux* I, 13–17.

[77] *HE* V.24 (ed. Colgrave and Mynors, p. 568); see C. V. Franklin and P. Meyvaert, 'Has Bede's Version of the *Passio S. Anastasii* come down to us in *BHL* 408?', *AB* 100 (1982), 373–400.

Anastasii provides one further link between him and the community of Cilician monks *ad aquas Salvias*.

The communities of oriental monks at Rome in the 640s did not simply pass their time in peaceful meditation; rather, they become deeply embroiled in one of the most violent doctrinal controversies which ever shook the Christian church, namely the monothelete controversy.[78] For centuries dissension had been mounting over the question of Christ's 'nature' (φύσις): whether, in simple terms, He was of one nature (divine), a view held by so-called monophysites, or two (divine and human). It proved impossible to reconcile the opposing points of view, and because religious dissension came to have serious political consequences, Emperor Heraclius and Patriarch Sergius determined to resolve the conflict by promulgating an authoritative opinion to the effect that there was in Christ one energy and one will (they thus attempted to shift discussion away from discussion of Christ's 'nature'). This imperial doctrine is known as monotheletism (from μόνος, 'one', and θέλειν, 'to will'). The doctrine seemed to find favour at first, but a powerful opponent soon came forward in the person of Sophronius, patriarch of Jerusalem (634–8). Sophronius amassed a dossier of some 600 patristic quotations which were claimed to refute the imperial, monothelete doctrine. Sophronius died in 638, but the opposition was carried on by Maximus the Confessor, one of the most able theologians of the Greek church. The forum of the opposition shifted from Palestine to Rome, principally because of the upheavals caused by the Arab invasions of Palestine and Syria, but also because the dyothelete (or: anti-monothelete) party found a sympathetic supporter in Pope Theodore (642–9), who was himself from Jerusalem. In the meantime both Heraclius and Sergius had died, but the subsequent emperor, Constans II (641–68), determined to put an end to dyothelete opposition by issuing in 648 a document called the *Typos*, which in effect outlawed opposition to the imperial doctrine of monotheletism. Pope Theodore died early in 649, but his successor, Martin I (649–55), convened a great council at the Lateran Palace in Rome in October 649, for the purpose of

---

[78] The bibliography on monotheletism is vast; for general orientation, see Herrin, *The Formation of Christendom*, pp. 206–19 and 250–9, and Haldon, *Byzantium in the Seventh Century*, pp. 56–9, as well as J. L. van Dieten, *Geschichte der Patriarchen von Sergios I. bis Johannes VI. (610–715)* (Amsterdam, 1972), pp. 179–218, and Sansterre, *Les Moines grecs et orientaux* I, 115–17.

reviewing comprehensively the imperial, monothelete doctrine. This Lateran Council was attended by 105 (mostly Italian) bishops, and their deliberations issued in a formal condemnation of monotheletism. In drawing up the *acta* or proceedings of the Lateran Council, the pope and his secretariat relied heavily on the advice and learning of the communities of oriental monks then living in Rome, and particularly on Maximus the Confessor himself.[79] The published *acta*[80] of the council contain a list of names of the scholars who participated in this way, and the list includes near its beginning the name of George, abbot of the monastery of Cilicians (St Anastasius *ad aquas Salvias*), together with those of abbots of other monasteries of oriental monks in Rome. Then follow names of individual scholars who served as advisors, including *Maximus monachus*, almost certainly identifiable with Maximus the Confessor. Now on the assumption that Theodore, future archbishop of Canterbury, was a member of the community of Cilician monks in Rome, he can hardly have been unaware of the proceedings of the Lateran Council. On the contrary, given his immense learning in Greek patristic sources – as it is known to us from the Canterbury biblical commentaries – he will have proved a very useful resource in these doctrinal matters. It is interesting to remark, therefore, that the list of signatories appended to the *acta* of the Lateran Council includes the name *Theodorus monachus*, immediately after the abbots and priests but preceding a list of deacons.[81] The position in the list probably implies that this Theodore played an important part in the proceedings. Could *Theodorus monachus* be identical with our Theodore, the future archbishop of Canterbury?

The Greek name 'Theodore' is of course a common one, but there is one piece of evidence which helps to confirm the identity. In the late 670s, when the monothelete controversy had been seething unresolved for over twenty years, an attempt at reconciliation was initiated by the emperor

---

[79] The role of Maximus has been established conclusively by R. Riedinger, 'Die Lateransynode von 649 und Maximos der Bekenner', in *Maximus Confessor. Actes du Symposium pour Maxime le Confesseur (Fribourg, 2–5 septembre 1980)*, ed. F. Heinzer and C. Schönborn, Paradosis 27 (Fribourg, 1982), 111–21, and *idem*, 'Die Lateransynode von 649. Ein Werk der Byzantiner um Maximos Homologetes', *Byzantion* 13 (1985), 519–34.

[80] *Concilium Lateranense a. 649 celebratum*, Acta Conciliorum Oecumenicorum 2nd ser. 1 (Berlin, 1984).

[81] *Ibid.*, p. 57 (*Theodorus monachus* occurs as no. 11 in the list).

Constantine IV.[82] Pope Agatho (678–81) responded positively to the imperial initiative by seeking the views of all western churches under his jurisdiction. A synod was held at the Lateran Palace at Easter in 680 in which all these views were canvassed (including those from England as affirmed by the synod of Hatfield in 679); following this Lateran synod Pope Agatho wrote to the emperor setting out the western position. He began by explaining that the theological issues at stake were immensely complex, and that their elucidation would require a thinker of correspondingly great subtlety and learning. Agatho went on to explain that there was within his church only one man with understanding of these complex matters, namely Archbishop Theodore: 'We were hoping, therefore, that Theodore, our co-servant and co-bishop, the philosopher and archbishop of Great Britain, would join our enterprise, along with certain others who remain there up to the present day'.[83] The only explanation of this extraordinary statement is that it was still remembered in papal circles in the late 670s that Theodore, by then archbishop of Canterbury, had many years previously been involved in drafting the *acta* of the Lateran Council of 649; and since all the others who had had similar involvement had died in the meantime, Theodore was the only Greek theologian still living who had first-hand knowledge of the original issues.[84]

There is also some evidence that Theodore had been involved in the monothelete controversy in the Canterbury biblical commentaries themselves. As we have seen, the progenitor of dyothelete opposition to the imperial doctrine was Sophronius, patriarch of Jerusalem, and at the time of the Lateran Council, the principal architect of the Council's *acta*, and their triumphant statement of the dyothelete position, was Sophronius's follower Maximus. It is therefore interesting to note that the Canterbury biblical commentaries reveal familiarity with both Sophronius and Maximus. Sophronius is quoted by name as the source of an opinion on the etymology of the place-name Emmaus (PentI 35); since this etymology

---

[82] See, conveniently, Herrin, *The Formation of Christendom*, pp. 275–8, as well as the more detailed account in F. X. Murphy and P. Sherwood, *Constantinople II et Constantinople III*, Histoire des Conciles oecuméniques 3 (Paris, 1974), 189–219.

[83] *Concilium Vniuersale Constantinopolitanum Tertium, Concilii Actiones I-XI*, ed. R. Riedinger, Acta Conciliorum Oecumenicorum 2nd ser. 2.1 (Berlin, 1990), 132–3: εἶτα ἠλπίζομεν ἀπὸ Βρεττανίας Θεόδωρον τὸν σύνδουλον ἡμῶν καὶ συνεπίσκοπον, τῆς μεγάλης νήσου Βρεττανίας ἀρχιεπίσκοπον καὶ φιλόσοφον, μετὰ ἄλλων ἐκεῖσε κατὰ τὸν τόπον διαγόντων, ἐκεῖθεν τῇ ἡμετέρᾳ ἑνωθῆναι μετριότητι.

[84] See also *Biblical Commentaries*, ed. Bischoff and Lapidge, pp. 78–80.

cannot be found in the surviving writings of Sophronius, there is some possibility that the information was conveyed to Theodore through personal contact, inasmuch as Sophronius spent some time in Constantinople in the early 630s when (on my reconstruction of his career) Theodore was studying there.[85] A possible further link between the two is Theodore's knowledge of the Greek verse-form known as anacreontics, of which Sophronius was an adept practitioner (see below, pp. 268–70). Maximus the Confessor is not quoted by name in the Canterbury biblical commentaries, but there are numerous striking points of contact between his writings and the commentaries.[86] For example, the statement in EvII 24 that there are two *natiuitates* in Christ – the 'natural' in the flesh, the 'spiritual' in baptism – is also found in the *Ambigua* of Maximus, and is a viewpoint wholly consonant with dyothelete doctrine.[87] If Theodore, like Maximus, was involved in drafting the *acta* of the Lateran Council, the two may have been in frequent contact in Rome during the 640s, and similarities in their theological outlook would be understandable. Such contact would also explain the fact that the *acta* of the synod of Hatfield endorsed, under Theodore's presidency, the doctrine that the Holy Spirit proceeded *both* from the Father *and* from the Son – the normal formula for signalling this double procession is *filioque* (see discussion by Chadwick, below, p. 88) – a doctrine which was anathema to most Greek church fathers but which was articulated on several occasions by Maximus the Confessor.[88] Once again, the simplest explanation of Theodore's doctrinal position is that he had arrived at it through discussions at Rome with Maximus. In short, the indirect evidence for Theodore's contacts with both Sophronius and Maximus helps to confirm that of Pope Agatho's letter to Emperor Constantine IV concerning Theodore's expertise in the theological issues of the monothelete controversy, and establishes that the future archbishop of Canterbury had indeed been centrally involved in the most important doctrinal controversy of the seventh century.

Although by 680 Theodore felt himself too old to travel to Rome and then on to Constantinople, the Oecumenical Council promoted by Pope Agatho and Emperor Constantine IV met in the Trullan Palace in Constantinople in 680 and formally condemned the imperial doctrine of monotheletism. Thus ended one of the most violent episodes in the history

---

[85] *Ibid.*, pp. 219 and 441–2 (comm. to PentI 35).   [86] *Ibid.*, p. 225.

[87] *Ibid.*, p. 512 (comm. to EvII 24).

[88] *Ibid.*, pp. 143–6.

of the Christian church. The aftermath of the Lateran Council of 649 had been particularly violent. Following the promulgation of the *acta* of that Council, Pope Martin I was arrested and taken to Constantinople, where he was tried for treason (inasmuch as the Lateran *acta* had contained a formal condemnation of a doctrine endorsed by imperial decree) and was condemned to death, though the death sentence was subsequently commuted to exile in the Crimea, where he died in 655.[89] The following year Maximus the Confessor was similarly tried in Constantinople on grounds of treason, and was exiled to Thrace; but he refused to abandon his opposition to monotheletism. Accordingly, his right hand was cut off (to prevent him from writing) and his tongue was cut out (to prevent him from speaking his opposition); he died in exile in Lazike at the remote eastern end of the Black Sea, in 662.[90]

It was only five years later that Abbot Hadrian suggested Theodore's name to Pope Vitalian as a possible candidate for the vacant see of Canterbury. Vitalian was a naturally cautious man, and his initial hesitation about the appointment of Theodore would be explained by the knowledge that Theodore had been involved in drafting the Lateran Council's *acta*, which in 667 were still under formal condemnation by Constans II, the emperor who had tried both Pope Martin and Maximus the Confessor for treason.[91] Such knowledge would also explain why Pope Vitalian insisted that Hadrian accompany Theodore to England, to ensure – in Bede's words – that Theodore 'did not introduce into the church over which he was to preside anything contrary to the truth of the faith in the manner of the Greeks',[92] words which seemingly refer to the dyothelete views of Maximus the Confessor and the other oriental (Greek-speaking)

---

[89] See Herrin, *The Formation of Christendom*, pp. 256–7, as well as W. M. Peitz, 'Martin I. und Maximus Confessor. Beiträge zur Geschichte des Monotheletenstreites in den Jahren 645–88', *Historisches Jahrbuch* 38 (1917), 213–36 and 429–58, esp. 223–6 and 436–58.

[90] See Herrin, *The Formation of Christendom*, pp. 251–9, as well as R. Devreesse, 'Le Texte grec de l'Hypomnesticon de Théodore Spoudée. Le supplice, l'exil et la mort des victimes illustres du monothélisme', *AB* 53 (1935), 49–80, and J. M. Garrigues, 'Le Martyre de Saint Maxime le Confesseur', *Revue Thomiste* 76 (1976), 410–52.

[91] On the character of Pope Vitalian, and especially his extreme deference to the emperor, see V. Monachino, 'I tempi e la figura del papa Vitaliano (657–72)', in *Storiografia e storia. Studi in onore di E. Dupré Theseider*, 2 vols. (Rome, 1974) II, 573–88.

[92] *HE* IV.1 (ed. Colgrave and Mynors, p. 330): 'ne quid ille contrarium ueritati fidei Graecorum more in ecclesiam cui praeesset introduceret'.

monks who had participated in drafting the *acta* of the Lateran Council. In any case, the pope's hesitations were eventually overcome and Theodore was duly consecrated archbishop of Canterbury on 26 March 668.

ENGLAND

Whereas the outlines of Theodore's career before his appointment to Canterbury have to be eked out of references in the Canterbury biblical commentaries, from the time of his arrival in England his activities are moderately well known from the writings of Aldhelm, Bede and Stephen of Ripon; furthermore, an ever-increasing corpus of literary works attests to his activities at Canterbury as scholar and teacher. It is not necessary to give here anything more than a brief synopsis of those activities, since many of them are treated in detail in the subsequent essays in this volume.[93]

Soon after their arrival, Theodore and Hadrian made a reconnaissance-tour of England, in order to familiarize themselves with the various dioceses under Canterbury's jurisdiction. An immediately striking problem was the fact that many bishoprics were vacant, and it was one of Theodore's first tasks to fill these vacancies.[94] Once the English episcopate had been repaired in this way, Theodore summoned a national synod at Hertford, probably in 673. At this synod Theodore, basing himself on a *liber canonum* or 'book of canon law' (on the identity of which, see discussion by Martin Brett, below, pp. 125–8), promulgated a number of rules intended to secure unanimity of practice throughout England in matters of orthodox belief, such as Easter dating, marriage and divorce, and so on. One of the canons of the synod, that more bishoprics should be created as the number of the faithful increased, brought Theodore into conflict with the irascible Bishop Wilfrid, who at that time was ruling a vast Northumbrian diocese. Theodore deposed Wilfrid in 677; but after

---

[93] See discussion in *Biblical Commentaries*, ed. Bischoff and Lapidge, pp. 133–9 (on Theodore's ecclesiastical administration), 139–55 (on his concern with orthodoxy and ecclesiastical legislation), and 173–89 (on the literary works produced in Theodore's school at Canterbury).

[94] On Theodore's ecclesiastical administration, see F. M. Stenton, *Anglo-Saxon England*, 3rd ed. (Oxford, 1971), pp. 130–42, as well as H. Mayr-Harting, *The Coming of Christianity to Anglo-Saxon England*, 3rd ed. (London, 1991), pp. 130–9, and N. Brooks, *The Early History of the Church at Canterbury* (Leicester, 1984), pp. 71–6.

Wilfrid had appealed successfully to Pope Agatho, a position of compromise was reached, whereby Wilfrid was restored to the diocese of York, but the rest of his former Northumbrian diocese was subdivided. The reconciliation between Theodore and Wilfrid was announced in letters sent by Theodore to Aldfrith, king of Northumbria (685–705), to Ælfflæd, subsequently abbess of Whitby (680–714), and to Æthelred, king of Mercia (675–704). The first two letters are lost; but Stephen of Ripon, in his *Vita S. Wilfridi*, preserves for us the letter to King Æthelred.[95] It is clear from this letter that Theodore was on intimate terms with the Mercian king, and also that Theodore's intimate familiarity with the Old Testament could be deployed to telling literary effect, especially in his allusions to the aged patriarchs Jacob and Isaac. The letter is important as being one of the very few texts which have come down to us attributed *nominatim* to Theodore.

If more such letters had survived, it would be easier to plot the progress and effect of Theodore's administrative reforms. Yet there can be no doubt that, as an administrator, Theodore was highly effective. The lasting effects of his administrative efforts were the breakup of the old, large dioceses and the corresponding increase in the number of bishops, as well as the provision for the annual convention of a general English synod (to be held at an unidentified location called *Clofesho*).[96] Reflecting on these achievements, Bede states, succinctly and accurately, that 'the English churches made more spiritual progress during his archbishopric than ever before'.[97]

A striking feature of Theodore's administration is his prevailing concern with orthodoxy, with the 'true and orthodox faith' (*fidem rectam et orthodoxam*), as Bede puts it.[98] This concern is attested by evidence of various sorts. There is no doubt, for example, that Theodore was concerned with the correct interpretation and implementation of ecclesiastical legislation. As we have seen, the rules promulgated by Theodore at the synod of

---

[95] *The Life of Bishop Wilfrid by Eddius Stephanus*, ed. B. Colgrave (Cambridge, 1927), p. 88 (ch. 43); see discussion in *Biblical Commentaries*, ed. Bischoff and Lapidge, pp. 136–8.

[96] See now S. D. Keynes, *The Councils of Clofesho*, The Brixworth Lecture 1993 (Leicester, 1994).

[97] *HE* V.8 (ed. Colgrave and Mynors, p. 474): 'Vt enim breuiter dicam, tantum profectus spiritalis tempore praesulatus illius Anglorum ecclesiae, quantum numquam antea potuere, ceperunt.'

[98] *HE* IV.17 [15] (*ibid.*, p. 384).

Hertford were drawn from a *liber canonum* or 'book of canon law', and among the texts studied and glossed at Theodore's Canterbury school were the canons of various early church councils. Theodore's knowledge of canon law, as embodied in texts such as these, is analysed thoroughly by Martin Brett in a subsequent chapter (below, pp. 120–40). Another aspect of Theodore's interest in ecclesiastical legislation is seen in the *Iudicia* which have come down to us – albeit at third hand – in Theodore's name. One part (the second) of these *Iudicia* is drawn once again from the canons of early church councils (and this provides further evidence of Theodore's knowledge of canon law), while the first part is a penitential, or handbook containing tariffs of private penance. This penitential was to prove widely influential on later collections of ecclesiastical legislation, both in Ireland and on the Continent. As Thomas Charles-Edwards shows (below, pp. 141–74), it reflects once again Theodore's extensive knowledge of eastern (Greek) penitential literature, and shows how Theodore's experience as a Greek monk helped to shape western penitential practice. Another area where Theodore's eastern background is likely to have been influential is that of the liturgy; unfortunately, so few Anglo-Saxon service books have survived from the early period (and none from before *c.* 700) that this influence must be a matter of conjecture. What can be known in this domain, and what can be safely conjectured (and what must remain a matter for further exploration), is set out clearly by Christopher Hohler (below, pp. 222–35).

We are on safer ground with respect to Theodore's achievements in the domain of scholarship and instruction. In recent years an increasing amount of attention has been given to the evidence of a group of little-studied Anglo-Saxon glossaries, known as the 'Leiden Family', and these glossaries have been shown to yield important information concerning the texts which were studied in Theodore's school at Canterbury.[99] The information which they contain is difficult of access, insofar as many of the relevant glossaries remain unpublished; but J. D. Pheifer (below, pp. 281–333) has given us for the first time a panorama of the glossaries in question, and shown how they complement and amplify our knowledge of the instruction on the text of the Bible which was given by Theodore and Hadrian at Canterbury. Other essays in the present volume elucidate for

[99] See M. Lapidge, 'The School of Theodore and Hadrian', *ASE* 15 (1986), 45–72, together with J. D. Pheifer, 'Early Anglo-Saxon Glossaries and the School of Canterbury', *ASE* 16 (1987), 17–44.

the first time Theodore's own scholarly activities. Jane Stevenson demonstrates persuasively (below, pp. 204–21) that Theodore was almost certainly the author of the so-called *Laterculus Malalianus*, a brief treatise which is partly chronographical, partly exegetical, and which draws on a wide knowledge of Greek patristic sources, including the *Chronographia* of John Malalas. Building in part on Stevenson's deployment of evidence, Carmela Vircillo Franklin has mounted the compelling argument (below, pp. 175–203) that Theodore was the (Latin) translator of the Greek *Passio S. Anastasii*, a text which reflects veneration for the patron saint of the Roman community of St Anastasius *ad aquas Salvias*, and which very possibly was brought to England by Theodore. Even so apparently trivial a text as the six-line octosyllabic poem addressed by Theodore to Bishop Hæddi can only properly be understood in the light of Greek metrics, in particular Byzantine anacreontics (below, pp. 260–80). Taken together, these texts illustrate brilliantly the impact of Theodore's Greek learning in Anglo-Saxon England, and help to validate Bede's high opinion of the achievements of his archbishopric. When these texts are placed alongside the recently published biblical commentaries on the Pentateuch and gospels, it becomes legitimate to regard the seventh-century school of Canterbury as one of the high points, perhaps the acme, of intellectual culture in the early Middle Ages.

2

The Syriac background

SEBASTIAN P. BROCK

The history of Christianity in late antiquity is all too often based on a bifocal model, consisting of the Greek East and Latin West. *Tertium non datur* – at least from a Chalcedonian viewpoint. Though for the most part separated ecclesiastically from the Greek and Latin churches as a result of the christological controversies of the fifth century, and politically from the Byzantine empire as a result of the Arab invasions in the third decade of the seventh century, the Syriac Orient[1] in this latter century was still very much part of the cultural world of Graeco-Roman civilization, and indeed the Syriac Orient should be seen as a co-heir, along with the Latin West, of the Greek East: large numbers of Greek texts, both religious and secular, were translated into Syriac as well as into Latin, and in many cases the same texts were selected, often employing the same sorts of translation techniques. In the case of Syriac, the choice of Greek theological texts to be translated was governed in part by the theological colour of the ecclesiastical community concerned. Here there are three groupings:

(1) the Syrian Orthodox (opprobriously nicknamed 'Jacobites' after the sixth-century bishop, Jacob Baradaeus, or 'Monophysites'),[2] who

---

[1] C. Moss's *Catalogue of Syriac Printed Books and Related Literature in the British Museum* (London, 1962) serves as a nearly complete bibliography of Syriac studies up to *c.* 1960; for subsequent years classified bibliographies can be found in *Parole de l'Orient* 4 (1973), 10 (1981–2) and 14 (1987), covering 1960–70, 1971–80 and 1981–5 respectively. For an introduction to Syriac studies, see the work by F. Young cited below, n. 26.

[2] The familiar tripartite division of the christological spectrum into Nestorian, Chalcedonian and Monophysite is a highly misleading oversimplification, since it wrongly equates the position of the Church of the East with 'Nestorianism', and that of the Syrian (and other Oriental) Orthodox with that of Eutyches. The Church of the East in fact follows the teaching of Theodore of Mopsuestia, not Nestorius, while the Oriental

rejected the Council of Chalcedon (AD 451), and saw themselves as the true heirs of Cyril of Alexandria's christological teaching, as expounded by Severus of Antioch (d. 538);

(2) the Church of the East (opprobriously called 'Nestorians' by their opponents), who rejected the Council of Ephesus (AD 431) and regarded Theodore of Mopsuestia as their guide in matters both theological and exegetical;[3]

(3) the Syriac-speaking Chalcedonian communities of Syria and Lebanon, who were, in the course of the late seventh and early eighth century, to divide into two bodies, the dyothelete Melkites who accepted the Sixth Oecumenical Council (AD 680) and the monothelete Maronites, who rejected it.[4]

Although the Greek-speaking church moved distinctly towards the Alexandrian end of the christological spectrum in the course of the sixth century,[5] the Latin-speaking church kept to a more Antiochene interpretation of the Council of Chalcedon, and so was in much closer sympathy with the Church of the East, geographically the more distant, than with the Syrian Orthodox. Thus we find that Theodore of Mopsuestia was acceptable to both the Latin church and the Church of the East, whereas

---

Orthodox (Armenian, Coptic, Ethiopian, Syrian) have, from the outset, repudiated the truly monophysite position of Eutyches (a single divine nature in the incarnate Christ), maintaining instead that in the incarnate Christ there is but one nature composed out of two (*scil.* human and divine), a position which might be called 'henophysite', to distinguish it from 'monophysite'.

[3] For the position of the Church of the East, see my 'The Christology of the Church of the East in the Synods of the fifth to early seventh Centuries. Preliminary Considerations and Materials', in *Aksum-Thyateira. A Festschrift for Archbishop Methodios of Thyateira and Great Britain*, ed. G. Dragas (Athens, 1985), pp. 125–42 (repr. in my *Studies in Syriac Christianity* (Aldershot, 1992), ch. XII).

[4] This is specifically stated in a recently published fragment, almost certainly of Maronite provenance; see my 'A Syriac Fragment on the Sixth Council', *Oriens Christianus* 57 (1973), 63–71 (repr. in my *Syriac Perspectives on Late Antiquity* (London, 1984), ch. XIII).

[5] See especially J. Meyendorff, *Christ in Eastern Christian Thought* (Crestwood, NJ, 1975), and A. Grillmeier, *Christ in Christian Tradition*, 2 vols. in 3 (London, 1987), vol. II.1. Justinian held unsuccessful conversations both with the Church of the East and with the Syrian Orthodox; for the former, see A. Guillaumont, 'Justinien et l'Eglise de Perse', *Dumbarton Oaks Papers* 23–4 (1969–70), 39–66, and for the latter, my 'The Conversations with the Syrian Orthodox under Justinian (532)', *Orientalia Christiana Periodica* 47 (1981), 87–121 (for this meeting we have, exceptionally, accounts of the proceedings from both sides), repr. in *Studies in Syriac Christianity*, ch. XIII.

his writings had been condemned by the Greek church in 553, and had always been anathema to the Syrian Orthodox.

The seventh century was a period of great literary creativity in all the Syriac churches, a fact all the more remarkable when one considers the upheavals caused, first by the Persian, and then by the Arab invasions. It was, furthermore, an irony of fate that the century which witnessed the political separation of the Syriac churches from the Byzantine empire was also the time when Syriac culture was at its most philhellenic, for the seventh century represents a climax in the gradual process of the hellenization of Syriac literary culture in late antiquity. With the notable exception of Bardaisan (d. 222),[6] the earliest surviving Syriac writers prefer to retain traditional Semitic literary genres and employ thought-patterns which are characteristic of ancient Near Eastern (including biblical) literature. Thus the great fourth-century Syriac authors, Aphrahat and (above all) Ephrem,[7] though certainly not untouched by, or unaware of, Greek literary culture of the time, preferred to write in an essentially Semitic mode. The fifth century and, even more so, the sixth, bring a marked change in atmosphere, largely due to the ever-increasing influence of Greek-speaking Christian culture;[8] owing to the divisive christological controversies of these centuries, the language and agenda of theological discourse in Syriac increasingly follows Greek thought-patterns and models, and it is only a rare figure like the Syrian Orthodox poet Jacob of Serugh (d. 521) who steadfastly holds out against this, even though in other respects he too can be shown to be strongly under the influence, in matters exegetical, of a Greek church father (ironically

---

[6] The 'Book of the Laws of the Countries' (or 'Dialogue on Fate'), from the School of Bardaisan, is modelled on the Greek genre of the philosophical dialogue; cf. B. R. Voss, *Der Dialog in der frühchristlichen Literatur* (Munich, 1970), pp. 51–9.

[7] Aphrahat's complete works are now readily available in French translation in Sources chrétiennes 349 and 359 (Paris, 1988–9). For Ephrem two English translations of some of the hymn cycles have recently appeared: K. McVey, *Ephrem the Syrian. Hymns*, Classics of Western Spirituality (New York, 1989), and my *St Ephrem the Syrian, Hymns on Paradise* (Crestwood, NJ, 1990). In both of these further bibliographical guidance can readily be found; see also my 'A Brief Guide to the Main Editions and Translations of the Works of St Ephrem', *The Harp. A Review of Syriac and Oriental Studies* 3 (1990), 7–29.

[8] For an overview of this process, see my 'From Antagonism to Assimilation: Syriac Attitudes to Greek Learning', in *East of Byzantium. Syria and Armenia in the Formative Period*, ed. N. Garsoian, T. Mathews and R. Thomson (Washington, DC, 1982), pp. 17–34 (repr. in *Syriac Perspectives on Late Antiquity*, ch. V).

Theodore of Mopsuestia).[9] This is a time when the Greek language itself has a profound influence on Syriac, as is witnessed not only in the proliferation during these two centuries of Greek loanwords, but also in the rapid increase in newly formed adjectives (the Syriac of the fourth-century writers employs very few), not to mention the many syntactic calques.[10] So great, indeed, has the influence of Greek on Syriac style become by the seventh century that it is sometimes hard to know, solely on internal grounds of language, whether a seventh-century Syriac text was an original Syriac composition or a translation from Greek.

Translations from Greek into Syriac during the fifth to seventh century abound, and indeed the changing translation techniques employed excellently reflect the ever-growing prestige of things Greek at the time. Whereas the earliest translations, up to the early fifth century, had almost all been rather free in character (sometimes, as in the case of some of Basil's works, remarkably so), and essentially reader-oriented, with the turn of the fifth to sixth century we can witness a distinct shift in practice, away from reader-oriented translations to ones that become more and more text-oriented, and the style of translation becomes more and more literal, with the ideal of *uerbum ad uerbum* replacing *sensus ad sensum*. By the time of the seventh-century translations such were the skills in sophisticated techniques of mirror translation that had been developed over the course of several generations, that the modern textual critic is enabled to reconstruct the underlying Greek text with a high probability of accuracy.[11]

These developments in translation practice can be observed both in biblical and in non-biblical translations from Greek. For the former,[12] the

---

[9] See especially T. Jansma, 'Etude sur l'Hexaméron de Jacques de Saroug', *L'Orient Syrien* 5 (1959), 3–42, 129–62 and 253–84.

[10] Some preliminary indications are provided in my 'Diachronic Aspects of Syriac Word Formation: an Aid for Dating Anonymous Texts', *V Symposium Syriacum*, Orientalia Christiana Analecta 236 (1990), 321–30.

[11] See my 'Towards a History of Syriac Translation Technique', in *III Symposium Syriacum*, ed. R. Lavenant, Orientalia Christiana Analecta 221 (1983), 1–14 (repr. in *Studies in Syriac Christianity*, ch. X); and, for the wider background, 'Aspects of Translation Technique in Antiquity', *Greek, Roman and Byzantine Studies* 20 (1979), 69–87 (repr. in *Syriac Perspectives on Late Antiquity*, ch. III).

[12] A summary survey of the Syriac biblical versions can be found in B. Aland and S. P. Brock, 'Bibelübersetzungen, syrische', in *Theologische Realenzyklopädie* V (1980), 181–96, or in my 'Syriac Versions', in *The Anchor Bible Dictionary* VI (1992), 794–9. For the New Testament, an excellent account is given by B. M. Metzger, *The Early Versions of the New Testament* (Oxford, 1977), ch. 1.

best documented books are the gospels, where the Old Syriac (perhaps early third-century) was gradually revised, in a rather haphazard way, eventually to result in an early fifth-century edition, subsequently known as the Peshitta, which rapidly became accepted as the standard New Testament version for all the Syriac churches. A century later, however, the Syrian Orthodox theologian Philoxenus of Mabbug (d. 523) was finding that some rather freely translated passages in the Peshitta were being used to support an Antiochene (to him, Nestorian) christological position; accordingly he sponsored a revision, undertaken by his *chorepiscopus* Polycarp in 507–8, to remedy this situation.[13] This version is unfortunately lost, apart from quotations, but it in turn served as the basis for yet a further, and much more rigorously literal, revision at the hands of Thomas of Harkel, working in Alexandria *c.* 616.[14] Remarkably, this version gained, over the course of the following centuries, considerable popularity in Syrian Orthodox circles, and it still features in certain lections in lectionary manuscripts continuing in use today.

With the Old Testament the situation is rather different, since the original Syriac translation (also known as the Peshitta) had been made from the Hebrew, rather than from Greek. It now appears (against the views of older scholarship) that the extant Peshitta manuscript tradition shows very little trace of any attempt to bring the text into closer alignment with the Septuagint;[15] on the other hand, a large number of distinctively Septuagint readings will have been familiar to Syriac readers through Syriac

[13] For further details, see my 'The Resolution of the Philoxenian/Harclean Problem', in *New Testament Textual Criticism. Essays in Honour of Bruce M. Metzger*, ed. E. J. Epp and G. D. Fee (Oxford, 1981), pp. 325–43.

[14] The standard edition remains that of J. White under the misleading (as it now turns out) titles *Sacrorum Evangeliorum Versio Syriaca Philoxeniana* and *Actuum Apostolorum et Epistolarum ... Versio Syriaca Philoxeniana* (London, 1778–1803), though for some of the Catholic Epistles there is now a critical edition by B. Aland, included in her *Das Neue Testament in syrischer Überlieferung, I. Die grossen katholischen Briefe* (Berlin, 1986), and an improved text of Revelation can be found in the photographic edition by A. Vööbus, *The Apocalypse in the Harklean Version*, CSCO 400 [Subsidia 56] (Louvain, 1978).

[15] See P. B. Dirksen, 'The Old Testament Peshitta', in *Mikra. Text, Translation, Reading and Interpretation of the Hebrew Bible in Ancient Judaism and Early Christianity*, ed. M. J. Mulder, Compendia Rerum Iudaicarum ad Novum Testamentum 2.1 (Assen and Philadelphia, PA, 1988), 255–97.

translations of Greek commentators on the Septuagint.[16] Around the turn of the fifth/sixth century we have fragmentary evidence of two rather different approaches to the problem posed by the increasing prestige of the Septuagint. In one (only) of the four manuscripts containing the Syriac translation of Gregory of Nyssa's Commentary on the Song of Songs, there is preserved a revised translation of the Song of Songs itself; here the reviser uses the Peshitta as his starting point, but provides every now and then distinctive phrases taken from the Septuagint.[17] A more radical procedure was adopted by the author of the so-called 'Syro-Lucianic' version of certain books of the Old Testament: this version, which may well have been sponsored by Philoxenus (who once quotes a passage where it has a very distinctive text),[18] follows the reverse procedure, for basically it is a new translation made from the Greek (using a manuscript belonging to the Lucianic recension), though the Peshitta's phraseology is retained where this is considered to correspond adequately to the Greek.

The seventh century witnessed two further translations of the Old Testament. The first of these is the Syrohexapla, so called because it is a translation of the revised Septuagint column of Origen's Hexapla.[19] This vast labour, which only survives in part, was undertaken by Paul of Tella, an associate of Thomas of Harkel, who was also working in Alexandria. Towards the end of the same century Jacob of Edessa (d. 708), one of the

[16] A good example is provided by the Septuagint reading at Gen. I.2, discussed by T. Jansma, 'Some Remarks on the Syro-Hexaplaric Reading of Gen. 1:2', *Vetus Testamentum* 20 (1970), 16–24; here the LXX reading, which has important theological consequences, was introduced through the Syriac translation of Theodore of Mopsuestia's *Commentary on Genesis*.

[17] A collation of part of the text (Cant. III.10 to end) is given by C. van den Eynde, *La Version syriaque du commentaire de Grégoire de Nysse sur le Cantique des Cantiques* (Louvain, 1939), pp. 25–9; a further folio from the same manuscript, containing Cant. I.17–III.10, is located in Mingana syr. 628; see my 'Mingana syr. 628: a Folio from the Revision of the Peshitta Song of Songs in (olim) Zurich Or. 76', forthcoming.

[18] This version can, in all probability, be identified as that sponsored by Philoxenus of Mabbug, who quotes its very distinctive text at Isaiah XLV.9 in his Commentary on the Prologue of John (ed. A. de Halleux, CSCO 380 [= Scriptores Syri 165] (Louvain, 1977), 90); see further R. G. Jenkins, 'Some Quotations from Isaiah in the Philoxenian Version', *Abr Nahrain* 20 (1981–2), 20–36.

[19] The Syrohexapla does not survive quite complete; a helpful survey of the materials is given by W. Baars, *New Syro-Hexaplaric Texts* (Leiden, 1968), which can now be supplemented by A. Vööbus's photographic editions of two further manuscripts (CSCO 369 and 449 [= Subsidia 45 and 68] (Louvain, 1975–83)).

greatest scholars of his time, carried out a further work of revision on certain Old Testament books.[20] Jacob's aim was evidently to provide a text for liturgical readings[21] which reflected both the strands of Syriac biblical tradition, that is, the Peshitta, translated from Hebrew, and the Syrohexapla, translated from Greek; at the same time he also made use of a Greek manuscript of the Septuagint containing a text of Lucianic complexion. Although Jacob's resulting version may seem a curious amalgam to the modern scholar, his work should not be judged in the light of modern expectations, for his interests and purpose were very different.

The pattern provided by the biblical translations, with the fashion for a highly literal translation technique reaching its climax in the early seventh century, can equally be traced in the many patristic and secular translations undertaken during this period. An astonishing number of translations of Greek patristic writings (mostly post-Nicene) were made in the course of three or so centuries, and it is certain that there must originally have been many more than those which still happen to survive. In many cases we find that earlier translations, made in the fifth or early sixth century, were subsequently revised and brought into much closer line with the original Greek. Thus, in the case of Gregory of Nazianzus's Homilies[22] we have an incomplete sixth-century version, and a complete seventh-century revision, the latter having been undertaken in 623–4 by Paul of Edessa while he was in Cyprus to escape the Persian occupation of Syria. It is significant that many features of Paul of Edessa's translation technique reflect the same practices which characterize the translation style of Thomas of Harkel and Paul of Tella.[23] Another writer for whom two

---

[20] A guide to the scattered material is provided by W. Baars, 'Ein neugefundenes Bruchstück aus der syrischen Bibelrevision des Jakob von Edessa', *Vetus Testamentum* 18 (1968), 548–54.

[21] The early (and often incomplete) manuscripts of this version contain elaborate lectionary tables enabling the reader to find the lection in the continuous Bible text; for this aspect, see my *The Bible in the Syriac Churches*, Schweich Lectures for 1989 (forthcoming).

[22] See below, n. 29.

[23] For Paul of Edessa's revision of Gregory's homilies, see my *The Syriac Version of the pseudo-Nonnos Mythological Scholia* (Cambridge, 1971), pp. 34–44 (the *scholia* are attached to certain of Gregory's homilies).

Syriac translations are preserved is Severus of Antioch; Severus's homilies, delivered during the years when he was on the patriarchal throne of Antioch (512–18),[24] have, with few exceptions, been lost in Greek, owing to the condemnation of his writings in 536; probably by that time the first of the two Syriac translations had been made, by Paul of Kallinikos. A century and a half or so later, this translation was revised by Jacob of Edessa.[25]

If one takes Siegmund's listing[26] of Greek patristic writings available in Latin translations for the most part made before the end of the seventh century, and compares this with what was available (and survives) in Syriac by the same time, there is a remarkably high degree of overlap. Only among the pre-Nicene fathers are there some surprising gaps on the Syriac side; thus, while Ignatius, Clement of Rome and Hippolytus are quite well represented,[27] Hermas, Justin, Irenaeus, Clement of Alexandria and Origen are conspicuous by their absence. For fourth- and fifth-century writers, however, virtually all the great names are represented, notably

---

[24] Details can be found in M. Brière's introduction to PO 29.1; the remaining homilies have subsequently been published in PO 35–8, though normally in Jacob's version.

[25] See C. J. A. Lash, 'Techniques of a Translator: Work Notes on the Methods of Jacob of Edessa in translating the Homilies of Severus of Antioch', in *Überlieferungsgeschichtliche Untersuchungen*, ed. F. Pashke, Texte und Untersuchungen 125 (Berlin, 1981), 365–83.

[26] A. Siegmund, *Die Überlieferung der griechischen christlichen Literatur in der lateinischen Kirche bis zum zwölften Jahrhundert* (Munich and Pasing, 1949). General surveys of translations into Syriac are given by J.-M. Sauget, 'L'Apport des traductions syriaques pour la patristique syriaque', *Revue de théologie et de philosophie* 110 (1978), 139–48, and F. Young, 'Syriac, a Tool for the Student of Early Christian Doctrine', in *Horizons in Semitic Studies*, ed. J. H. Eaton (Birmingham, 1980), pp. 39–58 (the same volume contains a general introduction to Syriac studies at pp. 1–33). The standard source for detailed information remains A. Baumstark, *Geschichte der syrischen Literatur* (Bonn, 1922; repr. Berlin, 1968); in the annotation given below, references are confined to only the more important subsequent literature.

[27] For Ignatius's Letters, the Syriac is a witness to the short recension (*CPG* I, no. 1025). The Syriac translation of Clement probably belongs to the seventh century. For Hippolytus in Syriac, see my 'Some New Syriac Texts attributed to Hippolytus', *Le Muséon* 94 (1981), 177–200, and A. de Halleux, 'Une Version syriaque revisée du Commentaire d'Hippolyte sur Suzanne', *Le Muséon* 101 (1988), 297–341.

Eusebius, Athanasius,[28] the Cappadocians,[29] John Chrysostom,[30] Epiphanius,[31] Theodore of Mopsuestia and Cyril of Alexandria.[32] In the case of Theodore, owing to the posthumous condemnation of his writings at the Fifth Council, almost all his surviving works are available only in Syriac or Latin translation.[33] With post-Chalcedonian Greek writers the choice was of course coloured by theological considerations; since very little of Chalcedonian literature has survived in Syriac,[34] and the Church of the East, centred outside the Byzantine empire, seems to have undertaken little in the way of translation from Greek in the sixth and seventh centuries,[35] it is the Syrian Orthodox choice of post-Chalcedonian Greek fathers which is best represented in extant manuscripts, with translations

---

[28] Syriac preserves Eusebius's *Theophania* and the long recension of the *Palestinian Martyrs*, both lost in Greek. The main works of Athanasius surviving in Syriac are ed. R. Thomson, CSCO 257–8, 272–3, 324–5 and 386–7 [= Scriptores Syri 114–15, 118–19, 142–3 and 167–8] (Louvain, 1965, 1967, 1972 and 1977, respectively).

[29] For Basil, see *Basil of Caesarea*, ed. P.J. Fedwick, 2 vols. (Toronto, 1981), esp. II, 444–55; for Gregory of Nazianzus, A. de Halleux, 'La Version syriaque des Discours de Grégoire de Nazianze', in *II Symposium Nazianzenum*, ed. J. Mossay, Studien zur Geschichte und Kultur des Altertums ns 2.2 (1983), 75–11; for Gregory of Nyssa, M. Parmentier, 'Syriac Translations of Gregory of Nyssa', *Orientalia Lovaniensia Periodica* 20 (1989), 143–93.

[30] Some indication of the Syriac translations are given by M. Geerard in *CPG* II.

[31] Including the *Treatise on Weights and Measures*, which survives complete only in Syriac; ed. with English translation by J. E. Dean (Chicago, 1935).

[32] R. Y. Ebied and L. R. Wickham, *A Collection of Unpublished Syriac Letters of Cyril of Alexandria*, CSCO 359–60 [= Scriptores Syri 157–8] (Louvain, 1975). The Commentary on Luke survives only in Syriac.

[33] To the editions listed by Geerard, *CPG* II, the following can now be added: L. Van Rompay, *Théodore de Mopsueste. Fragments syriaques du Commentaire des Psaumes*, CSCO 435–6 [= Scriptores Syri 189–90] (Louvain, 1982), and W. Strothmann, *Das syrische Fragment des Ecclesiastes-Kommentars von Theodor von Mopsuestia*, Göttinger Orientforschungen, Reihe Syriaca 28 (Göttingen, 1988).

[34] Most of these are preserved at St Catherine's Monastery, Sinai; cf. P. Bettiolo, *Una raccolta di opuscoli calcedonesi*, CSCO 403–4 [= Scriptores Syri 177–8] (Louvain, 1979). There is also a small number of Syriac texts of monothelete Chalcedonian provenance; cf. my 'A Monothelete Florilegium in Syriac', in *After Chalcedon. Studies in Theology and Church History offered to Professor Albert Van Roey*, ed. C. Laga, J. A. Munitz and L. Van Rompay, Orientalia Lovaniensia Analecta 18 (Louvain, 1985), 35–45 (repr. in *Studies in Syriac Christianity*, ch. XIV).

[35] An exception is Nestorius's *Liber Heracleidis*, translated *c.* 540.

of works by Timothy Aelurus[36] and (above all) Severus of Antioch.[37]

In the case of monastic literature the Latin West and the Syriac Orient are likewise heirs to a common Greek heritage. The Egyptian monastic tradition is well represented, with Lives of Antony[38] and of many other Egyptian fathers, Palladius's *Lausiac History*, the *Historia monachorum* and various collections of *apophthegmata*.[39] Evagrius, whose monastic teaching reached the West by way of Cassian, survives today almost entirely only in Syriac (and Armenian) translations,[40] and the popularity of this 'Father of those with spiritual understanding' (as one East Syrian monastic author called him),[41] is indicated both by the number of early manuscripts surviving and the fact that several works received revised, or even new, translations at a subsequent date.[42] Greek writers belonging to the native Syrian ascetic tradition are represented by Theodoret's *Historia religiosa*[43] and, especially, by the Macarian Homilies.[44] The Dionysian Corpus was translated into Syriac by Sergius of Resh'aina (d. 536), probably within a few decades of its composition; then, towards the end of the seventh

---

[36] See R. Y. Ebied and L. R. Wickham, 'Timothy Aelurus, Against the Definition of the Council of Chalcedon', in *After Chalcedon*, ed. Laga, Munitz and Van Rompay, pp. 115–66.

[37] A useful recent survey is given by F. Graffin in *Dictionnaire de spiritualité* XIV (Paris, 1989), 748–52; see also above, n. 24.

[38] R. Draguet's theory (accompanying his edition in CSCO 417–18 [= Scriptores Syri 183–4] (Louvain, 1980)), that the early Syriac version represents a Copticizing Greek text, has encountered considerable criticism; see, for example, the remarks of L. Abramowski in *Mélanges A. Guillaumont* (Geneva, 1988), pp. 47–56.

[39] Palladius's *Historia Lausiaca* is now ed. R. Draguet in CSCO 389–90 and 398–9 [= Scriptores Syri 169–70 and 173–4] (Louvain, 1978). For the *Historia monachorum* and the *apophthegmata*, there is only the edition based on a late manuscript of 'Enanisho's recension by E. A. Wallis Budge (cited below, n. 100).

[40] Details of editions can most readily be found in *CPG* II; for the letters, see now G. Bunge, *Evagrius Pontikos, Briefe aus der Wüste* (Trier, 1986).

[41] Dadisho', Commentary on the *Asceticon* of Abba Isaiah X.6 (as cited below, n. 99).

[42] See A. and C. Guillaumont, *Évagre le Pontique. Traité pratique ou le moine I*, Sources chrétiennes 170 (Paris, 1971), 319–34, and their *Évagre le Pontique. Le Gnostique*, Sources chrétiennes 356 (Paris, 1989), 52–62 and 68–71. The most dramatic case concerns the *Kephalaia Gnostica*, ed. A. Guillaumont, PO 28 (1958).

[43] Many of the lives circulated separately; cf. B. Outtier, 'Notule sur les versions orientales de l'Histoire Philothée (CPG 6221)', in *Antidoron. Hommages à M. Geerard I* (Wetteren, 1984), pp. 73–80.

[44] W. Strothmann, *Die syrische Überlieferung der Schriften des Makarios*, Göttinger Orientforschungen, Reihe Syriaca 21 (Göttingen, 1981).

century a thorough-going revision of this first translation[45] was made by Phokas of Edessa,[46] applying techniques of translation that had only been developed in the period subsequent to Sergius's death. Other Greek monastic writings which proved influential in Syriac translation were works by Abba Isaiah, Nilus and Mark the Monk.[47]

The only early Syriac church father to have the distinction of having some of his works translated into Greek was Ephrem (d. 373), one of whose writings in translation had already been admired by Jerome.[48] Very little, however, of the extant Ephrem Graecus and Ephrem Latinus is genuine Ephrem, and in most cases probably did not even start out in Syriac.[49]

Among the astonishingly large number of translations made from Greek into Syriac during the fifth to seventh century it is not surprising that hagiographical texts feature prominently, and many of these are texts which also found their way into Latin during the same period.[50] Thus, for

[45] Only excerpts of the two versions have so far been published; see J.-M. Hornus, 'Le Corpus dionysien en syriaque', *Parole de l'Orient* 1 (1970), 69–93, and W. Strothmann, *Das Sakrament der Myron-Weihe in der Schrift De Ecclesiastica Hierarchia des Pseudo-Dionysios Areopagita in syrischen Übersetzungen und Kommentaren*, Göttinger Orientforschungen, Reihe Syriaca 15 (Göttingen, 1977). A complete edition by G. Wiessner (Göttingen) has been promised.

[46] Although Phokas has usually been dated to the eighth century, there is now evidence that his work belongs to the late seventh, since it is quoted by Jacob of Edessa; see my 'Jacob of Edessa's Discourse on the Myron', *Oriens Christianus* 63 (1979), 20–36, esp. 21.

[47] The Syriac versions of Abba Isaiah's *Asceticon* are now ed. R. Draguet, CSCO 289–90 and 293–4 [= Scriptores Syri 120–3] (Louvain, 1968); those of Nilus's works are ed. P. Bettiolo, *Gli scritti siriaci di Nilo il Solitario* (Louvain, 1983). The Syriac translation of Mark's works remains unpublished.

[48] Jerome, *De uiris illustribus*, ch. 115.

[49] The best guide to this complex corpus is provided by D. Hemmerdinger-Iliadou, in *Dictionnaire de spiritualité* IV (Paris, 1960), 800–19, supplemented by her article in *Epeteris Hetaireias Byzantinon Spoudon* 42 (1975–6), 320–73, and *CPG* II, pp. 366–468. See also T. H. Bestul, 'Ephraim the Syrian and Old English Poetry', *Anglia* 99 (1981), 1–24; P. Sims-Williams, 'Thoughts on Ephrem the Syrian in Anglo-Saxon England', in *Learning and Literature in Anglo-Saxon England*, ed. M. Lapidge and H. Gneuss (Cambridge, 1985), pp. 205–26; and T. S. Pattie, 'Ephraem the Syrian and the Latin Manuscripts of "De Paenitentia",' *British Library Journal* 13 (1987), 1–23.

[50] A valuable overview of the influence of oriental hagiography on the West is provided by J. Gribomont, 'Panorama des influences orientales sur l'hagiographie latine', *Augustinianum* 24 (1984), 7–20. Details of publications of Syriac texts up to 1910 can be found in [P. Peeters], *BHO*.

example, the legend of the Seven Sleepers of Ephesus is found in three different sixth-century Syriac forms: a verse homily attributed to Jacob of Serugh (here there are eight youths; if genuine, this would be the earliest witness), and two translations made from Greek, incorporated into chronicles.[51] Other hagiographical texts popular both in Latin and in Syriac include Cosmas and Damian,[52] Cirycus (Cyriacus) and Julitta,[53] Febronia,[54] George,[55] the Maccabaean martyrs,[56] Pelagia,[57] the Forty Martyrs of Sebaste,[58] Sergius and Bacchus,[59] and the finding of the relics

---

[51] The most important Syriac texts were published by I. Guidi, in *Atti della R. Accademia dei Lincei, Memorie* 3rd ser. 12 (1884), 343–445; the series of articles by A. Allgeier in *Oriens Christianus* ns 6–8 (1916–18), though providing some further texts, obfuscate the issues of the early transmission of the text: see the remarks of P. Peeters in *AB* 41 (1923), 369–85.

[52] See M. van Esbroeck, 'La Diffusion orientale de la légende des saints Cosme et Damien', in *Hagiographie, cultures et sociétés, IVe au XIIe siècles* (Paris, 1981), 61–77.

[53] In Tarsus (cf. the remarks of Christopher Hohler, below, pp. 223–4). Another Cyriacus popular in both eastern and western hagiography in the seventh century was Judas Cyriacus, with whose help the dowager empress Helena was said to have discovered the True Cross; there are Syriac versions in sixth-century manuscripts of both the 'Finding of the Cross' and of his martyrdom; for the relationship of the latter to the Latin, see N. Pigoulewsky, 'Le Martyre de saint Cyriaque de Jérusalem', *Revue de l'Orient chrétien* 3rd ser. 6 (1927–8), 305–56.

[54] An English translation of the Syriac is given in S. P. Brock and S. A. Harvey, *Holy Women of the Syrian Orient* (Berkeley, CA, 1987), ch. 7.

[55] The earliest form of the Syriac text is ed. and trans. E. W. Brooks, in *Le Muséon* 38 (1925), 67–115.

[56] The cult of Shmuni (Greek Solomone) and her seven sons was particularly important at Antioch, as well as further east in the Syriac-speaking areas. Their portrayal in the frescoes of S. Maria Antiqua in Rome will probably have been inspired by refugees from the eastern Mediterranean littoral.

[57] An English translation of the Syriac is given in Brock and Harvey, *Holy Women*, ch. 2. The diffusion of the text is studied at length in the collaborative work *Pélagie la Pénitente, Metamorphose d'une légende*, 2 vols. (Paris, 1981–4); the results are summarized by P. Petitmengin, 'La Diffusion de la "Pénitence de Pélagie": résultats d'une recherche collective', *ibid.*, pp. 33–47.

[58] An English translation of the Syriac is forthcoming in a volume on the Forty Martyrs of Sebaste, ed. M. Mullett and A. Crabbe.

[59] Sergiopolis (Resafa) will have been known to Theodore as an important pilgrimage centre in northern Syria; for the imposing ruins, see T. Ulbert, *Resafa II. Die Basilika des heiligen Kreuzes in Resafa* (Mainz, 1986).

of John the Baptist[60] and those of Stephen.[61] Greek hagiography by strongly pro-Chalcedonian writers such as Cyril of Scythopolis of course remains untranslated in the Syriac non-Chalcedonian tradition,[62] though some of the less theologically minded Lives by Leontius of Neapolis do get translated and read.[63] Rather surprisingly, there is no trace in Syriac of the Life of Anastasius the Persian,[64] who had a great vogue in the West.[65] In a few cases Lives of saints started out in Syriac, and were subsequently translated, first into Greek and then into Latin (often getting considerably expanded on the way); in this category come the Acts of Thomas,[66] the Lives of Abraham and his niece Mary,[67] the Man of God (Alexius),[68] the Edessan martyrs Habbib, Shmona and Gurya,[69] and the Persian martyr Jacob Intercisus.[70] A particularly intriguing case is provided by another Persian martyr, Milus of Susa, who is known in the West from the Old

[60] On this text, see P. Peeters, *Le Tréfonds oriental de l'hagiographie byzantine*, 2nd ed., Subsidia hagiographica 26 (Brussels, 1950), 58–60. The Syriac has not yet been published.

[61] Peeters, *ibid.*, pp. 53–8.

[62] Fragments of a Syriac translation of Chalcedonian provenance, with the Life of St Sabas, are to be found among the new finds of Syriac manuscripts at St Catherine's Monastery, Sinai; cf. below, n. 117.

[63] Thus there are Syriac translations of his Life of Simeon the Fool (Salos) and of John the Almoner, preserved in Syrian Orthodox manuscripts.

[64] Martyred 28 January 628 at Beth Selokh (Bethsaloe in the Latin version; modern Kirkuk, Iraq); cf. C. V. Franklin and P. Meyvaert, 'Has Bede's Version of the "Passio S. Anastasii" come down to us in *BHL* 408?', *AB* 100 (1982), 373–400.

[65] See the discussion by Carmela Vircillo Franklin, below, pp. 175–203.

[66] The Latin *passio* and *miracula* differ considerably from extant Greek texts; cf. K. Zelzer, *Die alten lateinischen Thomasakten*, Texte und Untersuchungen 122 (Berlin, 1977), and his 'Zu die lateinischen Fassungen der Thomasakten', *Wiener Studien* 84 (1971), 161–79, and 85 (1972), 185–212.

[67] There is an English translation of the section on Mary in Brock and Harvey, *Holy Women*, ch. 1. This text was later to inspire one of Hrotswitha's plays; see M. Schmidt, 'Orientalischer Einfluss auf die deutsche Literatur: Quellengeschichtliche Studie zum "Abraham" der Hrotsvit von Gandersheim', *Colloquia Germanica* 1–2 (1968), 152–87.

[68] The legend does not, however, appear to have become known in the West until the late tenth century; see C. E. Stebbins, 'Les Origines de la légende de S. Alexis', *Revue belge de philologie et d'histoire* 51 (1973), 497–507, and the introduction to C. J. Odenkirchen, *The Life of St Alexius in the Old French Version* (Leiden, 1978).

[69] There is an English translation of the Syriac texts in F. C. Burkitt, *Euphemia and the Goth* (London, 1913).

[70] See P. Devos, 'Le Dossier hagiographique de S. Jacques l'Intercis', *AB* 71 (1953), 157–210, and 72 (1954), 213–56.

English Martyrology;[71] how and why knowledge of him travelled to England is a mystery, for although he received a short mention in the 'Synaxarium of Constantinople' and some Greek menologies, his Syriac Life was not among those known to have been translated into Greek.[72]

It would appear that translations into Syriac of secular Greek works, philosophical,[73] medical and scientific, were rarely undertaken before the sixth century. To the early sixth century, in any case, the work of Sergius of Resh'aina belongs. Besides translating the Dionysian Corpus[74] into Syriac (within what must have been only a few decades of its composition), Sergius also gained a reputation as a translator of Galen and as the author of an introduction to Aristotle's logical works.[75] The pivotal role played by the *Organon* in sixth-century education is nicely brought out by Sergius at the end of his Introduction, where he comments,[76] 'Without these [i.e. Aristotle's logical works] neither can the meaning of medical writings be attained, nor can the opinion of the philosophers be understood, nor, indeed, can the true sense be uncovered of the divine Scriptures, wherein lies the hope of our salvation – unless it should be that someone receives divine ability thanks to the exalted nature of his way of life, with the result that he has no need for human instruction. For education and advancement in the direction of all the sciences, as far as human ability is concerned, cannot take place without the exercise of logic.'

Most of the early books of the *Organon* in fact survive in two or more

---

[71] See discussion by C. Hohler, below, pp. 225–6.

[72] Ed. H. Delehaye, in PO 2 (1905).

[73] Although the Aristotelian commentator Probus has traditionally been put in the fifth century, there are good reasons for dating him to the sixth; see my 'From Antagonism to Assimilation' (cited above, n. 8), p. 26 with n. 102, and H. Suermann, 'Die Übersetzungen des Probus und eine Theorie zur Geschichte der syrischen Übersetzung griechischer Texte', *Oriens Christianus* 74 (1990), 103–14. For translations of medical literature (notably Galen, by Sergius of Resh'aina, on whom see below, n. 75), cf. M. Dols, 'Syriac into Arabic: the Transmission of Greek Medicine', *Aram* 1 (1989), 45–52.

[74] See above, n. 45.

[75] For Sergius's Introduction, see H. Hugonnard-Roche, 'Aux Origines de l'exégèse orientale de la logique d'Aristote: Sergius de Reš'aina', *Journal asiatique* 277 (1989), 1–17; and, for the translations from Galen (most of which are now lost), R. Degen, 'Galen im Syrischen', in *Galen: Problems and Perspectives*, ed. V. Nutton (London, 1981), pp. 131–66.

[76] London, British Library, Add. 14658, 60v–61r; the passage is paraphrased in the section on Aristotle in the *Anonymous Chronicle ad annum 1234*, ed. J. B. Chabot, CSCO 81 [= Scriptores Syri 36] (Louvain, 1953) I, 105.

Syriac translations, the earliest of which will almost certainly date from the sixth century, while the revisions were made in the course of the seventh and early eighth centuries (further revisions, or retranslations, were subsequently made in the ninth century).[77] Although the names of the sixth-century translators are not known (in most cases Sergius, to whom they are often attributed by modern scholarship, is unlikely to have been the author), those of the seventh-century revisers are known: thus for the *Categories*, we have an anonymous sixth/seventh-century version[78] (wrongly attributed in modern times to Sergius),[79] two revisions from the late seventh or early eighth century, by Jacob of Edessa[80] and by George, bishop of the Arab tribes,[81] and we know that there once existed two ninth-century translations/revisions, done by Hunayn ibn Ishaq and by a certain Yonan (or Yoba).[82]

The fate in Syriac of that long-lived textbook, Porphyry's *Eisagoge*, tells a similar story. The earliest translation, anonymous, is almost certainly a product of the sixth century;[83] in the seventh century, however, this

---

[77] Guides to this material can be found in H. Hugonnard-Roche, 'L'Organon. Tradition syriaque et arabe', in *Dictionnaire des philosophes antiques*, ed. R. Goulet, 2 vols. (Paris, 1989) I, 502–28, and in my 'The Syriac Commentary Tradition', in *Glosses and Commentaries on Aristotelian Logical Texts*, ed. C. Burnett, Warburg Institute Surveys and Texts 23 (London, 1993), 3–18.

[78] Preserved in a single seventh-century manuscript, the above-mentioned BL Add. 14658, not yet published; according to Hugonnard-Roche, 'L'Organon', the translator may have been Yonan, the correspondent of Severus Sebokht in the mid-seventh century (see below, n. 82).

[79] See H. Hugonnard-Roche, 'Sur les versions syriaques des Catégories d'Aristote', *Journal asiatique* 275 (1987), 205–22.

[80] Ed. K. Georr, *Les Catégories d'Aristote dans leur versions syro-arabes* (Beirut, 1948).

[81] This has been twice edited, by R. Gottheil, 'The Syriac Versions of the Categories of Aristotle', *Hebraica* 9 (1892–3), 166–215, and by G. Furlani, 'Le Categorie e gli Ermeneutici di Aristotele nella versione siriaca di Giorgio delle Nazioni', *Atti dell' Accademia Nazionale dei Lincei, Memorie* 6th ser. 5 (1933), 1–68.

[82] Neither of these survive (though if Yoba/Yonan belongs to the seventh, rather than the ninth, century), as Hugonnard-Roche proposes (see above, nn. 78 and 79), then this version does survive in BL Add. 14658.

[83] The sixth-century translation is published in my 'The earliest Syriac Translation of Porphyry's *Eisagoge*, I. Edition', *Journal of the Iraqi Academy, Syriac Corporation* 12 (1988), 315–66 (unfortunately my English introduction was missed out; see instead my 'Some Notes on the Syriac Translations of Porphyry's *Eisagoge*', in the *Festschrift for F. Jabre* (forthcoming).

version was considered inadequate, and was revised by the scholar-patriarch Athanasius II of Balad.[84]

A small, but telling, pointer to the extent to which the Latin West and the Syriac Orient shared a common Greek inheritance in the period under consideration is provided by the sigla used by George of the Arabs for glosses in his revised translation of the *Organon*: these bear a remarkable similarity to the sigla to be found in the Florentine manuscript of Boethius's translation of the *Analytica priora*.[85]

It is indeed remarkable that, in a century often regarded as reflecting a low ebb in Greek scholarship, there should have been such an extensive work of translation, revision, and commentary on the *Organon* on the part of Syriac scholars. It was in fact their work which laid the foundations for the subsequent flurry of translation activity at the Abbasid court in the ninth century, when scholars from the various Syriac churches played an essential role[86] in the early stages of the transmission of Greek philosophical and scientific writings to the Arab world – eventually to reach Europe by way of the twelfth-century Latin translations made from Arabic at Toledo and elsewhere.

The Syriac scholars of the seventh century who undertook this extensive work of translation, revision and commentary for the most part belonged to the Syrian Orthodox Church and received their training (and often carried out their work) in certain monasteries which over the course of time had gained a reputation for Greek learning. Perhaps the most important among these was the monastery of Qenneshre on the Euphrates[87] (to be differentiated from the town of Qenneshrin, Greek Chalkis); with this monastery, where the patriarch Julian (687–707/8) received training 'in

[84] Ed. A. Freimann, *Die Isagoge des Porphyrius in den syrischen Übersetzungen* (Berlin, 1897).

[85] For the sigla in the Florentine manuscript, see W. Shiels, 'A Set of Greek Reference Signs in the Florentine Manuscript of Boethius' Translation of the Prior Analytics', *Scriptorium* 38 (1984), 327–42.

[86] See, for example, G. Klinge, 'Die Bedeutung der syrischen Theologen als Vermittler der griechischen Philosophie an den Islam', *Zeitschrift für Kirchengeschichte* 58 (1939), 346–86, and De Lacy O'Leary, *How Greek Science Passed to the Arabs* (London, 1949), ch. 12. A new survey devoted specifically to the role of the Syriac translators is a desideratum.

[87] For the location, see my *The Syriac Version of the pseudo-Nonnos Mythological Scholia*, p. 10, n. 10. Other important monasteries with a reputation for Greek studies were Beth Malke (also known as Eusebona), and Mar Zakkai at Kallinikos (which specialized in Gregory of Nazianzus, according to the Life of Marutha, ed. F. Nau, PO 3 (1905), 70).

the Attic tongue',[88] both Paul of Edessa and Athanasius of Balad were associated.

By contrast with the situation in the Syrian Orthodox Church, where learning, both theological and secular, was concentrated in certain monasteries, that in the Church of the East was very different, for there it was the church schools, situated in several of the larger sees, which provided the seats of learning. Best known of these, but certainly not unique, was the School of Nisibis,[89] whose effective beginnings go back to the end of the fifth century, when it became the heir to the 'School of the Persians' at Edessa, which the emperor Zeno closed down in 489 on the grounds that it was a hotbed of Nestorianism. It was the School of Nisibis through which the Antiochene christological and exegetical traditions represented by Theodore of Mopsuestia eventually came to dominate the theological tradition of the Church of the East. In the mid-sixth century Mar Abba/ Patrikios, the friend of Cosmas Indicopleustes[90] and future Catholicos, probably introduced into the School's curriculum a new feature, namely the genre of the prefatory 'explanation' for the academic study of a particular work, set out under a series of headings, 'purpose', 'usefulness', 'authenticity', etc.[91] Mar Abba evidently took this over from his time studying in Alexandria, for the idea was borrowed from the introductory commentaries to Aristotle's logical works provided by Ammonius and his successors in Alexandria. The application of this method to biblical studies at Nisibis is excellently reflected in Junilius's *Instituta regularia*,[92] a Latin

[88] Barhebraeus, *Chronicon ecclesiasticum* (ed. Abbeloos and Lamy) I, 295.

[89] See A. Vööbus, *History of the School of Nisibis*, CSCO 266 [= Subsidia 26] (Louvain, 1965), and R. Macina, 'L'Homme à l'école de Dieu. D'Antioche à Nisibe', *Proche Orient Chrétien* 32 (1982), 86–124 and 263–301, and 33 (1983), 39–103. It should be noted that, contrary to statements often found, there is no evidence for the existence of a Christian medical school at Gondishapur in the sixth/seventh century.

[90] See W. Wolska-Conus, *La Topographie chrétienne de Cosmas Indicopleustès. Théologie et science au VIe siècle* (Paris, 1962).

[91] See E. Riad, *Studies in the Syriac Preface*, Studia Semitica Upsaliensia 11 (Uppsala, 1988), 39–72.

[92] Ed. H. Kihn, *Theodor von Mopsuestia und Junilius Africanus als Exegeten* (Freiburg, 1880). Cf. R. Macina, 'Cassiodore et l'Ecole de Nisibe', *Le Muséon* 95 (1982), 131–66, which, however, should be read in the light of G. Fiaccadori, 'Cassiodorus and the School of Nisibis', *Dumbarton Oaks Papers* 39 (1985), 135–7. For Junilius, see Averil Cameron, 'Byzantine Africa – the Literary Evidence', in *Excavations at Carthage 1978 conducted by the University of Michigan VIII*, ed. J. H. Humphrey (Ann Arbor, MI, 1982), pp. 29–62, esp. 46.

adaptation of a lost work by a certain Paul the Persian, who had been educated at the School of Nisibis.[93]

It would appear that, in contrast to the situation with the Syrian Orthodox, monasteries in the Church of the East in the seventh century were less concerned with the transmission of biblical and secular learning, producing instead a remarkable series of writers on the spiritual life, most famous of whom is Isaac of Nineveh (late seventh century),[94] a large part of whose writings were translated into Greek at the monastery of Mar Saba in Palestine in the eighth or ninth century. Isaac was by no means an isolated figure, and other important monastic writers of this century include Martyrius/Sahdona,[95] Dadisho'[96] (like Isaac, originally from Qatar) and Shem'on the Graceful.[97] The writings of these men in fact show them to be highly educated and well read in both Syriac and Greek patristic literature (the latter of course in translation), evidently available in their monastic libraries. Nor was secular literature entirely absent, for several of them quote from sayings of the pagan philosophers, and Isaac had available the Syriac translation of the Life of Secundus the Silent Philosopher.[98] The techniques of the scholarship of the Schools is also to be found in some of the monastic writers of this period. Dadisho' wrote commentaries both on

---

[93] To be distinguished from another Paul the Persian, author of a Syriac introduction to logic; cf. D. Gutas, 'Paul the Persian on the Classification of the Parts of Aristotle's Philosophy: a Milestone between Alexandria and Baghdad', *Der Islam* 60 (1983), 231–67, esp. 238–9, n. 14.

[94] An overview is provided by E. Khalifé-Hachem in *Dictionnaire de spiritualité* VII (Paris, 1971), 2041–54. An English translation (with good introduction) of the Greek version, by D. Miller, is available in *The Ascetical Homilies of St Isaac the Syrian translated by the Holy Transfiguration Monastery* (Boston, 1984); for a recent find of further Syriac homilies, see my 'Lost and Found: Part II of the Works of St Isaac of Nineveh', *Studia Patristica* 18 (1990), 230–3.

[95] Ed., with French translation, by A. de Halleux, CSCO 200–1, 214–15 and 252–5 [= Scriptores Syri 86–7, 90–1 and 110–13] (Louvain, 1960–5).

[96] His 'Discourse on Solitude' is trans. A. Mingana, *Early Christian Mystics*, Woodbrooke Studies 7 (Cambridge, 1934), 76–143. For further works by Dadisho', see below, n. 99.

[97] Some works by Shem'on (Simeon) are trans. Mingana, *Early Christian Mystics*, pp. 3–69; Shem'on clearly had some training in medicine. See also now P. Bettiolo, *Simone di Taibuteh. Violenza e grazia. La cultura del cuore* (Rome, 1993).

[98] See my 'Secundus the Silent Philosopher: Some Notes on the Syriac Tradition', *Rheinisches Museum* 121 (1978), 94–100, repr. in my *Studies in Syriac Christianity*, ch. IX.

Abba Isaiah's *Asceticon*[99] and the 'Paradise of the Fathers', the latter being a collection of monastic texts from Egypt put together by 'Enanisho' earlier in the century, containing such works as Palladius's *Historia Lausiaca*, the *Historia monachorum* (attributed to Jerome) and a collection of *apophthegmata*.[100]

The enormous effort expended by seventh-century Syriac scholars on translating from Greek, or revising earlier translations, should not obscure the fact that many of the very same men were important authors in their own right. Severus Sebokht (d. 666/7), besides translating from both Greek and Middle Persian and commenting on problems of Aristotelian logic,[101] also composed a number of treatises on mathematical and astronomical topics. In several of his works we can observe Severus reacting against Greek cultural chauvinism of his time, pointing out that the Greeks came to scientific learning long after the Babylonians and Indians; typical is a passage which provides what must be one of the earliest references to Indian numerals: 'At this point I shall refrain from speaking about the science of the Indians, who were not even Syrians, or about their exact discoveries in the science of astronomy – discoveries which show far more skill than those of the Greeks or Babylonians – and the logical method of their calculations and the way of counting which surpasses description (I refer to the method which uses nine signs). Had they been aware of these, this people [*scil.* the Greeks], who imagine of themselves that they alone have reached the summit of wisdom just because they speak Greek, would perhaps have been persuaded, even though rather late in the day, that there are other people who have some knowledge: it is not just the Greeks, but also some of the peoples who speak different languages as well.'[102]

---

[99] His interesting commentary on Abba Isaiah's *Asceticon* is ed. R. Draguet, CSCO 326–7 [= Scriptores Syri 144–5] (Louvain, 1972).

[100] There is an English translation by E. A. Wallis Budge (from his edition based only on late manuscripts; the contents of earlier manuscripts are somewhat different): *The Paradise or Garden of the Holy Fathers*, 2 vols. (London, 1907). For the manuscript tradition, see C. Butler, *The Lausiac History of Palladius*, Texts and Studies 6.1 (Cambridge, 1898), 77–84. See now N. Sims-Williams in *AB* 112 (1994), 33–64.

[101] A mistranslation misled earlier scholars into supposing he commented on the Rhetoric; the matter was set right by G. J. Reinink, 'Severos Sebokts Brief an den Periodeutes Jonan. Einige Fragen zur aristotelischen Logik', in *III Symposium Syriacum*, ed. R. Lavenant, Orientalia Christiana Analecta 221 (Rome, 1983), 97–108.

[102] Ed. F. Nau, 'La Plus Ancienne Mention orientale des chiffres indiens', *Journal asiatique* 10th ser. 16 (1910), 225.

Even more wide-ranging in his interests and writings was Jacob of Edessa: we have already seen that his translation revisions covered biblical writings, Severus of Antioch's *Homilies* and Aristotle's *Categories*. The meticulous nature of his translation work is splendidly illustrated in his revision of a collection of hymns by Severus of Antioch and others, surviving in an early manuscript which might possibly be an autograph.[103] His Syriac writings include a Chronicle (of which only a small fragment survives), works on liturgy, canon law, biblical studies, theology, literary criticism, grammar and logic.[104] A passing marginal note of his, attached to his revision of the Syriac translation of Severus's *Homilies*, reveals that he even had a knowledge of Hebrew, for he comments there in some detail on the Jewish reading of the Tetragrammaton.[105] Much of his scientific knowledge was incorporated into his largest surviving work, a learned commentary on the *Hexaemeron*,[106] which includes, alongside a great deal ultimately derived from earlier Greek writings, several interesting observations of his own on natural phenomena.

Apart from producing one outstanding theologian, Maximus the Confessor, the Greek world of the seventh century was suffering a time of 'éclipse passagière',[107] and so in the eastern Mediterranean world it was primarily among Syriac scholars that that part of the classical heritage which was to pass on the medieval world was best fostered. It is a matter of no small surprise that, in the century which witnessed such momentous political changes in the Middle East, Syriac scholars, who were living in the midst of such changes, managed to maintain this thread of continuity.

It remains to consider very briefly what sort of channels of communication might possibly provide links between the Syriac world and Theodore's England. Here I would tentatively suggest three which might be worth exploring. The first would be centred on the person of Theodore

---

[103] See E. W. Brooks, *The Hymns of Severus and others in the Syriac Version of Paul of Edessa as revised by Jacob of Edessa*, PO 6–7 (1909–11).

[104] A summary overview of his works is given by F. Graffin in *Dictionnaire de spiritualité* VIII (Paris, 1974), 33–5.

[105] Homily 123, in PO 29 (1960), 194–202. E. Nestle had drawn attention to the interest of the passage much earlier: 'Jakob von Edessa über den Schem hammephorasch...', *Zeitschrift der Deutschen Morgenländischen Gesellschaft* 32 (1878), 465–508 and 735–6.

[106] Ed. J. Chabot, trans. A. Vaschalde, CSCO 92 and 97 [= Scriptores Syri 44 and 48] (Louvain, 1928–32).

[107] P. Moraux, *D'Aristote à Bessarion* (Quebec, 1970), p. 17; cf. the remarks of G. Cavallo, below, pp. 54–9.

himself, and his origins in Tarsus. Although Tarsus will have lain outside the Syriac-speaking area, a native of that town could hardly have been unaware of the existence of a developed scholarly literature in Syriac. The mention in the Canterbury biblical commentaries (PentI 413) of outsize melons in Edessa[108] perhaps suggests that Theodore had even visited this home of Syriac culture.[109] Ecclesiastical allegiance, however, would have ensured that any contact he might have had with the Syriac world would not have been with the body which was most active in scholarship, the Syrian Orthodox. Here it is particularly unfortunate that we have so little surviving evidence from the Syriac-speaking Chalcedonian community in Syria at this time, for any contacts that might have existed would have been with them.[110]

A second channel of contact would also be linked, at least potentially, with Theodore, but this time with his stay in Rome. From a variety of sources it is known that considerable numbers of monks and others reached Italy and Rome as refugees from the Arab invasions. In many cases these people travelled by way of North Africa and Sicily, and most famous among their number was Maximus the Confessor who, it now appears,[111] was a native of Palestine, rather than of Constantinople. Although the majority of these refugees will have been Chalcedonians, there were evidently also some belonging to the Church of the East; thus in the Syriac Life of Maximus the Confessor (of monothelete provenance) we learn of a monastery in Hippo Diarrhytus housing some eighty monks described as 'Nestorians' who included among their number some students from Nisibis (presumably from its famous theological School).[112] Later on in

---

[108] See *Biblical Commentaries*, ed. Bischoff and Lapidge, p. 35. Jacob of Edessa, by contrast, in his Commentary on the *Hexaemeron*, mentions outsize fruit as something to be found in India, Cush and Sheba (ed. Chabot, p. 136).

[109] On Edessa, see J. B. Segal, *Edessa, 'The Blessed City'*, (Oxford, 1970), as well as discussion in *Biblical Commentaries*, ed. Bischoff and Lapidge, pp. 27–37.

[110] Some interesting details of the Melkite community in Edessa in 723 are provided in a colophon published by R. W. Thomson, 'An Eighth-Century Melkite Colophon from Edessa', *JTS* ns 13 (1962), 249–58; among other things, this colophon reveals that there were separate Greek and Syriac choirs.

[111] On the basis of an early Syriac Life, of monothelete provenance, ed. and trans. in my 'An early Syriac Life of Maximus the Confessor', *AB* 91 (1973), 299–346 (repr. in my *Syriac Perspectives on Late Antiquity*, ch. XII). The evidence of the Syriac Life for Maximus's origins is accepted, for example, by I. Dalmais, in *Dictionnaire de spiritualité* X (Paris, 1980), 836–7.

[112] Syriac Life of Maximus, ch. 19.

the Life of Maximus we are told that these students continued on to Rome, where 'they were received by Martin as having the same faith as he [i.e. dyothelete], and he gave them a monastery, called in the Latin tongue *Cellae nouae* (QLWNWBWS), which means "nine cells".[113] And they remained in their error, leading astray all they could. . .' The presence of 'Nestorian' monks in Rome is in fact well attested from other sources, where they are connected with the *Boetiana* monastery[114] (in *c.* 676/8, however, they were dispersed). We can of course only speculate whether or not Theodore ever came into direct contact with any of these representatives of the Syriac churches during his time in Rome. This evidence is, nonetheless, of considerable interest, since it points to the shared interest in the Antiochene christological and exegetical tradition,[115] represented par excellence by the writings of Theodore of Mopsuestia. Here it should also be recalled that earlier in the century, in 629, Heraclius had very nearly concluded a theological concordat with the Church of the East,[116] and that there has recently come to light some striking evidence of contact between monks of the Church of the East and the Chalcedonian monastery of St Catherine on Mt Sinai.[117]

A third channel of contact is provided by the evidence of literary texts which are known to have travelled from the Syriac Orient to the Latin West. Some of these, notably pieces of hagiography, have already been mentioned. A remarkable further instance, although falling just beyond the end of the seventh century, is the Apocalypse of pseudo-Methodius, a Syriac product from Mesopotamia and belonging to the end of the seventh century; this influential work, containing the legend of the last Roman

---

[113] *Ibid.*, ch. 24.

[114] J. M. Sansterre, *Les Moines grecs et orientaux à Rome aux époques byzantine et carolingienne (milieu du VIe s. – fin du IXe s.)*, 2 vols., Académie Royale de Belgique, Mémoires de la classe des lettres, Collection in octavo 2nd ser. 86 (Brussels, 1983), index, s.n.

[115] See discussion by Michael Lapidge, above, pp. 4–5, and *Biblical Commentaries*, ed. Bischoff and Lapidge, pp. 14–26 and 243–9.

[116] See C. Mango, 'Deux Etudes sur Byzance et la Perse sassanide', *Travaux et mémoires* 9 (1985), 91–118, esp. 105–17.

[117] The presence of a work by the East Syrian theologian par excellence, Babai the Great, is announced among the new finds of Syriac manuscripts at St Catherine's Monastery: see Mère Philothe, 'Les Nouveaux Manuscrits du Mont Sinai', in *III Symposium Syriacum*, ed. Lavenant, pp. 333–9, esp. 338.

emperor, was very soon translated into Greek, and thence into Latin.[118] Unfortunately, however, in this and in virtually every other case, the precise routes by which these texts reached western Europe and, sometimes, Theodore's England, are unknown. Colonies of Syrian merchants are well attested in the Rhone valley, and this might well have been the route by which hagiographical texts travelled. One could conjecture that the 'Syrian' (*Syrus*) with whose help Gregory of Tours put the legend of the Seven Sleepers of Ephesus into Latin, was one such Syrian merchant (presumably Greek-, rather than Syriac-speaking). A less direct route by which texts from the eastern Mediterranean world reached the British Isles is suggested by certain biblical apocrypha, where distinctive text-forms are sometimes attested in common by Syriac (or other oriental) and early Irish witnesses, with Spain the possible intermediary.[119] In such cases, however, it may well be that no real contact is implied, and it is simply a case of outlying areas preserving early forms of texts which have been lost, or subsequently developed, elsewhere.

'In the Okeanos, to the North of Spain, because of its proximity to the inhabited world, God made some islands which are trodden [*scil*. by human beings] and inhabited, Hibernia (YWB'RNY') and Albion ('LW'YWN), which are called the Brettanikoi.' Such is the extent of Jacob of Edessa's knowledge of the British Isles in the geographical section of his Commentary on the *Hexaemeron*.[120] Yet, although his younger contemporary, Bede, might not have had any better a knowledge of Jacob's Syria, the writings of these two men in particular serve to show how much scholars working in the late seventh century at either end of what had once

---

[118] See P. Alexander, *The Byzantine Apocalyptic Tradition* (Berkeley, CA, 1985), which includes an English translation of the Syriac; see also the contributions by G. J. Reinink, M. Laureys and D. Verhelst, in *The Use and Abuse of Eschatology in the Middle Ages*, ed. W. Verbeke *et al.* (Leuven, 1988), and A. N. Palmer, *The Seventh Century in the West-Syrian Chronicles* (Liverpool, 1993), pp. 222–50.

[119] This applies, for example, to some of the texts of the *Transitus Mariae*; cf. M. McNamara, *The Apocrypha in the Irish Church* (Dublin, 1975), p. 122. In general for this route, see J. N. Hillgarth, 'The East, Visigothic Spain and the Irish', *Studia Patristica* 4 [= Texte und Untersuchungen 79] (1961), 442–56.

[120] Commentary on the *Hexaemeron*, ed. Chabot, p. 112.

been the eastern and western extremities of the Roman empire still shared a common intellectual heritage.[121]

[121] A much briefer survey, but covering some different points and from a different perspective, can be found in my 'Syriac Culture in the Seventh Century', *Aram* 1 (1989), 268–80.

Addendum to n. 98 (above p. 47): It should be noted that the pagan oracle from the *Theosophia*, found in Oxford, Bodleian Library, Laud gr. 35, 226v, is also attested in a Syriac collection of pagan prophecies put together *c.* 600; see my 'A Syriac Collection of Prophecies of the Pagan Philosophers', *Orientalia Lovaniensia Periodica* 14 (1983), 203–46, at 229 and 238–9 (§7), repr. in my *Studies in Syriac Christianity*, ch. VII. The link is significant because Laud gr. 35 was brought to England from Rome in the latter half of the seventh century, perhaps by Theodore himself; for references, see *Biblical Commentaries*, ed. Bischoff and Lapidge, p. 170.

3

Theodore of Tarsus and the Greek culture of his time

GUGLIELMO CAVALLO

It is a wholly reasonable assumption that Theodore of Tarsus acquired his knowledge of Latin at Rome, where he spent a number of years before setting off – together with Hadrian, abbot of the monastery of *Hiridanum* near Naples – for England and Canterbury, where he became archbishop on his arrival in 669.[1] On the other hand, it is extremely difficult to recover anything concerning when and where he acquired his learning in Greek, which was the language and culture of his native Cilicia. His career, and hence the period in which his education took place, spans broadly the seventh century (he was born in Tarsus *c.* 602 and died in Canterbury in 690); but there is insufficient evidence to state with conviction where he studied, whether in Athens[2] or Constantinople[3] or elsewhere, or to ascertain what course(s) of study he followed. In the absence of any direct evidence, therefore, it is necessary to attempt to reconstruct the intellectual climate of the Greek-speaking Mediterranean world of his time, extending from Constantinople and its eastern provinces to Sicily and Rome in the West. Such reconstruction will help to illuminate the circumstances of his education, even if – given the limitations of our knowledge – it is not possible to attain certainty in any respect.

One fact must be noted at the outset: namely the recognizable asym-

[1] On the activity of Theodore and Hadrian in England, see N. Cilento, *Civiltà napoletana nel medioevo nei secoli VI-XIII* (Naples, 1969), pp. 14–16; A. Guillou, 'L'Ecole dans l'Italie byzantine', *SettSpol* 19 (1972), 291–311, at 299–301; and C. Mango, 'La Culture grecque et l'Occident au VIIIe siècle', *SettSpol* 20 (1973), 683–721, at 685–8.

[2] Mango ('La Culture grecque', p. 685, n. 9) is sceptical on this point.

[3] See M. Lapidge, 'The Study of Greek at the School of Canterbury in the Seventh Century', *The Sacred Nectar of the Greeks: the Study of Greek in the West in the early Middle Ages*, ed. M. W. Herren (London, 1988), pp. 169–94, at 169; *Biblical Commentaries*, ed. Bischoff and Lapidge, pp. 41–64, and above, pp. 11–19.

metry in the eastern Byzantine world, between Constantinople and the outlying provinces during the period between the late sixth century and the late eighth, in the domain of literary culture, authors and texts. That is to say, in Constantinople itself we can see the slow triumph of *agroikía* ('rusticity'), whereas in the outlying provinces the evidence points to cultural continuity.[4] Let us look more closely at the two poles of this asymmetry. The cultural policies of Justinian (527–65) had already undermined the ancient traditions of Greek culture in the capital. The significant points in the implementation of these policies are the closing of the Academy in Athens in 529, the persecution of 'Hellenic' grammarians, rhetoricians and jurists in 546, and the burning of pagan books in the *Kynegion* in 562.[5] On the other hand, the collapse of urban life, which became ever more conspicuous from the late sixth century onwards,[6] necessarily involved the disappearance of places suitable for the conception, realization and circulation of written culture, and hence of texts and books. In fact the last florescence of 'Hellenic' culture in the capital is attested in the reign of Heraclius (610–41), as revealed by artistic production in various media (especially silverwork and mosaics), literary works (the historical writings of Theophylact Simocatta, the epic panegyrics of George of Pisidia) and institutional arrangements such as the appointment of Stephen of Alexandria as *didáskalos* in Constantinople. But this outburst of 'Hellenism' was ephemeral and left no trace of influence on subsequent generations. Even Stephen – who is to be identified with Stephen of Athens, the 'sophist', 'philosopher' and 'physician' – bears witness to the cultural traditions of Alexandria rather than Constantinople, for it was at Alexandria where he taught before his appointment to Constantinople, where he attempted to re-establish his (Alexandrian) school, 'cette forteresse de la science païenne et profane', as one scholar has

---

[4] The recent revaluation of seventh-century Byzantine schools and culture by W. Treadgold ('The Break in Byzantium and the Gap in Byzantine Studies', *Byzantinische Forschungen* 15 (1990), 289–316, esp. 307–10) unfortunately takes no account of the profound differences between Constantinople and outlying provincial milieux at this time as regards the education of certain learned individuals and of literary production in general, and his conclusions are therefore questionable.

[5] On all this, see my study 'La circolazione libraria nell'età di Giustiniano', in *L'imperatore Giustiniano. Storia e mito*, ed. G. G. Archi (Milan, 1978), pp. 211–12; see also Averil Cameron, *Procopius and the Sixth Century* (London, 1985), pp. 19–32.

[6] C. Mango, *Byzantium. The Empire of New Rome* (London, 1980), pp. 66–78.

recently described it.[7] And when Stephen died, there was no one who could be found to carry on his instruction, with the result that Heraclius was obliged to invite one Tychikos to Constantinople from faraway Trebizond. Tychikos had formerly been a student of Stephen, and was expert in learning both sacred and secular (as may be surmised from the contents of his library); when, therefore, Tychikos refused the imperial invitation, it was henceforth to him and his school in Trebizond that young scholars turned for instruction.[8] A little later, in the eighth century, the so-called *Parastáseis sýntomoi chronikaí* provide evidence that late antique inscriptions had become incomprehensible at Constantinople itself, insofar as no one could be found to read them; and the crude style in which these *Parastáseis sýntomoi chronikaí* are composed reveals clearly that the level of written culture in the capital at that time was exceedingly low.[9] Finally, concerning the 'University of Constantinople', which was reorganized by Theodosius II in 425: were it not for the imperial decree of that year stipulating its establishment, we would scarcely know anything of its existence;[10] a university, in other words, which between late antiquity and the Byzantine Middle Ages seems to be little more than an historical phantom. The sixth-century notice concerning the 'chair' of John Lydus is the latest datable evidence pertaining to a state-operated school of higher education, and to the building in which this school was located, namely the Capitolium.[11] The presence of Stephen of Alexandria as *didáskalos* in Constantinople at some point during the reign of Heraclius – from *c.* 619/20 until approximately 638 – does not necessarily imply official instruction either at a state university or at a patriarchal school.[12]

---

[7] On Stephen of Alexandria, see the excellent study by W. Wolska-Conus, 'Stéphanos d'Athènes et Stéphanos d'Alexandrie. Essai d'identification et de biographie', *Revue des études byzantines* 47 (1989), 5–89 (the quotation is from p. 80).

[8] H. Berbérian, 'Autobiographie d'Anania Sirakac'i', *Revue des études arméniennes* ns 1 (1964), 189–94, at 192–3.

[9] See *Constantinople in the Early Eighth Century: the Parastaseis Syntomoi Chronikai*, ed. Averil Cameron and J. Herrin (Leiden, 1984), pp. 27–9 and 38–45.

[10] Mango, *Byzantium*, p. 130.

[11] John Lydus, *Mag.* III.29 (ed. Wünsch, p. 117). See C. Mango, *Le Développement urbain de Constantinople (IVe-VIIe siècles)* (Paris, 1985), pp. 30 (with n. 44) and 58.

[12] Wolska-Conus, 'Stéphanos d'Athènes', pp. 15–17; see also the discussion of Stephen of Alexandria by P. Speck, *Die Kaiserliche Universität von Konstantinopel. Präzisierungen zur Frage des höheren Schulwesens in Byzanz im 9. und 10. Jahrhundert* (Munich, 1974), pp. 65–6 (with n. 52).

Even the existence of the 'patriarchal school' has been considered by some scholars as a myth.[13]

In the eastern provinces of Byzantium, by contrast, even during the course of those centuries which have been called 'Dark Ages', one can, in spite of the Persian and Arab invasions, trace certain vital threads of transmission of Greek authors and texts – either because particular urban structures and educational activities, and hence literary culture, were preserved; or else because various, more or less extensive, scholarly collections of books survived the turmoil and disasters in those centres (some of them preserving Hellenistic-Roman tradition) which had formerly housed state or municipal schools; or finally because copies of classical texts were prized by the new conquerors, to the point even of being translated into their own languages. In other words, there was a continuity of Greek culture in those centres and provinces even after they had been lost to the (Roman/Byzantine) empire; and I might add that it is in these centres and provinces where certain roots of the ninth-century Byzantine renascence must be sought.

The evidence to support these assertions is not lacking, though it is often of an indirect rather than direct nature. It should be noted at the outset, however, that no thorough study has ever been made of how many surviving manuscripts (including fragmentary ones) may be attributed to outlying, eastern centres during the period between the sixth century and the eighth. Furthermore, one's perspective is hindered by the fact that the majority of witnesses seems to have originated – judging by the mere accident of preservation – in Egypt. If the datings assigned to the surviving witnesses are correct, there must have been in circulation at that time some fifty literary and reference manuscripts, not counting biblical, liturgical and other theological works.[14] The number is not large, and we must reckon with a decline in book production (and in writing of all kinds) even in those areas and centres of ancient Hellenistic culture: but not its total disappearance. The picture which we can reconstruct from indirect evidence shows in every case the circulation of written culture. Lives of saints of the iconoclastic period witness to the continuity not only of

[13] P. Lemerle, *Le Premier Humanisme byzantin. Notes et remarques sur enseignement et culture à Byzance des origines au Xe siècle* (Paris, 1971), pp. 95–6.

[14] In matters concerning the so-called 'papyri' (that is, papyri and parchment fragments of Graeco-Egyptian provenance), I am indebted to the kindness of Paul Mertens (University of Liège) for much information.

elementary education, but also of instruction at a higher level in sacred and secular disciplines.[15] It is significant, however, that the oldest hagiographical texts in question, those dating from the eighth century, refer principally to saints who received their education in outlying areas rather than in the capital. That this continuity existed above all in areas and cities in the provinces of the Byzantine empire is clear from evidence of various kinds, as we shall see.

In Alexandria, the famous school survived that of Athens by becoming christianized. It has been observed that, 'the compromise character of the Alexandrian school as opposed to the diehard orthodoxy of Athens is the dominating fact in the history of fifth- and sixth-century philosophy':[16] with the result that Alexandria remained a centre of institutionalized education at least until the seventh century. This movement of christianization is perceptible particularly in the case of John Philoponus, in the fields of philosophy and medicine; and the vitality of the school of Alexandria even in the seventh century can be measured from the presence there of scholars such as the above-mentioned Stephen (originally from Athens) as well as Paul of Aegina. Indeed the fact that these two men went to Alexandria to complete their studies, and not to Constantinople, confirms the point that at that time the capital did not have much to offer in the way of advanced learning. It has been argued, on good evidence, that 'large sections of technical libraries of the 7th century have survived *en bloc* till the period of the transliteration';[17] accordingly, even if new works were not being composed in Greek, numerous Greek books of scientific and philosophical content were being preserved.[18] From Arab sources we know that it was still possible at a later time to find and acquire at Alexandria books of this kind.[19] Moreover, it was principally from

[15] Lemerle, *Le Premier Humanisme byzantin*, pp. 97–104.

[16] See *The Greek Commentaries on Plato's Phaedo, I. Olympiodorus*, ed. L. G. Westerink (Amsterdam, Oxford and New York, 1976), p. 23; *idem*, 'Philosophy and Medicine in Late Antiquity', *Janus* 51 (1964), 169–77; and the earlier study of H.-D. Saffrey, 'Le Chrétien Jean Philopon et la survivance de l'école d'Alexandrie au VIe siècle', *Revue des études grecques* 67 (1954), 396–410.

[17] *Ibid.* p. 169.

[18] See G. Strohmaier, 'Byzantinische arabische Wissenschaftsbeziehungen in der Zeit des Ikonoklasmus', in *Studien zum 8. und 9. Jahrhundert in Byzanz*, ed. H. Kopstein and F. Winkelmann (Berlin, 1983), pp. 179–83.

[19] H. Meyerhof, 'La Fin de l'école d'Alexandrie d'après quelques auteurs arabes', *Archeion* 15 (1933), 1–15, at 7.

Alexandria of the Byzantine and Islamic periods that philosophical and medical knowledge spread, as is shown *inter alia* by the prestige enjoyed by the writings of John Philoponus in the Near and Middle East – even if this prestige sometimes rested on false attributions and misrepresentations. In any event, it was above all from Greek exemplars of Alexandrian origin that the principal Syriac and Arabic translations of these writings were made.[20]

Further (indirect) light is thrown on the seventh-century school of Alexandria and its programme of studies by evidence from Armenia. Although some doubt exists concerning the precise chronology of Armenian translations of scholarly works of the so-called 'hellenizing school', it nevertheless seems certain that the authors translated into Armenian from the second half of the sixth century onwards were linked in some way with the Alexandrian school. It should also be noted that the translations in question relate specifically to the scheme of the 'seven liberal arts', that is, to the three literary disciplines of grammar, rhetoric and dialectic, as well as to the four scientific disciplines of arithmetic, music, geometry and astronomy. These last four, which constitute in effect the *quadrivium*, were introduced into the Armenian curriculum by Ananias of Shirak, who flourished in the first half of the seventh century, and who – through the agency of his master Tychikos, in his turn a student of Stephen – had been in contact with the scientific instruction of the school of Alexandria. The scholastic 'canon' of Ananias, in other words, was that of Alexandria: a further indication that the programme of studies elaborated in Alexandria was still continuing to exert influence in the Byzantine empire.[21]

Another aspect of the influence of the school of Alexandria, and in particular of the Alexandrian commentaries on Aristotle's *Categoriae* and

---

[20] On this complex matter, see M. Meyerhof, 'Von Alexandrien nach Bagdad. Ein Beitrag zur Geschichte des philosophischen und medizinischen Unterrichts bei den Arabern', *Sitzungsberichte der Preussischen Akademie der Wissenschaften*, phil.-hist. Klasse, 23 (1930), 389–429, and *idem*, 'Joannes Grammatikos (Philoponos) von Alexandrien und die arabische Medizin', *Mitteilungen des Deutschen Instituts für Ägyptische Altertumskunde in Kairo* 2 (1932), 1–21.

[21] See the fundamental study by J.-P. Mahé, 'Quadrivium et cursus d'études au VIIe siècle en Armenie et dans le monde byzantin d'après le K'nnikon d'Anania Sirakac'i', *Travaux et mémoires* 10 (1987), 159–206; see also P. Lemerle, 'Notes sur les données historiques de l'autobiographie d'Anania de Shirak', *Revue des études arméniennes* ns 1 (1964), 195–202; *idem*, *Le Premier Humanisme byzantin*, p. 7; and Wolska-Conus, 'Stéphanos d'Athènes', pp. 20–33.

Porphyry's *Isagoge*, is seen in the philosophical handbooks which were produced between the end of the sixth century and the beginning of the eighth. These handbooks or *compendia* of logic consist primarily of philosophical definitions accompanied by examples; and although in some sense they represent a notable retraction in philosophical teaching when set alongside the original commentaries, they nevertheless came to play a significant role in the transmission of Aristotelian thought during the course of the seventh century.[22] *Compendia* of this sort were also evidently known in Syria and Palestine at this time; in the opinion of one scholar, they 'form the likeliest bridge between the Alexandrian lectures on the one hand and the *Dialectica* of John Damascene on the other'; and it is probable that the Alexandrian tradition of Aristotelian commentary spread even as far as Antioch.[23] The *compendia* are also interesting for the light which they throw on authors who are known to have had access to them, such as Theodore of Raithu, Maximus the Confessor, Anastasius Sinaita and Theodore Abû Qurra, bishop of Harran. Even more striking is the fact that these same *compendia* were the source of the revival of Aristotelianism which emerged at Constantinople after AD 800.

The intellectual formation of a well-known figure such as John Moschus, who flourished in the late sixth and early seventh centuries, bears witness to the vitality of Greek culture in outlying areas of the Near and Middle East. John Moschus is the author of the *Pratum spirituale*, a work written in a simple and unpretentious style but which attests, particularly in its recourse to rhetorical devices, to its author's scholarly reading, a reflection in turn of his scholarly apprenticeship at places such as Alexandria itself, where he studied with Stephen in person, but also in Cilicia, Palestine and Syria (where he was in contact with the circle of Gregory of Antioch).[24] In any case there is no anecdote in the *Pratum* which implies that he stayed in Constantinople (a stay which, in any case,

---

22 M. Roueché, 'Byzantine Philosophical Texts of the Seventh Century', *Jahrbuch der österreichischen Byzantinistik* 23 (1974), 61–76 (with the quotation on p. 67); *idem*, 'A Middle Byzantine Handbook of Logic Terminology', *ibid.* 29 (1980), 71–98.

23 Saffrey, 'Le Chrétien Jean Philopon', p. 409.

24 H. Chadwick, 'John Moschus and his Friend Sophronius the Sophist', *JTS* ns 25 (1974), 41–74; see also the introduction to *Giovanni Mosco: Il Prato*, ed. R. Maisano (Naples, 1982), esp. p. 47. There is a recent, comprehensive treatment of Greek culture in seventh-century Palestine: B. Flusin, *Saint Anastase le Perse et l'histoire de la Palestine au début du VIIe siècle*, 2 vols. (Paris, 1992); on John Moschus, see esp. II, 23–5, 40–6 and 59–64; on Sophronius, see II, 36–8 and 47–9, and *passim*.

has only recently been demonstrated).[25] The vitality of scholarly activity and the circulation of texts in these areas are also witnessed by the career of another figure from the same historical and intellectual milieu as John Moschus, namely Sophronius 'the Sophist', who was John's student and colleague. Sophronius completed his studies in his native Damascus as well as in Alexandria, as is clear from the evidence of John Moschus as well as from references in Sophronius's own writings.[26] This Sophronius has been identified – not, however, without some expression of dissent – with Sophronius, patriarch of Jerusalem (634–8),[27] who in his youth is known to have been a teacher of rhetoric (hence the epithet 'Sophist').[28] In any event Sophronius is known as the author of works in both prose and verse, as well as of a commentary on the grammar of Dionysius Thrax. It is likely, in fact, that his reputation for learning played some part in his election as patriarch of Jerusalem. This same Sophronius appears to have owned and carried with him a collection of books which deserves to be considered 'as a valuable acquisition to culture in the province'.[29] It is worthwhile briefly to consider the verse of Sophronius, that is in effect his anacreontics, as a reflection of the literary culture of his day.

Our knowledge of Byzantine anacreontics depends largely on a manuscript now in the Vatican, Biblioteca Apostolica Vaticana, Barberini gr. 310, written at Constantinople in the late tenth century. (Our concern here, however, is solely with the anacreontics preserved in the first part of

[25] E. Follieri, 'Dove e quando morì Giovanni Mosco?', *Rivista di studi bizantini e neoellenici* ns 25 (1988), 3–39, at 36–7.

[26] See Wolska-Conus, 'Stéphanos d'Athènes', pp. 47–59.

[27] Doubts about the identification of Sophronius the Sophist with Patriarch Sophronius were expressed by I. Sevcenko, 'Storia letteraria', in *La civiltà bizantina dal IV al IX secolo. Aspetti e problemi* (Bari, 1977), pp. 141–2 and 144–5; more recently, however, the identification has been put beyond doubt by J.-M. Sansterre, *Les Moines grecs et orientaux à Rome aux époques byzantine et carolingienne (milieu du VIe siècle – fin du IXe siècle)*, 2 vols. (Brussels, 1983) II, 110–11, n. 47 (with discussion and bibliography).

[28] S. Vailhé, 'Sophrone le Sophiste et Sophrone le Patriarche', *Revue de l'Orient chrétien* 7 (1902), 360–85, at 365–6, and 8 (1903), 32–69 and 356–87, at 368. On the rhetorical culture of Sophronius the Sophist, see C. von Schönborn, *Sophrone de Jerusalem. Vie monastique et confession dogmatique* (Paris, 1972), pp. 55–60; J. Duffy, 'Observations on Sophronius' Miracles of Cyrus and John', *JTS* ns 35 (1984), 71–90; and Wolska-Conus, 'Stéphanos d'Athènes', pp. 47–59.

[29] Averil Cameron, 'Byzantine Africa – the Literary Evidence', in *Excavations at Carthage* (1978) VII, ed. J. H. Humphrey (Ann Arbor, MI, 1982), pp. 29–62, at 56.

the Barberini codex.)[30] As it is preserved, the manuscript is defective; but a detailed list of contents (1r-7r) prefacing the collection gives some notion of its original contents. From this it is clear that the earliest authors represented were from Palestinian (or Syro-Palestinian) schools, since they include poets such as John of Gaza and especially Sophronius of Damascus and Jerusalem, whose verse is followed by that of one 'Sophronius monk and iatrosophist' (to be identified with the aforementioned Sophronius?), as well as poets who flourished during the eighth and ninth centuries such as Elias Syncellus of Jerusalem and Michael Syncellus, also of Jerusalem. To the earliest names represented in the collection should be added that of George *grammatikós*, a poet of Greek-Egyptian origin. The poetic tradition of anacreontic verse, therefore, was established firmly in Syria, Palestine and Egypt earlier than at Constantinople, where examples of this type of poetry are not attested before the late ninth century.

The careers and writings of John Moschus and Sophronius have drawn our attention to the region of Syria and Palestine, and this region requires further attention in other important respects. It was in Palestine during the seventh century that Maximus the Confessor was educated.[31] In Palestine, too, a substantial body of hagiography was composed at this time, and there is also evidence for the composition of various scholarly manuals. The continuity of Greek culture in this region during the seventh century is also confirmed by the presence there of intellectual milieux even later, in the eighth century.[32]

If we turn now to the Byzantine West, it is – surprisingly – not at Ravenna, seat of the exarchate, where we find the strongest evidence of Greek culture. Ravenna, in fact, remained a city of Latin language and of

---

[30] On this manuscript and its contents, see the recent study by C. Gallavotti, 'Note su testi e scrittori di codici greci', *Rivista di studi bizantini e neoellenici* ns 24 (1987), 29–83. On Greek anacreontics, see also discussion by Lapidge, below, pp. 265–73.

[31] S. Brock, 'An Early Syriac Life of Maximus the Confessor', *AB* 91 (1973), 299–346.

[32] On literary culture in Palestine in the seventh and eighth centuries, see the fundamental study by C. Mango, 'Greek Culture in Palestine after the Arab Conquest', in *Scritture, libri e testi nelle aree provinciali di Bisanzio*, ed. G. Cavallo, G. De Gregorio and M. Maniaci (Spoleto, 1991), pp. 149–60. See also G. L. Huxley, 'On the Erudition of George the Synkellos', *Proceedings of the Royal Irish Academy* 81C (1981), 207–17, and W. Hörandner, 'Eléments de rhétorique dans les siècles obscurs', *Orpheus* ns 7 (1986), 293–305, as well as the important work by Flusin, cited above, n. 24.

'sentimenti latini',[33] even though during the reign of Heraclius the exarchal court was inevitably open to the influence of the reawakened Hellenism of Constantinople, which is reflected at Ravenna in the production of various manuscripts and inscriptions.[34] On the contrary, it was particularly in southern Italy, in the area extending from Rome to Sicily, where – thanks to waves of immigrants from the eastern Greek regions fleeing the incursions and conquests of the Persians and Arabs – one finds the best evidence for the presence and circulation of Greek literary culture. In Sicily there was already a substratum of Greek civilization, which the waves of new immigrants succeeded in reactivating: as Jean Irigoin has observed, 'continuité hellénique et apports byzantins se mêlent ainsi d'une façon inextricable'.[35] The uses made of Greek were not merely linguistic, but also more broadly cultural, encompassing education both of a private nature but also possibly linked to episcopal sees,[36] as well as the circulation of texts and books which, though they are not directly identifiable, must evidently have been studied in these areas from the seventh century onwards,[37] as is clear from the quality of the education itself, from 'the uncommonly high level of learning' enjoyed by a number of popes of Greek and Sicilian origin, from portrayals of saints as being well educated, as well as from literary production which, though problematic in certain respects, is nevertheless well attested. This literature includes various hagiographical writings,[38] biblical commentaries,[39] hymns[40] and possibly

---

[33] A. Pertusi, 'Bisanzio e l'irradiazione della sua civiltà in Occidente nell'alto medioevo', *SettSpol* 11 (1964), 75–133, at 120–1.

[34] See my study 'La cultura scritta a Ravenna tra antichità tarda e alto medioevo', in *Storia di Ravenna II*, ed. A. Carile (Venice, 1991), pp. 79–125.

[35] J. Irigoin, 'La Culture grecque et l'Occident latin du VIIe au XIe siècle', *SettSpol* 22 (1975), 425–46, at 429.

[36] Guillou, 'L'Ecole dans l'Italie byzantine', pp. 295–302.

[37] V. von Falkenhausen, 'Il monachesimo greco in Sicilia', in *La Sicilia rupestre nel contesto delle civiltà mediterranee*, ed. C. D. Fonseca (Galatina, 1986), pp. 143–59 (with the quotation from p. 146).

[38] Guillou, 'L'Ecole dans l'Italie byzantine', pp. 304–5.

[39] S. Gennaro, 'Influssi di scrittori greci nel «Commento all'Ecclesiaste» di Gregorio di Agrigento', *Miscellanea di studi di letteratura cristiana antica* 2 (1951), 169–79.

[40] A. Guillou, 'La Sicile byzantine. Etat de recherches', *Byzantinische Forschungen* 5 (1977), 95–145, at 132; A. Acconcia Longo, 'Il Concilio calcedonese in un antico contacio per S. Eufemia', *AB* 96 (1978), 305–31, esp. 326; J. Irigoin, 'La Culture byzantine dans l'Italie méridionale', in *La cultura in Italia fra tardo antico e alto medioevo*, 2 vols. (Rome, 1981) II, 587–603, at 592.

anacreontic verse, if the ninth-century poems by Constantinus Siculus and Theodosius, a grammarian from Syracuse, do indeed draw – as they seem to do – on an earlier tradition stretching back nearly to Sophronius.[41] In short, during the earlier seventh century and up until the Arab Conquest, Byzantine Sicily was 'a nursery of intellectuals'[42] and a centre of 'flourishing literary culture',[43] even if this culture was the possession of a restricted élite.

From Sicily we turn to Rome. In the *Acta* of the Lateran Council of 649 there are references not only to various oriental monks living then in Rome, but also to the existence of Greek monasteries.[44] These *Acta* are thus a valuable source for estimating the level of Greek culture and the nature of Greek books in circulation at that time in Roman religious houses. The recent studies of Rudolf Riedinger on the Lateran Council have demonstrated – against what was hitherto believed – that the Latin text of the *Acta* is not the original draft of the Council's deliberations but a translation of a body of materials in Greek assembled apparently in the time of Pope Theodore (642–9), before the convention of the Council itself during the papacy of Martin I (649–53). In light of Riedinger's demonstration,[45] the hypothesis that it was Maximus the Confessor and the Greek monks of his circle who drafted the original, Greek, text of the *Acta*, seems ever more likely.

All this has a direct bearing on our estimate of the circulation of Greek books in seventh-century Rome.[46] Certain of the books cited in the *Acta* could have been available in one or other of the Greek monasteries of Rome, and need not necessarily have formed part of the papal library

[41] B. Lavagnini, 'Anacreonte in Sicilia e a Bisanzio', *Atti dell'Accademia di scienze, lettere e arti di Palermo* 4th ser. 38.2 (1978–9), 471–84.

[42] F. Burgarella, 'Aspetti della cultura greca nell'Italia meridionale in età bizantina', in *Fatti, patrimoni e uomini intorno all'abbazia di S. Nilo nel medioevo* (Grottaferrata, 1988), pp. 19–46, at 27.

[43] von Falkenhausen, 'Il monachesimo', p. 157.   [44] Sansterre, *Les Moines* I, 9–31.

[45] R. Riedinger, 'Aus den Akten der Lateran-Synode von 649', *Byzantinische Zeitschrift* 69 (1976), 17–38; 'Griechische Konzilsakten auf dem Wege ins lateinische Mittelalter', *Annuarium Historiae Conciliorum* 9 (1977), 253–301, esp. 254–62; and 'Die Lateranakten von 649: ein Werk der Byzantiner um Maximos Homologetes', *Byzantina* 13 (1985), 519–34.

[46] For convenience I refer simply to Sansterre, *Les Moines* I, 176–9, and II, 201–2 (discussion of the preceding bibliography).

housed in the Lateran, as Giovanni Battista De Rossi believed.[47] (One can confidently attribute to the papal library only those books mentioned explicitly in the *Acta* as having belonged to it: this is the case with a copy of the pseudo-Dionysius, for example.) The documentation which was produced at the Council could hardly have been (even partially) prepared by Maximus the Confessor prior to his arrival in Rome, as various scholars have supposed; by the same token the florilegium of patristic and heretical passages which was read out during the fifth session of the Council must have been assembled by the Greek monks in Rome itself, where many of the texts cited were arguably available, even if it is impossible to say which of them were preserved in the Lateran and which had been brought or transmitted by the Greek monks. The level of Greek learning possessed by these monks, to judge from the *Acta*, was relatively high, not only in matters of theological doctrine but also in grammar and rhetoric.

Some decades after the Lateran Council, the *Acta* of the Sixth Oecumenical Council held at Constantinople in 680–1 are an equally valuable source concerning the presence of Greek books at Rome and in the papal library. In 678, in preparation for that Council, the emperor Constantine IV requested of Pope Donus that he send to him a substantial delegation of ecclesiastics equipped with the relevant books. Pope Agatho, who in the meantime had succeeded Donus, sent a less sizeable delegation than that which had been requested, but it was composed substantially of Greeks, who took with them a good number of books of the church fathers and of the relevant heresiarchs: and with the exception of a copy of Ambrose, all the authors in question were Greek. Furthermore, in the writings drawn up for presentation at the Sixth Council, Agatho refers to still other Greek texts which, by implication, were evidently available at Rome.

The sum of this evidence shows clearly that at Rome in the seventh century, 'les oeuvres grecques circulaient ... plus qu'on ne pourrait le penser';[48] and we need not exclude the possibility that there was at this time even some amount of book production in the Greek monasteries and churches of Rome. It might also be mentioned that there is from this period a substantial body of Greek inscriptions in Rome, such as those dating from the papacy of Martin I in S. Maria Antiqua, or those from the

[47] G. B. De Rossi, 'De Origine historia indicibus scrinii et bibliothecae Sedis Apostolicae', in H. Stevenson, *Codices Palatini Latini Bibliothecae Vaticanae* I (Rome, 1886), esp. pp. lxiv-lxxi.

[48] Sansterre, *Les Moines* I, 178.

so-called 'second decoration' of S. Saba, or those on the frescoes of the underground church of S. Maria in via Lata.[49]

One should note, finally, that the oriental influences detectable at this time either in Sicily or Rome derive not from Constantinople, but from the Byzantine provinces: Egypt, Palestine, Syria, Asia Minor. From these regions, moreover, came the largely anonymous waves of refugees, who included such outstanding figures of Greek learning as Maximus the Confessor, as well as – presumably – Theodore of Tarsus.

We are now in a position to return to Theodore of Tarsus. As we have seen, he was born *c.* 602 in Cilicia, and presumably left his native land, either in face of the Persian invasion of 613, or the subsequent Arab invasions.[50] It was said of Theodore that he was a 'philosopher',[51] which implies that he was an educated man involved in the activity of teaching. It also implies, however, a knowledge of various disciplines, from philosophy to rhetoric, from mathematics to medicine. Moreover, Bede[52] tells us that Theodore was trained in sacred and secular learning. But where and from whom had he acquired this learning?

Between 619/20 and the end of the 630s, when Stephen of Alexandria was teaching at Constantinople, Theodore was in the midst of his own studies; and it is permissible to believe that he could have followed the lectures of Stephen in the capital during the brief florescence of Hellenism under Heraclius. His course of studies could have included the *quadrivium*, which was still being taught in the seventh century, as is clear from the evidence of the 'canon' of Ananias of Shirak. It is not out of the question that Theodore could have met in Constantinople such learned individuals as John Moschus and Sophronius, who passed through the capital at approximately that time.[53] But Theodore could also have met scholars such as these elsewhere. Theodore's education need not have taken place exclusively in Constantinople. During the years of his scholarly apprenticeship the Byzantine provinces were enjoying a more lively level of Greek culture than was the capital itself; and Theodore, like his learned contemporaries, will certainly have had the opportunity of studying in various

[49] See my study 'Le tipologie della cultura nel riflesso delle testimonianze scritte', *SettSpol* 34 (1988), 467–516, esp. 484–90.
[50] Mango, 'La Culture grecque et l'Occident', p. 685.
[51] The evidence is listed by Sansterre, *Les Moines* II, 211, n. 155.
[52] Bede, *HE* IV.1 (ed. Colgrave and Mynors, p. 330).
[53] Follieri, 'Dove e quando', pp. 3–39.

regions and centres of the Byzantine world, whether in the East or in the West. At Rome Theodore may not only have acquired some knowledge of Latin; he could also have carried on his studies of Greek. Furthermore, Hadrian could have exercised some influence on his training, since like Theodore Hadrian was learned in both Greek and Latin. Hadrian, who was the companion of Theodore's journey to England, had received his early training in Byzantine Africa, which in the seventh century was an important foyer of learning and literary activity.[54] Finally, both Theodore and Hadrian were refugees who could both have spent time in Sicily, which at that time 'was a stopping point and halfway house for the Africans and easterners on their way to Rome'.[55] Sicily and Rome, in any case, were closely linked by a shared cultural inheritance.[56] In the final analysis, even if there is no possibility of ascertaining the precise means, times, places and programmes of study of Theodore of Tarsus, the Greek cultural background from which he originated was a decisive factor in his own education as well as in the inheritance of learning which he passed on to his school at Canterbury.[57]

[54] Cameron, 'Byzantine Africa', pp. 53–60.   [55] *Ibid.* p. 59.
[56] Sansterre, *Les Moines* I, 45–6.
[57] See Lapidge, 'The Study of Greek', as well as *idem*, 'The School of Theodore and Hadrian', *ASE* 15 (1986), 45–72, and *Biblical Commentaries*, ed. Bischoff and Lapidge, pp. 5–81, and *passim*.

4

Rome in the seventh century

THOMAS F. X. NOBLE

Let us begin by considering four texts that together symbolize both the concrete and the imaginary history of Rome in the seventh century. The first is the account in the *Liber pontificalis* of the visit of Emperor Constans II to Rome in 663 during the pontificate of Vitalian (657–72), the very pope who sent Theodore to England.[1] Some years earlier Constans had seized and brutalized Pope Martin I because of that pontiff's unbreakable opposition to imperial religious policy and because of his having summoned a Lateran council to proclaim that opposition. Vitalian sought better relations with Constantinople and, immediately after his election, he wrote to Constans and to Patriarch Peter in ambiguous and conciliatory terms. He omitted all mention of the Lateran Council of 649. Constans responded with rich gifts and with a confirmation of the privileges of the Roman see. A few years later the emperor visited Rome. Vitalian received him with all due honours but had to endure three calculated blows. Constans issued a privilege for Maurus of Ravenna that made the archbishop of that city autocephalous, effectively independent of Rome. The emperor also laid harsh tax requirements on southern Italy, Sicily, Sardinia and North Africa. Finally, the emperor plundered the pagan and Christian monuments of Rome, stripping them of their bronze coverings and fittings and leaving them weakened and suitable only for salvage.[2]

The other three texts are itineraries written in Rome in the middle of the seventh century. One is a guide to the cemeteries outside Rome and

---

[1] *Le Liber Pontificalis* (hereafter *LP*), ed. L. M. O. Duchesne, 2nd ed., 3 vols. (Paris, 1955–7) I, 343– 4.

[2] Not quite all of these details are in the *LP*. For the letters to Constans and Peter and for the affairs of Ravenna, see P. Jaffé, *Regesta Pontificum Romanorum* (hereafter Jaffé, *RP*) I (Leipzig, 1895), nos. 2085, 2086, 2096 and 2097.

the other two are lists of the principal churches and martyrs' tombs inside and outside the city. These texts[3] are riddled with problems and I only wish to observe that at just the time when pagan, imperial Rome was being dismantled, Christian, apostolic, martyrial Rome was being advertised to residents and visitors alike. Cassiodorus once spoke of Rome's 'vast population of statues' (*populus copiosissimus statuarum*)[4] and if he had had a seventh-century successor, that author might well have spoken instead of Rome's *populus copiosissimus sanctorum*. The emperor who was then in Rome was no benevolent protector of his people. He taxed them mercilessly, destroyed their city, failed to protect them from the Lombards and imposed upon them odious religious doctrines. The pope, on the contrary, and the saints and martyrs of Rome, would alone have to suffice to protect the city and its people from their enemies. The import of these texts may be more symbolic than real but our task must now be to look for the historical realities to which those symbols point.

As in the physical history of the city, so too in its political, social and cultural evolution, seventh-century Rome saw the dismantling of old structures and the erection of new ones. The principal themes are these: the decline of the civil administration and its replacement by military and ecclesiastical ones that only occasionally cooperated harmoniously; the decline of the senatorial aristocracy and its replacement by, once again, military and ecclesiastical ones that had not achieved social integration and cohesion by the end of the seventh century; the elaboration of an essentially ecclesiastical culture that drew upon but was nevertheless different from the patristic and classical cultures of antiquity; and a progressive reorientation of papal interests away from the Mediterranean and toward the kingdoms, churches and peoples of western Europe. Each of these themes, as I shall suggest in my conclusions, has relevance for Theodore's mission to England.

Understanding these themes, or understanding the Roman background to Theodore's mission, requires a bit of historiographical stage-setting. The seventh century has never been easy to study, partly because it is rather poorly endowed with source materials and partly because it is

---

[3] *Il catalogo dei cimiteri di Roma, Notitia ecclesiarum urbis Romae* and *De locis sanctis martyrum quae sunt foris civitatis Romae: Ecclesiae quae intus Romae habebantur*, in *Codice topografico della città di Roma* II, ed. R. Valentini and G. Zuchetti, Fonti per la storia d'Italia 88 (Rome, 1942), 49–66, 67–99 and 101–31.

[4] *Variae* VII.xiii.1.

difficult to know where to place this period within any kind of historical continuum. Put a bit differently, the problem is that it is hard to know what questions should be asked of the seventh century. Some years ago the annual Spoleto conference was devoted to finding ways of thinking about the seventh century and in hundreds of learned pages a score of scholars came to no firm conclusions.[5]

I should argue that the seventh century has fallen into a crevice between two historiographical mountains. These mountains became fully visible only after scholars such as Peter Brown, André Chastagnol and Henri-Irenée Marrou reconsidered and renamed the period from about 300 to 600 'late antiquity'.[6] The point of their work has been to stress that these centuries were not a time of decline and despair but rather of achievement, creativity and continuity. For a long time other scholars had been signalling the achievements of the eighth century: Byzantine revival under the Isaurians; Islamic recovery under the early Abbassids; Frankish renewal under the Carolingians; and English advance under the Mercians.[7] The seventh century could once confidently be dismissed as the darkest moment in the long Dark Ages, but now it seems to have been cut loose from all moorings. Is it a beginning or an end? By what standards are its successes and failures to be measured?

One way, at least, to attempt to come to terms with the seventh century is to study one place in detail. My focus will rest upon Rome and to a lesser extent upon Italy in the period from 604 to 701. Why these dates? They represent the accession and death of Popes Sabinian and Sergius I and include all the seventh-century popes except Gregory I who was elected in

---

[5] *Caratteri del secolo VII in Occidente*: SettSpol 5 (Spoleto, 1958).

[6] There is no point in presenting here a bibliographical essay. Among the most original or synthetic works, these might be noted: A. Chastagnol, *L'Evolution politique, sociale et économique du monde romain de Dioclétien à Julien: la mise en place du régime du Bas-Empire (284–363)* (Paris, 1982); H.-I. Marrou, *Décadence romaine ou antiquité tardive? IIIe-VIe siècle* (Paris, 1977); P. Brown, *The World of Late Antiquity* (London, 1971); idem, *The Making of Late Antiquity* (Cambridge, MA, 1978). With specific reference to Rome and Italy these questions have been discussed by S. D'Elia, 'Problemi di periodizzazione fra tardo antico e alto medioevo' and by O. Capitani, 'La storiografia altomedievale: Linee di emergenza dalla critica contemporanea', both in *La cultura in Italia fra tardo antico e alto medioevo*, 2 vols. (Rome, 1981) I, 99–122 and 123–47.

[7] Some sense of the sweep of these issues can be had from R. E. Sullivan, 'The Carolingian Age: Reflections on its Place in the History of the Middle Ages', *Speculum* 64 (1989), 267–307.

590. It is also the case that Theodore of Tarsus was alive during some portion of all of these pontificates. Using a papal chronology is not arbitrary because papal history was the creative and dynamic one in seventh-century Rome: it was the presence of the papacy that attracted Theodore and other easterners to Rome and it was a pope who sent Theodore to England. I hope in the end to show that a detailed understanding of seventh-century Rome can be very helpful in contemplating the English career of the first truly great archbishop of Canterbury.

At the conclusion of the brutal and brutalizing Gothic Wars, Justinian had by a pragmatic sanction attempted to restore traditional Roman government to Italy.[8] This would have involved a civilian administrative hierarchy and a separate military structure. By the end of the century, however, circumstances in Italy had produced a quite different set of arrangements. Beginning in the winter of 568–9 the Lombards, a Germanic confederation whose first members had entered Italy as federate troops in the army of Narses, had begun their conquest of Italy. Because the Lombards were never totally united and because they entered Italy and spread out over a fairly extended period of time, they represented a particularly difficult challenge for the authorities in Italy. Neither the Lombards nor the imperial military establishment ever thought of staking everything on a winner-take-all engagement and so constant small-scale warfare became the most familiar feature of life throughout the peninsula. The chief governmental result of this situation was the concentration of almost all power in the hands of military officers.[9]

---

[8] For the Pragmatic Sanction and its attendant problems, see T. F. X. Noble, *The Republic of St Peter: the Birth of the Papal State, 680–825* (Philadelphia, PA, 1984), p. 3 and n. 9 (with literature). For Italian and Roman history there are some good modern studies, but one must still turn to older works for detailed narratives: T. Hodgkin, *Italy and her Invaders*, 6 vols. (New York, 1889), esp. vols. V and VI; F. Gregorovius, *History of the City of Rome in the Middle Ages*, trans. G. W. Hamilton, 4 vols. (London, 1902) II, 1–213; L. M. Hartmann, *Geschichte Italiens im Mittelalter*, 4 vols in 6 (Gotha, 1897–1915) II, pts 1 and 2, 1–121; O. Bertolini, *Roma di fronte a Bisanzio e ai Langobardi*, Storia di Roma 9 (Bologna, 1941), 189–432. Among modern works: P. Llewellyn, *Rome in the Dark Ages* (London, 1971), pp. 1–228; C. Wickham, *Early Medieval Italy: Central Power and Local Society* (London, 1981), pp. 1–145; O. Capitani, *Storia dell'Italia medievale* (Bari, 1986), pp. 3–104; G. Tabacco, *The Struggle for Power in Medieval Italy: Structures of Political Rule*, trans. R. B. Jensen (Cambridge, 1989), pp. 1–108.

[9] The key study is now T. S. Brown, *Gentlemen and Officers: Imperial Administration and Aristocratic Power in Byzantine Italy A.D. 554–800*, Publications of the British School at

By the 580s the empire had begun to administer Italy from Ravenna through officers called exarchs.[10] These officers were not surrounded by a *comitatus* of civilian officials but by a staff of military officers. As the seventh century progresses it is more and more difficult, and finally impossible, to find any evidence of the old civilian hierarchy of officialdom. At Rome, for example, the urban prefect was still a crucial official in the second half of the sixth century – Gregory the Great had held this office – but the prefect vanished at some point in the seventh century. This militarization of public life in Byzantine Italy is one of the key developments of the age.

Who were the new military officers? First of all, they were not the old official aristocracy. The Roman senatorial aristocracy had been dealt a series of blows which were collectively fatal to it. The settlement of the Visigoths in southern Gaul and Spain and of the Vandals in North Africa had severely diminished the international connections and wealth of the old senatorial class. Then the Gothic Wars ravaged their holdings in Italy itself and before any social reconstruction could take place the Lombards took possession of much of the best land in the peninsula and thereby prevented such senatorial avatars as might have existed from reconstituting their economic position. The Roman Senate had ceased meeting by the seventh century and the last identifiable senator was the father of Pope Severinus.[11] This once mighty class, always the political and ideological bearers of the Roman heritage, simply vanished. Second, then, the new class of military officers were not the old aristocracy in a new guise. They were new men who had risen to positions of power and prominence through the military hierarchy and who had then solidified their positions by landholding.[12]

This account of the massive change in the nature of the public personnel

Rome (Rome, 1984), but much of value is still to be found in P. Rasi, *Exercitus Italicus e milizie cittadini nell'alto medioevo* (Padua, 1937).

[10] L. M. Hartmann, *Untersuchungen zur Geschichte der byzantinischen Verwaltung in Italien* (Leipzig, 1889), pp. 4–34; and Noble, *Republic of St Peter*, pp. 4–5.

[11] Brown, *Gentlemen and Officers*, p. 24.

[12] The books by Wickham and Tabacco (cited above, n. 8) are especially strong on the great social changes in Italy, as is Brown's *Gentlemen and Officers*, especially for the elite. To these should be added K. Bosl, *Gesellschaftsgeschichte Italiens im Mittelalter*, Monographien zur Geschichte des Mittelalters 26 (Stuttgart, 1982), 1–56, and A. Casatagnetti, *L'organizzazione del territorio rurale nel medioevo: Circonscrizioni ecclesiastiche e civile nella 'Langobardia' e nella 'Romania'* (Turin, 1979).

of seventh-century Italy is deceptively simple because it conceals several underlying trends. One significant aspect of this new aristocracy is its local nature. Apart from the exarchs who were always sent to Italy from Constantinople, the officer corps of the *Exercitus Italicus* was recruited locally. It seems too that these officers tended to serve in areas quite close to their original homes. The discovery that the army was recruited from and led by the Italian population has two critical implications, one historiographical and one historical. As for the former, it means that one cannot speak of a Hellenization of the Italian leadership in the Byzantine period. There may have been some migration into Sicily and the south as a result of the rise of Islam, the conquests of Bulgars and Slavs in the Balkans and perhaps too because of theological persecutions in the Byzantine world. But the Italian elite was Italian.[13] As to the latter, it means that there was from the beginning of the seventh century the possibility of sharp opposition between the needs and interests of the imperial regime in the east and needs and interests of the Italian leadership. This situation put the exarchs in an almost impossible position, as can be seen in the numerous cases where their troops refused to follow them and where the bishops of Ravenna and Rome ignored them with impunity. There is no point in speculating on whether or not Italy would have been more easily and effectively governed by alien personnel sent from the outside, because that is not what happened. Italy was governed by locals who on most occasions quite naturally pursued their own interests. This means that Guillou's arguments about the degree of separatism in Italy must be modified slightly. Italians were not so much consciously rejecting the Byzantine government as pursuing local interests which were increasingly incompatible with imperial interests.[14]

[13] The 'Hellenization' (in any case an anachronistic concept) of early medieval Italy has been debated for years. Old contributions are: L. T. White, 'The Byzantinization of Sicily', *AHR* 42 (1936), 1–42; P. Charanis, 'On the Question of the Hellenization of Sicily and Southern Italy during the Middle Ages', *AHR* 52 (1946), 74–86. More recently A. Guillou has championed this cause: 'Demography and Culture in the Exarchate of Ravenna', *SM* 3rd ser. 10 (1969), 201–19 and 'L'Italie méridionale byzantine ou Byzantins en Italie méridionale?', *Byzantion* 44 (1974), 152–90. I concur with Brown's critique of these views: *Gentlemen and Officers*, pp. 64–77.

[14] That such a localization of interests took place is not in doubt, but there are controversies about its origins. These debates are rooted in the question of Hellenization. The alternative views can be well grasped from A. Guillou, *Régionalisme et indépendance dans l'Empire byzantin au VIIᵉ siècle: L'exemple de l'Exarchat et de la Pentapole d'Italie*, Istituto

A second key trend was that the military elite solidified its position by acquiring land and in time by expanding its landholdings. C. J. Wickham has characterized this situation nicely. He says that 'soldiers of all military ranks, with their links with the rich, taxation-based, patronage network of the administration and the church, found it easy to buy, marry, lease or extort their way into landownership'.[15] This is certainly true, but it is not very helpful as a description of individual cases, very few of which can be portrayed in detail. We do know now that soldiers were not automatically given landed allotments and this makes it even more difficult to learn how individuals got started in the landholding business.[16] It is known that many prominent persons were in possession of substantial tracts of church lands which they held against various forms of lease. But did they become prominent because they had acquired these lands or did they acquire leaseholds because they were already prominent? The scanty sources are not going to make it easy to answer these questions, but the fact is that we do not know enough about the traffic in land in seventh-century Italy even though we do know that its possession was a fundamental standard of wealth and influence. The evidence also makes clear that no one in seventh-century Italy rivalled the extraordinary landholdings of the old senatorial aristocrats and that no individuals rivalled the holdings of the Roman and Ravennese churches.

Available evidence suggests strongly that the army in seventh-century Italy was a genuine meritocracy and that it provided opportunities for significant social mobility.[17] In this sense the army in Italy was a bit like the official hierarchy in the late empire except that, now, there was no senatorial order operating as a final brake on upward mobility. T. S. Brown has noted that in the eighth century members of some families

storico italiano, studi storici 75–6 (Rome, 1969) and T. S. Brown, 'The Interplay between the Roman and Byzantine Traditions and Local Sentiment in the Exarchate of Ravenna', *SettSpol* 34 (Spoleto, 1988), 127–60. In *Gentlemen and Officers*, Brown devotes close prosopographical analysis to Roman figures from the seventh century and his findings agree with his evidence from Ravenna.

15 Wickham, *Early Medieval Italy*, p. 76.
16 Brown, *Gentlemen and Officers*, pp. 91–3. The point is important on its own terms and also because it means that one cannot press too hard the argument that the establishment of the exarchates of Carthage and Ravenna was the basis for the 'theme' system elaborated in seventh-century Byzantium. For a good discussion of the subject, see W. Treadgold, *The Byzantine Revival* (Stanford, CA, 1988), pp. 14–17 and 26–36.
17 Brown, *Gentlemen and Officers*, pp. 61–81, esp. 78–80.

began trying to create pedigrees for themselves.[18] It is not surprising that in time families began to assert birth as a requirement for nobility, but the late and limited way that this was asserted in Italy points directly to its irrelevance at an earlier time and then to the difficulty of re-establishing it as a key criterion. The clerical hierarchy seems to share much with the military in this regard. Honorius (625–38) and Severinus (640) were the last demonstrably noble popes[19] before the brothers Stephen II and Paul I in the middle of the eighth century, and whereas the former two were the last representatives of the old aristocracy, the latter were the first popes chosen from the new social elite.

Saying that the institutions of seventh-century Italy provided opportunities for social mobility is perhaps another way of saying that they provided outlets for talent and ambition. The decline of the old civil hierarchy and the disappearance of the senatorial order did not mean that there were no longer people of ability who sought ways to use their talents for the public good and also to achieve personal power and prestige. The emerging elite of seventh-century Italy was after all the heir of both Symmachus and Gregory the Great. That is, they will have seen service as both a burden and an opportunity. Let us look for a moment at service, particularly in the clergy, as an opportunity.

It has long been recognized that the Gallo-Roman or Hispano-Roman aristocracies found in clerical service abundant opportunities to maintain the kinds of public positions that their class had held since the principate.[20] Such persons were still educated in a special way for their kind of service. They were uniquely the bearers and guardians of a cultural tradition. They bore distinctive titles and wore distinctive dress. They appeared eminently and publicly before their communities on festive

---

[18] *Ibid.*, pp. 164–74.

[19] According to statements in *LP* I, 323 ('ex patre Petronio consule') and 324 (depending upon the identification of Abienus as the descendant of a sixth-century senatorial family).

[20] M. Heinzelmann, *Bischöfsherrschaft in Gallien: Zur Kontinuität römischer Führungsschichten vom 4. bis zum 7. Jahrhundert: Soziale, prosopographische und bildungsgeschichtliche Aspekte*, Beihefte der Francia 5 (Munich, 1976); *idem*, 'Bischof und Herrschaft vom spätantiken Gallien bis zu den karolingischen Hausmaiern: Die institutionelle Grundlagen', in *Herrschaft und Kirche: Beiträge zur Entstehung und Wirkungsweise episkopaler and monastischer Organisationsformen*, ed. F. Prinz, Monographien zur Geschichte des Mittelalters 33 (Stuttgart, 1988), 23–82; and R. Van Dam, *Leadership and Community in Late Antique Gaul* (Berkeley, CA, 1985).

occasions. And they remained a class, an *ordo*, in the Roman sense. It was not until the seventh century that this situation was replicated to a degree in Rome, partly because it took much longer for the vestiges of the imperial order to decline there. But in Rome there was a difference. The clerical society that emerged was not aristocratic in origin as it was in Gaul or Spain. It became that later but that is another story. In Gaul you were not important because you were a bishop; you were a bishop because you were important. In Rome, on the contrary, your importance was increasingly measured by your place in the local ecclesiastical hierarchy.

The clergy of the Roman church were educated for their tasks at a time when public education was in full decline, not so much because people had plunged into the Dark Ages and were thus expected to snuff out the tapers of learning, as because the massive official hierarchy that had always supported public education had disappeared and its training schools had rather predictably disappeared too. Now if persons in Rome, or in Ravenna for that matter, wanted a specific kind of training they could get this almost exclusively in a clerical setting.[21] And it was a kind of specialized education that made its recipients distinctive in both contemporary and historical contexts. The seventh century was an important time in the elaboration of the protocol of the Roman church, in other words of the ceremonial definition of office and hierarchy. The clergy of the Roman church wore distinctive clothes and appeared in public ceremonies that were reserved to them alone. The seventh century was therefore a decisive moment in the making of the elite of medieval Rome.

The seventh century was also a time when the Roman clergy expanded a number of its traditional roles in ways that gave it increasing power and influence. Scholars have long been debating whether bishops acquired

---

[21] The fundamental study remains P. Riché, *Education and Culture in the Barbarian West*, trans. J. J. Contreni (Columbia, SC, 1976). Important perspectives are offered by: D. Illmer, *Formen der Erziehung und Wissensvermittlung im frühen Mittelalter: Quellenstudien zur Frage der Kontinuität der abendländischen Erziehungswesens*, Münchener Beiträge zur Mediävistik und Renaissanceforschung 7 (Munich, 1971); *La scuola nell' Occidente latino dell'alto medioevo = SettSpol* 19 (Spoleto, 1972); M. Pavan, 'La scuola nel tardo antico', in *La cultura in Italia* (as cited above, n. 6) II, 553–60; A. Guillou, 'La cultura nell'Italia bizantina dal VI all'VIII secolo', *ibid.* II, 575–86; and J. Irigoin, 'La Culture byzantine dans l'Italie méridionale', *ibid.* II, 587–603.

their considerable influence by usurpation or by delegation.[22] The fact is that both processes were at work. Certainly the imperial government delegated to bishops a variety of caritative and financial responsibilities as well as jurisdiction in a number of kinds of minor legal cases. As various kinds of public authorities were less and less in evidence, the roles of bishops expanded accordingly. In Gaul this sometimes meant that the effective powers of courts were called into question while in Rome it produced a situation where the food supply for the city, the repair of the aqueducts and even street repairs fell to the papal administration instead of to the Byzantine authorities. I do not see this as either delegation or usurpation in any strict sense. What I do see is a very traditional – in the Roman world – adjustment of the ever-shifting line between public and private responsibilities.[23]

The lands of the Roman church, for example, its patrimonies, were always called by Gregory I an endowment for the poor. By the middle of the seventh century a new charitable institution was being elaborated in Rome, the *diaconia*, precisely to mobilize the landed wealth of the church on behalf of Rome's poor.[24] By the end of the seventh century, the Arab conquests had cut off Egypt and North Africa as sources of grain and had seriously endangered Sicily's ability to provide for Rome. Thus the papal patrimonies were increasingly feeding the whole urban population. This was a public role but simultaneously a private one. Roman society had always been a massive network of patron-client ties and the situation in seventh-century Rome was no different. People could look to the church as the source of divine patronage but also to countless papal bureaucrats as the source of daily sustenance. The church became the great patron in all

[22] Among many discussions of this debate, F. Prinz is excellent: 'Herrschaftsformen der Kirche vom Ausgang der Spätantike bis zum Ende der Karolingerzeit: Zur Einführung ins Thema', in *Herrschaft und Kirche* (as cited above, n. 20), pp. 1–21.

[23] Two superb investigations of this theme for late antiquity are: J. Matthews, *Western Aristocracies and Imperial Court, AD 364–425* (Oxford, 1975) and R. MacMullen, *Corruption and the Decline of Rome* (New Haven, CT, 1988). The subject is badly in need of treatment for the early medieval period. For Rome itself a good but severely limited study is G. Jenal, 'Gregor der Große und die Stadt Rom', in *Herrschaft und Kirche*, pp. 109–45.

[24] The best overall study of the *diaconiae* remains O. Bertolini, 'Per la storia delle diaconie romane nell'alto medioevo sino alla fine del secolo VIII', in his *Scritti scelti di storia medioevale*, ed. O. Banti, 2 vols. in 1 (Livorno, 1968) I, 19–61. See also Noble, *Republic of St Peter*, pp. 231–4.

sorts of ways. It kept the Lombards at bay, got periodic tax reductions, kept the waters flowing through the aqueducts and protected people from theological errors. No emperor or exarch could possibly compete for the loyalty of the Romans regardless of any vestigial attachment to a Roman ideal. To put this a little differently, we can see here a concrete manifestation of the realities symbolized by Constans's destruction of classical Rome at the very time when others were trumpeting celestial Rome.

Let me briefly sum up the social changes I have been identifying as critical to the history of seventh-century Rome. The decline of the civil administration in the face of the military necessities occasioned by the ubiquitous Lombard menace dealt a final blow to the old civil aristocracy. The immediate result of this situation was the emergence of a new military and clerical elite that seems to have risen by merit more than by birth or wealth. The persons who formed this new elite were locals. Neither the military nor the clerical leadership was introduced from the outside. This new elite, especially in its clerical guise, came to monopolize a host of public and private functions that secured for it both power and prestige on the local scene and that made that elite the focal point for opposition to the imperial regime. The seventh century, therefore, was a critical period in the social and political history of Italy.

In ecclesiastical history the record is more ambiguous as regards positive achievements. We might begin with some very basic details about the popes and the papacy in the seventh century.[25] The period from 604 to 701 had twenty popes whose pontificates averaged only 4.9 years. These short pontificates need not in themselves have been disruptive because the popes elected were, as far as we can tell, all career ecclesiastical bureaucrats and they would have been similarly trained and prepared for their office. Indeed the historical record does not show any radical novelties on the part of any pope. But the short pontificates do mean that there were frequent elections and these, judging from the accounts in the *Liber pontificalis*, were frequently turbulent. Emperors, exarchs, clerical factions, military officers, ordinary soldiers and mobs got involved in the process at one time or another. Moreover, each time there was an election a time-consuming process of imperial approval had to be initiated. Because of the time needed for elections and approvals, the papal throne was vacant for 10.6

---

[25] These details are easily compiled from the statements at the beginning of every *vita* in *LP*. For a discussion of why the *LP* is structured the way it is, see T. F. X. Noble, 'A New Look at the *Liber Pontificalis*', *Archivum Historiae Pontificiae* 23 (1985), 347–58.

years in the seventh century, for a longer time than all but three of the century's pontificates. Near the end of the century Benedict II got the emperor to agree that the person elected should be consecrated without delay and it is interesting to note that the average vacancy of 184.2 days dropped to 71.5 thereafter.[26]

The *Liber pontificalis* records fewer personal details about the seventh-century popes than it does for those of the eighth century, but a few general trends can be discerned. I have already noted that no pope after Severinus can confidently be assigned to the nobility. Honorius, Severinus's predecessor, donated among other things almost 2,000lbs of silver to various Roman churches. Peter Llewellyn has suggested that this may have been his way of disposing of a paternal legacy but, in any case, no other pope of the age dispensed that kind of largesse, and probably none had it to dispense.[27] The popes were also locals for the most part, despite a persistent tendency to talk about an eastern swamping of the clergy in this period. Of our twenty popes, thirteen were from Rome or its immediate surroundings and a further four from Sicily. One each came from Dalmatia, Greece and Syria. About these latter three virtually no personal details are known, but there is certainly nothing in their conduct that marks them as 'eastern'.[28] A couple of other cases are revealing, though, of what is wrong with the old argument. Sergius, says the *Liber pontificalis*, was a Syrian born in Sicily.[29] I do not see how one can regard him as an easterner in the first place and he entered the Roman clergy at least eleven years before his election. Conon, says the same source, was born in Sicily the son of a Thrakesion.[30] Knowing his father's army unit does not make it possible to say for certain that the family's origins were in Asia Minor and, in any event, Conon was Sicilian, not eastern. Perhaps one might suggest that the papal electors showed at times some preference for Sicilians because of the greater likelihood that they would have good Greek and thus better means of dealing with the continuous theological provocations launched from the East. But this is only a guess and I see no reason to

---

[26] *LP* I, 363–4; cf. Jaffé, *RP*, no. 684. These actions represented a correction of the situation as negotiated a few years before under Pope Agatho: *LP* I, 354–5.

[27] Llewellyn, *Rome*, p. 94.

[28] The most recent statement of this old view is J. Richards, *The Popes and the Papacy in the Early Middle Ages, 476–752* (London, 1979), pp. 270–1. I have spelled out fully my reasons for disagreeing with it in *Republic of St Peter*, pp. 185–8.

[29] *LP* I, 371.   [30] *LP* I, 368.

suppose that there were not always people in Rome who could construe a Greek text. More critically, however, I cannot detect any decisive changes in policy or outlook at any point in the seventh century.

A few interesting perspectives can be gained by making some elementary tabulations based on the *Regesta pontificum*. Only 145 papal letters survive from this whole century, or about seven per pope. One might compare that with the more than 800 that survive from Gregory I alone. Text-book accounts of the seventh century might well lead one to believe that eastern affairs, both political and diplomatic as well as theological ones, dominated the Roman Church in the seventh century. The surviving letters tell a different story. Thirty-six, the largest single group, were sent to Constantinople or to eastern prelates because of the monothelete struggles, and ten of these were sent in one great burst of activity by Martin I in his attempt to enlist support. In other words, 87% of all surviving letters went to four basic places and three-quarters of all letters did not go to the East. In very broad terms these letters provide some support to Pirenne's old idea of a *volte-face de la papauté*.[31]

Just as revealing as the destinations of these letters are the subjects with which they deal. It is interesting to note that only thirteen seventh-century letters were taken up in later canonical collections, and only six by Gratian.[32] This was not a time for profound ideological formulations or even for timeless administrative formulae. Two basic kinds of issue can be discerned and each is revealing. First, there are a good many letters dealing with the on-going monothelete controversy, but apart from a brief moment when Honorius sought grounds for an accommodation with the East, the letters have a uniformly disengaged and authoritative character. What I mean is that the popes simply refused to discuss the issues at hand. The canons of the Lateran Council of 649, for example, simply and briefly affirmed traditional positions, and the encyclical letter that accompanied the canons is very much like letters that Martin sent to a number of eastern prelates.[33] It says basically that scripture and the councils have transmitted a catholic faith but that the devil has led heretics to challenge it. In

---

[31] I refer to a famous section in his *Mohammed and Charlemagne* (New York, 1957), pp. 210–24.

[32] I take these details from Jaffé, *RP*, who always notes when a particular papal letter was taken up by later canonical collections. His findings may have been corrected in small ways but are still about right.

[33] Mansi, *Concilia* X, 790D-798B and 863C-1183C.

other words, the Chalcedonians are right, the monotheletes are wrong, and there is no point in discussing matters further. These letters are not, as is sometimes maintained, evidence for theological backwardness in Rome. They are evidence for a certain institutional and ideological inflexibility but that is a different thing altogether. The second thing revealed by these letters is the real and constant daily business of the papal bureaucracy. Routine matters of ecclesiastical administration, ranging from appointments in England to monastic privileges in Gaul, to marital customs in Spain, to patrimonial management in Italy, are the most frequently raised kinds of business in these letters. Most of this material was so intensely ordinary that later compilers of canonical collections found little in it they could use.

In terms of ecclesiastical administration, then, the seventh century has nothing to offer that is as dramatic as the social and political alteration of Italy that I discussed earlier. But this apparent absence of innovation is itself revealing. Despite frequent elections and vacancies in the papal office, despite imperial and exarchal raids upon Rome, despite imperial interference in church administration – for example in removing Ravenna from Rome's jurisdiction – and despite theological provocations, the papal government went relentlessly along its way attending to the routine business of the church. The sixth century and also the eighth were much richer in both institutional innovations and ideological pronouncements on *regnum* and *sacerdotium* than the seventh, but the seventh century is instructive about what it must have been like most of the time to work in the Lateran and to do the church's business. The lustre of great trans-Mediterranean events can distract the historian's attention from the fact that the popes and their legion of officials spent most of their time managing their estates and sorting out routine ecclesiastical claims.[34]

A third subject that requires brief address concerns the cultural life of Rome in the seventh century. I shall remark upon both the public culture

[34] I am arguing here for my own view of what is significant in this period of papal history, and in many later periods too. I am objecting to the excessive concentration on ideology that characterized the work of W. Ullmann, especially in his *The Growth of Papal Government in the Middle Ages*, 3rd ed. (London, 1970). I also object to the anachronisms of both Catholic and Protestant papal historians who see the early Middle Ages as a stage on the inevitable – and, respectively, positive or negative – march to the 'Papal Monarchy' of the high Middle Ages. My forthcoming chapter in the *New Cambridge Medieval History* will afford me an opportunity to develop these themes.

of Rome and the papal administration and also the more elevated realms of thought and letters.

The most important development in the realm of public culture came in the elaboration of official ceremonial. By the late seventh century *Ordo Romanus I* had been developed to guide the celebration of stational liturgies in the Roman church.[35] On these occasions the pope and much of his administration went in solemn procession from the Lateran to one or another of those churches in Rome that belonged to the *Sancta Romana Ecclesia* in the strict sense. Peter Llewellyn has said, and I agree, that *Ordo Romanus I* represented the development 'of a state function of the city, surrounding the pope's person with the mystique of sovereignty, ecclesiastical and civil'.[36] The clarity, precision and sophistication of the *Ordo* surely mark it out as inspired by and perhaps as a rival to imperial ceremonial. And the importance of the *Ordo* can only have been enhanced by the relative ceremonial vacuum left by the disappearance of the civil administration. Civic ritual, as historians of late antiquity and of early modern Europe have shown, is a powerful way of forging and articulating a sense of community.[37] The popes also began to wear the *camelaukion*, or pale, camel-hair pointed cap that would evolve into the tiara.[38] This was another sign of ceremonial and ideological sensitivity. It has been suggested that the papal court, beginning with Vitalian, began to develop its musical repertoire as another means of rivalling the imperial court.[39] And there can be no serious doubt that the Roman synods that became more and more frequent in the seventh century were being used as a focal point for the political life of Rome, central Italy and much of the rest of Italy too.[40] These synods were surely taking up some of the actual and symbolic roles once played by the Roman senate. Richard Krautheimer has said that

[35] M. Andrieu, *Les Ordines Romani du haut moyen âge*, 5 vols. (Louvain, 1931–61) II, 52–64 (discussion) and 66–108 (text).

[36] Llewellyn, *Rome*, p. 126.

[37] S. MacCormack, *Art and Ceremony in Late Antiquity* (Berkeley, CA, 1981); M. McCormick, *Eternal Victory: Triumphal Rulership in Late Antiquity, Byzantium and the Early Medieval West* (Cambridge, 1986); and E. Muir, *Civic Ritual in Renaissance Venice* (Princeton, NJ, 1981).

[38] B. Sirch, *Der Ursprung der bischöflichen Mitra und päpstlichen Tiara*, Kirchenrechtlichen Quellen und Studien 8 (St Ottilien, 1975).

[39] Llewellyn, *Rome*, pp. 123–4.

[40] *Ibid.*, p. 129; Noble, *Republic of St Peter*, pp. 242–3.

the seventh century popes were great builders.[41] It is certainly true that some of them made extensive donations to the church and that many of them repaired churches in Rome. In part this was simple necessity. The maintenance of all the buildings that together made up the *Sancta Romana Ecclesia* must have been a staggering burden and expense. But there was more to it, I suspect. There was the evergetism always practised by the elite classes in late antique cities.[42] In endowing and refurbishing churches Rome's clerical elite were announcing in a very clear way their own power, prestige and influence. And someone had to do all the physical work so building projects provided plenty of opportunities to expand and consolidate ties of patronage. In all sorts of ways the papal administration was calling attention to itself in seventh-century Rome and in so doing paving the way for the takeover of the whole region in the eighth century.

Rome's public culture is intimately related to both the socio-political and the ecclesiastical life of the city and its elaboration shows how carefully one must look for signs of creativity and advance. On the whole, as I said before, ecclesiastical administration showed few innovations in the seventh century while social and political life changed a good deal. The issues I have lumped together as public culture show the ecclesiastical administration responding to and adapting itself to those changes in the wider society. What is interesting is the way that that administration reassembled various bits of imperial ceremonial in ways appropriate to the leadership of their own local society.

In matters of high culture seventh-century Rome seems a pretty depressed place. But, we might ask, what kind of a place was it supposed to be? What kind of a place had it been? One of the constantly remarkable features of Roman history, from Republican times forward, is how few native Romans played key roles in making Roman culture. Italians and provincials had always been more numerous and important and in late antiquity regional centres such as Milan or Ravenna, Arles or Bordeaux or Trier, had usually had more to offer. It is true that no seventh-century pope wrote a book, at least as far as we know. Gregory I of course wrote lots of them. Is that fact attributable to something in the culture of sixth-century Rome or to the papacy at that time, or is it entirely attributable to Gregory himself? If seventh-century popes were not great

---

[41] R. Krautheimer, *Rome: Profile of a City, 312–1308* (Princeton, NJ, 1980), p. 87.
[42] P. Garnsey and R. Saller, *The Roman Empire: Economy, Society and Culture* (Berkeley, CA, 1987), pp. 33–4 and 101–2.

pastoral theoreticians or theologians or exegetes, or were not great liturgists or lawyers, does this make them second-rate and backward? Answering that question requires comparisons, but what are the correct ones to draw? How many popes, in almost two millennia, have been significant intellectual figures? The answer is not many, and there is nothing in the job description that calls for intellectual brilliance. Popes needed diplomatic and managerial skills and these are not necessarily things you learn from books or that you write books about. Thus to say that seventh-century, papal Rome was not a flourishing intellectual centre is to describe the obvious but to explain little. Part of the explanation has already been given: neither Rome nor the popes nor the papacy were customarily focal points for significant intellectual achievement. But civil and ecclesiastical Rome were at the centre of many networks of ideas and it is legitimate to ask what kinds of ideas entered Rome and how many of them took root there.

Legitimate to ask but hard to answer. Riché once said that one thing people sought in Rome was manuscripts and that almost any book could be found there.[43] That is a more confident judgement than I am willing to make; even so, what can we say for certain about the learning or knowledge of any individual just because that person had access – we think – to a given book? The seventh century saw the creation or expansion in Rome of several Greek monasteries and, according to Krautheimer, the development of a considerable Greek neighbourhood between the Palatine and the Torre delle Milizie.[44] Most of the immigrants are thought to have been fugitives and they brought with them certain eastern cults and relics. But what was their permanent impact on the culture of the city? As I am sceptical about an eastern swamping of the clergy so too I am doubtful, lacking concrete proof, about an eastern domination of Rome's intellectual life.[45] And there really is very little evidence. In Sicily a thriving Greek culture flourished through the early Middle Ages. We can prove that, but evidence for Rome is almost totally lacking. It is true that certain

---

[43] Riché, *Education and Culture*, p. 351: 'one could almost certainly find whatever texts one needed in Rome'.

[44] Krautheimer, *Rome*, pp. 87–90. Monastic immigrants solidified and expanded these neighborhoods, as J.-M. Sansterre has shown: 'Le Monachisme byzantin à Rome', *SettSpol* 34 (1988), 701–46.

[45] Both Llewellyn, *Rome*, p. 133 and Riché, *Education and Culture*, pp. 345–52 take this position, but I consider it to be exaggerated.

important figures visited Rome: Theodore himself, John Moschus and Maximus the Confessor. But John and Maximus spent little time there, none executed his major writings there, none joined or founded a school as far as we know. Whether they had any influence is extremely difficult to say. Maximus provides a case in point. There is no doubt that he was the most distinguished orthodox theologian during the monothelete controversy and one of the greatest of all early Christian thinkers. He spent years, though, in North Africa, called by Ostrogorsky the 'refuge of Orthodoxy' and went to Rome only for the Lateran Council of 649.[46] There was no known difference between the fundamental positions held in Rome and those held by Maximus, and (as I have already observed) the popes had no intention of arguing a case against monotheletism. Maximus produced lengthy treatises but these were not strictly required by the circumstances. And there is an interesting difference between Martin and Maximus. The former wrote to the imperial court and showed considerable political sensitivity – not that it did him any good in the long run – in blaming absolutely nothing on the emperor but rather in excommunicating the patriarchs Paul and Sergius and blaming the disturbances on them.[47] Maximus meanwhile spun a theory, not wholly original with him it is true, that the emperor as a layman had no business interfering in dogmatic issues.[48] In the eighth century Gregory III would echo those sentiments but they fell on deaf ears in the first instance. Thus in one case at least we can locate a major intellectual figure in Rome and we can point to a case where he was without influence.

Perhaps I can sum up my point by referring to a letter of Pope Agatho to Constantine IV that has always been interpreted, most recently by Riché, as evidence of the ignorance of the Roman and western clergy. I read the letter very differently.[49] Agatho said that amidst the press of such great worldly concerns it is not surprising that members of the clergy have no time for theological speculation. Besides, the scriptures and the councils have handed down a faith that needs no revision or correction. Agatho was not saying that the clergy was ignorant. He was saying that they were attending to their proper responsibilities. If I have not misread the

---

[46] G. Ostrogorsky, *History of the Byzantine State*, trans. J. Hussey (New Brunswick, NJ, 1969), pp. 118 and 119–20.

[47] Mansi, *Concilia* X, 794–5.   [48] Maximus, *Acta*, PG 90, 113 and 117.

[49] Jaffé, *RP*, no. 2109; text in PL 87, 1161–4; cf. Riché, *Education and Culture*, pp. 347–8.

situation, then I think that is a perfectly normal and predictable thing for a seventh-century pope to have said.

The Rome which Theodore visited, for a good many more years than the conventional wisdom teaches according to Michael Lapidge,[50] with whose views I am in accord, will have been a considerable school for the later archbishop. He would have seen first-hand a realm of constantly shifting political geography. Power relationships were neither clear nor constant. Most of the key roles in society were exercised either by military men or by ecclesiastical figures but not by a hierarchy of civil officials. Military leaders, from local ones to the emperor, could be a real nuisance but some cooperation with them was necessary and desirable. There were limits, however, to the kinds of cooperation that could be contemplated. Generally, the clergy did not suffer gladly interventions in dogmatic issues or matters of ecclesiastical administration. Details mattered. The Roman church had a vast array of routine business that simply had to be done. Little of it was glamorous or interesting but most of it was essential. No less dedicated to the momentum of routine was the attitude of the Roman church toward basic dogmas. Rome adopted a posture that was conservative and traditional. Key matters that had long been settled were not to be opened up for fresh discussion. Finally, *Rome*, and the papal court, will have been places where sensitivity to and sympathy with historical and cultural differences were daily features of life. Theodore himself must have been at least trilingual and if he made history in England then we should not lose sight of the fact that he had lived several different histories in the Mediterranean world. He was not, however, unique.

Theodore's achievement in England will be explored in other essays in this volume, but perhaps I can conclude by pointing directly to aspects of his work that appear to square with the Rome from which he departed. He found in the north a land of shifting and unsettled political conditions where military men gained and lost power often and unpredictably. He found a world where churches and churchmen were both respected and abused. He found dogmatic irregularity and royal interference in doctrinal questions. He discovered numerous impediments to the free and orderly functioning of ecclesiastical institutions. He landed in a world that was by no means without a rich and estimable culture, but nevertheless a place where some of the formal, intellectual requirements most critical to the

50 See *Biblical Commentaries*, ed. Bischoff and Lapidge, pp. 65–81, as well as the comments of Michael Lapidge, above, pp. 19–26.

church were barely in evidence. He found, finally, a land of linguistic and ethnic diversity. Surely it is no accident that every single area of activity that attracted Theodore's attention in England had at least a rough precedent in Rome. Theodore was a man of deep learning, vast experience and sterling personal qualities but by the time Vitalian sent him to England he was also, in a sense, a Lateran professional.

5

Theodore, the English church and the monothelete controversy

HENRY CHADWICK

In his *Historia ecclesiastica*, Bede tells his readers that the church is the cement to unite the squabbling tribes in the old Roman province of Britannia, especially through the link to St Peter mediated through Gregory the Great sending Augustine to Kent, and through Pope Vitalian sending Theodore of Tarsus in 668, 'the first archbishop to whom the entire Church of the English consented to give obedience'.[1] In Bede's pages the troubles of the church in the Mediterranean south seldom surface in the narrative. An exception is the account of the Council called by Theodore to meet at Hatfield[2] on 17 September, probably in 679, where the assembled bishops affirmed their faith in the five oecumenical councils and also in Pope Martin I's Lateran Council (649) whose condemnation of the doctrine that Christ, though fully human and fully divine, had only one will, created a storm with Byzantium and dreadful suffering for Martin.[3] Bede records the Council's further assent to the double procession of the Spirit or 'filioque', on which the six councils were silent, but which Augustine's influence had erected into a non-controversial proposition in the western churches at large, even if they had not yet been added to the Credo.[4]

---

[1] *HE* IV.2 (p. 332).

[2] *HE* IV.17–18 [15–16] (pp. 384–90). No doubt the Hatfield near Doncaster in south Yorkshire is meant, where the Anglo-Saxon Chronicle places the defeat in 633 of Edwin of Northumbria. In view of the considerations submitted in this paper, the location of the synod in the sphere of influence of Bishop Wilfrid of York is probably significant.

[3] On the Lateran Council in general, see *Biblical Commentaries*, ed. Bischoff and Lapidge, pp. 69–80 and 139–46; its *acta* are ed. R. Riedinger, *Concilium Lateranense a. 649 celebratum*, Acta Conciliorum Oecumenicorum 2nd ser. 1 (Berlin, 1984).

[4] Bede, *HE* IV.17 [15] (p. 386): 'glorificantes Deum Patrem sine initio, et Filium eius unigenitum ex Patre generatum ante saecula, et Spiritum Sanctum procedentem ex Patre

Bede continues by adding that Benedict Biscop had returned from pilgrimage to Rome bringing with him the precentor (*archicantator*) of St Peter's, John, commissioned by the pope (probably Agatho) to examine the orthodoxy of the English churches and to report back to Rome. The precentor brought to England the decrees of the Lateran Council of 649, and a copy was made for the monastery at Jarrow. The decisions at Hatfield, recorded by Bede, showed how sound the English were. For Bede the episode showed the authority of Theodore vindicated both by his orthodox doctrine and by papal authority.

From Bede it would seem that Theodore's authority had been questioned, and that the significance of the Council of Hatfield was confined to its settling of a little local difficulty. Set in the context of the monothelete controversy which had been racking the church in the Mediterranean world for more than a century and especially since 633, the emphasis of the Council at Hatfield looked very different.

Since the ending of the Acacian schism in 518–19 it had been agreed between Rome and Constantinople that there could be no compromise on the strict adherence to the Chalcedonian definition that the Christ who is known or acknowledged to be 'in two natures' is nevertheless one person, one hypostasis. At the Council of Constantinople in 553 Justinian's bishops met every imaginable demand of the anti-Chalcedonian party other than the one supreme gravamen: the anti-Chalcedonians hated '*in* two natures', and felt themselves justified in their suspicions by the language of the more extreme adherents of Chalcedon and its two-nature christology, Nestorianizers who spoke as if the human soul of Christ could be almost independent of the incarnate Word.

The split between the defenders and the critics of Chalcedon had vast social and political consequences for the Greek churches, and since the anti-Chalcedonians had no greater bugbear than the diphysite 'Tome' of Pope Leo the Great, the controversy produced deep suspicions and tensions between Rome and a succession of Byzantine patriarchs trying to unite their fractured flocks. A succession of formulas for rapprochement were all doomed by the virtually fundamentalist intransigence of the anti-Chalcedonians. But in 633 the patriarch Cyrus of Alexandria succeeded in achieving union between the Chalcedonian minority and the more sub-

et Filio inenarrabiliter.' On Augustine's treatment of the 'double procession', the creed and the Council of Hatfield in general, see J. N. D. Kelly, *Early Christian Creeds*, 3rd ed. (London, 1972), pp. 358–67.

stantial 'monophysite' body who followed the tradition of Theodosius of Alexandria and Severus of Antioch – a group of essentially very moderate sympathies who anathematized the extremist Eutyches and other radical monophysite groups and, except for their 'hang-up' over Chalcedon's preposition 'in', were very orthodox indeed.

The basic proposition in the union at Alexandria in 633 was that the Christ who is 'in two natures and of two natures' has one *energeia*: that is, there is no psychological tension or conflict within the one person; the miracles and the human sufferings are alike the experiences of a single person, not of a divided mind; the centre of action within him is one not two. The proposition was underpinned by a quotation from a letter in the writings of Dionysius the Areopagite (the authenticity of which had been penetratingly questioned by an otherwise unknown presbyter Theodore known to Photius but without persuasive effect). This letter affirmed that in Christ there was 'a new theandric energeia'.[5] The Areopagite phrase evidently gave major support to the reconciliation, but alarmed fundamentalist Chalcedonians, notably Sophronius, who seized the happy chance of a vacancy in the patriarchate of Jerusalem to get himself elected and therefore to distribute a synodical letter in 634 announcing his installation and vehemently attacking the Alexandrian union. Monophysite children were mocking the Chalcedonians in the street for having accepted a formula which they took to be a victory for their side. Sophronius could not endure it. His *synodica* is one of the angriest documents of the age.[6] It did not immediately alert the papacy to the

[5] Dionysius Areopagita, *Ep.* iv *ad Gaium* (PG 3, 1072C). Cyrus's Union formula is cited in full in the *acta* of the thirteenth session of the Council of 681. There can be no question of the brilliance of its drafting. The critique of the authenticity of the writings of Dionysius the Areopagite by the presbyter Theodore (probably of the sixth century) is known only through Photius, *Bibliotheca*, cod. 1. His arguments are so cogent that it is surprising to find no one apparently writing a reply.

[6] Sophronius's argument is dominated by the axiom, more philosophical than theological, that each nature has its own activity or operation. On Sophronius, see the brief discussion by G. Cavallo, above, p. 61, as well as Christoph von Schönborn, *Sophrone de Jerusalem, vie monastique et confession dogmatique* (Paris, 1972), whose erudition is deeply sympathetic to Sophronius and unsympathetic to the anxieties of the anti-Chalcedonians. Sophronius's *synodica* appears in full in the *acta* of the eleventh session of the Council of Constantinople, 681 (PG 87, 3148–3200); the complete *acta* of this Council are in the process of being edited by Rudolf Riedinger, the first part of which appeared as *Concilium Vniuersale Constantinopolitanum Tertium, Concilii Actiones I-XI*, Acta Conciliorum Oecumenicorum 2nd ser. 2.1 (Berlin, 1990), the second part in 1992.

difficulty, and in 634 Pope Honorius lent his support to Cyrus's happy formula, also upheld by the patriarch of Constantinople, Sergius.[7] The hitherto monophysite patriarch of Antioch was brought to accept 'in two natures' by the Alexandrian formula of one *energeia*.[8]

But at Constantinople a senior civil servant named Maximus who left his secular career to become a monk was wholly persuaded by Sophronius, and led a dissident opposition.[9] He moved to North Africa, and went on to Rome where he found a ready ear in the popes of the 640s. They had become mountingly embarrassed by Honorius's letters to Constantinople, and the election of a new pope in July 649 provided the occasion for a synodical protest: to speak of one activity, one will in Christ was implicitly to deny His human will and therefore to compromise the purity of the Chalcedonian definition, with its insistence on the full reality of the Lord's humanity. Pope Martin found himself arrested by a large military force (acting on instructions of the emperor, Constans II) in June 653, and put on trial in Constantinople on a charge of high treason. He suffered grim physical tortures but, worst of all, abandonment by the Roman church which, under imperial pressure, elected a successor while Martin was still alive. The bold words of the Lateran Council were quietly dropped.

The successes of Arab arms now became a crucial factor. The axiom was undisputed that the defence of the empire depended on the favour of heaven. Was that favour being withdrawn because of the monothelete doctrine, or because of those opposed to it? Each side was ready to accuse the other of provoking celestial wrath. The emperor Constantine IV

---

[7] Honorius's letters are cited in the *acta* of the twelfth session of the Council of 681; during the eighth session Honorius was invoked by the arch-monothelete, Macarius, patriarch of Antioch. That made Honorius's condemnation inevitable. It is nevertheless remarkable that the Roman legates brushed aside at least two proposals to condemn monothelete doctrine but no names.

[8] Theophanes, *Chronicon* AM 6021 (ed. de Boor, p. 329), using Anastasius Sinaita (PG 89, 1153A).

[9] On Maximus the Confessor a large literature has come to be. The bibliography is accessible in M. L. Gatti, *Massimo il Confessore. Saggio di bibliografia generale ragionata e contributi per una ricostruzione scientifica del suo pensiero metafisico e religioso* (Milan, 1987), as well as more briefly in G. C. Berthold, *St Maximus the Confessor: Selected Writings*, Classics of Western Spirituality (London and New York, 1985), pp. 227–33. Note that in the present discussion I follow the account of Maximus's early life given in the later Greek hagiography (*BHG*, no. 1234), rather than that in the monothelete Syriac life recently discovered by Sebastian Brock (cited below, n. 16; cf. also Brock's discussion above, pp. 50–1).

(668–85) came to think the monothelete cause dubious. To a great council at Constantinople in 680 he invited the pope (from 27 June 678, Agatho) to send legates.

Agatho needed to show the Greek churches that the western churches, even though they were now living under numerous independent barbarian kingdoms, were unanimous in rejecting monotheletism. Those living under barbarian rule were precisely those untouched and unpolluted by the compromises imposed by the Byzantine government (to which several of Agatho's predecessors had bent the knee). He was glad to be able to tell the emperor at Constantinople that among the Langobards, Slavs, Franks, Goths and Britons (distinct from the *Angli*) there was no dissent from the total rejection of monotheletism by himself and his own synod of Italian bishops. He told Constantinople that he had nursed the hope of being joined by Theodore, 'our fellow-bishop and philosopher, from the large island of Britannia' with others who live in those parts. But the journey to and from this remote oceanic region was too long. Among the signatures to Agatho's Italian synod, held at Rome on 27 March 680, stands that of 'Wilfrid bishop of York, legate of the venerable synod *per Britanniam*'.[10]

Agatho needed Wilfrid's signature: here was the testimony of Northumbria that monotheletism had no place in its doctrine. The pope also needed Theodore, archbishop of Canterbury, and his synod at Hatfield, giving the same basic attestation. Neither Agatho nor Bede had an interest in the sharp tensions between Theodore and Wilfrid. After all, Stephen of Ripon's *Vita S. Wilfridi* makes it clear that Wilfrid had been ejected from his see at York in 678, and was not to return to it.[11] He was at loggerheads with Theodore's policy of dividing very large dioceses, and resented the high-handed action of the archbishop of Canterbury who had split the diocese of York into three without his consent. Wilfrid took his appeal to Agatho in 679, where the Roman Council sought to reconcile the two standpoints, telling Wilfrid that his diocese was indeed so large that he must appoint three coadjutor-bishops, but telling Theodore that

[10] Agatho's synodal letter from his Council of March 680 (*CPG* IV, no. 9418) is given in the fourth session of the *acta* of the Council of Constantinople of 681, ed. Riedinger, *Concilium Vniuersale Constantinopolitanum Tertium, Concilii Actiones I-XI*, pp. 122–59; see also PL 87, 1215–48.

[11] Stephen of Ripon, *Vita S. Wilfridi*, ch. 24 (ed. B. Colgrave, *The Life of Bishop Wilfrid by Eddius Stephanus* (Cambridge, 1927), pp. 48–50).

things must be done at York with Wilfrid's willing acquiescence.[12] Like Agatho, Bede himself wanted to see the best in both Theodore and Wilfrid, minimising Wilfrid's intransigent and contentious role and praising his trumpet-tongued insistence on English acceptance of Roman authority in such matters as the dating of Easter.

No reader of the letters of Agatho and the *acta* of the Council of Constantinople in 680–1 would be given reason to think that the pope was faintly anxious about the orthodoxy of the English church. For Agatho it is the unanimous testimony of these far-flung barbarian Christian communities under their bishops, among whom there are some like Theodore with an excellent education and a philosophical mind, which vindicates the authority of Peter's see in opposing clever heresy in the Greek East. For Bede, however, the mission of John the precentor was to carry out an investigation, as if someone had given Agatho reason to fear that all might not be well. Happily, to Bede's evident gratification, the decisions of the Council of Hatfield proved how meticulously orthodox the English churches were, and although the precentor died on his journey back to Rome (and because of his devotion to St Martin was buried at Tours),[13] the report he had written was safely transmitted to the pope.

Two questions arise from these considerations. The first is whether perhaps the suggestion of some failure or lapse in orthodoxy in England might have come from Wilfrid.[14] When he brought his appeal against Theodore to Rome, might he have insinuated that the Greek monk from Tarsus, who had not been Pope Vitalian's first choice for the archbishopric and had been sent *faute de mieux* with Hadrian to keep an eye on him, was not absolutely sound at all points and spoke with an uncertain sound on essential matters where divergence is not tolerable? The second question arises from Bede's remarkable emphasis on the Council of Hatfield's endorsement of the 'filioque'. That was not a way of talking about the Holy Trinity that would have come naturally to a Greek monk from

---

[12] The *acta* of the Roman synod of 679 are in W. Levison, *Aus rheinischer und fränkischer Frühzeit* (Düsseldorf, 1948), pp. 288–92, with an important critical discussion.

[13] See the fine study of burial in proximity to saints by Yvette Duval, *Auprès des saints corps et âme: l'inhumation 'ad sanctos' dans la chrétienté d'Orient et Occident du IIIe au VIIe siècle* (Paris, 1988).

[14] I have explored this suggestion further in 'Theodore of Tarsus and Monotheletism', *Logos. Festschrift für Luise Abramowski* (Berlin and New York, 1993), pp. 534–44.

Tarsus, though in the West until the middle of the seventh century there is no evidence of the least awareness that this Augustinian doctrine was uncongenial to the Greek churches.

The first evidence that there could be a problem about the 'filioque' emerges in the monothelete controversy. Maximus the Confessor, the Byzantine bureaucrat turned monk who, like Pope Martin, suffered terribly for his opposition to monotheletism, gives us the crucial information that at the time of his election Pope Martin I had included in his *synodica* an affirmation that the Holy Spirit proceeds from the Father and the Son; that the arrival of this document in the East had raised several eyebrows; and that the monotheletes had used it to undermine the pope's moral right to sit in judgement on their orthodoxy when he was himself so irreverent and disrespectful to an oecumenical council as to be corrupting the text of its creed.[15]

In none of the western texts produced by Agatho in 680 for the Council of Constantinople is there the least hint of the 'filioque'. In 681 the see of Rome wished to be firm for its christological tradition, but not to invite unpleasant charges of making improper changes in a creed that had sacrosanct status.

The evidence is compatible with the hypothesis that Theodore of Canterbury needed the Council of Hatfield to affirm the 'filioque' because that would silence criticisms taken to Rome by the contentious Wilfrid of York. The 'filioque' was not stressed at Hatfield to help Pope Agatho for whose delicate task this emphatic affirmation could only be an embarrassment, handing needless weapons to the arsenal of his Greek critics in the patriarchate of Antioch, men with a sharp eye for weaknesses in Roman defences, such as the notorious fact that until 677 a nest of Nestorian Greek monks had been unmolested in Rome itself.[16] Accordingly, the

---

[15] PG 91, 136. Maximus's fidelity to Roman authority led him also into an adventurous defence of Pope Honorius (PG 91, 328–9).

[16] See the life of Pope Donus (676–8) in *Liber pontificalis* (ed. L. Duchesne, *Le Liber Pontificalis*, 2 vols. (Paris, 1886–92, with a third vol. containing bibliography and indexes by C. Vogel, Paris, 1955–7) I, 348). These Nestorians were 'in monasterio qui appellatur *Boetiana*' – evidently founded by Boethius's family. Their presence in Rome was only too well known to the eastern monotheletes, as is shown by ch. 24 of the Maronite life of Maximus edited by S. P. Brock ('An Early Syriac Life of Maximus the Confessor', *AB* 91 (1973), 299–346 [repr. in his *Syriac Perspectives on Late Antiquity*, no. XII], at 318), where their Roman monastery is named *Cellae novae*; cf. also discussion by Brock, above, pp. 50–1.

insistence on the 'filioque' at Hatfield almost certainly belongs to the tensions between Theodore and Wilfrid and was the kind of help that in 680 Agatho would have preferred not to receive.

6

The importation of Mediterranean manuscripts into Theodore's England

DAVID N. DUMVILLE

The despatch of Christian missionaries necessarily meant also the despatch of books, for in as much as Christianity was a religion which referred constantly to its Holy Scriptures, employed also a range of books detailing its church services, and had developed a body of law-texts governing its own actions, there was an irreducible minimum of written materials without which even the most practically minded group of missionaries would wish to function. Even if we had no other information on the point, therefore, we should assume that the first Roman missionaries sent by Pope Gregory I to England would have been equipped with a quantity of fundamental Christian texts, probably including high-status books designed to impress by their quality, size and decoration. Bede, who is necessarily our informant, offered no remarks on this matter when speaking of the arrival of Abbot Augustine and his party in 597; but in his account of the reinforcements sent by Gregory in 601 and led by Abbot Mellitus he specified that among 'uniuersa quae ad cultum erant ac ministerium ecclesiae necessaria' brought by them were *codices plurimos*.[1] It has long been thought that among the books brought to Kent in the opening years of the mission was the sixth-century manuscript of the gospels, now known as 'St Augustine's Gospels' – Cambridge, Corpus Christi College 286.[2] From time to time other candidates for comparably early importation have been suggested, but none of these attributions can

---

[1] *HE* I.29.

[2] *CLA* II, no. 126. Cf. F. Wormald, *The Miniatures in the Gospels of St Augustine, Corpus Christi College MS. 286* (Cambridge, 1954), and G. Henderson, *Losses and Lacunae in Early Insular Art* (York, 1982).

96

be demonstrated beyond doubt.[3]

A further consideration is that Augustine, his fellows, and their successors at least until the death of Archbishop Honorius in 653, were drawn from the Roman Mediterranean world, if not indeed from Rome itself.[4] They were accordingly participants in a culture which, even in its secular aspect, enjoyed a significant level of access to literacy. We cannot imagine that they would easily have forsaken this in the mission field, even in a largely illiterate society. For our purpose this has two dimensions.

Relatively high levels of secular literacy in late Roman and sub-Roman southern Europe had meant that documentary record of commercial and real-estate transactions had become routine, at both private and public levels.[5] A result of this was that the Roman missionaries in England were likely to expect to be able to document the sources and nature of their – their churches' – possessions. From late in the seventh century we do indeed acquire direct evidence for the transplantation to England of the land-charter, albeit mutated into a form rather different from that of its continental ancestor. There has been some dispute as to whether this practice began during the first seventy years of English Christianity or rather was initiated during the regime of Archbishop Theodore (669–90). The arguments for a diversity of sources for the English solemn diploma seem impressive in sum and likely to point to the form's development in England in the earlier Christian generations.[6] What is particularly striking is that the diploma, used in England as a generally royal conveyance of rights over land, dues and people to the church, was turned into a

---

[3] For discussion of the types of manuscript which Augustine could have brought, see H. Mayr-Harting, *The Coming of Christianity to Anglo-Saxon England*, 3rd ed. (London, 1990), pp. 168–74.

[4] Bede, *HE* III.20. Cf. recent comparative discussion by D. N. Dumville *et al.*, *Saint Patrick, A.D. 493–1993*, Studies in Celtic History 13 (Woodbridge, 1993), 80–2.

[5] For the primary documentation, see *Chartae Latinae Antiquiores*, ed. A. Bruckner and R. Marichal (Olten, 1954–).

[6] P. Chaplais, 'Who introduced Charters into England? The Case for Augustine', *Journal of the Society of Archivists* 3 (1965–9), 526–42, repr. in *Prisca Munimenta*, ed. F. Ranger (London, 1973), pp. 88–107 (cf. 28–34); S. Kelly, 'Anglo-Saxon Lay Society and the Written Word', *The Uses of Literacy in Early Mediaeval Europe*, ed. R. McKitterick (Cambridge, 1990), pp. 36–62, at 39–43. For the context, see W. Levison, *England and the Continent in the Eighth Century* (Oxford, 1946), pp. 224–33.

document of considerable formality designed (as it would appear) to impress rather than in any narrow sense to authenticate:[7] to this end it was at first written throughout in Uncial script. Surviving originals of the first 150 years of English Christianity are very few,[8] which is not entirely unexpected; to the troubled histories of many Anglo-Saxon churches in at least the first three centuries of their history, we may add the very real possibility that the earliest documents were written on papyrus, a rather perishable medium, in imitation of Mediterranean practice.[9]

The second dimension which I wish to discuss, of the transference of literate assumptions to the English context, concerns the scripts practised and read by the Roman missionaries (not to mention the Gauls among them) and the extent to which these were transferred to the mission-field. Christian literature was in principle written in Uncial or Half-uncial script in late antiquity and the sub-Roman period: biblical and liturgical texts were usually in Uncial, while biblical commentary and other *theologica* might be executed in Half-uncial.[10] We should expect that churches established by Roman ecclesiastics would, when acquiring book-producing capacity, have expected to practise both scripts. Furthermore, necessary educational adjuncts – for schools would have been early requirements if the mission was to prosper – would have included (as an absolute minimum) grammatical texts: it is likely that imported copies of these would have been written in a script of lesser status, Cursive Half-uncial for example.[11] In any event, we must imagine that the members of the Roman

---

[7] F. M. Stenton, *The Latin Charters of the Anglo-Saxon Period* (Oxford, 1955), pp. 49–50, made this point.

[8] E. A. Lowe, *English Uncial* (Oxford, 1960); cf. D. H. Wright, 'Some Notes on English Uncial', *Traditio* 17 (1961), 441–56 (and pls. III-VI), and B. Bischoff, *Mittelalterliche Studien*, 3 vols. (Stuttgart, 1966–81) II, 328–39 and pls. X-XI.

[9] M. Deanesly, 'Early English and Gallic Minsters', *Transactions of the Royal Historical Society* 4th ser. 23 (1941), 25–69, at 26–30 (cf. 53–8). Cf. Kelly, 'Anglo-Saxon Lay Society', pp. 41–2, who did not however refer to Deanesly's work.

[10] On these scripts, see B. Bischoff, *Latin Palaeography: Antiquity and the Middle Ages* (Cambridge, 1990), pp. 66–78. Still indispensable, if now incomplete, are the pioneering lists of majuscule manuscripts: L. Traube, *Vorlesungen und Abhandlungen*, 3 vols. (Munich, 1909–20) I, 157–263 (pp. 163–71 on Rustic Capitals and 171–261 on Uncial); E. A. Lowe, 'A Hand-list of Half-uncial Manuscripts', *Studi e Testi* 40 (1924), 34–61. Cf. Lowe, *English Uncial*, p. 7. For Half-uncial as a rival of Uncial in the sixth century, see J. Brown, *A Palaeographer's View* (London, 1993), p. 54.

[11] On Cursive Half-uncial (Lowe's 'Quarter-uncial'), see Bischoff, *Latin Palaeography*, pp. 75–6, and, more fully, Brown, *A Palaeographer's View*, pp. 179–241 and 284–7. For

mission, in so far as they were literate and particularly in as much as any of them were scribes, would have used a cursive script of some sort not only for many everyday purposes but also for copying texts of relatively low status. Nevertheless, what is striking is that evidence is largely wanting for the importation, reception and use of even (continental) Half-uncial in England, let alone script-forms of lesser status.

The implication of this lack remains unclear. Imported books written in these scripts have not been identified or have been destroyed over the centuries. The same might apply to manuscripts written in England by the missionaries themselves, which might not have displayed features distinguishing them from continental products. English scribes, once trained, may not have written in a way which enables their products to be identified as other than continental. It would only have been when the conventions of Insular script, arriving in England from the Gaelic world (or, perhaps less probably, from the British churches), began to penetrate scriptoria in the heartlands of the Roman mission that the possibility of distinctively English scribal products would have arisen. As far as I am aware, the question of when that happened has never been formulated.

Practitioners of each of the two script-systems would have met in mid-seventh-century Northumbria following the arrival of Gaelic missionaries in 634/5.[12] But here the Irish element rapidly became dominant, although at least one prominent Roman missionary remained active in Deira and from the 650s churchmen with continental experience increasingly challenged aspects of Irish ecclesiastical practice.[13] Nevertheless, it seems to have been Benedict Biscop's foundation of monasteries of strongly southern European character, first at Wearmouth in 674 and then at Jarrow in 681/2,[14] which effectively brought Romanizing scribal practice to Northumbria, and this in time challenged and mutated Insular

one school-text, Arator's *Historia apostolica*, in continental Cursive Half-uncial of *c.* 600 and of fifteenth-century Canterbury (St Augustine's) provenance, see *ibid.*, pp. 203 and 230, and *CLA* Suppl., no. 1740; Oxford, Bodleian Library, e Museo 66 (S.C. 3655), offsets of binding fragments.

12 For the events, see Bede, *HE* II.20 and III.

13 On James the Deacon, see *ibid.* II.16 and 20 (cf. III.25 and IV.2), and on the controversies of the episcopates of Fínán and Colmán in Northumbria, *ibid.* III.25 and 27.

14 *Venerabilis Baedae Opera Historica*, ed. C. Plummer, 2 vols. (Oxford, 1896) II, 361 and 365. See also P. Wormald, 'Bede and Benedict Biscop', in *Famulus Christi*, ed. G. Bonner (London, 1976), pp. 141–69, at 151–2.

script.[15] In the South matters must have proceeded differently. In Kent, East Anglia and Wessex Roman practice should have been dominant. However, from the first in Wessex we observe a series of Northumbrian and Irish connections, and for as much as a dozen years within the period 658 x 670 Wessex was without a bishop recognized by Canterbury.[16] By *c.* AD 700 Insular script was being written in Wessex.[17] Likewise in East Anglia, although the Roman mission established itself there in the time of Archbishop Honorius (627 x 631–653), the presence (and possibly the antecedent presence) of St Fursa, a bishop from southern Ireland, would have made this an area of mixed tradition: Fursa worked for many years, within 630 x 655, in East Anglia and established a monastery there which outlasted him, as Bede made clear.[18] By the time of Archbishop Theodore's arrival at Canterbury, in 669, the Insular and late Antique script-systems are likely to have already met, in varying circumstances, in Northumbria, East Anglia and Wessex, and perhaps to have begun mutual interpenetration. Theodore's creation of a single English church which looked to Canterbury and of a school at Canterbury which attracted, *inter alios*, Irish pupils would by themselves have ensured that Kent was opened up to the experience of the churches of the other English kingdoms.[19] The flexibility of the Insular system of scripts, with its emphasis on a very practical minuscule, may have commended itself to all during the next generation or two. The earliest known specimen of Insular script written in Kent dates from 697.[20]

[15] See discussion by Brown, *A Palaeographer's View*, pp. 195 and 197–8.

[16] Bede, *HE* III.7, for the early episcopal history of Wessex.

[17] Brown, *A Palaeographer's View*, pp. 191, 213 and 232, on Boniface's having learnt to write Insular minuscule in Wessex before 700.

[18] On East Anglia, see Bede, *HE* III.18–20. For a recent discussion of Fursa, see P. Ó Riain, 'Les Vies de saint Fursy: les sources irlandaises', *Revue du Nord* 68 (1986), 405–13. Bede suppressed the information (which lay before him in *Vita I S. Fursei*) that Fursa was a bishop. On education in East Anglia, see P. F. Jones, 'The Gregorian Mission and English Education', *Speculum* 3 (1928), 335–48.

[19] On church unification, see Bede, *HE* IV.2. For Irish pupils at Canterbury, see the discussion in *Aldhelm: the Prose Works*, trans. M. Lapidge and M. Herren (Cambridge, 1979), pp. 143–6 and 160–4, including translation of *Epistola V* (to Heahfrith); *Aldhelmi Opera*, ed. R. Ehwald, MGH, Auct. Antiq. 15 (Berlin, 1919), 486–94.

[20] London, British Library, Stowe Charter 1: *Chartae*, ed. Bruckner and Marichal III, no. 220; P. H. Sawyer, *Anglo-Saxon Charters. An Annotated List and Bibliography* (London, 1968), no. 19. See also *ibid.*, no. 21 (*Chartae*, ed. Bruckner and Marichal III, no. 189), of AD 700 or 715. Both are written in Insular hybrid minuscule and both are

Did the adoption of Insular scripts necessarily sound the death-knell for the late Antique system in England? That English Uncial continued to be written, at least into the middle years of the eighth century, is certain. Indeed some of the most striking developments in English Uncial took place *c.* 700 in Northumbria and major manuscripts might be produced in the South as late as the mid-century.[21] But if the late Antique system had any future, more of it would have to be in regular use than merely the elaborate and expensive Uncial. It is hard to imagine that a continuing flow of continental Half-uncial manuscripts did not reach England. What, then, was the fate of that script on English soil? We should expect continuity at the hands of foreign scribes and successful imitation by those whom they trained. If such occurred, it has remained undetected. Instead, palaeographers have identified two books, at least one of which had been written by *c.* 700, in script apparently imitative of continental Half-uncial. These are Oxford, Bodleian Library, Douce 140 (S.C. 21714),[22] subsequently annotated by St Boniface (†754), and Cambrai, Bibliothèque municipale, 470 (441).[23] The implication of the scribes' difficulties in producing convincing performances in continental Half-uncial is, however, that they were already practitioners within another script-system, presumably the Insular. It seems likely to have been the very flexibility of the finely graded Insular minuscule system which rendered continental Half-uncial largely unnecessary in England – as Insular Half-uncial came increasingly to be in status an Insular equivalent of Uncial, so Insular hybrid minuscule stepped into the everyday shoes of Half-uncial.[24] After the middle of the eighth

from the church of Lyminge; on that house's Northumbrian connections, see P. Wormald, *Bede and the Conversion of England: the Charter Evidence*, Jarrow Lecture 1984 (Jarrow, 1985), p. 17. For an example of a literary manuscript in Insular minuscule thought to be of Kentish origin, see *CLA* II, no. 123.

[21] For an account of developments in this script, see Lowe, *English Uncial*.

[22] Lowe, *CLA* II, no. 237, dating it *c.* 700 ('VII–VIII'). Cf. Lowe, 'A Hand-list', p. 47 (no. 68), in a survey from which manuscripts in Insular Half-uncial were explicitly excluded (*ibid.*, p. 37); M. B. Parkes, *Scribes, Scripts and Readers* (London, 1991), pp. 126–7 (attributing it now to the beginning, now to the end, of the seventh century); and Brown, *A Palaeographer's View*, pp. 195 and 213 (cf. pl. 50).

[23] Lowe, *CLA* VI, no. 740, dating it to the first half of the eighth century; cf. Lowe, 'A Hand-list', p. 40 (no.16); Parkes, *Scribes, Scripts and Readers*, p. 126, n. 18; and Brown, *A Palaeographer's View*, p. 195, dating it 'seventh–eighth century' (*c.* 700?).

[24] See T. J. Brown, 'Late Antique and Early Anglo-Saxon Books', in *Manuscripts at Oxford: an Exhibition in Memory of Richard William Hunt (1908–1979)*, ed. A. C. de la Mare and B. C. Barker-Benfield (Oxford, 1980), pp. 9–14, at 9.

century in England, both Uncial and Insular Half-uncial were increasingly marginalized, as presumably expensive and difficult scripts.[25] In short, in English hands majuscule scripts were rendered superfluous by the development of Insular minuscule. While for lack of evidence we are left uncertain as to what lesser (non-Insular) scripts than Uncial were being written in southern England during the first century of English Christianity, what does seem certain is that in the slightly longer term the adoption there of the Insular script-system was the cause of the failure of continental Half-uncial and Cursive to develop in England.

It is possible that there is one further factor involved here, and that we should take the hint from the use of Uncial script for diplomas. If it were believed that in the mission-field everything had to be organized in such a way as to impress the heathen and the newly converted, there may have been great pressure when writing books in England to use only the most stately script, namely Uncial. While Half-uncial books of continental origin must have been imported and used, they may therefore in general not have been multiplied in English scriptoria. That Cursive had been displaced from its role in charters may be an indication of its more general rejection; but, if so, it is hard to see how its place was filled in southern England before the adoption of Insular minuscule.

Nevertheless, the import of books from the Continent, and in particular from Rome, during the first two generations of the mission seems a certainty. Likewise, the Gaelic ecclesiastics, who came especially but by no means exclusively from Iona, would have brought books too, albeit of a very different character: their script, whether invented in Britain in the late fifth and sixth centuries or created in Ireland in the later sixth and earlier seventh,[26] was to have a dominant future in the British Isles. Before

---

[25] However, the script continued to be practised as part of the English heritage in churches of the German mission-field: Lowe, *English Uncial*, pp. 13–14 and 24–5. Further to Bernhard Bischoff's suggestion to Lowe that this tradition lay behind the Carolingian redevelopment of Uncial (Lowe, *English Uncial*, p. 14, n. 3), see R. McKitterick, 'Frankish Uncial: a New Context for the Echternach Scriptorium', *Willibrord, zijn wereld en zijn werk*, ed. P. Bange and A. G. Weiler (Nijmegen, 1990), pp. 374–88, and 'Carolingian Uncial: a New Context for the Lothar Psalter', *British Library Journal* 16 (1990), 1–15.

[26] For differing views, see on the one hand Lowe, *CLA* II, p. xi (2nd ed., p. xv), and Bischoff, *Latin Palaeography*, pp. 77 and 83–95, and on the other Brown, *A Palaeographer's View*, pp. 179–241 and 284–7, who developed the ideas of L. Bieler, 'Insular Palaeography, Present State and Problems', *Scriptorium* 3 (1949), 267–94, esp. pp.

its comprehensive triumph, however, it had to coexist with Uncial, during which time Roman concepts of calligraphy and book-production were to have a profound impact on Insular script and codicology.[27]

While that process was running its course, a new movement arose among English ecclesiastics, that of private book-collection. We meet only a few examples, some of them by merest chance; but among these few were one or two major collectors. He who most engages our attention in this regard is Benedict Biscop, founder-abbot of Monkwearmouth and Jarrow. Likewise St Wilfrid must not be neglected, for the famous continental travels of this famously wealthy prelate gave many opportunities to import books to England, although it must be admitted that neither his biographer nor Bede encourages us to think in these terms.[28] Abbot Ceolfrith may have been another: we know that he made one trip to Rome with Benedict Biscop, and his biographer tells us that in the course of his abbacy at Monkwearmouth–Jarrow (688/9–716) he doubled the already very large library which Benedict had created for that church;[29] but it is not certain that these were comparable acquisitions rather than new products of the scriptoria of the twin-monastery. Another great traveller, Oftfor, educated at a Northumbrian church, Whitby, became in due course bishop of Worcester (691-*post* 693): he was reputed to be a man of considerable learning who had travelled to Rome and perhaps therefore acquired books which presumably would have come to rest eventually at Worcester Cathedral.[30] Another episcopal collection built up in the early eighth century was that of Acca at Hexham (709–31), which was praised by Bede:[31] whether it remained safely there when Acca was expelled in 731

273–4. Bieler there noted (p. 271) that in 1947 Lowe (*CLA* IV, p. xxiii) had himself suggested that in fifth-century Cursive Half-uncial lay the predominant inspiration of Insular minuscule; by the end of his life Lowe had implicitly withdrawn that view, however.

[27] Cf. above, n. 15.

[28] We owe to Stephanus, however, the story of Wilfrid's commissioning, for the church of Ripon, a new gospel-book 'in letters of purest gold on purpled parchment and illuminated' to be encased in gem-encrusted gold: *Vita S. Wilfridi*, §17 (*The Life of Bishop Wilfrid*, ed. and trans. B. Colgrave (Cambridge, 1927), pp. 34–7).

[29] *Historia abbatum*, §15: *Venerabilis Baedae Opera Historica*, ed. Plummer I, 379; for discussion, see *ibid*. II, 365 (cf. 361).

[30] See the discussion by P. Sims-Williams, *Religion and Literature in Western England, 600–800*, CSASE 3 (Cambridge, 1990), 193–4.

[31] *HE* V.20.

is unknown. Perhaps the most notable library to be brought together in Northumbria after the formation of Benedict Biscop's collection was that established at York: it has been speculated that this was created by Archbishop Ecgberht (732–66, bishop 732–5),[32] but it comes into the view of our sources only *c.* 778, as the possession of Archbishop Ælberht who bequeathed it to Alcuin; to the last-named we owe a sort of metrical catalogue of his library (as it was in 781 x 793), which may have been transported to Tours after 796.[33]

Among lesser collectors and importers an interesting example was identified by Ludwig Traube and Paul Lehmann:[34] Cuthwine, bishop of Dunwich (716 x 731),[35] is known to have acquired two illustrated Italian manuscripts of Christian Latin poets.[36] He may have possessed many more, and he is likely to be representative of a much larger group of those

---

[32] Cf. Levison, *England and the Continent*, p. 153. On his regime, see Mayr-Harting, *The Coming*, pp. 241–2 and 263 (cf. 251–2, 260 and 273).

[33] On the date of the poem, see *Alcuin: The Bishops, Kings, and Saints of York*, ed. and trans. P. Godman (Oxford, 1982), pp. xxxix–xlvii. For discussion of the library, see M. Lapidge, 'Surviving Booklists from Anglo-Saxon England', in *Learning and Literature in Anglo-Saxon England*, ed. M. Lapidge and H. Gneuss (Cambridge, 1985), pp. 33–89, at 45–9.

[34] L. Traube, 'Palaeographische Anzeigen. III', *Neues Archiv der Gesellschaft für ältere deutsche Geschichtskunde* 27 (1901/2), 264–85, at 276–8; P. Lehmann, 'Wert und Echtheit einer Beda abgesprochenen Schrift', *Sitzungsberichte der Bayerischen Akademie der Wissenschaften*, philosophisch–philologische Klasse (1919), 4. Abhandlung.

[35] On him and his identity see also Mayr-Harting, *The Coming*, pp. 191–2 (and p. 309, nn.1–3); Levison, *England and the Continent*, pp. 132–4; A. S. Cook, 'Bishop Cuthwini of Leicester (680–691), Amateur of Illustrated Manuscripts', *Speculum* 2 (1927), 253–7, who argued for an alternative candidate.

[36] Bede, *Liber quaestionum*, §2 (ed. Lehmann, 'Wert und Echtheit'), referred to Cuthwine bringing an illustrated manuscript, perhaps of Arator's *Historia apostolica*, from Rome to England: see Mayr-Harting, *The Coming*, p. 191, for a translation of the relevant passage. R. N. Bailey has speculated that Bede borrowed the book from Cuthwine: *The Meaning of Mercian Sculpture*, Sixth Brixworth Lecture (Leicester, 1988), p. 4. In Antwerp, Museum Plantijn-Moretus, M. 17. 4, we have a copy, made at Liège in the early ninth century (but after 814), of an illustrated manuscript of Caelius Sedulius's *Carmen paschale* once owned by Cuthwine: on the Antwerp book, see C. Caesar, 'Die antwerpener Handschrift des Sedulius', *Rheinisches Museum für Philologie* ns 56 (1901), 247–71; J. J. G. Alexander, *Insular Manuscripts, 6th to the 9th Century* (London, 1978), p. 83 (no. 65) and pls. 285–301; Bischoff, *Mittelalterliche Studien* III, 9 ('Die älteste Handschrift aus Lüttich').

who collected while travelling as pilgrim or ecclesiastical administrator. Wilhelm Levison drew attention to two anonymous pilgrims to Rome before 705 who had brought back with them *uolumina numerosa*, according to Æthilwald in his *Carmen rhythmicum II*.[37] While the Roman pilgrimage may have become commonplace by 731, a generation earlier it had been less usual: then at least, collection of books seems to have been a significant aspect of such journeys.[38]

Books might still be imported by foreigners in the second half of the seventh century. According to the Life of St Bertila,[39] abbess of Chelles (*c.* 660–*c.* 710), she was asked by English kings to despatch disciples to found monasteries in their territories: with them she sent relics and 'many volumes of books'.[40] E. A. Lowe stressed what he saw as the considerable importance for the history of English script and libraries of the visit to Northumbria, and specifically to Monkwearmouth–Jarrow, of John, *archicantor* ('precentor') of St Peter's, Rome;[41] this is perhaps to build a great deal on the remark that John 'left behind him a good number of instructions which he had committed to writing and which are still preserved in the library of the same monastery in memory of him',[42] but there can be no doubt that he was at least responsible for some new matter in the Monkwearmouth–Jarrow library. Finally, the spotlight falls on Theodore and Hadrian who established such a remarkable school at Canterbury, something of whose curriculum we learn from its most famous *alumnus*, Aldhelm. Although neither Aldhelm nor Bede tells us anything about books being imported by this learned pair – and no doubt a good many manuscripts had accumulated at Canterbury since Augustine's day – it is

---

[37] Levison, *England and the Continent*, p. 134 and n. 2; cf. *Aldhelmi Opera*, ed. Ehwald, p. 531 (*Carmen rhythmicum* II, Æthilwald to Wihtfrith, lines 107–16).

[38] See Sims-Williams, *Religion*, pp. 193–4, for interesting commentary on Bede, *HE* IV.23 (21).

[39] *Vita S. Bertilae*, §6: ed. W. Levison, *Passiones Vitaeque Sanctorum Aevi Merovingici*, ed. B. Krusch and W. Levison, MGH, SRM 6 (Hannover, 1913), 106–7.

[40] Levison, *England and the Continent*, p. 132, n. 2. Cf. Sims-Williams, *Religion*, pp. 110 and 204, with translation of the relevant passage.

[41] *English Uncial*, p. 7; on John, cf. Levison, *England and the Continent*, pp. 15–16.

[42] *Historia abbatum*, §6: *Venerabilis Baedae Opera Historica*, ed. Plummer I, 369; trans. C. Albertson, *Anglo-Saxon Saints and Heroes* (New York, 1967), p. 231. Cf. Bede, *HE* IV.18 (16), for a more expansive account.

hard to imagine that their vast learning and extraordinary curriculum were unsupported by a substantial library.[43]

Throughout the seventh century and the early eighth, therefore, before the cultural flow changed direction, a considerable movement of books from southern Europe to England must be envisaged.[44] Only a tiny number of such manuscripts has been identified, however. Can Vikings, Normans and Henry VIII be responsible for their almost total loss, along with the steady attrition caused by the passage of time? To answer the question we must first consider the few which are known.

Gneuss[45]	Shelfmark	Content	Date (Origin)
83	Cambridge, Corpus Christi College 286	Euangelia	vi (Italy)
87	Cambridge, Corpus Christi College 304	Iuuencus	viii[1] (Italy)
245	Durham, Cathedral Library, B.iv.6, fol. 169*	Maccabaei	vi (Italy)
281	London, British Library, Additional 15350, fols. 1 and 121	Vitae patrum	vii/viii (Italy?)
297	London, British Library, Additional 40165.A.1	Cyprianus	iv *ex.* (Africa?)
529	Oxford, Bodleian Library, Auct. D.2.14 (*S.C.* 2698)	Euangelia	vii (Italy)
654	Oxford, Bodleian Library, Laud Gr. 35 (*S.C.* 1119)	Acta Apostolorum	vi/vii (Sardinia?)
834	Kassel, Landesbibliothek, Theol. Fol. 65	Hegesippus	vi (Italy)
848[46]	Louvain-la-Neuve, Bibliothèque de l'Université, Frag. H. Omont 3	?	vii/viii
944	Würzburg, Universitätsbibliothek, M.p.th.q. 2	Hieronymus	v (Italy)
945	Würzburg, Universitätsbibliothek, M.p.th.f. 68	Euangelia	vi (Italy)

[43] For discussion, see M. Lapidge, 'The School of Theodore and Hadrian', *ASE* 15 (1986), 45–72.

[44] A comparable transfer to northern Francia has also been noted: see Wormald, 'Bede and Benedict Biscop', pp. 149–50.

[45] In this column I give the reference-number assigned by H. Gneuss, 'A Preliminary List of Manuscripts written or owned in England up to 1100', *ASE* 9 (1981), 1–60.

[46] In Gneuss's list, this item is treated as ninth-century and Old English. For fuller details, see B. Schauman and A. Cameron, 'A newly-found Leaf of Old English from Louvain', *Anglia* 95 (1977), 289–312, at 297–300 and pl. [2]: the evidence is on the verso which bears writing in continental Half-uncial of *c.* AD 700.

This is a poor remnant of a body of imported books which must by the end of the seventh century have been numbered in thousands rather than hundreds. To later ages many such manuscripts would have seemed to be objects of very high status and their destruction might be considered all the more surprising.[47] What is more, there is no large number of manuscripts written before *c.* 700 and surviving now in British libraries from which significant additions might be made to the foregoing list.

Other means are of course open to us if we wish to pursue the results of the importation of books from Mediterranean sources in the seventh century. We can seek in English manuscripts the physical results of copying from earlier continental books in majuscule scripts, or testimony to the same effect from the textual history of a work found in a later Insular-script copy, or art-historical evidence of the direct derivation of English illumination from Mediterranean models: all are available to indicate the former presence in England of southern European books of high status. Textual content may be equally demonstrative of geographical source: Northumbrian gospelbooks provide evidence of the impact of Neapolitan liturgy,[48] and one gospel manuscript shows that it is a copy from an exemplar corrected at Eugippius's monastery in AD 558.[49]

Another course is to examine the literary works known to English authors of the seventh and eighth centuries and to assume that each or most of these would originally have been carried to England as a manuscript-import from southern Europe. Occasionally our sources offer significant help in reconstructing the process of transmission. In Bede's so-called *Historia abbatum* – otherwise *Vita sanctorum abbatum monasterii in Wiremutha et Gyruum* – we read accounts of Benedict Biscop's six visits to Rome: in his notices of the fourth, fifth and sixth, Bede reported on Benedict's acquisitions of books. We are further reminded of his book-collecting activities in accounts of his instructions to his monks during his last years and in the statement of the virtues of Abbot Ceolfrith's regime.

---

[47] This conclusion must, however, be tempered by knowledge of the extent of destruction to which English manuscripts were subject at various periods: that the two equally massive siblings of *Codex Amiatinus* could disappear almost without trace is an indication that the unimaginable was indeed possible.

[48] See *Biblical Commentaries*, ed. Bischoff and Lapidge, pp. 155–60.

[49] Levison, *England and the Continent*, p. 142, on Paris, Bibliothèque nationale, lat. 9389 (*CLA* V, no. 578).

Quod ubi duobus annis monasterium rexit, tertium de Brittannia Romam iter arripiens solita prosperitate conpleuit librosque omnis diuinae eruditionis non paucos uel placito praetio emptos, uel amicorum dono largitos retulit. Rediens autem ubi Viennam peruenit, empticios ibi quos apud amicos commendauerat, recepit (§4).[50]

Et ut ea quoque quae nec in Gallia quidem repperiri ualebant, romanis e finibus aecclesiae suae prouisor inpiger ornamenta uel munimenta conferret; quarta illo, post conpositum iuxta regulam monasterium, profectione conpleta multipliciore quam prius spiritalium mercium fenore cumulatus rediit. Primo[51] quod innumerabilem librorum omnis generis copiam adportauit (§6).[52]

. . . non multo post temporis spatio quinta uice de Brittannia Romam adcurrens, innumeris sicut semper aecclesiasticorum donis commodorum locupletatus rediit; magna quidem copia uoluminum sacrorum; sed non minori, sicut et prius, sanctarum imaginum munere ditatus (§9).[53]

Bibliothecam quam de Roma nobilissimam copiosissimamque aduexerat, ad

---

[50] *Venerabilis Baedae Opera Historica*, ed. Plummer I, 367; trans. Albertson, *Anglo-Saxon Saints and Heroes*, p. 228 (reproduced here with minor modifications): 'After ruling this monastery for two years, Benedict set out on his third trip from Britain to Rome and completed it with his usual good fortune. He brought back with him a good number of books pertaining to all branches of sacred literature, some of which he had purchased at a favourable price and some of which had been given him as gifts by friends. On the way home he stopped at Vienne to pick up books which he had bought there and left in the keeping of friends.' This is an account of Benedict's fourth visit to Rome, made in AD 671/2.

[51] This is the beginning of a list of five things.

[52] *Venerabilis Baedae Opera Historica*, ed. Plummer I, 368–9; trans. Albertson, *Anglo-Saxon Saints and Heroes*, pp. 230–1: 'And as for yet other items – ornaments for his church and protective charters – which would not be found even in Gaul, he resolved, like the indefatigable provider that he was, to bring them from Rome. So, as soon as he had his monastery organized in the pattern of the rule, he made his fourth trip to Rome and returned laden with a much more profitable freight of spiritual merchandise than before. First of all, he brought back a vast number of books of every kind.' This is an account of Benedict's fifth visit to Rome, on which he was accompanied by Ceolfrith, AD 678/9.

[53] *Venerabilis Baedae Opera Historica*, ed. Plummer I, 373; trans. Albertson, *Anglo-Saxon Saints and Heroes*, p. 235: 'Not long after [Benedict] went to Rome for the fifth time from Britain and returned richly laden as always with a huge treasure of ecclesiastical goods. Again there was a great wealth of sacred books, and no less rich a collection than before of holy paintings.' This is an account of Benedict's sixth visit to Rome, AD 684–6. On *imagines*, see P. Meyvaert, 'Bede and the Church Paintings at Wearmouth–Jarrow', *ASE* 8 (1979), 63–77.

instructionem aecclesiae necessariam, sollicite seruari integram, nec per incuriam fedari, aut passim dissipari praecepit (§11).[54]

Qui et ipse tertius [abbas], id est Ceolfridus ..., deinde utrique monasterio ... uiginti et octo annos sollerti regimine praefuit; et cuncta quae suus prodecessor aegregia uirtutum opera caepit, ipse non segnius perficere curauit... bibliothecam utriusque monasterii, quam Benedictus abbas magna caepit instantia, ipse non minori geminauit industria; ita ut tres pandectes nouae translationis, ad unum uetustae translationis quem de Roma adtulerat, ipse super adiungeret ... dato quoque Cosmographiorum codice mirandi operis, quem Romae Benedictus emerat, terram octo familiarum ... ab Aldfrido rege in scripturis doctissimo in possessionem monasterii beati Pauli apostoli comparauit; quem comparandi ordinem ipse, dum aduiueret, Benedictus cum eodem rege Aldfrido taxauerat, sed priusquam complere potuisset obiit (§15).[55]

Benedict Biscop's purchase of books at Vienne has been used to account for a singular aspect of Bede's reading.[56] M. L. W. Laistner[57] argued that Bede used as a major source for his own commentary on Proverbs the rarely

---

[54] *Venerabilis Baedae Opera Historica*, ed. Plummer I, 375; trans. Albertson, *Anglo-Saxon Saints and Heroes*, p. 238: 'He gave orders that the excellent and most extensive library which he had brought from Rome, and which is so necessary for the education of the Church, should be jealously preserved intact, and should not be allowed to fall into disrepair through neglect, or be dispersed.'

[55] *Venerabilis Baedae Opera Historica*, ed. Plummer I, 379–80; trans. J. Stevenson, *The Church Historians of England* I.2 (London, 1853), 614–15, repr. in *Bede's Ecclesiastical History of the English Nation*, trans. J. Stevens *et al.*, Everyman's Library 479 (London 1910), 359–60: 'The third of these, Ceolfrith, ... ably governed, during twenty-eight years, both these monasteries, and, whatever works of merit his predecessor had begun, he, with no less zeal, took pains to finish.... the library of both monasteries, which Abbot Benedict had so actively begun, under his equally zealous care became doubled in extent. For he added three Pandects of a new translation which he had brought from Rome.... Moreover, for a beautiful volume of the Geographers which Benedict had bought at Rome, he received from King Aldfrith, who was well skilled in Holy Scripture, in exchange, a grant of land of eight hides ... for the monastery of St Paul's. Benedict had arranged this purchase with the same King Aldfrith before his [own] death, but died before he could complete it.' Cf. *Vita S. Ceolfrithi*, §20: *Venerabilis Baedae Opera Historica*, ed. Plummer I, 395, and trans. Albertson, *Anglo-Saxon Saints and Heroes*, p. 259.

[56] On the southern Gaulish connection in Bede's writing, see M. L. W. Laistner, in *The Intellectual Heritage of the Early Middle Ages*, ed. C. G. Starr (Ithaca, NY, 1957), pp. 133–4; and on Bede's possible knowledge of Avitus of Vienne, see *ibid.*, p. 124.

[57] *Ibid.*, pp. 136–8. He was followed by Mayr-Harting, *The Coming*, p. 211. For the text, see *Salonii Episcopi Genavensis Commentarii in Parabolas Salomonis et in Ecclesiasten*, ed. C.

encountered work long attributed to a fifth-century predecessor, one Salonius, bishop of Geneva. The supposed presence of this obscure text in Bede's library could therefore be explained by Salonius's associations with Vienne. However, in more recent years Bede's work has been shown to be the source of the other commentary, whose attribution to Salonius has accordingly been abandoned;[58] the possibility has also been advanced that it was written as late as *c.* 1100 and that Honorius Augustodunensis was its author.[59]

The massive collection of volumes, largely (one must presume) in majuscule scripts, which Benedict Biscop assembled and made the basis of the library or libraries of Monkwearmouth and Jarrow, would have provided a remarkable series of models for scribes. Whether or not Benedict himself determined that the house-scriptoria should practise Uncial script, the presence there of so many Uncial codices would have created great pressure on scribes to imitate it. What is more, the importance of Rome as a source of Benedict's books helps to explain why the specifically Roman Uncial of the late sixth and seventh centuries exercised such an influence on the script of Monkwearmouth–Jarrow.[60] While we should not ignore the papacy as a source of Roman books for the Italian (and, in the case of Felix, Burgundian) bishops in southern England, nevertheless their imported manuscripts are unlikely to have migrated to Northumbria in any quantity. It would be better to suppose that it was the manuscripts brought back from Rome by Benedict (and perhaps also by Wilfrid, if he was interested in books) which served to introduce northern England to Roman script and thus to create the conditions in which

Curti (Catania, 1964). A relationship between Bede's commentary and that attributed to Salonius was also demonstrated, apparently independently of Laistner, by J. Hablitzel, 'Bedas Expositio in Proverbia Salomonis und seine Quellen', *Biblische Zeitschrift* 24 (1938/9), 357–9.

58 J.-P. Weiss, 'Essai de datation du Commentaire sur les Proverbes attribué abusivement à Salonius', *Sacris Erudiri* 19 (1969/70), 77–114; for his first doubts about Salonius's authorship, see 'L'authenticité de l'oeuvre de Salonius de Genève', *Texte und Untersuchungen zur Geschichte der altchristlichen Literatur* 107 [= *Studia Patristica* 10] (1970), 161–7.

59 V. I. J. Flint, 'The True Author of the Salonii Commentarii in Parabolas Salomonis et in Ecclesiasten', *Recherches de théologie ancienne et médiévale* 37 (1970), 174–86.

60 On Roman Uncial, see A. Petrucci, 'L'onciale Romana. Origini, sviluppo e diffusione di una stilizzazione grafica altomedievale (sec. VI-IX)', *Studi medievali* 3rd ser. 12 (1971), 75–134 (with twenty plates). On its impact at Monkwearmouth–Jarrow, see Parkes, *Scribes, Scripts and Readers*, pp. 94–5.

Northumbrian Uncial would flourish and develop in the late seventh and earlier eighth centuries.

While all these approaches may give us glimpses of the English *Nachleben* of Mediterranean manuscripts imported in the seventh century, they do little or nothing to explain what became of such books thereafter. To gain some purchase on this issue, we must proceed speculatively. A pointer is offered by the continental, and particularly the German, locations of three of the eleven manuscripts listed above as imports into early Anglo-Saxon England.[61]

It has long been apparent that there were English churchmen in the continental mission-fields who had possession of various late Antique or sub-Roman high-status manuscripts.[62] The question is how these books were acquired. For the most part the issue has been treated with a cautious scholarly conservatism, few indeed having been admitted to be manuscripts which were transmitted from the Mediterranean basin to England and thence to continental *Germania*. Nevertheless, the possibility exists, and in a few instances it has been demonstrated beyond cavil. A famous example, where the manuscript in question is no longer known to survive, is provided by an illuminated copy of Caelius Sedulius's *Carmen paschale*, executed at Liège in the ninth century; it contains also a copy of a subscription by a former owner, one Cuthwine, almost certainly the bishop of Dunwich whom we met earlier as the importer from Italy of an illuminated copy of the poetry of Arator.[63]

Two ancient manuscripts which are found in the hands of eighth-century English missionaries on the Continent help us to envisage what may have happened. These examples differ from those few already mentioned in that there is no conclusive proof that they were ever in Anglo-Saxon England itself. At Vienna there now survives a fifth-century Uncial copy of Livy's *Historiae* containing an *ex-libris* inscription of one Theutbertus (Old English Theodberht, presumably), bishop of Dorestad.[64] And in

---

[61] Gneuss, 'A Preliminary List', no. 654 (*CLA* II, no. 251), a member of that list, should be added to the items currently in German locations, for it was in Germany from the eighth century to the sixteenth, before entering the collection of Archbishop William Laud (1573–1645).

[62] Cf. Lowe, *English Uncial*, p. 3, for example, and *CLA* VIII, p. vi.

[63] See above, p. 104 and n. 36.

[64] Lowe, *CLA* X, no. 1472. For the minuscule inscription, not in Insular script, see *Analecta Liviana*, ed. T. Mommsen and G. Studemund (Leipzig, 1873), pp. 3–5 and pl. IV. Cf. discussion by P. Lehmann, 'Das älteste Bücherverzeichnis der Niederlande', *Het*

the Vatican Library we meet an Uncial manuscript (written *c.* 600) of minor works of St Augustine,[65] with an added list (written, according to Paul Lehmann, in early eighth-century Insular script) of books belonging to an English missionary in the Low Counties.[66]

When publishing his inventory of pre-ninth-century literary manuscripts in German libraries, E. A. Lowe noted that about half of the four hundred items listed belonged to the Anglo-Saxon tradition: further, he observed that the English missionaries in Germany had brought ancient Italian manuscripts with them.[67] The point has been restated in more recent work:[68] here I propose to take it a stage further by examining all manuscripts written before *c.* 700 to see whether they bear any sign of having resided in places where Insular script in its English interpretation was written. The result is the list opposite.

Commentary on these nineteen items shows both the possibilities and the difficulties which their evidence produces.

1   This manuscript is the increasingly discussed 'Vergilius Romanus' for which dates from the fourth century to the sixth have been proposed. Most recently, a case for a sub-Roman British origin has been vigorously advanced, largely on art-historical grounds.[71] If the book is indeed British,[72] it does not meet the needs of the present discussion. However, some evidence which suggests its presence in the British Isles in the eighth

---

Boek 12 (1923), 207–13, at 210–11, and J. Crick, 'An Anglo-Saxon Fragment of Justinus's *Epitome*', *ASE* 16 (1987), 181–96, at 190–2.

[65] *CLA* I, no. 84: Vat. Pal. lat. 210.

[66] Lehmann, 'Das älteste Bücherverzeichnis der Niederlande', p. 212, followed by Crick, 'An Anglo-Saxon Fragment', p. 191; but Lowe, *CLA* I, no. 84, wrote that the list was in a ninth-century Irish hand.

[67] Lowe, *CLA* VIII, p. vi: 'they also took along to Germany ancient Italian manuscripts selected from the books which they had received from the missionaries of the seventh century sent to England by Popes Gregory and Vitalian'.

[68] Crick, 'An Anglo-Saxon Fragment', pp. 191–3.

[69] Lowe, *CLA*, cited by volume and number.

[70] For the current shelf-mark, see B. Bischoff *et al.*, 'Addenda to *Codices Latini Antiquiores* (II)', *MS* 54 (1992), 286–307, at 306.

[71] K. R. Dark, *Civitas to Kingdom: British Political Continuity 300–800* (Leicester, 1994), pp. 184–91, with bibliography and discussion of previous scholarship.

[72] Its palaeographical kinship with the so-called 'Vergilius Palatinus' (*CLA* I, no. 99: Vat. Pal. lat. 1631) was noted by Lowe and needs consideration in this context; the provenance of that book was Lorsch.

century and its availability to Heiric of Auxerre in the ninth, as well as its eventual Saint-Denis provenance, may indicate that it was transmitted to the Continent in the period of the missions. If the book is Italian or Gaulish rather than British, it would indeed fall within our terms of reference and would be valuable as an example of an illustrated import.[73]

2   Paul Lehmann gave this manuscript prominence by showing that it belonged to the Carolingian court-librarian, Gerward. It was at a continental house under Anglo-Saxon influence, probably Lorsch, by the ninth century. It contains a book-list in Insular script which Lehmann dated to the first half of the eighth century and attributed to an English missionary in the Netherlands.[74] This view has been widely disseminated: if correct, it would place the manuscript within our terms of reference; however, E. A. Lowe described the list as having been written by a ninth-century Irishman.[75] The question remains to be resolved.

3   Two fragments constituting about half of one leaf survive. The manuscript has two original points of contact with the so-called 'Oxford Gospels of St Augustine', in its gospel-*capitula* (shared also with the [Cambridge] 'Gospels of St Augustine') and in its script.[76] The modern provenance of this item is German: a history conformable with our present needs is therefore possible but unevidenced.

4   This item, represented now by mere binding-fragments, was recovered from an English manuscript of late twelfth-century date. The date of the Spanish book's importation into England has not been demonstrated, but it would be surprising if that had occurred later than the eighth century.[77] It should be added to the list of specimens given above, p. 106.

5   E. A. Lowe suggested that this manuscript might have reached its

---

[73] For the relevance and importance of this consideration, cf. above, pp. 104–5, on Cuthwine.

[74] See above, n. 66.   [75] *CLA* I, no. 84. See above, n. 66.

[76] For the 'Oxford Gospels', see *ibid*. II, no. 230 (Gneuss, 'A Preliminary List', no. 529); for the 'Cambridge Gospels', see *CLA* II, no. 126 (Gneuss, 'A Preliminary List', no. 83).

[77] Another Uncial manuscript of possibly Spanish – but possibly Italian – origin (*CLA* II, no. 127: Cambridge, Corpus Christi College 304) reached Anglo-Saxon England, but not necessarily much before *c.* 900, as recent work by Sarah Billington (Trinity College, Cambridge) has shown. It may therefore have to be deleted from the list on p. 106, above.

North French provenance by way of England.[78] It bears Insular-script additions (including one Old English gloss) of eighth-century date.

6   This South Italian book has had a complex history, probably largely at Rome but perhaps with an excursion into English possession. An addition on 105v indicates that it was used by an Anglo-Saxon in the second half of the eighth century. Other additions show that the manuscript was in Rome in the ninth and tenth centuries.[79] It is therefore a question where the eighth-century English user was working.

7   It would be surprising if this volume had ever reached England. On the evidence of its script it was written 'in a Burgundian centre under Insular influence'. It bears seventh-century Merovingian-period corrections in Cursive, while in the mid-ninth century it was at Lyon. Nevertheless it has running titles and correction 'in late eighth-century Anglo-Saxon minuscule' and ninth-century marginal matter shows distinct English influence.[80]

8   This Italian manuscript of St Jerome's Chronicle was certainly in Insular hands in the eighth century and has an eventual German provenance. However, E. A. Lowe suggested that the script of the Insular corrections was 'probably Irish'.[81]

9   Written perhaps at Lyon, this manuscript was probably eventually broken up at Reichenau. Lowe thought that a liturgical entry (2v) of eighth- or ninth-century date 'seems Insular'.[82]

10   This canon-collection was copied in the pontificate of Gregory the Great. A century later it was in a location where Cursive was written, as a marginal note attests.[83] In the eighth century, it acquired a *probatio pennae* (159v) in Insular script and an Uncial note (found also in the eighth-century Northumbrian book now Köln, Dombibliothek, 213) naming one 'Sigibertus'.[84]

11   Written in or before 546/7 this substantial volume acquired corrections in eighth-century English Uncial (239r) and in ninth-century Insular

---

[78] *CLA* VI, no. 735. Gneuss ('A Preliminary List', no. 799) has dated this 'viii?', the age of its English additions, and identified the original texts as works of St Ambrose; for the one Old English gloss, see N. R. Ker, *Catalogue of Manuscripts containing Anglo-Saxon* (Oxford, 1957), p. lxiii (no. 6*).

[79] *CLA* VIII, no. 1031.   [80] *Ibid.* VIII, no. 1061.   [81] *Ibid.* VIII, no. 1075.

[82] *Ibid.* VIII, no. 1113.   [83] *Ibid.* VIII, no. 1162.

[84] On the latter, see *ibid.* VIII, no. 1163.

minuscule of Fulda type.[85] Its numerous Insular cursive minuscule additions seem likely to be partly in the hand of St Boniface (†754).[86]

12   This South French copy of *Breuiarium Alarici* has French additions of subsequent centuries: Cursive or Merovingian script of the seventh century and (on 331v) a rewritten section in pre-Caroline minuscule. The front flyleaf, however, bears pen-trials in Anglo-Saxon script of the early ninth century, although these seem to point to Würzburg rather than an Insular location.[87] It is possible, then, that this manuscript was imported into England in Theodore's day – it is arguable that the text was known in England[88] – only to be returned to the Continent in the following century; but the distribution of the evidence from the manuscript itself renders this unlikely.

13   A palimpsest, this manuscript was rewritten at Luxeuil in the characteristic minuscule of that house. An Insular-minuscule correction of eighth-century date occurs on p. 280, which has been used to hint at a Würzburg connection. A later eighth-century continental correction shows Insular influence in its script.[89] On the whole, this is an improbable candidate for early importation into England.

14   These 'Gospels of St Kilian' have been thought to be of North French origin. By the late eighth century the manuscript 'was in a scriptorium where Anglo-Saxon scribes were active'; its presence at Würzburg is first documented in the late eleventh century.[90]

15   Written in Italy, this unique copy of the works of the heresiarch Priscillian was still there in the eighth century if an addition in 'crude Italian cursive minuscule' is correctly dated. Nevertheless in that century it had 'reached a centre where Anglo-Saxon script was known'.[91] Whether the travels of this codex have any connection with Irish flirtations with Priscillianist reading is doubtful,[92] although an explanation for interest in

---

85   *Ibid.* VIII, no. 1196.

86   On this, see Parkes, *Scribes, Scripts and Readers*, pp. 121–42.

87   *CLA* IX, no. 1324.

88   A. S. Cook, 'Aldhelm's Legal Studies', *Journal of English and Germanic Philology* 23 (1924), 105–13; M. R. James, *Two Ancient English Scholars. St. Aldhelm & William of Malmesbury*, Glasgow University Publications 22 (Glasgow, 1931), 13–14; and Lapidge, 'The School of Theodore and Hadrian', p. 53.

89   *CLA* IX, no. 1419.   90   *Ibid.* IX, no. 1429.   91   *Ibid.* IX, no. 1431.

92   On these flirtations and their possible context and consequences, see D. N. Dumville, 'Biblical Apocrypha and the Early Irish: a Preliminary Investigation', *Proceedings of the Royal Irish Academy* 73 C (1973), 299–338, at 322–30.

its decidedly unorthodox contents is certainly needed. It could have travelled to the British Isles in the eighth century, but closer investigation of its Insular additions is needed to determine the precise nature of the palaeographical evidence.

16 The Vienna copy of bks XLI-XLV of Livy's History has had a much discussed but still poorly understood history. According to E. A. Lowe it bears dry-point marginalia in 'Anglo-Saxon minuscule'; these have apparently not been successfully dated. Secondly, it bears an eighth-century ownership-inscription of *Theutberti episcopi de Dorostat* who has been thought an English missionary bishop. It was later at Lorsch.[93]

17 An eighth-century liturgical note on 1r of this gospel-book was thought by E. A. Lowe 'to be in Insular majuscule'.[94] It is therefore possible that this presumptively French manuscript travelled to the British Isles not long after its production.

18 Although an origin in Southern France has been thought possible for this manuscript, a codicological feature reported by Lowe could be interpreted as Insular. Its omission signs have been compared with those of *Codex Amiatinus*. In the eighth century it received 'corrections and added liturgical formulae in Anglo-Saxon minuscule' and Uncial.[95]

19 This is a codex of some complexity which gained it three entries in *Codices Latini Antiquiores*.[96] The principal manuscript (fols. 1–172) is an early seventh-century copy of Augustine's *De baptismo paruulorum*. It acquired entries in 'Merovingian cursive' of perhaps *c*. AD 700 and pen-trials in 'tiny Anglo-Saxon minuscule' of eighth-century date, was copied at Lorsch in the ninth century, and received additions in a tenth-century German hand.[97] To it are prefixed two bifolia of apparently long-standing connection with the manuscript: on fols. I-II is matter from Eutropius in African or Spanish Uncial of *c*. AD 500,[98] while fols. III-IV contain a *Benedictio cerei paschalis* in seventh-century Cursive written in Spain (or perhaps Italy). On the lower half of IVv are found 'various

[93] *CLA* X, no. 1472. For further details, see above, n. 64. [94] *Ibid*. X, no. 1561.
[95] *Ibid*. XI, no. 1627. The codicological feature in question is pricking in both margins, a characteristically Insular practice. For *Codex Amiatinus* (*CLA* III, no. 299), cf. Lowe, *English Uncial*, pp. 8–13; R. L. S. Bruce-Mitford, 'The Art of the Codex Amiatinus', *Journal of the British Archaeological Association* 3rd ser. 32 (1969), 1–25 and pls. I-XX.
[96] *CLA* XI, nos. 1628a, 1628b and 1629. [97] *Ibid*. no. 1629.
[98] *Ibid*. no. 1628a. The textual and script-division in fact takes place between IIIr and IIIv.

probationes pennae in Anglo-Saxon majuscule and minuscule of the eighth century', one of which caused Lowe to think of Würzburg. 'Later Merovingian and Germanic cursive' additions also occur.[99] If all this evidence be taken together, there is a window for possible Insular transmission in the eighth century, but an eventual location in western Germany seems probable.

This very mixed group produces one resounding message: more work is needed on the Insular element in each of these manuscripts. In particular, very precise description is needed of the Insular-script additions in each instance, so that the best possible determination may be made of whether or not these indicate a sojourn in the British Isles, rather than in the Insular mission-fields. Some problems remain in distinguishing English from Irish contributions[100] and, in two cases, of being certain that the original execution of each book was not itself Insular.[101] At the German end of these books' travels, Lorsch and Würzburg loom large: the former in particular has enjoyed a significant place in classicists' consideration of the Insular route long proposed for the transmission of ancient Latin literature, but scepticism as to the applicability of this model has in recent years been eroding confidence in it and focussing attention on the extensive practice of the Insular script-system on the Continent.[102] It is important that in both these contexts the limits and strengths of the evidential value of palaeographical data be kept in mind.

What the fragmentary case-histories of these nineteen manuscripts indicate is the potential for doubling the list (given above) of early imported Mediterranean manuscripts which have already been identified beyond reasonable doubt.[103] Of the eleven manuscripts there in question, four are now represented only by binding fragments. Of the remaining seven, four are in British libraries; three of these four seem certain to have had a continuous English history from an early date indicated by annotations or other alterations or augmentations. The three in German

---

[99] *Ibid.* no. 1628b.   [100] See nos. 2, 8, 9, 15 and 17.

[101] See nos. 1 and 18.

[102] For discussion of this large issue, see D. N. Dumville, 'The Early Mediaeval Insular Churches and the Preservation of Roman Literature: towards a Historical and Palaeographical Reevaluation', in *Formative Stages of Classical Traditions: Latin Texts from Antiquity to the Renaissance*, ed. O. Pecere and M. D. Reeve (Spoleto, forthcoming).

[103] For the list, see above, p. 106. For reasonable doubt about even a member of this group, however, see above, n. 77.

libraries have been netted by a more demanding version of the same process. It is clear, then, that so far the principal method of identifying such imports has been palaeographical, relying on the efforts of early Anglo-Saxon readers in annotating the manuscripts which they had to hand. But the possibility has to be recognized that many books may have acquired no additions in the course of an Insular history. Increasingly, the method of identifying such books' sojourns will be text-historical; their Insular descendants will be recognized and the line of transmission might even be identified in quotations in the works of Anglo-Latin authors. In that area, however, gains come slowly. For the moment, the directly palaeographical approaches have not run their course. In particular, majuscule-script exemplars of Insular manuscripts will be identified and given precision.

Nevertheless, it must be recognized that, even with the most substantial augmentation of the lists offered here, we shall recover knowledge of only a fraction of the body of imported manuscripts to which our seventh- and eighth-century literary sources draw attention. Whether in England or in the regions of the continental mission-field the circumstances of the next millennium were not conducive to comprehensive survival of manuscripts from the founding era of Christianity. If two of the three great Bibles executed at the wish of Abbot Ceolfrith could disappear almost without trace, what hope might there be for lesser books?[104] Fragments will continue to be discovered, broadening our knowledge of what has been lost.[105] We can take some steps to re-examine the corpus of survivors for further witnesses, but we must reconcile ourselves to extensive losses of the Mediterranean manuscripts of Archbishop Theodore's England.

---

[104] On Ceolfrith's Bibles, see Lowe, *English Uncial*, pp. 8–13 and 19, and *CLA* II, no. 177, and III, no. 299.

[105] The increasing importance of fragments in the corpus is indicated by the discoveries published by Lowe, *CLA*, Supplement, and in the two series of 'Addenda' to that work. see *MS* 47 (1985), 317–66, and 54 (1992), 286–307.

7

Theodore and the Latin canon law

MARTIN BRETT

When scholars first considered the canon law known to Archbishop Theodore, they could act with decision. The materials on which to form a view were slight and little understood, and the matter could be dismissed briefly. Since then the subject has been transformed, though good editions are still thin on the ground. The complexity of the problems is now clear, but correspondingly the answers are more elusive. The systematic study of the sources of canon law in England in the seventh and eighth centuries in the light of this learning is still in its infancy. Only the most preliminary of sketches can be attempted here.

What I have tried to do is to lay out the elements of the problem, to examine very briefly the bearing of the testimony of the Councils of Hertford and 'Hatfield', the glossaries of Leiden and Paris and the *Iudicia Theodori* on the question, and to end with a guess about the outcome of further work.

To begin with the context. Since the pioneering studies of Johnson and Bright,[1] our knowledge of the scale and range of canonical study in the seventh century has been enlarged out of all recognition. One consequence is that we can see how various a world Theodore came from. Bede's account

---

[1] The cross references to the supposed sources in Dionysius were inserted in the text of J. Johnson, *A Collection of all the Ecclesiastical Laws, Canons, Answers or Rescripts, with other Memorials concerning the Government, Discipline and Worship of the Church of England* (London, 1720), I (unpaginated), and repr. from there in *Councils and Ecclesiastical Documents relating to Great Britain and Ireland*, ed. A. W. Haddan and W. Stubbs, 3 vols. (Oxford, 1869–71) III, 118–21. W. Bright, *Chapters of Early English Church History*, 3rd ed. (Oxford, 1897), pp. 278–83 provided a more exact and fuller account. H. Vollrath, *Die Synoden Englands bis 1066*, Konziliengeschichte Reihe A, Darstellungen (Paderborn, 1985), p. 70, n. 134 refers only to the identifications repr. from Johnson by Haddan and Stubbs.

of the new archbishop's journey to England provides a convenient framework for defining some of its elements. As he made his way to England he
passed through at least four distinct zones in the study of canonical texts.[2]

His Greek background and Syrian contacts might well have made him
familiar with the flourishing Eastern tradition of law, represented for
instance by the vast collection in eight books of *Apostolic Constitutions*. Of
this only small fragments had been absorbed in the Latin law, but
Finsterwalder at least believed that the larger work, and the Greek texts
of St Basil, were to influence the *Iudicia*.[3] The possibility that they had
a wider influence is of great importance, but I have not attempted to
discuss it.

When Theodore reached Italy, he would have found the Latin law
represented by a whole variety of collections, the products of what is still
often described as a 'Gelasian renaissance' at the end of the fifth century.
Of these the most important and influential in the long run was the work
of Dionysius Exiguus, a new translation of the canons of the Greek
councils from Nicaea to Chalcedon, supplemented by a body of material
from Africa, and particularly by some hundred canons, the *Registri ecclesiae
Carthaginiensis excerpta*, which Dionysius may well have been responsible
for disguising as the canons of the Council of Carthage of 419.[4] To his

---

[2] *HE* IV.1 (pp. 330–3). For a compact recent guide to the early canon law, see
J. Gaudemet, *Les Sources du droit de l'Eglise en Occident du IIe au VIIe siècle* (Paris, 1985).

[3] *Ibid.*, pp. 21–5 and 85; *Les Constitutions apostoliques*, ed. M. Metzger, 3 vols., Sources
chrétiennes 320, 329 and 336 (Paris, 1985–7); P. W. Finsterwalder, *Die Canones
Theodori Cantuariensis und ihre Überlieferungsformen* (Weimar, 1929), pp. 204–5. Finster-
walder's references to sources for individual canons in the text derive principally from
Wasserschleben's earlier edition. See too the valuable review by W. Levison, repr. from
ZRG Kan. Abt. 19 (1930), 699–707 with some additions in his *Aus rheinischer und
fränkischer Frühzeit* (Düsseldorf, 1948), pp. 295–303. For Basil, see P. J. Fedwick, 'The
Translation of the Works of Basil before 1400', and R. E. Reynolds, 'Basil and the Early
Medieval Latin Canonical Collections', both in *Basil of Caesarea: Christian, Humanist,
Ascetic*, ed. P. J. Fedwick, 2 vols. (Toronto, 1981) II, 439–512 and 513–32,
respectively. For the earlier, eastern, collections E. Schwartz, 'Die Kanonessammlungen
der alten Reichskirche', *ZRG* Kan. Abt. 25 (1936), 1–114, remains fundamental.

[4] F. Maassen, *Geschichte der Quellen und der Literatur des canonischen Rechts im Abendlande bis
zum Ausgange des Mittelalters* (Graz, 1870), pp. 422–76; H. Wurm, *Studien und Texte zur
Dekretalensammlung des Dionysius Exiguus*, Kanonistische Studien und Texte 16 (Bonn,
1939); H. Mordek, *Kirchenrecht und Reform im Frankreich: Die Collectio Vetus Gallica, die
älteste systematische Kanonessammlung des fränkischen Gallien*, Beiträge zur Geschichte und
Quellenkunde des Mittelalters 1 (Berlin, 1975), 241–9 and 151–60. There is a critical

second recension Dionysius added a collection of papal decretal letters. By the time Theodore reached Italy this collection was already being adapted and enlarged in some versions.[5]

Dionysius however did not dominate the Italian field without challenge. In terms of surviving manuscripts a number of other collections, some containing widely different material, such as the *Collectio Quesnelliana*[6] or the *Sanblasiana*,[7] were as widely known in the sixth and seventh centuries.

edition of the first version of Dionysius by A. Strewe, *Die Canonessammlung des Dionysius Exiguus in der ersten Redaktion*, Arbeiten zur Kirchengeschichte 16 (Berlin, 1931). The councils of the second version are still usually consulted in the edition of C. Justel from Oxford, Bodleian Library, e Mus. 103 (s. x), *Codex canonum ecclesiasticorum Dionysii exigui. Item epistola synodica S. Cyrilli et concilii Alexandrini contra Nestorium*, 2nd ed. (Paris, 1643), repr. in G. Voell and H. Justel, *Bibliotheca iuris canonici veteris in duos tomos distributa*, 2 vols. (Paris, 1661) I, 97–180, and thence in PL 67, 135–230 (for the decretals, see below p. 132, n. 44). There are critical editions of various of the councils by C. H. Turner in *Ecclesiae Occidentalis Monumenta Iuris Antiquissima*, 2 vols. in 7 pts (Oxford, 1899–1939), in *Concilium Universale Chalcedonense*, ed. E. Schwartz, Acta conciliorum oecumenicorum 2 (Berlin, 1932–8) II.2, 49–60 [141]-[152], and in *Concilia Africae, A. 345–A. 525*, ed. C. Munier, CCSL 149 (Turnhout, 1974). This edition is severely treated in the belated review by H. Mordek in *ZRG* Kan. Abt. 72 (1986), 368–76. For Dionysius and the African canons, see, too, F. L. Cross, 'Fact and Fiction in the African Canons', *JTS* ns 12 (1961), 227–47, esp. 234–6.

5 I cite the decretals from the Migne text, but the editions of the decretals of the second collection of Dionysius are a bibliographical nightmare. For the problem, see the Appendix, below, pp. 138–40.

6 Maassen, *Geschichte*, pp. 486–500; Turner, *Monumenta* I.1.1, xi–xiv; *Concilium Universale Chalcedonense*, ed. E. Schwartz, Acta conciliorum oecumenicorum 1 (Berlin, 1922–30) V.2, xiiii–xvii; Wurm, *Studien*, esp. pp. 82–7 and 210–23; W. Stürner, 'Die Quellen der Fides Konstantins', *ZRG* Kan. Abt. 55 (1969), 64–206, at 74–9; Mordek, *Kirchenrecht*, pp. 8 and 238–40. Edited first by P. Quesnel in *Sancti Leonis magni Romani papae opera* (Paris, 1675) II, 3–242 from the latest and worst surviving copy, Oxford, Oriel College 42 (Malmesbury, s. xii), on which see R. Thomson, *William of Malmesbury*, (Woodbridge, 1987), pp. 64–6, collated with Paris, BN, lat.3842A (s.ix). A better edition is based on Vienna, Österreichische Nationalbibliothek 2141 (s. ix; see *CLA* X, no. 1505, formerly Iur. can. 39) by P. and G. Ballerini in *Sancti Leonis magni Romani pontificis opera*, 3 vols. (Venice, 1753–7) III, 13–472 (repr. in PL 56, 359–746). Abbot Sæwold of Bath gave Saint-Vaast at Arras a *Quesnelliana* around 1066 (P. Grierson, 'Les Livres de l'abbé Seiwold de Bath', *RB* 52 (1940), 96–116, esp. 104–5 and 109–10, and M. Lapidge, 'Surviving Booklists from Anglo-Saxon England', *Learning and Literature in Anglo-Saxon England*, ed. M. Lapidge and H. Gneuss (Cambridge, 1985), pp. 33–89, esp. 58–62); Arras, Bibl. Mun. 644 (572), *CLA* VI, no. 713, is a *Quesnelliana* of *c.* 800

When Theodore crossed the Alps and reached Arles on the lower Rhône he was at one of the leading centres engaged in the collection of canonical material anywhere in the West, not merely historical collections such as those of Saint-Maur, Lyon or Albi,[8] but also more systematic collections such as those of the *Statuta ecclesiae antiqua*,[9] the so-called 'Second Council of Arles',[10] and outstandingly the *Vetus Gallica*. Very possibly composed *c.* 600 at Lyon on the basis of material collected in Gaul, this early systematic compilation included the canons of a flourishing tradition of Gallo-Roman and Merovingian councils.[11] The earliest elements of the

from the abbey, but is said to be (at least in part) in the script of Saint-Amand (cf. B. Bischoff, 'Panorama der Handschriftenüberlieferung aus der Zeit Karls des Grossen', *Karl der Grosse: Lebenswerk und Nachleben* (Düsseldorf, 1965) II, 233–54, esp. 239). It was very probably brought to England from Saint-Bertin in the tenth century. Though the *Quesnelliana* is generally treated as an Italian collection in recent accounts, Maassen, *Geschichte*, pp. 491–4 makes a case for Gaul 'mit einiger Sicherheit'; cf. also C. H. Turner, 'Arles and Rome: the first Developements of Canon Law in Gaul', *JTS* 17 (1916), 236–47.

[7] For the *Sanblasiana*, see particularly Maassen, *Geschichte*, pp. 504–12; Wurm, *Studien*, esp. pp. 88–9 and 261–4; Stürner, 'Die Quellen der Fides', pp. 79–82; Mordek, *Kirchenrecht*, pp. 240–1; Gaudemet, *Sources*, pp. 139–40. In general, see too H. Mordek, 'Il diritto canonico fra tardo antico e alto medioevo. La svolta «dionisiana» nella canonistica', *La cultura in Italia fra tardo antico e alto medioevale*, Atti del Convegno tenuto a Roma, Consiglio Nazionale delle Ricerche, dal 12 al 16 Novembre 1979 (Rome, 1981) I, 149–64, esp. 159–61, and H. Fuhrmann, 'Das Papsttum und das kirchliche Leben', *SettSpol* 27 (1981), 419–56, esp. 431–3. For the *Concordia canonum* of Cresconius as another seventh-century Italian collection, see below, n. 14.

[8] Maassen, *Geschichte*, pp. 613–24, 775–7 and 592–603, respectively; C. H. Turner, 'Chapters in the History of Latin MSS. I. The Manuscripts of the Jesuit Collège de Clermont in Paris', *JTS* 1 (1899–1900), 435–41 and 'III. The Lyons-Petersburg MS of Councils', *JTS* 4 (1902–3), 426–34; Mordek, *Kirchenrecht*, pp. 15–16, 39–43, 45–6 and 53–6; Gaudemet, *Sources*, pp. 142–4. Few of these collections can be placed precisely, but the Lyon–Arles axis was clearly central.

[9] *Concilia Galliae, A. 314–A. 506*, ed. C. Munier, CCSL 148 (Turnhout, 1963), 162–80, repr. from his *Les Statuta ecclesiae antiqua*, Bibliothèque de l'Institut de droit canonique de l'Université de Strasbourg 5 (Paris, 1960), which contains more detail.

[10] *Concilia Galliae, A. 314–A. 506*, pp. 111–30; Gaudemet, *Sources*, p. 84; K. Schäferdiek, 'Das sogenannte zweite Konzil von Arles und die älteste Kanonessammlung der arletenser Kirche', *ZRG* Kan. Abt. 71 (1985), 1–19, summarizing the earlier literature.

[11] Mordek, *Kirchenrecht*, *passim*; O. Pontal, *Die Synoden im Merowingerreich*, Konziliengeschichte Reihe A, Darstellungen (Paderborn, 1986).

later *Hispana* collection also show clear signs of the influence of cis-Pyrenean activity too, possibly even at Arles.[12]

When Theodore moved north to Paris he was still in an area of canonical activity, if slighter and more recent, attested by such collections as those of Reims, Saint-Amand, Beauvais or the manuscript of Pithou.[13] The archbishop's companion, Abbot Hadrian, could have provided even more, for the African church had displayed a particular interest in collecting and studying the conciliar records of the church, evidenced in historical collections such as the Carthage *Excerpta* or *Breviary of Hippo*, and in systematic ones such as those of Fulgentius Ferrandus and perhaps the mysterious Cresconius.[14]

The point of this restatement of the obvious is simple; the range of books from which Theodore might in principle have taken his texts was remarkably wide. Many non-Italian collections incorporated local material, and there was a wide circulation of Merovingian, African and Spanish legislation throughout Gaul and even Italy. The claim of Peitz in particular that the Dionysian collections enjoyed from the outset a position of peculiar authority has found little support in recent scholarship. Mordek's

[12] The *Hispana* contains a substantial Frankish element; cf. Maassen, *Geschichte*, pp. 680–1; the question has aroused some national fervour. Against the polemic of J. Tarré, 'Sur les origines arlésiennes de la collection canonique, dite *Hispana*', *Mélanges Paul Fournier* (Paris, 1929), pp. 705–24, see G. Martínez Díez, *La Coleccion Canonica Hispana*, Monumenta Hispaniae sacra, Ser. canonica 1 (Madrid, 1966) I (Estudio), 288–91, for whom only the councils of Gaul in the 'Collection of Corbie' have any influence, and that indirectly. Cf. Schäferdiek, 'Das sogenannte zweite Konzil', pp. 13–19.

[13] Maassen, *Geschichte*, pp. 604–11, 638–40 and 778–84, showing the dependence of the later collections of Saint-Amand and Beauvais on an earlier common source which ended with the Council of Chalon-sur-Sâone of 647/53; Mordek, *Kirchenrecht*, pp. 10, 56, 72–3 and 249–50; Pontal, *Die Synoden*, pp. 193–7 and 280–3; Gaudemet, *Sources*, pp. 146–9. Though none of these can be placed exactly, they seem to belong to Western Gaul, and further north than the Rhône valley.

[14] Maassen, *Geschichte*, pp. 771–4, 799–802 and 806–13; C. Munier, 'La Tradition littéraire des canons africains', *Recherches augustiniennes* 10 (1975), 1–22; Mordek, *Kirchenrecht*, pp. 253–5; Gaudemet, *Les sources*, pp. 79–83 and 137–9. The predominantly Italian circulation of Cresconius is shown by R. Kottje, 'Einheit und Vielfalt des kirchlichen Lebens in der Karolingerzeit', *Zeitschrift für Kirchengeschichte* 76 (1965), 323–42, esp. 339–40, and the new edition by K. Zechiel-Eckes, *Die Concordia canonum des Cresconius*, Freiburger Beiträge zur mittelalterlichen Geschichte 5 (Frankfurt, 1992), holds that the work is itself Italian. The *Breviatio* of Ferrandus is ed. Munier in *Concilia Africae*, pp. 284–311.

investigation of the sources for the *Vetus Gallica* is only the most obvious demonstration of the range of texts to which a bishop might turn in search of authoritative law at the beginning of the seventh century.

When, therefore, the earlier commentators on Bede and the glossaries assumed without debate that Theodore would look first and chiefly at the Dionysian collections, they were going far beyond the evidence. For what it is worth, the only one of the collections I have listed which survives in an early manuscript written in England is the *Sanblasiana*.[15] The case for dependence on the collections of Dionysius needs to be established.

The materials on which the argument should rest have a paradoxical character. The only sources directly and unambiguously attributable to Theodore are his councils at Hertford and 'Hatfield', as reported by Bede.[16] For reasons I will outline shortly, however, these support few conclusions. As we move out from the councils, the information becomes more precise, but its connection with the archbishop becomes progressively more uncertain.

There is much that can be said of the reading of Theodore's 'circle' on the basis of the glossaries, something on the sources for the *Iudicia*, much more on the continental sources for the thought of the compiler of the *Hibernensis*. To provide anything like a firm context for the study one would have to examine the whole range of the evidence for the Anglo-Saxon church before 750, a subject far beyond the scope of this paper.

In what follows I report no more than the fruits of a first reconnaissance on the councils, the glossaries and the *Iudicia*. Even with this limitation there is much more that could be said, and even more room for further enquiry.

Bede's account of the Council of Hertford begins with a narrative describing the summons of the bishops 'una cum eis, qui canonica patrum statuta et diligerent et nossent, magistris ecclesiae pluribus'.[17] There follows what appears to be a formal record of its acts, with an elaborate

---

[15] See below, p. 136, n.57.

[16] *HE* IV.5 (pp. 348–55) and IV.17 (pp. 384–7). C. R. E. Cubitt ('Anglo-Saxon Church Councils *c.* 650–*c.* 850' (unpubl. PhD dissertation, Cambridge Univ., 1990), pp. 130–2) argues that Hatfield in Yorkshire is as probable as Hatfield in Hertfordshire (cf. the remarks of Henry Chadwick, above, p. 88), and that the site is best treated as unidentified.

[17] *HE* IV.5 (p. 348): 'together with many teachers of the church who knew and loved the canonical institutions of the fathers'.

protocol and eschatocol which have allowed some systematic analysis of its diplomatic,[18] so one is encouraged to suppose that we are not far from Theodore's own text. If we can read it closely, it is of great importance, for he says there that he urged the assembled bishops to unity and to the maintenance of whatever was decreed and defined by holy and proven fathers, and asked them each in turn if they would observe 'quae a patribus canonice sunt antiquitus decreta'.[19] When they agreed, unsurprisingly, he offered them at once 'eundem librum canonum'. For Theodore, it seems, the tradition of the fathers was a specific book, not a state of mind or disposition. Out of this book he propounded ten canons, which he had noted each in its place, and urged that they be observed with special diligence. The ten canons follow.

What is at once striking is that the words of these canons cannot be identified with any known text, or collection of texts. In several cases the *sententia* is entirely familiar, as with the second:

Ut nullus episcoporum parrochiam alterius inuadat, sed contentus sit gubernatione creditae sibi plebis.[20]

Bright, and Johnson before him, had no difficulty in pointing to the opening of c. 14 of the 'Canons of the Apostles', which Dionysius had put at the front of his collection, as a possible source:

Episcopo non licere alienam parroeciam propria relicta peruadere.[21]

This is nearer the words of Theodore than the other conciliar texts which returned to this theme with obstinate regularity, but the second half of the canon has no verbal parallel I can find until a letter of Leo I: 'suis igitur terminis quisque contentus sit'.[22]

The rule is well-known, but its formulation is idiosyncratic. Similarly with c. 8:

---

[18] P. Chaplais, 'The Origin and Authenticity of the Royal Anglo-Saxon Diploma', *Journal of the Society of Archivists* 3.2 (1965), 48–61, esp. 50. The forms of these early synodal acts are discussed in more detail by Cubitt in 'Anglo-Saxon Church Councils', pp. 96–113.

[19] *HE* IV.5 (p. 350): 'the canonical decrees which had been laid down by the fathers in ancient times'.

[20] 'That no bishop intrude into the diocese of another bishop, but that he should be content with the government of the people committed to his charge.'

[21] Turner, *Monumenta* I.1, 14.   [22] Dionysius (Leo I), c. 38 (PL 67, 294).

Ut nullus episcoporum se praeferat alteri per ambitionem, sed omnes agnoscant tempus et ordinem consecrationis suae.[23]

The closest parallel in earlier legislation comes from the African canons incorporated in the 'Council of Carthage' by Dionysius as chs. 86 and 89.[24] Again, if this is indeed the source, it has been treated with great freedom.

Other cases introduce a different problem. Bright, for whom the identity of the *liber* of the prologue with Dionysius was axiomatic, found a difficulty with c. 9. The sense of the canon, 'Ut plures episcopi crescente numero fidelium augerentur',[25] was certainly not to be found explicitly in Dionysius, and he was reduced to suggesting that canons forbidding the subdivision of dioceses under particular circumstances could be interpreted by implication as permitting it in others. In fact several African canons incorporated by Dionysius provide a better parallel than any he suggested, but their wording is far away.[26]

The last canon, on marriage, if it depends on Dionysius at all, is a compendium of scattered references particularly from the decretals of his second version, rather than any kind of quotation.[27]

Canon 3 is particularly problematic:

---

[23] 'That no bishop claim precedence over another bishop out of ambition; but all shall take rank according to the time and order of their consecration.'

[24] Dionysius (Council of Carthage), cc. 86 and 89, in PL 67, 208–9; *Concilia Africae*, ed. Munier, pp. 206–7. Both canons are attributed to the Council of Mileva, represented in the Spanish tradition by *Hispana*, ed. Martínez Díez III, 438–54.

[25] 'That more bishops shall be created as the number of the faithful increases.'

[26] Dionysius (Council of Carthage), cc. 53, 56 and 98, and cf. c. 118 (PL 67, 197, 199, 214 and 219– 20); *Concilia Africae*, ed Munier, pp. 189–90, 192–3, 216 and 224. All stress the need for the consent of the bishop whose see is being diminished.

[27] *Canones apostolorum*, c. 48, Council of Ancyra, c. 18 and Council of Neocaesarea, c. 2 (Turner, *Monumenta* I.1, 1 and 31, and II.1, 107 and 121), Council of Chalcedon, c. 27 (*Concilium Universale Chalcedonense*, ed. Schwartz II.2, 16 [152]), Dionysius (Innocent I), c. 24 (PL 67, 247), and Dionysius (Leo I), cc.18–19 (PL 67, 288–9) and 42–5 (PL 67, 296–7)). Bright, *Early Chapters*, pp. 282–3, following Johnson (see above, p. 120, n. 1), suggested the influence of the letters of Basil, which may well be right. No known Latin *liber canonum* contains the relevant passages, though cc. 1–68 of Basil's canonical letters appear in the widely influential sixth-century *Synagoge* of John Scholasticus (*Ioannis Scholastici Synagoga L titulorum ceteraque eiusdem opera iuridica*, ed. V. Benesevic, Abhandlungen der Bayerischen Akademie, phil.-hist. Abteilung n.s. 14 (Munich, 1937)). The origins of John's work are almost certainly Antiochene. For a

Ut quaeque monasteria Deo consecrata sunt nulli episcoporum liceat ea in aliquo inquietare nec quicquam de eorum rebus uiolenter abstrahere.[28]

There is no text in the current collections I can find which incorporates this principle; the earlier councils and popes were more concerned to enforce the obedience of monks to their bishop than to protect them from his avarice.[29] Though the idea could certainly be extracted from the correspondence of Gregory I,[30] the fact remains that if Theodore found it in his book of the law, this book has not yet been identified.

Nothing contradicts the idea that he was inspired by the *Dionysiana*, but there is no proof, and if this was his book of the law, he drew upon it for general principles, not precise formulations. There is a striking congruence between the apparent freedom with which Theodore was treating his sources here and the use of the earlier law in the *Iudicia Theodori*, as Finsterwalder described it.[31] The conclusion commands some confidence; if we have lost innumerable books, it remains striking that not one of the canons of Hertford shows a direct verbal connection with any of the Latin survivors.

The case of the Council of 'Hatfield' is instructive in this regard, for we are told something of its immediate origin. According to Bede, Theodore had heard of the rise of the monothelete heresy at Constantinople and resolved to hold a council to ensure the orthodoxy of his own church. He

recent summary of the ancient discipline of marriage, see J. Gaudemet, *Le Marriage en Occident* (Paris, 1987).

28 'That no bishop shall in any way interfere with any monasteries dedicated to God nor take away forcibly any part of their property.'

29 The canon of a Council of Carthage in 535, first found in Vatican City, Biblioteca Apostolica, lat. 5845 (Capua, s. x¹), a copy of the second *Dionysiana* with an important appendix, is a qualified exception: H. Mordek, 'Libertas monachorum. Eine kleine Sammlung afrikanischer Konzilstexte des 6. Jahrhunderts', *ZRG* Kan. Abt. 72 (1986), 1–16, esp. 13–15, completed by S. Kuttner, 'The Council of Carthage 535: a Supplementary Note', *ibid.* 73 (1987), 346–51, who shows that it also occurs in Vatican, Barberini lat. 679 (see next note). There is no evidence that the text had any wider early circulation, and again there is no verbal connection with Theodore's canon.

30 Particularly in *Registrum* V. 49 (JE 1362), VIII. 17 (JE 1504) and VIII. 32 (JE 1521); the first is found as an addition to Vatican, Barberini lat. 679 (Italy, s.viii/ix, formerly xiv.52, 2888), a copy of the Vatican collection which has some additions characteristic of the enlarged *Dionysiana* (Ballerini, in PL 56, 140–1; Maassen, *Geschichte*, pp. 302 and 513; Stürner, 'Die Quellen der Fides', pp. 150–1).

31 Finsterwalder, *Die Canones Theodori*, p. 199.

preserves an incomplete account of its *acta*, including a formal reaffir-
mation of the faith of the five oecumenical councils and the decrees of Pope
Martin's Lateran Council in 649, and a reference to the presence of Abbot
John of St Martin at Rome, sent at the command of Pope Agatho. Abbot
John also brought with him the text of the Lateran Council.[32]

Although, then, Bede describes John as brought by Benedict Biscop to
instruct his churches in the chant, he also appears to have been one of those
emissaries whom Pope Agatho sent to the distant provinces of the church,
presumably to investigate their position on the monothelete controversy
on which he was in dispute with Constantinople. The points at issue
turned on the most precise phrasing, and there is an echo of the text of
649, but it is no more than that.[33] The formulation of Theodore's council
is distinctly idiosyncratic. Here too the archbishop is clearly treating one
of his sources with a good deal of freedom.

With the glossaries the position is almost entirely reversed. Here we
have no explicit general principles, but rather isolated words, presumably
quoted more or less exactly. I have taken two, those at Leiden and Paris,
for examination.[34]

---

[32] See the discussion by Henry Chadwick, above, pp. 89–93.

[33] *Concilium Lateranense a. 649 celebratum*, ed. R. Riedinger, Acta conciliorum oecumenicorum 2nd ser. 1 (Berlin, 1984), 369:

Si quis non confitetur secundum sanctos patres proprie et uere patrem et filium et spiritum
sanctum, trinitatem in unitate, unitatem in trinitate, hoc est unum deum in tribus subsistentiis
consubstantialibus et aequali gloriae,

compared with 'Hatfield':

confitemur secundum sanctos patres proprie et ueraciter Patrem et Filium et Spiritum Sanctum
Trinitatem in Unitate consubstantialem et Unitatem in Trinitate, hoc est unum Deum in tribus
subsistentiis uel personis consubstantialibus aequalis gloriae et honoris

(*HE* IV. 17 (p. 386)).

Cf., however, discussion in *Biblical Commentaries*, ed. Bischoff and Lapidge,
pp. 139–46, where a much different emphasis is placed on the relationship.

[34] *A Late Eighth Century Latin-Anglo-Saxon Glossary preserved in the Library of the Leiden
University (MS Voss. Qᵒ Lat. No. 69)*, ed. J. H. Hessels (Cambridge, 1906); and Paris,
BN, lat.2685, fols. 47–8. See M. Lapidge, 'The School of Theodore and Hadrian', *ASE*
15 (1986), 45–72, esp. 54–66 and 68–70, and discussion by J. D. Pheifer, below,
pp. 281–333. The identification of the sources in Hessels's edition was written with
knowledge of the work of P. Glogger, *Das Leidener Glossar Cod. Voss. lat. 4o 69*,
Programm des kgl. humanistischen Gymnasiums St Stephan, 3 vols. (Augsburg,
1901–7) II, 1–5 (see Hessels, *Leiden*, p. xvii and n.).

There are three preliminary cautions. Firstly, though both manuscripts show clear signs of a connection with Theodore, they are of the late eighth or ninth century, allowing in principle for a good deal of contamination. Secondly, the identification of single words in the sources is always hazardous; two-word phrases inspire more confidence, but occur only rarely. Thirdly, the character of these possible sources is very uncertain. They are not only numerous but complex. Although there are several distinct Latin translations of the early Greek councils, the surviving books turn from one to the other with great frequency, even within a single council. It must be supposed that any lost collections shared this characteristic to the full. Even so, something can be done.

The first section from the canons in the 'Leiden Glossary' is roughly in alphabetical order. There may be some contamination of the text. Once or twice it is quite certain that the interpretation at least is derived from another source altogether.[35] A further section of entries from the canons, this time in the order of the source,[36] appears after glosses from Gregory I's *Dialogi*, and it seems possible that the interpretation at least of one canonical term reflects the usage of Gregory rather than the canons.[37] Leiden returns briefly to the canons again in a later miscellaneous section.[38] At first sight these distinct groups might suggest distinct sources, but the overwhelming majority of the words can be explained on the basis of a single collection.

This is essentially the second collection of Dionysius, containing both the councils and the papal decretals. A number of the African canons put

---

[35] If the lemma of Hessels, *Leiden*, i. 49 (p. 2): 'epistilia – grece, quae super capitella columnarum ponuntur', came from a canonical collection originally, the source presumably read 'epistolia' (or some such); it occurs widely. The interpretation comes from Isidore's *Etymologiae* XV.viii.15 and XIX.x.24, and treats it as 'epistyle'. The interpretation of Hessels, *Leiden*, i.95 (p. 2), 'portentuose – monstruose: exempli causa cum sex digitis nati' (also from *Etymologiae* XI.iii.6–7) is inappropriate to the supposed context, where it is used figuratively (cf. below, p. 131, n. 41).

[36] Hessels, *Leiden*, xxxix.53–73 (p. 42); cf. Glogger, *Das Leidener Glossar* II, 69, citing the Munich and Einsiedeln glossaries for a distinct heading 'De Sinodalibus' at this point, and Lapidge, 'The School of Theodore and Hadrian', pp. 68 and 70.

[37] Hessels, *Leiden*, i.104 (p. 3), and cf. xxxix.22 (p. 41): 'presbytera', in the title to Council of Laodicea (Dionysius, c. 114; PL 67, 166) apparently meaning 'priestess', and parallel to deaconess, is interpreted as priest's wife, as in Gregory I, *Dialogi* IV. 11.

[38] Hessels, *Leiden*, xli.1–6 (p. 43); cf. Glogger, *Das Leidener Glossar* II, 69, citing the Munich and Einsiedeln glossaries at this point, and Lapidge, 'The School of Theodore and Hadrian', pp. 68 and 70.

under contribution in all three sections are very rarely found outside the Dionysian complex, being absent for instance from the *Sanblasiana*.[39] A few very odd words make it near certain, however, that this was not a so-called 'pure' version of the second Dionysian collection (of which no complete copy survives),[40] but one of the mass of 'enlarged' versions, some of which contain a distinctive form of the *Vetus defensio fidei* of Chalcedon[41] and the synodal letter before the Council of Gangres which is otherwise more usually found in the 'Isidorean' version.[42]

These enlarged forms are an unusually dense thicket, still in part unexplored,[43] and it is impossible to define what range of texts any

---

[39] See above p. 123, n. 7.   [40] Wurm, *Studien*, p. 31, n. 1.

[41] The word 'machomenus', unknown to lexicographers except from the glossary, occurs in *Concilium Universale Chalcedonense*, ed. Schwartz II.2, 64 [156] from the *Hadriana* and *Dionysiana aucta*, and only there so far as is known. The words 'delirantes', 'portentuose', 'promulgantes' are also in the same version, though elsewhere too. The word 'adnisus' is found in the Dionysian version of c. 12, but not in the other forms; 'inoleuit', unidentified by Hessels, is also found in the *Tomus Damasi* (Turner, *Monumenta* I.2.1, 281 and 284), which occurs in the enlarged *Dionysiana* as well as a number of other collections. For the *Vetus Fides*, see too Stürner, 'Die Quellen der Fides', pp. 71–104.

[42] Hessels, *Leiden*, i.48, 'extorris', and 57, 'genuinum decus' (p. 2), are found in the prefatory letter to the council of Gangres which is not in the 'pure' *Dionysiana*. The letter does, however, occur in the version of the *Dionysiana* which lies behind the *Hadriana*, and in several copies of the other enlarged *Dionysiana* forms. For the text and manuscripts, see Turner, *Monumenta* II.2, 162. The entry 'olografia – totum scriptio' occurs in Hessels, *Leiden*, xxxix.72 (p. 42) at the end of a sequence from the 'Council of Carthage'. The word is rare anyway, but it does occur at the end of the Council of Carthage in the aberrant version of some enlarged *Dionysiana* texts (but not in the *Hadriana*); see the Ballerini in 'De antiquis tum editis, tum ineditis collectionibus et collectoribus canonum ad Gratianum usque tractatus' II.3.10 (*Sancti Leonis opera* III, cii, repr. PL 56, 119). For criticism of Maassen's treatment of some enlarged versions of the *Dionysiana* as enlarged *Hadriana* texts, see particularly Turner, *Monumenta* I.1.2, vi–vii; R. Massigli, 'Sur l'Origine de la collection canonique dite *Hadriana augmentée*', *Mélanges d'archéologie et d'histoire (École française de Rome)* 32 (1912), 364–83; Wurm, *Studien*, pp. 35–6; A. Chavasse, 'Les Lettres de Saint Léon le Grand dans le supplément de la *Dionysiana* et de l'*Hadriana* et dans la collection du manuscrit du Vatican', *Revue des sciences religieuses* 38 (1964), 154–76; Mordek, *Kirchenrecht*, p. 243. Other references are collected in H. Mordek, 'Dionysio-Hadriana und Vetus Gallica – historisch geordnetes und systematisches Kirchenrecht am Hofe Karls des Grossen', *ZRG* Kan. Abt. 55 (1969), 39–63, esp. 42–3.

[43] For instance, *A Catalogue of Canon and Roman Law Manuscripts in the Vatican Library*, ed. S. Kuttner and R. Elze, Studi e Testi 322 and 328 (Vatican City, 1986– [in progress])

manuscript of this later version of the collection might have contained. Even in terms of what we do know, it seems clear that the original second Dionysian collection underwent several distinct additions and revisions. In the version that was to have the greatest future the revisions included particularly the incorporation of versions of some conciliar texts different to those of Dionysius, and the additions a series of decretals after those of Anastasius II. Ultimately, one variation of this was to become the ancestor of the *Hadriana* of 774, but the process of accretion began much earlier. A copy of this form which had no additions later than the letters of Pope Hormisdas (d. 523) lies behind the early ninth-century 'Codex Sessorianus' from Nonantola. Such a text would provide 129 of the 133 words glossed in the Leiden *glossae collectae* from councils.[44]

Strictly, there is no decisive method of excluding the *Hadriana* itself as a source for Leiden, for the manuscript of the glossary is almost certainly later than 774, and the differences between the 'pure' *Dionysiana* and the later versions which can be shown to be relevant to the glossary are all also found in the *Hadriana*. Nevertheless, it is far more probable that Leiden depends on a *Dionysiana* which had received some of the additions and alterations later found in the *Hadriana* than on the *Hadriana* itself. No other source as late as 774 has yet been identified in Leiden, and the latest element in the *Hadriana* proper, Gregory II's council of 721, cannot be shown to have been used by the glossator. Though the edition of the *Hadriana* councils is profoundly unsatisfactory, at least one of the Leiden

---

I, 86–94, identifies Vat. lat. 1343 (Italian, s. x/xi) as another incomplete copy of the *Dionysiana aucta*, hitherto unnoticed.

[44] Rome, BN Vittorio Emanuele II, 2102 (Sess. LXIII), on which see Turner, *Monumenta* I.1.2, vi–vii; E. Loew, *The Beneventan Script. A History of the South Italian Minuscule* (Oxford, 1914, repr. with corrections and additions by V. Brown in *Sussidi Eruditi* 33–4 (Rome, 1980), 114, 202 and 304); G. Gullotta, *Gli antichi cataloghi e i codici della abbazia di Nonantola*, Studi e Testi 182 (Vatican, 1955), 187–204; G. Cencetti, 'Scrittoria e scritture nel monachesimo Benedettino', *SettSpol* 4 (1957), 187–219, esp. 202–5 and pl. V; Mordek, *Kirchenrecht*, p. 153 and n. The manuscript is Wurm's Ds (*Studien*, p. 31). Like all but the earliest Dionysian manuscripts it contains Hormisdas c. 4 (JK 800, PL 67, 342), which provides a source for Leiden i.14, 'arcimandritis'. The manuscript has been added to from several sources, including the *Vetus Gallica* and *Hadriana*; it seems to have been copied from an enlarged *Dionysiana* which had some, but not all, the *Hadriana* additions (the original numeration and the preliminary *capitulatio* extend only as far as the decretals of Hormisdas), and a number of details in the conciliar section link it with the enlarged *Dionysiana* rather than the *Hadriana* proper; cf. the passages cited on p. 131, nn. 41 and 42.

words is only reported in the *Dionysiana aucta*, and not in the *Hadriana*.[45] The conclusion is of some importance. Although there are structural reasons for believing that an enlarged *Dionysiana* of the kind existed quite early, no manuscript of it earlier than the 'Leiden Glossary' is yet known.

Of the four words not identifiable in such a *Dionysiana* one is not easy to explain on any hypothesis,[46] but three relatively unusual words present a different problem. All three are only found together in the 'Vatican' collection's form of the Chalcedon *Defensio fidei*,[47] though two of them also occur in other versions (but not the enlarged *Dionysiana*). If these are not a later intrusion, the glossator either had a manuscript with two versions of the *Defensio* or he consulted two collections.[48]

The Paris glossary begins in striking fashion (47r):

In Dei nomine. Pauca de canonibus concilii incipiunt. Canon grece, latine regula – multorum in unum.

The invocation, and the following passage from Isidore's *Etymologiae* VI.xvi.1. and 12–13, suggest at once that we are dealing with an early

---

[45] *Conciliae Germaniae quae celsissimi principis Joannis Mauritii, archiepiscopi Pragensis sumptu cl. Joannes Fridericus Schannat magna ex parte primum collegit, dein P. Josephus Hartzheim S.J. eiusdem Celsissimi impensis plurimum auxit, continuavit, notis, digressionibus criticis, charta et praefatione chorographicis illustravit* I (Cologne, 1759), 131–235, based on three manuscripts from Cologne and the earlier editions. For 'olografia', see above p. 131, n. 42.

[46] Hessels, *Leiden* i.39 (p. 1), 'diuus – imperator qui post mortem ut deus habetur', appears in texts collected in the aberrant mid-sixth-century 'Collectio Avellana', e.g. *Epistulae imperatorum, pontificum aliorum inde ab A. CCCLXVII usque ad A. DLIII datae, Avellana quae dicitur collectio*, ed. O. Guenther, CSEL 35 (Vienna, 1895–6) I, 57 and 89, and repeatedly in the enigmatic letter addressed to Emperor Maurice, *Gregorii I papae Registrum Epistolarum*, ed. P. Ewald, MGH, Epistolae (Berlin, 1891–9) I, 19–20 (bk I, no. 16a), but I have not found it in any collection otherwise likely to be known to Theodore.

[47] The words 'aemulum' and 'secretalem' are found in the Vatican, *Sanblasiana*, *Quesnelliana* and Hague versions, but not in either the enlarged Dionysian or 'Isidorean' forms. 'Primicerius' occurs in the Vatican and 'Isidorean' forms but not in the others: *Concilium Universale Chalcedonense*, ed. Schwartz II.2, 6 [98], 11–13 [103]–[105] and 83–6 [175]–[178].

[48] One major puzzle occurs in Hessels, *Leiden*, xxxv.46 (p. 34): 'Thia – matertera'. In the Paris glossary this occurs under the canonical extracts (as do a few other entries from Leiden's ch. xxxv), apparently by reference to Council of Nicaea, c. 2 in several versions, though not that of Dionysius. If this is not a later intrusion, and the source is rightly identified, the glossator must have had more than one version of Nicaea before him. Hessels, *Leiden*, p. 205 identified the source as Eusebius, which would explain the lemma but not the interpretation. It would not help with the Paris entry.

---

variation of the *Hadriana*, where both elements occur in a number of manuscripts, though a little way apart.[49] However, in the Paris copy they are followed by another extract from the *Etymologiae* VI.xvi.6–9, with the heading: 'Ait ita Isidorus de quattuor principalibus sinodis'.

Neither the heading nor quite this form of Isidore is reported from the *Hadriana* manuscripts.[50] However, the two passages do occur, in reverse order but with some of the same modifications, in the Preface to the early seventh-century *Hispana*, itself sometimes attributed to Isidore.[51] In the event, these rather confusing indications that the Paris glossary proper refers to a collection quite unlike that of Leiden prove largely illusory.

The early elements of the glossary are arranged in part in the order of the councils of the source, each with its rubric, though the later section, especially that part taken from the decretals, disintegrates into disorder. Again some form of the second collection of Dionysius explains the great majority of the entries, and some are found nowhere else in the earlier stages of their transmission.[52] There are fewer entries than in the corresponding section of Leiden, and not a great deal of overlap; while Leiden makes little demonstrable use of the decretals of the second *Dionysiana*, Paris draws on them more heavily. There is no evidence that the decretals

---

[49] W. Lippert, 'Die Verfasserschaft der Canonen gallischer Concilien des V. und VI. Jahrhunderts', *Neues Archiv* 14 (1889), 9–58, esp. 16–24; E. Seckel, *Die erste Zeile Pseudoisidors, die Hadriana-Rezension In nomine Domini incipit praefatio libri huius und die Geschichte der Invokationen in den Rechtsquellen*, Aus dem Nachlass mit Ergänzungen herausgegeben von Horst Fuhrmann, Sitzungsberichte der deutschen Akademie der Wissenschaften zu Berlin, Klasse für Philosophie, Geschichte, Staats-, Rechts- und Wirtschaftswissenschaften, 1959 (Berlin, 1959), esp. pp. 25–9; Mordek, 'Dionysio-Hadriana', pp. 49–53 and *Kirchenrecht*, pp. 151–60.

[50] Seckel, *Die erste Zeile*, pp. 27–8 notes that the passage does occur as part of his 'Stück IV' in the *Hadriana* copies, but as part of a longer extract.

[51] The earlier literature is conveniently surveyed by Martínez Díez in *Hispana* I, 257–62 and 306–18, who edits the Preface at III, 43–6. For criticism of the Isidore thesis, see the literature cited in Mordek, *Kirchenrecht*, p. 252.

[52] For example, the entries under Council of Ancyra include (47v): 'parantes' (c. 1), 'funestis' (c. 3) and 'notabiles' (c. 17). These are peculiar to the Dionysian version, while almost all other forms (including the *Sanblasiana*) are variants on the 'Isidorean' version (Turner, *Monumenta* II.1, 55, 59 and 105); similarly 'aut hemiolia' (48r) reflects the Dionysian version of Nicaea c. 17: 'aut hemiolia' (Turner, *Monumenta* I.1.2, 270). As is so often the case, one manuscript of the *Quesnelliana* has been contaminated by the same reading (*ibid.*, p. 136 n.).

included the council of Gregory II peculiar to the *Hadriana*, but the possibility remains, for Paris as for Leiden.[53]

If an enlarged *Dionysiana* could account for all but three of the fifty entries in the Paris glossary, the three are a warning against over-confidence. One of them is still unexplained,[54] but the other two present a different problem. The first is the entry: 'De sigmaticis: de subintroductis mulieribus'. The interpretation is the heading of canon 3 of the Council of Nicaea in the version of Dionysius, but 'sigmaticis' appears to be a rough approximation to the heading of the Greek συνεισακτων. The nearest known parallel in the Latin sources is 'fynecitas' in the *capitulatio* to Nicaea in the *Sanblasiana* form of the so-called 'Isidorean' version, but it is remote.[55]

The second is the word 'exaucteratus'. This occurs in the 'Isidorean' version of the Council of Antioch, used in such Italian collections as the *Quesnelliana*, the collections of Freising, Diessen and so on, as well as the *Hispana*, but in neither the Dionysian collections nor the *Sanblasiana* (which is here based on the 'Prisca'). In short, as with Leiden, the *Dionysiana* is the preponderant, but not quite the unique, source of the Paris glossary.[56] While, however, the erratic entries of Leiden suggest

---

[53] The *lemma* 'genuini – nobiles', at the beginning of the council, is found in a slightly variant form in Leiden (above, p. 131, n. 42). While this points to a copy which was not a 'pure' *Dionysiana*, the 'Isidorean' preface is found both in the enlarged *Dionysiana* and the *Hadriana*.

[54] It has the entry for 'THIA', also in Leiden (above, p. 133, n. 48). The apparent order of the entries breaks down after the heading 'DE ANTIOCOENO CONCILIO', but the puzzling entries are: 'destinabitur – uoluebunt' (probably from Council of Antioch c. 97, 'destinabunt') and the unidentified 'conspirabitis – oculte consiliabitis'. Two are possibly to be explained by errors. For 'murcus – immundus et rixosus', compare 'Quorum doctrinae nefariae auctor Marcus dudum de urbe pulsus' in Innocent I (JK 318; Dionysius c. 49; PL 67, 256). For 'tafidus – credulus uel potentior', compare Boniface (JK 353; Dionysius c. 1, PL 67, 265): 'Vobis, inquit, religiose imperantibus modo tutus est populus, tam fidus Deo quam tibi.'

[55] Turner, *Monumenta* I.2, 187 and 257. The 'Isidorean' version is also found in the *Quesnelliana* and elsewhere, and the word gave rise to a jungle of bizarre scribal conjectures.

[56] Turner, *Monumenta* II.2, 246; 'detractare – id est blasphemare', under 'Canones apostolorum' in Paris, might be derived from 'si quisquam salubribus preceptis satisfacere detrectarit' in Leo I (JK 398; PL 54, 596), which is in the enlarged *Dionysiana* (see Maassen, *Geschichte*, p. 256). Oddly, the usage appears to be rare in the canons.

contamination by a Vatican version of Chalcedon, those of Paris point rather to the *Quesnelliana*, Freising or Saint-Maur collections, which alone have the 'Isidorean' forms of both Nicaea and Antioch.

So far, with all the hesitations appropriate in a field of defective editions, or even none, we can do no more than add a good deal of proof and some precision to the view of earlier scholars. In Theodore's circle, as the glossaries reflect it, an enlarged version of the second *Dionysiana* was indeed a central text, and no other will explain so much of the material of the glossators.

With the Penitential of the 'Discipulus Umbrensium' the case is quite different. As Finsterwalder noticed, most of his citations are far too free to allow a precise indication of his source, but several years ago Michael Lapidge pointed to a passage from the Council of Ancyra which suggested direct dependence on the *Sanblasiana*, and particularly on the only copy of it thought to have been written in England.[57] A second quotation from the Council of Nicaea goes a long way to confirm his conclusion.[58] To put the matter more strongly, if one applies Occam's razor to the work of the Discipulus, his identifiable quotations and references from the canons need come from no other source.[59] A curious gap opens between the glossaries and the Penitential.

My conclusions, if they may be so dignified, are, then, that the Council of Hertford contains no direct quotations from any known law-book, that the glossaries reflect overwhelmingly the use of an enlarged *Dionysiana*, though there are slight traces of other sources, and that the Penitential's

---

[57] Lapidge, 'The School of Theodore and Hadrian', p. 66 citing the Discipulus I.xv.4 (Finsterwalder, *Die Canones Theodori*, p. 311) from Council of Ancyra c. 24 compared with the copy which is now Cologne, Dombibl., 213 (*CLA* VIII, no. 1163) in Turner, *Monumenta* II.1, 112. The Cologne manuscript is usually treated as Northumbrian, but R. McKitterick, 'Knowledge of Canon Law in the Frankish Kingdoms before 789: the Manuscript Evidence', *JTS* ns 36 (1985), 97–117, at 109–15, building on Bischoff's observation that an Insular scribe working over the sea could not be excluded, makes a case for its continental origin. The evidence of the 'Discipulus' weighs against this.

[58] Discipulus I.v.14 (ed. Finsterwalder, p. 297): 'Si quis a fide dei discesserit sine ulla necessitate – adhuc extra communionem' is also closer to the *Sanblasiana* form of the 'Isidorean' text of Council of Nicaea, c. 11 than to any other we know (Turner, *Monumenta* I.2, 213).

[59] For the use of Basil by the Discipulus, cf. Reynolds in *Basil of Caesarea* II, 521–2, and above, p. 121.

only discernible source for the canons of the early councils and decretals is the *Sanblasiana*.

These conclusions are undoubtedly too restrictive on a larger canvas. The detailed investigation of the sources of Anglo-Saxon legal learning has hardly begun yet, and the absence of satisfactory editions of much of the material will make it a frustrating business. The secular law of the empire clearly played its part, as well as Greek learning.[60] Other texts from England may well suggest other and wider reading, as the Irish *Collectio Hibernensis* certainly does.

The *Hibernensis* can only be used for the purpose with great caution. While it shows unmistakable signs of the influence of Theodore, it is far from clear that it can be associated with him at all closely. Further, the stages of its growth are still not yet elucidated, and the text printed in the edition probably represents the work of several hands (which it may have been from the outset). Nevertheless, it is remarkable that it cites a number of the Merovingian synods of Gaul which do not seem to occur in the sources we have considered so far.[61] No detailed account of the canonical sources of the collection has yet been published, but it seems clear that it rested on a much wider selection of them than can be discerned in the texts more directly associated with Theodore.[62]

[60] Finsterwalder, *Die Canones Theodori*, pp. 204–5.

[61] *Die irische Kanonensammlung*, ed. H. Wasserschleben, 2nd ed. (Leipzig, 1885), esp. pp. xvi–xxi. The modern literature on the manuscripts is extensive (much of it listed in Mordek, *Kirchenrecht*, pp. 255–9); see too R. E. Reynolds, 'Unity and Diversity in Carolingian Canon Law Collections: the Case of the *Collectio Hibernensis* and its Derivatives', *Carolingian Essays: Andrew W. Mellon Lectures in Early Christian Studies*, ed. U.-R. Blumenthal (Washington, DC, 1983), pp. 99–135. The published studies do little to elucidate the canonical sources of the collection in detail. A comparison of a random sample of XXI. 27, XXXVII. 39, XXXIX. 15, XLII. 9 and XLIII. 2 with the editions by Munier in *Concilia Galliae* shows that the texts are so freely rehandled as to make identification of the exact source exceptionally difficult. See also discussion by Thomas Charles-Edwards, below, pp. 142–7.

[62] The compiler sometimes cites an early conciliar text under the simple inscription 'Dionisius', as in XXVIII.5.a, 10.a. XXVIII.10a is closer to the first Dionysian version than the second (Turner, *Monumenta* II.1, 109). Elsewhere citations from canons included in the *Dionysiana* are either robust paraphrases (e.g. XXVIII.5.a and XLII.18), or nearer the second Dionysian form, as with XLI.5.a (Turner, *Monumenta* II.2, 303–5). Frequent citations of the 'Statuta ecclesiae antiqua' as canons of a council at Carthage (e.g. I.10 and X *passim*) suggest the use also of a collection such as the *Hispana*. No conclusions can be drawn from such random notes given the present state of the edition.

The question of the legal authorities to which the Anglo-Saxon church turned in the years between the coming of Theodore and the Anglo-Saxon missions in Francia is an important one, with implications that extend far beyond England. It is not a subject on which the sources allow much precision, but a great deal of further work is needed. In the course of time we may well have to contemplate a more crowded landscape than has been drawn here.

NOTE ON THE EDITION OF THE DIONYSIAN DECRETALS IN THE EDITION BY VOELL AND JUSTEL OF 1661

The Dionysian decretals are generally cited from the edition by G. Voell and H. Justel in 1661 from the papers of the elder Justel. Christopher Justel's original edition of 1628 depended wholly on his own manuscript (now Oxford, Bodleian Library, e Musaeo 103), which has only the councils. At the end of his second edition he printed the *capitula* of the decretals as far as Anastasius II from an unknown source (though it was late enough to include the added decretals of Zosimus and Leo I, discussed below). He added: 'omissis Decretorum integris capitibus, quae ex veteri codice canonum Ecclesiae Romanae, qui Moguntiae primum excusus est, anno 1525, et postea Parisiis an. 1619, facile cuivis fuerit repetere' (PL 67, 229–30; see C. H. Turner, 'Chapters in the History of Latin MSS of Canons. V', *JTS* 30 (1929), 337–46, at 340n.).

In the version printed in 1661 the *capitula* and this passage were reprinted (though the *capitula* were omitted in Migne's version), but were followed by texts of the decretals, distinguishing between the decretals up to Anastasius II (as they occur in the early form) and the added decretals to Gregory II (from the *Hadriana* version). This led Turner (*ibid.* p. 341), and Kuttner after him (cited in Gaudemet, *Sources*, p. 136, n. 19), to suggest that Voell and Justel used *Canones apostolorum, veterum conciliorum constitutiones, decreta pontificum antiquiora, de primatu Romanae ecclesiae*, ed. J. Wendelstinus [Cochlaeus] (Mainz, 1525), or the reprinted version by F. Pithou in *Codex canonum vetus ecclesiae Romanae quae ei codici accesserunt sequens epistola indicabit* (Paris, 1609), to provide the texts.

Cochlaeus printed his text from three copies of the enlarged *Dionysiana–Hadriana*, the form of the Dionysian second collection sent by Pope Hadrian to Charlemagne in 774, of which there are innumerable copies (Maassen, *Geschichte*, pp. 441–54, and Mordek, *Kirchenrecht*, pp. 241–9). Two of his copies came from

Mainz and one from Erbach, and he noted some variants in the margin. However, there is no distinction in either edition of this form between the original decretals and the additions, as there is in the version of 1661. While the break might have been inferred from Justel's *capitulatio*, the texts of the two versions diverge quite often (e.g. Innocent I, c. liv, where Cochlaeus in both editions reads 'Nostro aevo lex' and the margin offers the alternative reading 'sed nostra lex', while 1661 reads 'Nostre vero lex'). The 1661 version notes none of the variants of Cochlaeus, though some of his marginal readings appear in the text without comment.

Wurm (*Studien*, p. 51, n.74) held that the edition of 1661 was based on a late and corrupt *Hadriana*. For some evidence for his conclusion compare: Innocent I, c. 20, where 1609 lacks the date of the edition of 1661; c. 45, inscription, where 'Antiocheno' in 1661 is missing in 1609; and outstandingly the decretal of Gelasius. The 1609 edition (here agreeing with some manuscripts of the *Hadriana*) places this after the decretals of Hilary, Simplicius and Felix, and has the inscription of the early form of the *Dionysiana*, while the 1661 text has it directly after Leo I, with the inscription of a later form (Wurm, *Studien*, pp. 65, 68 and 76).

It seems to follow that the edition of 1661 is based on the second *Dionysiana* proper for the councils, but on a poor manuscript of the *Hadriana* for the decretals. As the Ballerini noted long ago (PL 56, 199–200), and Wurm after them (*Studien*, pp. 70 (no.23a), 75 (no.37a) and 79), the 1661 edition therefore included in the decretal section which does belong to the early *Dionysiana* some letters which were added later, notably Zosimus c. 4 and Leo I c. 49, as well as the appendix from Hilary onwards. These additions accumulated slowly; the *Hadriana* marks a late stage in the process.

The 1661 text is also full of readings proper only to the *Hadriana*. To detect these the principal resources remain the out-dated editions of the relevant early papal letters: P. Coustant, *Epistolae Romanorum pontificum et quae ad eos scriptae sunt a S. Clemente I. usque ad Innocentium III quotquot reperiri potuerunt* (Paris, 1721) for the popes to Sixtus III; P. and H. Ballerini, *Sancti Leonis opera* I, 607–1438 (repr. in PL 54, 551–1506); and A. Thiel, *Epistolae Romanorum pontificum genuinae et quae ad eos scriptae sunt a S. Hilario usque ad Pelagium II* (Braunsberg, 1868), of which only the volume to Hormisdas ever appeared.

None provides anything like an adequate apparatus, but each is in part based on copies of the second Dionysian collection proper, not the *Hadriana*. Coustant knew Paris, BN, lat. 3837 (Anjou, s. ix[1]), the Ballerini used for their edition of Leo's letters Vatican lat. 5845 (see above, p. 128, n. 29), though they knew of the Paris copy (PL 54, 557). The manuscripts labelled 'F1' and 'F2' of Thiel's apparatus represent two states of the Dionysian collection prior to the *Hadriana*, which may be identified in the readings of his H copies, though his 'H7' is the enlarged *Dionysiana* from Nonantola (see above, p. 132, n. 44), not a true

Hadriana (Thiel, *Epistolae*, pp. xxii and xxxv-vi). The merits, and weaknesses, of the procedures of these early editors are conveniently discussed by K. Silva-Tarouca in 'Beiträge zur Überlieferungsgeschichte der Papstbriefe des IV., V. and VI. Jahrhunderts', *Zeitschrift für katholische Theologie* 43 (1919), 467–81 and 657–92, esp. 467–80.

The nearest we yet have to a critical guide through the readings of the manuscripts is provided by Wurm, *Studien*, pp. 62–80, though he deals only with the inscriptions and explicits of the decretals. The number of editions of individual decretals exceeds the limit of a brief note, but those of Innocent I (JK 293; Dionysius cc. 20–7; PL 67, 245–8) and Leo I (JK 402; Dionysius c. 48; PL 67, 277–80) in H. Wurm, 'Decretales selectae ex antiquissimis Romanorum pontificum epistulis decretalibus', *Apollinaris* 12 (1939), 40–93 are of particular value as a control on the editions of Coustant and the Ballerini. There is an enormous amount of work to be done before these texts can be used with confidence, and no detailed examination of the Dionysian versions of the decretals can be based on the current edition.

8

The Penitential of Theodore and the
Iudicia Theodori

THOMAS CHARLES-EDWARDS

Penitentials have often had a bad press, from the ninth century to the nineteenth. As Theodulf of Orleans remarked, 'many faults are read in the penitential which it is not becoming for the man [the penitent] to know';[1] or, as Plummer put it more vividly, 'The penitential literature is in truth a deplorable feature of the mediaeval church. Evil deeds, the imagination of which may perhaps have dimly floated through our minds in our darkest moments are here tabulated and reduced to system. It is hard to see how anyone could busy himself with such literature and not be the worse for it.'[2] Theodore's Penitential suffers from further handicaps. Although there are several penitential texts claiming a connection with Theodore, not one of them was written by him.[3] The most extensive of these texts, that compiled by the *Discipulus Umbrensium*, 'Disciple of the Northumbrians', makes it quite clear, not merely that Theodore did not write the work, but that the Disciple's knowledge of Theodore's views was second- or third-hand.[4] Yet even if no text was written by Theodore himself, a version of

---

[1] Theodulf of Orléans, *Capitulare*, in PL 105, 219; trans. J. T. McNeill and H. M. Gamer, *Medieval Handbooks of Penance* (New York, 1938), p. 397.

[2] *Venerabilis Baedae Opera Historica*, ed. C. Plummer, 2 vols. (Oxford, 1896) I, clvii–clviii.

[3] P. W. Finsterwalder, *Die Canones Theodori Cantuariensis und ihrer Überlieferungsformen* (Weimar, 1929), p. 1. For a recent summary, see R. Kottje, 'Paenitentiale Theodori', *Handwörterbuch zur deutschen Rechtsgeschichte* III (1983), cols. 1413–16; see also C. Vogel, *Les 'Libri paenitentiales'* (Turnhout, 1978), pp. 68–70. Important earlier work includes F. Liebermann, 'Zur Herstellung der Canones Theodori Cantuariensis', *ZRG* 12 (1922), 387–409; G. Le Bras, 'Notes pour servir à l'histoire des collections canoniques, I. Iudicia Theodori', *Revue historique de droit français et étranger* 4th ser. 10 (1931), 95–131.

[4] Disciple, *Pref.* (ed. Finsterwalder, *Die Canones Theodori und ihre Überlieferungsformen*, pp. 287–8). I refer to this text, Finsterwalder's U, as the Disciple, and use a citation such as 'II.xii.2' for book, chapter and clause. I take *Humbrenses* as 'Northumbrians'

his penitential teaching was already known outside England within a generation of his death. Rules were already quoted as Theodore's in the A-Recension of the *Collectio Canonum Hibernensis*, compiled before 725.[5] The source for the *Hibernensis* was not, however, the work of the Disciple, but Finsterwalder's D, entitled *Iudicia Theodori*, but generally known as the *Capitula Dacheriana* after D'Achéry, its first editor.[6] As a result this text has the earliest terminus ante quem of all the Theodoran penitential literature. Theodore, however, was also an important named source for the two main eighth-century Irish penitentials, the 'Bigotian' and 'Old Irish' Penitentials;[7] for both, the version used was the work of the Disciple, Finsterwalder's U. The texts associated with his name also had some influence on Frankish penitentials of the same period.[8] By the mid-eighth

rather than as a term for the Deirans, as proposed by Lapidge, 'The School of Theodore and Hadrian', p. 48, because of Ecgfrith's title in the proceedings of the Synod of Hatfield, 'Ecgfrido rege Humbronensium' (Bede, *HE* IV.17 [15]). Levison may have been entirely right, however, in suggesting in his review of Finsterwalder, *ZRG* 19 (1930), repr. in his *Aus rheinischer und fränkischer Frühzeit* (Düsseldorf, 1948), p. 301, that the Disciple's teachers may have been at the School of York.

[5] *Collectio Canonum Hibernensis* [hereafter *Hibernensis*], ed. F. W. H. Wasserschleben, *Die irische Kanonensammlung*, 2nd ed. (Leipzig, 1885), LIV.12–14; in I.22 he is cited, but not by name. For relevant comparisons, see Appendix II (below, pp. 172–4). The date of the Hibernensis is fixed by the names of its two compilers, one of whom, Ruben, died in 725. It is unlikely to have been written before 716, since the other compiler, Cú Chuimne, who died in 747, was from Iona and the Paschal dispute had evidently already been resolved (cf. *Hibernensis* XX.6); see J. F. Kenney, *The Sources for the Early History of Ireland: Ecclesiastical* (New York, 1929), no. 82.

[6] This was already perceived by Bradshaw, *apud* Wasserschleben, *Die irische Kanonensammlung*, p. lxx, and by Wasserschleben himself, *ibid.* n. **; but unfortunately, in the notes to his text, it is only I.22c which is traced to the *Iudicia Theodori* rather than to the work of the Disciple. Bradshaw's discovery was ignored by, among others, Liebermann, 'Zur Herstellung der Canones Theodori', p. 400, and Le Bras, 'Notes pour servir à l'histoire des collectiones canoniques'.

[7] See Bieler's edition of the former and Binchy's translation of the latter in *The Irish Penitentials*, ed. L. Bieler (Dublin, 1963), *passim*.

[8] For a general survey, see R. Pierce, 'The Frankish Penitentials', *Studies in Church History* 11 (1975), 31–9. For the influence of Theodore, see, for example, the *Sangallensis Collectio Tripertita*, ed. H. J. Schmitz, *Die Bussbücher und das kanonische Bussverfahren nach handschriftlichen Quellen* (Düsseldorf, 1898), pp. 182–4, as well as the *Paenitentiale Martenianum*, ed. W. von Hörmann, *ZRG* 4 (1914), 358–490 [text; the editor's discussion includes a table of correspondences between the *Paenitentiale Martenianum* and U (*ZRG* 1 (1911), 207–19). See also R. Kottje, *Die Bussbücher Halitgars von Cambrai und des Hrabanus Maurus: ihre Überlieferung und ihre Quellen* (Berlin, 1980), p. 204–9, where

century at the latest, therefore, more than one text existed offering a report of Theodore's penitential teaching, and in some cases actual decisions made by him.[9]

Difficulties are not confined to the origin of the texts. There is also uncertainty about Theodore's own standpoint on the practice of penance. It is customary to distinguish between two forms of penance: the public penance prevalent in the early church, and private penance, which first appears in texts with a British background and subsequently in Ireland and among Irish *peregrini* on the Continent.[10] On this view, public penance was the only form upheld in the early church, whereas private penance was Celtic and medieval. Why then did Theodore, no champion of Celtic diversities, and moreover specifically commanded to uphold Roman practice, give the respectability of his name to Insular penitential teaching?[11]

These two difficulties, the more narrowly textual and that of Theodore's standpoint, are interconnected. The greater the distance which can be put between Theodore and the penitential texts which appealed to his name, the less arduous will be the task of explaining why a monk of eastern origin and Roman residence should not merely accept but even recommend Celtic penitential practice.[12] Such links between our problems make it necessary to begin with the texts and leave wider issues until later. I shall concentrate on that compiled by the Disciple of the Northumbrians, because by the mid-eighth century it had become the principal source of

it is argued that Hrabanus derived his Theodoran material from the *Paenitentiale Martenianum*; and H. Mordek, *Kirchenrecht und Reform im Frankenreich: Die Collectio Vetus Gallica, die älteste systematische Kanonessammlung des fränkischen Gallien. Studien und Edition* (Berlin, 1975), pp. 52 and 664.

[9] Disciple, I.xiv.29.

[10] For a brief statement of the contrast, see C. Vogel, *Les 'Libri paenitentiales'*, pp. 34–5; an excellent short account is that of J. Gaudemet, *L'Eglise dans l'empire romain (IVe-Ve siècles)*, Histoire du droit et des institutions de l'église en occident 3 (Paris, 1958), 667–81; for a recent survey, see R. Kottje, 'Bußbücher', *Lexikon des Mittelalters* II (1983), 1118–22. For a short, but good, account of the Irish penitentials, see K. Hughes, *Early Christian Ireland: Introduction to the Sources* (London, 1972), pp. 82–9; and for their reception on the Continent, R. Kottje, 'Überlieferung und Rezeption der irischen Bußbucher auf dem Kontinent', in *Die Iren und Europa im früheren Mittelalter*, 2 vols. (Stuttgart, 1982) I, 511–24.

[11] Disciple, I.v.2: 'qui numquam Romanorum decreta mutari a se saepe iam dicebat uoluisse'; cf. McNeill and Gamer, *Medieval Handbooks of Penance*, p. 184, n. 46; Bede, *HE* IV.1 (p. 331).

[12] Disciple, I.vii.5 ('Theodorus laudavit'); not in D.

information about Theodore's penitential teaching. I shall first, however, give a brief account of the *Iudicia Theodori*.

Whereas the Disciple's work is organized in Roman fashion, by books and titles, the *Iudicia Theodori* are simply a series of sentences with no overt structural framework. Finsterwalder claimed that the collection was put together on the Continent and that very few intervening copies lay between the two manuscripts, both Breton, Paris, BN, lat. 12021[13] and Paris, BN, lat. 3182,[14] and the original. Since Finsterwalder's edition, Bieler has made a detailed study of the order of the texts in these two manuscripts and has shown that the *Iudicia Theodori* belong to a group containing also the *Collectio Canonum Hibernensis* (A-Recension), the *Canones Adamnani*, a group of canons of the Council of Ancyra, extracts from the Penitential of Vinnian, and *Canones Hibernenses I* and *II*.[15] The group of texts to which the *Iudicia Theodori* belonged was, at least proximately, Breton: this was Bieler's conclusion, and his argument has been strengthened by Fleuriot's demonstration that the *Excerpta de libris Romanorum et Francorum*, found in several related manuscripts including Paris, BN, lat. 12021 and 3182, and previously known as *Canones Wallici*, were Breton by origin.[16] On the other hand, our two manuscripts have different versions of the *Excerpta* in different positions in the sequence of texts. In other words, the unambiguously Breton element may well be a secondary addition. The other texts are mainly Irish, and it is therefore quite likely that the group was already formed when they came from Ireland to Brittany. The two manuscripts of the *Iudicia* would then derive the texts in question independently from this import before it received the addition, made separately, of the *Excerpta*.

One important advantage of getting the textual history clear is that it is then easier to assess the evidence for the *Iudicia Theodori*, as well as the significance of a major piece of evidence about the *Collectio Canonum Hibernensis*. The group of texts with which we are concerned, mainly Irish

---

[13] Datable to the early tenth century (s. x^in) and written by a Breton scribe; formerly Sangermanensis 121, previously from Corbie. Jackson gives the Old Breton glosses in this manuscript an appreciably earlier date than those in BN, lat. 3182: K. H. Jackson, *A Historical Phonology of Breton* (Dublin, 1967), p. xxxvi.

[14] Datable to the tenth century (s. x) and written by a Breton scribe; provenance Fécamp.

[15] *Irish Penitentials*, ed. Bieler, pp. 22–4.

[16] L. Fleuriot, 'Un Fragment en latin de très anciennes lois bretonnes armoricaines du VIe siècle', *Annales de Bretagne* 78 (1971), 601–60; see also D. N. Dumville, 'On the Dating of the Early Breton Lawcodes', *Etudes Celtiques* 21 (1984), 207–21.

but with additions from elsewhere, occurs in two forms, of which that containing the *Iudicia Theodori* is Version B. The core of the group is made up as follows (using the abbreviation *Hib.* for the *Collectio Canonum Hibernensis* and *Adamnán* for the *Canones Adamnani*):

VERSION A[17]	VERSION B[18]
Hib.	*Hib.*
Excerpta	*Iudicia Theodori*
Adamnán	*Adamnán*

There are good textual reasons for associating both the *Iudicia Theodori* and the *Canones Adamnani* with the *Hibernensis*. The *Iudicia Theodori* were the latest text to be quoted in the A-Recension of the *Hibernensis*, while the *Canones Adamnani* were the latest text quoted in the B-Recension.[19] Both were probably available in Ireland before the group of texts, including the *Iudicia Theodori*, was taken to the Continent. So much is certain for the *Iudicia*, quoted in the A-Recension of the *Hibernensis*, and probable for the *Canones Adamnani* since they, like the *Iudicia*, appear to be a report by a pupil of what the teacher has said and are unlikely to be later than the generation after Adomnán's death (704), namely the early eighth century.[20] This suggests that both were imports from Ireland to Brittany in the company, as in the manuscripts, of the *Hibernensis*. In other words, the *Iudicia Theodori* probably came to Brittany, and subsequently to Francia, as a satellite of the *Hibernensis*. The canons of the Council of Ancyra, another of these satellite texts, were used by the *Hibernensis* and perhaps by the

---

[17] Oxford, Bodleian Library, Hatton 42; London, British Library, Cotton Otho E. xiii; Orléans, Bibliothèque municipale 221; and Paris, BN, lat. 3182, pt i. It is important for the relationship between the A- and B-recensions of the *Hibernensis* that the B-Recension appears in a sub-group of Version A. Cf.:

Otho E. xii	Hatton 42
Hib. A	*Hib.* B
Excerpta	*Excerpta*
Adamnán	Adamnán
Hib. B (in part)	

[18] Paris, BN, lat. 12021; cf. also Paris, BN, lat. 3182, pt ii, but without the *Hibernensis* already in pt i of the same composite collection of texts.

[19] H. Bradshaw, *apud* Wasserschleben, *Die irische Kanonensammlung*, p. lxx.

[20] *Canones Adamnani*, cc. 16–20 (*The Irish Penitentials*, ed. Bieler, pp. 178–80).

Iudicia Theodori.[21] In Version A, however, the *Iudicia Theodori* were displaced, after the group had arrived in Brittany, by the *Excerpta* – a Breton text. It would be possible to argue that the *Iudicia Theodori* were also, like the *Excerpta*, a secondary addition to an earlier core consisting of the *Hibernensis* and the *Canones Adamnani*, but this is made unlikely by the textual relationship between the *Hibernensis* and the *Iudicia Theodori*. Since that relationship makes it likely that the *Iudicia* were brought to Brittany from Ireland, along with the purely Irish texts, it is simpler to suppose that the text came in the company of the *Hibernensis*, which is where we find it in the manuscripts. Version B, therefore, is the core of the group as it left Ireland; Version A, on the other hand, a revision made in Brittany.

There is a further argument in favour of regarding Version B as an earlier, and, moreover, an Irish group of texts. In Paris, BN, lat. 12021, at the end of its copy of the *Hibernensis* and immediately before the *Iudicia Theodori*, is written the colophon 'Hucvsq; nuben et cv. cuiminiae et du rinis'. After contributions from several scholars, this was finally explained by Thurneysen as 'Hucusque Ruben et Cu Cuimne Iae et Dairinis', 'Up to this point Ruben of Dairinis and Cú Chuimne of Iona'.[22] The function of the colophon was to mark the division, within this group of texts, between the *Hibernensis* and the *Iudicia Theodori*. Yet it is likely that the colophon was already in the copy brought from Ireland to Brittany, given the detailed knowledge of Irish persons and places. Hence it is also likely that the group of texts, within which the colophon serves as a marker, was also present in the book brought from Ireland to Brittany.

Finsterwalder thought that the *Iudicia* were a continental compilation. His arguments, however, when they have any weight,[23] are directed against the notion that the text was English in origin. Thus he pointed to the description of Theodore in the text as *episcopus Saxonum* and argued that an Englishman would not have described the archbishop as a mere

---

[21] *Hibernensis* XXVIII.5*a*; XLVI.32*c*; and LXIV.5. I am indebted to Luned Davies for her help with the sources of the *Hibernensis*. Finsterwalder (*Die Canones Theodori*, p. 205) gives the sections of U dependent upon the Council of Ancyra, some of which are also in D, but the list evidently needs sifting.

[22] R. Thurneysen, 'Die irischen Kanonensammlung', *Zeitschrift für celtische Philologie* 6 (1908), 1–5; the order of the names of the persons and places is ABBA.

[23] The argument that the manuscripts are continental does not allow for the fact that nearly all surviving Irish manuscripts from before 900 were preserved on the Continent; it is, moreover, demolished by the use made of the *Iudicia* by the *Hibernensis*.

episcopus.[24] The argument is irrelevant to a possible Irish origin; moreover, the Annals of Ulster describe Theodore in his obit as *episcopus Brittaniae* and he is described as *episcopus* in the *Hibernensis* itself.[25]

In its extant form, therefore, the *Iudicia Theodori* derive from Brittany and previously from Ireland. They attest both the rapid reception of Theodore's teaching in Ireland and one route by which it reached Francia. The difficult issue of the ultimate origin of the text must be left until we have considered the longest version of Theodore's teaching, that of the Disciple.

The complete text of the Disciple's work (Finsterwalder's U) consists of a prologue, two books and an epilogue. Both prologue and epilogue contain explanation and justification of the Disciple's work, but before considering what he says, it is crucial to notice one thing from the outset. Only bk I is a penitential; bk II is a collection of canons.[26] That is to say, it is only in bk I that we have a series of typical penitential rules of the form, 'If anyone should commit such-and-such a sin, let him do penance for so many days or years'. The pairing of sin and penance, usually in the two parts of a conditional sentence, is characteristic of such rules. In bk II, however, we have general rules of conduct without any specification of a penance, or indeed any penalty at all. Since the two books are so different, it is not surprising that the manuscript transmission should show that they attracted distinct readerships: bk II frequently occurs without bk I.[27] It would indeed be remarkable if the two books had not interested different readers. After all, the Celtic penitentials are directed at priests who are, as it is often said, doctors of souls.[28] Its rules were not promulgated to the church at large, not even to the clergy. A penitential, therefore, envisaged a smaller readership than did a collection of canons.

---

[24] Finsterwalder, *Die Canones Theodori*, p. 17.

[25] *The Annals of Ulster*, ed. S. Mac Airt and G. Mac Niocaill (Dublin, 1983), s.a. 691; similarly in the Annals of Tigernach; Wasserschleben, *Die irische Kanonensammlung* LIV.13 *b* 14.

[26] See Finsterwalder, *Die Canones Theodori*, pp. 80–2. Levison showed, against Finsterwalder, that the Epilogue and the Prologue were by the same author: *Aus rheinischer und fränkischer Frühzeit*, p. 299.

[27] See the list of manuscripts in McNeill and Gamer, *Medieval Handbooks of Penance*, pp. 434–5.

[28] Columbanus, B, Prol.; Cummian, Prol. Title, VII.16; and Jonas, *Vita Columbani*, I.5, 10; II.1, 8, 15, 19, 25 (ed. B. Krusch, MGH SRG (1905), pp. 161, 170, 232, 245, 265, 273 and 290).

With this in mind, we may approach what the Disciple has to say in his prologue and epilogue.[29] They are stylistically of a piece: our Disciple has too much literary ambition, and too infirm a grasp of Latin grammar, to be able to write lucid prose. Some quite important issues may, therefore, be difficult to resolve. The opening salutation in the prologue is addressed to 'universis Anglorum catholicis propriae [=proprie] animarum medicis'.[30] The salutation is appropriate to a penitential, with its readership composed of 'animarum medici', but less so to the second book consisting of canons. The body of the prologue may be divided into three sections: in the first the Disciple defines the nature of the work; in the second he explains how the material was gathered together; and in the third he tells us, to the accompaniment of profuse apologies for his rash incompetence, what he himself has done to the raw material he had at his disposal. The emphasis on the penitential in bk I is apparent: for his doctors of souls he has a 'medicamen' or 'medicamenta' or a 'curatio cicatricum'; he is concerned with a law, foreshadowed by the law of Moses, the Law of Penance; in justification he appeals to Christ's words 'Penitentiam agite'. At this stage the canons of bk II seem entirely forgotten.

When he turns to the sources of his compilation, he has a complicated story to tell. The major part derives, 'so it is said', from the answers given by Theodore to questions put to him by a priest called Eoda who is already dead. The phrase 'so it is said' presumably implies that the Disciple did not gain his information directly from Eoda but through an intermediary. In addition there were 'those things which that man (*iste uir*) had asked out of a booklet of the Irish (*ex Scottorum libello*) which has been widely distributed'. The same verb, *sciscitare*, is used for the questioning put in relation to the booklet of the Irish and for the questioning of Theodore by Eoda. It therefore seems likely that *iste uir* is still Eoda putting questions to Theodore. It would be natural to suppose that Eoda chose the points from the Irish booklet on which he questioned the archbishop. On the other hand, we cannot go as far as to separate Theodore from the *libellus* and to suggest that only Eoda had any direct interest in a text from so suspect a source. In the first place, the prologue itself tells us that Theodore gave it as his opinion that the author of the *libellus* was an 'ecclesiasticus homo', a man whose beliefs were in accord with the teaching

---

[29] It is important to note that both Prologue and Epilogue are the work of the Disciple: see above, n. 12. The text itself refers to the Prologue at I.vii.5.

[30] Ed. Finsterwalder, *Die Canones Theodori*, p. 287.

of the church. Secondly, in one place in bk I Theodore is said to have approved a particular commutation of a penance (the substitution of prayers or corporal punishment in place of a period of penance). The Disciple then adds the comment, 'These are instances of what we said in the Preface about the Irish booklet, in which, as in other texts, he sometimes gave more severe rulings about the worst sins, sometimes, however, took a more lenient view, as seemed appropriate, in respect of the weak.'[31] Here Theodore's engagement with the Irish booklet is more direct; and we are also warned, both of the existence of other texts used by Theodore and also that the severity of the penance may often have been changed.

The third section of the Prologue explains what the Disciple did with his material. He begins by saying that reports of Theodore's penitential teaching aroused an insatiable curiosity among both men and women. The consequence was a rush of pupils to 'a man of knowledge unparalleled in our age'. The enthusiasm of these pupils did not engender only an oral tradition of Theodore's teaching, for 'there was found in the hands of many people that varied and muddled account of those rules written down together with, in the second book, the issues on which he had given a ruling (*statutae causae*)'.[32] This sentence is crucial evidence and has demonstrably been misunderstood. One possible translation suggests that the Disciple conceived his contribution to have consisted in introducing greater order into a collection which already had the form of two books.[33] This is not the only way of interpreting the sentence, so it is necessary to look at it in detail. The sentence, describing the situation as the Disciple found it, is as follows:

Vnde et illa diuersa confusaque degestio regularum illarum cum statutis causis libri secundi conscripta inuenta est apud diuersos.

There are two possible interpretations. The first separates the *diuersa confusaque degestio* from the *statutae causae*; it therefore takes the term *conscripta* as signifying that there already existed in writing, side by side,

---

[31] Disciple, I.vii.5 (not in **D**).

[32] My translation differs from that of McNeill and Gamer, *Medieval Handbooks of Penance*, p. 183: they treat the phrase *libri secundi* as a genitive depending on *degestio*; my translation assumes that it depends on *statutis causis*.

[33] Finsterwalder, *Die Canones Theodori*, pp. 80–8, and Levison, *Aus rheinischer und fränkischer Frühzeit*, p. 299, however, prefer to regard the Disciple as responsible for the arrangement in two books. This is tempting, if only because the other versions of

the confused *degestio* of the rules of penance and the *statutae causae libri secundi*. The division into two books would then have existed in the text found *apud diuersos*, for the *degestio* would correspond to the Disciple's bk I, while the *statutae causae* would correspond to his bk II. The confusion and muddle would be attributed to the *degestio* alone – there would be no implication that the confusion arose from combining in one disordered *degestio* the rules of penance and the *statutae causae*. The Disciple, then, would not be responsible for the division into two books. The other possible interpretation would understand the reference to a second book as being solely to bk II in the Disciple's own work. The implication would then be that the *statutae causae*, which only now, in the Disciple's work, were gathered together into a separate book, were previously written together (*conscripta*) with the confused *degestio* of penitential rules. This interpretation would thus take the sentence as follows: 'And hence there was found among many that digest of those rules [of penance], varied in content and muddled in order, written [in a single text] together with the issues of [my] second book which he adjudged.' The advantage of the first interpretation is that it does not require any assumptions which do not accord naturally with the text: the Latin is allowed to speak as directly as it can. The advantage of the second interpretation is that it allows the *diuersa confusaque degestio* to be seen as just such a text as the *Iudicia Theodori*, in other words as a text without any separation into distinct books and thus one which mingled penitential and canonical rules. It is, in any case, clear from a later sentence in the Prologue that the Disciple was responsible for the *tituli*, the headings given to the chapters within the two books, as well as for selecting what he thought most useful from all the material at his disposal. He was thus, on his own account, responsible to some degree for ordering the material; and this ordering would, on the second interpretation, have included the arrangement into two books.

A further way of interpreting the sentence has been proposed by McNeill and Gamer. This has the effect, like the second interpretation, of avoiding the conclusion that the division into two books went back before the Disciple. Their translation is: 'Hence there has been found in divers quarters that conflicting and confused digest of those rules of the second

---

Theodore's penitential teaching, Finsterwalder's **D**, **G** and **Co**, are not in two books; but Finsterwalder's discussion of the crucial passage in the Prologue is cursory in the extreme (*Die Canones Theodori*, p. 81).

book compiled with the cases adjudged.'[34] The difficulty with this version is that it requires *libri secundi* to be dependent on *regularum illarum* rather than on *statutis causis*. Using brackets to segregate the Latin corresponding to 'compiled with the cases adjudged', the sentence runs:

Vnde et illa diuersa confusaque degestio regularum illarum [cum statutis causis] libri secundi [conscripta] inuenta est apud diuersos.

There is, however, no justification for so unnatural a reading of the text. The Disciple, then, selected the more useful sections from an existing work which may already have been in two books and arranged the whole under titles. The confusion which troubled him in his source was evident principally in the *degestio*, the penitential bk I. Again, it is bk I which occupies the foreground so far as the Disciple is concerned.

As for the *Iudicia Theodori*, it requires a particular reading of the Disciple's Prologue – and, what is more, not the most natural one available – to sustain the theory that the *Iudicia* were the confused *degestio* on which the Disciple worked. The *Iudicia* are, however, very early;[35] they have a manuscript transmission which points to Ireland and then Brittany; and, finally, nearly all of the material contained in the text is also in the Disciple's work and the wording is very similar. There evidently is, therefore, a textual link between the *Iudicia* and the Disciple's work, even though the *Iudicia* may not be the *degestio*. An hypothesis which may account for the facts is that the *Iudicia* were the work of an Irish pupil of Theodore, who took his material from the texts circulating among other pupils before they acquired a two-book form.[36] Moreover, he also acquired his material before it received an extra injection of material from the *libellus Scottorum*, namely the Penitential of Cummian, used, apparently by Eoda, in his questioning of Theodore. In this respect, the *Iudicia* are not as Irish in content as is the work of the Disciple. The implication of this line of argument, then, is that the *Iudicia* give us an insight into the penitential teaching of Theodore at an earlier stage than that represented by the Disciple. We may labour under the disadvantage that none of the material was actually written by Theodore himself, but we do at least have some

---

[34] McNeill and Gamer, *Medieval Handbooks of Penance*, p. 183.

[35] Cf. Lieberman, 'Zur Herstellung der Canones Theodori Cantuariensis', p. 400.

[36] Contrast Liebermann's view (*ibid.*, pp. 401–2), that the Disciple was an Irishman writing in Canterbury.

evidence to show how his approach to penitential practice developed during the 670s and 680s.

All this raises the difficult issue of the relationship between Eoda, the *libellus Scottorum* and the work, possibly in two books, found among a number of Theodore's pupils. Was Eoda simply one of these pupils? And, if so, why is he given such prominence in the second section of the Prologue, but in the third section seems lost in the crowd of those sitting at the feet of 'the man of knowledge unparalleled in our age'? Some kind of answer to this question is possible if we consider further the *libellus Scottorum*.

The *libellus* has interested students of Theodore's Penitential, naturally enough given its prominence in the Prologue. Yet, in the main text itself it is cited only once and then only in a comment evidently added by an editor. There is a clear contrast here with St Basil, who is cited by name five times in all, three times in bk I and twice in bk II.[37] In the main body of the text, therefore, Basil is an acknowledged authority; the *libellus* is not. Even in the Prologue the *libellus* must be defended by the statement that Theodore considered its author to be an 'ecclesiasticus homo'. Finsterwalder and others have identified the *libellus* with the Penitential of Cummian, and I have no doubt that they have been right to do so.[38] It is, however, worth pausing to consider the reasons for the identification. Cummian's Penitential is organized around the scheme of eight principal vices set out in the fifth of Cassian's *Conlationes*, and which also underlie bks V–XII of his *Instituta*.[39] Cassian was a principal source for the Celtic penitentials as a whole, but Cummian was the first to make the eight vices the basis of his structure. The dependence is made all the clearer by Cummian's use of Cassian's Greek term *philargyria* for avarice, the third of

---

[37] Disciple, I.ii.7; I.viii.14 (D 171, which also refers to Basil); I.xiv.3 (D makes a mess of this ruling and also omits the name of Basil); II.vii.3 (not in D); II.xii.6 (approximately D 164, not 167 as Finsterwalder asserts).

It seems that Theodore must have used Basil directly, rather than in the collection of canons composed by John Scholasticus *c.* 565, the Συναγωγὴ κανόνων, since the latter used only the second and third of the letters to Amphilochius: H.-G. Beck, *Kirche und theologische Literatur im byzantinischen Reich* (Munich, 1959), pp. 422–3. The penitential ascribed to the Patriarch John the Faster is of a later period and cannot have been used by Theodore: Beck, *ibid.*, pp. 423–4.

[38] Finsterwalder, *Die Canones Theodori*, pp. 200–3.

[39] Bieler, *The Irish Penitentials*, p. 5.

the eight.[40] In the work of the Disciple the first four vices reappear, but in disguise. The vice of gluttony becomes drunkenness; anger becomes homicide.[41] A particular sinful form of action is substituted for the parent vice. Whereas Cummian is oriented towards habits – virtues and vices – the work of the Disciple is directed at actions. And yet the four remain, relative to one another, in the original order inherited from Cassian, even though a section on perjury, included under avarice in Cummian, is given a separate title by the Disciple.[42]

All this suggests that, while Cummian's Penitential was a source of the material, it was not used by the Disciple himself when he set about his task of ordering 'the varied and muddled account'. The Disciple knew of the existence of Cummian; he may at some stage have made personal use of his penitential; but apparently he did not use it when revising the existing account of Theodore's teaching in two books. A principal element in that task, according to the Prologue, was the insertion of appropriate titles. They, however, are not merely different from those in Cummian but are based on a different approach to morality. There is also the question why only the first four of Cassian's vices appear, disguised, in the Disciple's work, whereas all eight are in Cummian. An answer is easier if the Disciple was not working with the text of Cummian before him, but there is a further point. The Disciple was responsible both for the titles and for selecting the *utiliora* from the confused mass of material before him. As one works through Cummian, there is a distinct change after the fourth vice, *ira*. The next three sections, on *tristitia*, *accidia* and *iactantia*, are very short and contain hardly any specific penances. Any editor confronted by such material, concerned for *utiliora* and unmindful of Cassian's eight vices, would naturally omit it altogether. With the last of Cassian's eight vices, *superbia*, the problem is more difficult: Cummian contains extensive material much of which should have escaped the Disciple's blue pencil. Yet here, too, the difficulty would be considerably more acute if the Disciple had had Cummian's work in front of him and could have appreciated the crucial position of *superbia* in the whole structure. A useful point of comparison in all this is the Bigotian Penitential which drew much material from the Disciple's work and showed great reverence for the authority of Theodore, but nonetheless maintained the scheme of the eight

---

[40] Cummian, III (ed. Bieler, *The Irish Penitentials*, p. 116).   [41] Disciple, I.i.iv.
[42] Disciple, I.vi (not in **D**); cf. Cummian, III.8–11.

principal vices and so restored sentences on perjury from Theodore's Penitential to their position under *auaritia*.[43]

The Disciple's debt to Cummian seems, therefore, to be at second-hand. A closer connection between the Disciple and Cummian might, however, be suggested by the single reference to the Irish *libellus* in the body of the Penitential. The first two sentences of I.vii.5 come straight from Cummian except that whereas Cummian refuses to approve or condemn the commutation of twelve three-day fasts in place of a year, Theodore is said to have approved. Similarly, Cummian's preference is for sick penitents, unable to endure normal penance, to give a half of all they possess in alms as against the view of others that they should give the value of a man or a slave-woman;[44] Theodore, however, is said to have given the two rulings side by side without expressing a preference. In the last sentence of I.vii.5 we are told that:

These texts are from the work we mentioned in the Preface, (namely) from the Irish booklet, in which, as in other cases, he sometimes gave a more severe ruling concerning the worst sins, but sometimes, as seemed appropriate to him, he imposed a more lenient degree of penance for the weak.

This note must be the work of the Disciple himself, since it refers to what he said in the Prologue. On the other hand, it also seems to show a direct knowledge of Cummian, in that the Disciple knows that these parts of his text derive from Cummian and also knows that Theodore's penances were not always the same as those given by the earlier work. There is, therefore, a conflict of evidence: the Disciple's disregard for Cassian's eight vices suggests that he did not have Cummian before him when revising a work already existing in two books; the knowledge of Cummian in this passage suggests the opposite.

A possible solution can perhaps be found if we distinguish between the Disciple, apparently not himself a pupil of Theodore but very close to him in time, and those among whom the collection in two books, on which the Disciple worked, was circulating. Only the latter, among them probably Eoda, were in a position to know from direct experience what was Theodore's use of, and attitude to, the *libellus Scottorum*. The Disciple,

---

[43] Bigotian Penitential, III.iii.1–4.

[44] The *ancilla* is the much-used *cumal* of early Irish law, where 1 *cumal* is the top value of the *arer*, a compensation payment given, for example, to the first foster-parents of the slain person.

perhaps precisely because he was not a pupil of Theodore, displays a close interest in the interaction between the archbishop and those who came to him seeking expertise in the healing of souls. In the Prologue he is eager to tell his readers about Eoda and his questioning of Theodore even though it seems that Eoda was not known personally to the Disciple. A plausible hypothesis is that the Disciple was faced with the sentence referring to Theodore's approval of the commutation ('Item XII. triduana pro anno pensanda, Theodorus laudauit'), and discovered from a pupil of Eoda or of Theodore the source of the commutation thus approved and the way in which Theodore treated the *libellus Scottorum*. On that basis the Disciple would then be able to make his comment in the Prologue on Theodore's use of the Irish penitential. My explanation, then, is that the Disciple's references to the *libellus* were based on information he received, directly or indirectly, from one or more of Theodore's disciples, not on inferences from his own comparison between Theodore's Penitential and that of Cummian. We know from the Prologue, composed by the Disciple, that Eoda and Theodore, in their conversations, made use of the *libellus*. Such personal information strongly suggests a reliance on someone who could transmit Eoda's reminiscences to the Disciple.

I have pursued this argument in order to place the use of Cummian's Penitential where it belongs – within the context of the interaction between Theodore and his pupils. That interaction, in which Eoda may have been prominent, created the text, perhaps already in two books, on which the Disciple was subsequently to work. It also created a wider interest in Theodore's penitential teaching extending to people who were not his pupils, a wider interest which the Disciple exemplifies. That interest found expression both in texts, more or less unsatisfactory, and verbal reports of Theodore's opinions.

At this point it is worth recalling that the *Iudicia Theodori* do not show the same indebtedness to the Penitential of Cummian as does the Disciple's work. The *Iudicia* cite Basil but not Cummian.[45] The impact of Cummian, however, is likely to have produced the arrangement in two books. To see this we may compare two concordances, the first thirty sentences of the *Iudicia* compared with the other Theodoran texts, and, secondly, the first thirty sentences of the Disciple (U) compared with the *Iudicia* (D).

---

[45] See the table in Appendix I (below, p. 171).

D	U	U	D
1	II.iii.1–2	I.i.1	
2	II.iii.3	2	
3	II.iii.4	3	
4	II.iii.5	4	
5	II.iii.6	5	
6	II.iii.7[46]	6	
7	II.iv.5	7	
8	II.iv.6	8	
9	II.ii.10	9	
10	II.ii.14	I.ii.1	82
11	I.x.1, 2 [= all of I.x]	2	
12	II.viii.1	3	
13	II.viii.2	4	
14	I.xi.1	5	
15	II.viii.3	6	153
16	II.viii.4	7	
17	II.i.3	8	
18	II.i.4	9	
19	II.viii.7	10	
20	II.xi.7	11	
21	II.xi.1	12	
22	II.xi.4	13	
23	II.xi.8[47]	14	27
24	II.viii.6	15	
25	II.xii.1–2	16	
26	I.xii.4	17	64
27	I.ii.14	18	
28	II.xii.18	19	
29	II.xii.26	20	
30	II.xii.27	21	

What these concordances show is that the decisive difference between **D** and **U** is that the former mixes penitential and canonical material in a single sequence of rules, while the latter uses a principle of organization derived from Cassian *via* Cummian and so separates penitential from canonical material. There is a further implication of the concordances,

[46] See **D** 41 for II.iii.8.   [47] Together with the last clause of II.xi.7.

namely that the *Iudicia* give pride of place to canonical rules (which then appear in bk II of the Disciple's work), whereas the Disciple made bk I his penitential and, to judge from the Prologue, saw it, rather than bk II, as his principal concern. Bk II was mostly already in **D**, whereas most of bk I was lacking in **D**. All this is likely to be due to the impact of Cummian. As soon as Cummian's arrangement of his penitential according to the scheme of eight principal vices made any real impact on the Theodoran mixed penitential and canonical texts, it would naturally lead to a division between a penitential book, on the one hand, and a book of canons on the other. Cummian's adaptation of Cassian's scheme offered a framework for a penitential but was irrelevant to canons. Hence, to apply the scheme required a separation of penitential from canonical material. Yet, according to the Prologue in **U**, Cummian was already exerting an influence while Theodore was still alive, and therefore before the Disciple got to work. This supports the argument advanced above, that the two-book arrangement predated the Disciple. We have no copy of it merely because it was replaced by the Disciple's work. To make sense of the material, therefore, it is necessary to posit three main stages in its development:[48]

I   A text or texts giving pride of place to canons rather than penitential rules, without any division into books or chapters and without any debt to Cummian. This stage is represented by the *Iudicia Theodori* as well as by another text, less well dated, the *Canones Gregorii*.

II   The confused *degestio* in two books, one penitential, the other canonical; the first book being indebted to Cummian.

III   The work of the *Discipulus Umbrensium*. The existing chapter-headings, indebted to Cummian but not showing direct knowledge of him, were added by the Disciple.

Stages I and II reflect direct interaction between Theodore and his pupils; stage III comes after the archbishop's death.

There is no reason to suppose that Eoda's contribution to this growth of a Theodoran penitential tradition, both oral and written, was separate from the formation of the text in two books. One must presume that the division into two books was responsible for the same division in the Disciple's work. Thus the Disciple must be very heavily indebted at the very least to the text in two books; and yet he gives Eoda the first place in the interrogation of *pater Theodorus*. The Disciple may well, therefore, have

---

[48] Cf. Liebermann, 'Zur Herstellung der Canones Theodori', p. 399.

thought that Eoda had a principal part in the formation of the text in two books. What we have, then, in U is a text edited no later than the middle of the eighth century by someone who had good access to information about Theodore, his pupils and their reaction to his teaching, and in particular had a text written by one or more of those pupils and circulating among them. Indeed, the strong probability is that he had more than one text, for he himself refers to the existence of more than one *codex*.[49] The Disciple's own contribution was, according to himself, editorial. We may not have the very words written by Theodore, but what we do have is a quite exceptional wealth of information on the impact of his *iudicia*, both canonical and penitential, over several years upon a wide group of pupils.

If the influence of Cummian's Penitential was acknowledged by the Disciple, that of Basil is openly accepted in the text itself.[50] Basil's three letters ('On the Canons') to Amphilochius bishop of Iconium had acquired the authority of law in the eastern church.[51] I shall take one major example of Basil's influence on Theodore: marriage and divorce.[52] Basil's own position was a complex one and could not adequately be represented in brief penitential rules. He had to confront issues where different authorities claimed obedience: there was Roman law, as in the case when a slave married without the consent of his master (no marriage according to Basil);[53] there was custom, both of local society and of the church;[54] there were ecclesiastical canons also, which in Basil's eyes did not always address the questions to which he was seeking an answer.[55] In all this Basil is no root-and-branch reformer: in logic, he says, the adulterous man should be treated in just the same way as the adulterous woman, but he is not, and there is no prospect that custom will be changed.[56]

On the issue of remarriage the crucial question was bound to be the interpretation of Matthew V.32 and XIX.9: a man may not put away his wife except for fornication. If, then, a man's wife committed adultery and he put her away, was he entitled to take another wife? And if he contracted

---

[49] Disciple, II.xii.5 and 7.   [50] For references, see above, n. 20.

[51] They are ed. V. Courtonne, *Saint Basile: Lettres*, 3 vols. (Paris, 1957–66) II, 120–31, 153–64 and 208–18 (= nos. clxxxviii, cxcix and ccxvii). The paragraphs of these three letters have been given a single consecutive numbering.

[52] Cf. J. Gaudemet, *Le Mariage en Occident* (Paris, 1987), pp. 70–88.

[53] Basil, *Lettres*, ed. Courtonne, no. cxcix.40.

[54] *Ibid.*, no. cxcix.21.   [55] *Ibid.*, no. ccxvii.77.

[56] *Ibid.*, no. clxxxviii.9 (and cf. 21).

a second marriage, could his former wife remarry? And if the adultery of a wife allowed, or even required, the husband to repudiate her, what of the adultery of a husband?

On these issues earlier penitentials in the British Isles had taken a rigorist line.[57] No second marriage is allowed even when a spouse is put away for adultery. Basil, however, allowed remarriage for a man whose wife had left him, but not for the woman whose husband had done the same.[58] This line is reflected by Theodore's teaching (reported in both the *Iudicia Theodori* and the Disciple, and therefore presumably early), even though the rigorist line was upheld by the Council of Hertford in 673.[59] Since Theodore's Penitential was soon available in Irish circles accustomed to a stricter rule, it is possible to trace the impact of this particular view. It was not without support at first but was ultimately rejected. The so-called Second Synod of St Patrick provides the first evidence for the influence of Theodore. It was quoted in the *Collectio Canonum Hibernensis* of *c.* 720, normally with the ascription *Synodus Romana*, that is to say, a synod of the Roman party within the Irish church.[60] In one of its clauses it seems to reflect Theodore's line on remarriage. After quoting Matthew XIX.9 it adds, thinking of the qualifying clause 'except for fornication', 'as if it were permitted for that reason. Therefore, if he marries another woman, as if it were after the death of his former wife, they do not forbid it.'[61] The phrase, 'they do not forbid it', may be understood in two ways. First, 'they' may be authorities acknowledged by a text; so, for example, 'they do not forbid (the eating of) horse(flesh)'.[62] Secondly, however, this *synodus*

---

[57] Vinnian, 42–5; Cummian, II.29; cf. *Hibernensis* XLVI. 32.

[58] Basil, *Lettres*, ed. Courtonne, no. clxxxviii.9.

[59] Disciple, II:xii.5–6 (D 163 and 164); Bede, *Historia ecclesiastica* IV.5 (c. 10 of the Synod); cf. Bede, *Comm. in Marc.* X.9–10 (quoted by Plummer, *Venerabilis Baedae Opera Historica* II, 236).

[60] See Bieler's apparatus, *The Irish Penitentials*, pp. 184–96.

[61] *Synodus II S. Patricii*, c. 26 (ed. Bieler, *Irish Penitentials*, p. 194); my translation differs slightly from that of Bieler. I am also reluctant to accept the view expressed in Bieler's note (p. 255): translating 'hac si liciat ob hanc causam' (scil. *fornicatio*) by 'as if it were for that reason', he interprets the clause as follows: 'the words *hac* (= *ac*) *si liciat ob hance causam* are probably the criticism of a reader, who, like Vinnian (c. 43 f.) advocated the stricter observance, and have crept into the text in the course of its transmission'. In my view the clause can be interpreted purely as an explanation of 'nisi ob quam causam fornicationis' and may be rendered '(the wording of the verse is phrased) as if it be permissible for that reason'. Cf. also c. 28.

[62] Disciple, II.xi.4 = D 22 = *Hibernensis* LIV.13.*b*.

Romana shows elsewhere a desire to reconcile the custom of the writer's own province ('us') with that of another ('they'). So, talking of the prohibition on marrying kin, it says, 'Understand what the law saith, neither less nor more: but what is observed among us, that they be separated by four degrees, they say they have never seen or read.'[63] By 'they' the text may be referring simply to churches unaware of the rules set out in Theodore's Penitential, according to which the Romans (as opposed to the Greeks) prohibited marriage to kin within four degrees.[64] The clause allowing remarriage – which talks of what 'they' consider allowable – is probably using 'they' for unnamed authorities; if so, it may have been using Theodore's Penitential. Alternatively, it may reflect, not a direct borrowing, but a more general influence of Theodore's teaching among those Irishmen who would be most likely to accept his authority – the *Romani* within Ireland.[65]

It may be possible to go a little further. The Second Synod of St Patrick received its modern name because of the colophon: 'Finit Patricii Synodus.' This has strong support in the manuscript tradition and is easier to explain if the synod had a close connection with one or more Patrician churches, especially Armagh, which had gone over to the Roman party by the end of the seventh century.[66] Once that had happened Armagh was the leading church of the *Romani* in northern Ireland, just as Iona was the most important church in the other camp (even though its abbot, Adomnán, was himself a *Romanus* by *c.* 690). The text which shows the most emphatic rejection of the laxer rule given in the Second Synod of St Patrick is the *Canones Adamnani*. This collection is similar to Theodore's Penitential in that it makes no claim to have been written by Adomnán, abbot of Iona, but is rather a report by others of rulings and opinions ascribed to

---

[63] *Synodus II S. Patricii*, c. 29.   [64] Disciple, II.xii.26 = D 29.

[65] On the Irish *Romani*, see K. Hughes, *The Church in Early Irish Society* (London, 1966), pp. 47–9, 105–10 and 125–33.

[66] Hughes (*ibid.*, pp. 115–16), proposes the limits 640 × 688. The first depends upon the letter of the pope-elect John to a number of Irish churchmen headed by Tomméne, bishop of Armagh, quoted in part by Bede, *Historia ecclesiastica* II.19. It has been called into question by the argument of D. Ó Cróinín, '"New Heresy for Old": Pelagianism in Ireland and the Papal Letter of 640', *Speculum* 60 (1985), 505–16, that the issue arose out of the 'Greek' paschal limits in the Easter table of Victorius of Aquitaine. We cannot, however, infer from Ó Cróinín's argument that all those addressed by the papal letter were followers of Victorius, for one of them was Ségéne, presumably the abbot of Iona and a leading defender of the Celtic Easter.

Adomnán. One of the rulings ascribed to the abbot of Iona is a firm rejection of remarriage for the husband whose wife has deserted him: 'Her husband shall not marry another woman while she lives.'[67] It adds, apparently on its own account rather than as a report of Adomnán's view: 'Therefore we do not know whether that ruling of which we read *in quaestionibus Romanorum* has been confirmed by acceptable or by false witnesses.' This may plausibly be seen as a reference to the view reported in the Second Synod of St Patrick, itself a *synodus Romana*. A possible reconstruction of the situation would therefore go as follows: Theodore's views on remarriage (themselves reflecting Basil's) became known in some circles among the Irish *Romani*, including Armagh. Some, at least, were inclined to accept them, in spite of the more rigorist views traditional among Irish churchmen since at least the sixth century (there appears to have been no compromise with the secular law of marriage on this question).[68] These more rigorist views are attested, among other places, in the Penitential of Cummian, but although Theodore approved, in general terms, of that text, he preferred to follow Basil on this issue. The church of Iona opposed any relaxation of the traditional Irish line and this opposition prevailed, at least in theory. The *Collectio Canonum Hibernensis* of *c.* 720 used Theodore's Penitential and the Second Synod of St Patrick. Moreover, it is usually very ready to report varying opinions. Yet, on this issue, neither Theodore's Penitential nor the Second Synod of St Patrick is cited. The laxer view is dismissed and the traditional line is firmly upheld.[69] If Theodore's views had found a sympathetic hearing at Armagh

---

[67] *Canones Adamnani*, c. 16 (ed. Bieler, *The Irish Penitentials*, p. 178). Cf. Adomnán, *Vita S. Columbae* II.41 (ed. A. O. and M. O. Anderson, *Adomnán's Life of Columba*, rev. M. O. Anderson (Oxford, 1991), pp. 164–6).

[68] I am not aware of what evidence there may be to justify the suggestion made by Donnchadh Ó Corráin, 'Marriage in Early Ireland', in *Marriage in Ireland*, ed. A. Cosgrove (Dublin, 1985), p. 20, that before the seventh century the Irish church tolerated divorce and remarriage. On his theory a single set of Irish lawyers compiled the vernacular tracts and the Latin canons; when compiling the vernacular tracts, they adhered to a supposed early tolerant attitude to remarriage, but when writing Latin they maintained a later and harsher view. This ingenious idea might be acceptable if there were any evidence from before AD 600 for the supposed tolerant view.

[69] *Hibernensis* XLVI. 4, 8, 10, 12, 14 and 15. The only point on which the *Hibernensis* seems not to have taken a rigorist line is on the question whether a person whose spouse entered the religious life by consent might then marry another: cf. *Hibernensis* XLVI. 5, with the Disciple, II.xii.8.

but had been rejected at Iona, the line taken by the *Hibernensis* is explicable. One of the compilers of the *Hibernensis* was a monk of Iona.[70]

Theodore's views on penance and canon law seem, therefore, to have been rapidly disseminated in Ireland as in England. That is only what we might expect, given Aldhelm's report of Theodore's being 'hemmed in by a mass of Irish students' and the evidence of the Disciple that Theodore's pupils were especially anxious to hear his penitential teaching.[71] The *Iudicia Theodori* may be the text taken home by one such Irish pupil. In the Bigotian and Old Irish Penitentials we see, later in the eighth century, the influence of the Disciple's text, by then perhaps the most authoritative penitential even in Ireland.[72] In the Bigotian Penitential, Theodore is quoted by name, unlike Cummian, just as in the Disciple's text Basil is quoted by name, not Cummian. In the Old Irish Penitential Theodore and Cummian are both named, but the superior authority of the learning associated with Theodore is nicely illustrated by the ascription of Cummian's Penitential in two of the manuscripts to St Basil.[73]

Yet there is one fundamental point on which Theodore is held to have turned his back on St Basil and to have embraced Celtic novelties: the abandonment of public in favour of private penance.[74] The public penance of the early church was unrepeatable and applied solely to major sins. (Those guilty of lesser sins expiated them by giving alms.) Penance involved a renunciation of all weapons and of sexual relations during the period of penance. According to the normal pattern the sinner sought to be admitted to the ranks of the penitents and was only allowed to proceed with the consent of his or her spouse and after careful questioning. Once admitted, the penitent moved through distinct stages of penance, from the lowest, the 'weepers' who remained outside the doors of the church, to the highest, those who were allowed to stand with the full members of the church but were not yet allowed to communicate. A long-term exclusion from communion coupled with a slow progress towards eventual reinteg-

---

[70] Cú Chuimne: see Thurneysen, 'Zur irischen Kanonensammlung'.

[71] R. Ehwald, *Aldhelmi Opera*, MGH, Auct. Antiq. 15 (Berlin, 1919), 493, trans. M. Lapidge and M. Herren, *Aldhelm: the Prose Works* (Cambridge, 1979), p. 163.

[72] Bigotian Penitential, I.i-ii; I.v.2 and 8; I.vii; II.ii etc.; the Old Irish Penitential, I.4; II.21 and II.2.

[73] Bieler, *The Irish Penitentials*, p. 108.

[74] For what follows, see Vogel, *Les 'Libri paenitentiales'*, p. 35.

ration among the communicants were the characteristics of this form of penance. This system was upheld by Basil and his penances included the different stations or stages by which the penitent was gradually brought back within the fold of the communicant church.[75] Theodore, on the other hand, is held to have abandoned this system in favour of the private penance of the Irish and the Britons. The latter was repeatable, could be used for minor as well as for major sins, and was controlled by priests rather than by bishops.

No doubt there is much truth in this contrast between Insular penance and the system of the early church, but the contrast can be made too sharp and too simple. First, it is necessary to ask what kinds of publicity were envisaged by the earlier system. There is the publicity entailed by the open confession of sin before the local church, whether that sin was already known to one's fellow-Christians or not. This is found in monasteries, but never seems to have been normal in the secular church.[76] There is also the publicity implied by membership of the order of penitents, a separate group attached to the church, yet not fully of it, as were the catechumens. In Frankish Gaul in the sixth century clerical penitents allowed their hair to grow while lay penitents were tonsured.[77] A clerical penitent thus publicly acknowledged that he was suspended from his order, and the lay penitent did the same in reverse. Finally, there is the publicity consequent upon a ceremony of reconciliation in which the bishop brought back the wandering sheep into the fold.

I shall take these forms of publicity in reverse, beginning with the reconciliation of the penitent by the bishop. A *locus classicus* for the obsolescence of this aspect of the ancient system of penance is the Disciple, I.xiii (*De Reconciliatione*; not found in D). We are told that the Greeks and the Romans use different parts of the church for the ceremony, that it occurs on Maundy Thursday and is performed by the bishop, and that it is only allowed once the period of penance has been completed. Only in an emergency may the bishop delegate the job of reconciling a penitent to a priest. We then have a sudden surprise, for the paragraph concludes with the statement, 'Thus there is no public provision for reconciliation in this

---

[75] Basil, *Lettres*, ed. Courtonne, no. ccxvii.56–8.
[76] Gaudemet, *L'Eglise dans l'empire romain*, p. 675.
[77] C. Vogel, *La Discipline penitentielle en Gaule des origines la fin du VIIe siècle* (Paris, 1952), p. 108; Isidore, *De ecclesiasticis officiis* II.17.

province, since there is likewise no public penance.'[78] Support for this conclusion is offered by an earlier clause which declares that, 'According to the canons penitents ought not to communicate before the completion of their penance; we, however, for mercy's sake, give permission after a year or six months.'[79] Yet such a permission would be quite incompatible with any firm adherence to the old stations or stages by which the penitent was gradually reincorporated. To be a communicant was to be a full member of the church; to be a penitent had been to be attached to the church, seeking readmission, yet not fully accepted – on trial like a catechumen.

What then should one make of the references to the stages of penance contained in the Penitential? The first reproduces three of the four stations given in Basil's Letters 'On the Canons';[80] the second seems to be either muddled or corrupt, talking as if *penitentes* stood for one of the stages of penance, such as the *auditores* 'the hearers' who were dismissed just after the catechumens and before the eucharist proper.[81] It may be that the text is simply reproducing as best it can earlier decrees.[82] On the other hand, there is some slight evidence to suggest that these clauses in Theodore's Penitential are not just fossils, half-understood echoes of a form of penance long abandoned. Both of these clauses concern heretics, a topic which is immensely more important in Theodore's Penitential than it is in any of the Irish ones. Yet it is precisely when an Irishman came up against heretics in Frankish Gaul that we have another suggestion of the old system of public penance. In the Penitential of Columbanus we are told that 'If any layman in ignorance has communicated with the followers of Bonosus or other heretics, let him rank among the catechumens, that is, separated from other Christians, for forty days, and for two other forty-day periods in the lowest rank of Christians, that is, among the penitents, let

---

[78] Disciple, I.xiii.4 (not in **D**). It is uncertain what the text means by 'province'; but it can hardly embrace both the Irish and the Anglo-Saxons, as implied by Kottje, 'Überlieferung und Rezeption der irischen Bußbücher', p. 512.

[79] Disciple, I.xii.4; cf. **D** 26 and **G** 123.

[80] *Extra ecclesiam* = προσκλαίων; *auditor* = ἄκροωμενος; and *extra communionem* = συνέστως (the third, ὑποπίπτων, is omitted).

[81] Disciple, I.v.14 (not in **D**).

[82] The Disciple, I.v.14, quotes the Nicene Council; among the Latin versions edited by C. H. Turner, *Ecclesiae Occidentalis Monumenta Iuris Antiquissima*, 2 vols. in 7 pts (Oxford, 1899–1939) I, 212–13, the wording is closest to the *Interpretatio Isidori*, but not so close as to prove that the Disciple did have access to a version made from the Greek in Canterbury.

him wash away the guilt of his unsound communion and thus after imposition of hands by a Catholic bishop let him be restored to the altar.'[83]

We have here the episcopal reconciliation of a penitent heretic familiar from the early church. The bishop has not been shouldered aside by the priest. We also have the equivalent of two of the stations or stages of penance. The 'hearers' under the old system were dismissed immediately after the catechumens, namely after the readings from scripture and before the offertory.[84] The next stage was that of the penitents allowed to stand with the rest of the congregation for the eucharist, but not allowed to communicate. Whereas Basil calls them 'the co-standers', here they are called the penitents. Instead of Basil's four stages we now only have two. A similar simplification of the old system may be behind Theodore's Penitential, for it has three stages in place of Basil's four. The terms are also partially different from Basil's. All this suggests a system of penance which is changing rather than a system which is dead and is being replaced by something quite different, the private penance of the British and Irish churches. The full process of the stages of penance is applied to reconciled heretics, but not to the orthodox sinner; the divide between heretic and orthodox has perhaps come to be perceived as different in kind from that between the sinner and the virtuous and also greater in seriousness. If the old system had been dead, and the Penitential of Theodore had, nonetheless, incorporated the odd fossil from the past, one would have expected a faithful reproduction of Basil's four stages, since his authority is openly acknowledged in the text.

Moreover, if we do treat these references to the stages of penance as more than antiquarianism, we can explain a difficulty in the Disciple's text. The Disciple seems to be getting into a mere muddle in talking of those penitents who were within the church but separated from the congregation as *auditores* in I.v.10, but as *penitentes* in I.v.14. Yet there are reasons why we should hesitate before concluding that the Disciple has fallen into

---

[83] Penitential of Columbanus, B, c. 25; this clause is regarded by J. Laporte, *Le Pénitentiel de S. Colomban: Introduction et édition critique* (Tournai, 1958), pp. 62–3, and, following him, by Bieler, *The Irish Penitentials*, p. 5, as an accretion, but for no very good reason.

[84] Vogel, *La Discipline pénitentielle en Gaule*, p. 109, denies that ordinary penitents were dismissed, citing the Council of Epaone (AD 517), c. 29: the *lapsi* depart, implying, according to Vogel, that other penitents did not. I cannot see that the text can sustain his interpretation.

confusion. First, Columbanus also uses *penitentes* for one of the stages of penance. Secondly, a possible solution is that the normal penitent now only went through one or two stages, and not four. The stage in which most penitents found themselves, or in which they were most distinctive as a group, thus found itself designated by the term *penitentes*. Heretics, however, because their heresy had excluded them from the church, were still compelled to go through a more exacting process of reintegration into the church by stages, as follows:

Columbanus

If a layman has communicated with heretics,

(a) *in ignorance,*

(b) *deliberately,*

(1) Forty days among the catechumens.

(1) Full penance continues for a year.

(2) Two further periods of forty days 'in the last *ordo* of Christians, that is, among the penitents'.

(2) Abstinence from wine and meat for another two years.

(3) After imposition of hands by a bishop, the penitent is allowed to communicate.

The penances for deliberately communicating with heretics would presumably have had the effect of placing the ex-heretic among, first, the catechumens and then 'the penitents' in the last *ordo* of Christians. It is not clear whether the full penance would have coincided with being placed among the catechumens, and the lesser penance with being placed in the last *ordo*.

Theodore

The heretic has (a) also persuaded others to become heretics or (b) merely been a heretic himself (I.v.10 and 14).

(a)

(b)

(1) Four years 'outside the Church';

three years 'outside the Church'.

(2) Six years among 'the hearers';

seven years among 'the penitents'.

(3 a & b) Two years excluded from communion.

If we put these two side by side, it becomes evident that Columbanus's 'among the catechumens' corresponds to Theodore's 'outside the Church'. Similarly, Columbanus's 'among the penitents' corresponds to Theodore's 'among the hearers' (a) and 'among the penitents' (b). Columbanus's penance before episcopal reconciliation, followed by communion, includes periods corresponding to Theodore's time during which penitents remain excluded from communion.

A further, and more general, argument arises from an issue which is sometimes neglected but was of deep concern for Theodore: the size of dioceses. Vogel's picture of the decay of the old system of penance in sixth-century Gaul is based upon contrasting the practices found in the works of Caesarius of Arles with the much more scanty references later in the century, notably in Gregory of Tours and in the councils. Yet the contrast may be as much geographical as chronological. Caesarius of Arles could take for granted the conditions of Provence, in particular small dioceses. Here the bishop might perhaps himself be able to reconcile all those who underwent penance after major sin. But in the large dioceses more characteristic of the rest of Gaul, it is scarcely conceivable that a bishop could ever have discharged this function in the way envisaged by some of the texts emanating from provinces in which the small diocese was normal. If a Gregory of Tours had seen it as his duty to reconcile all those who committed *fornicatio* in the diocese of Tours, he would scarcely have had time for anything else. We are not dealing here with anything properly described as decay of the ancient system, but merely with a necessary consequence of large dioceses which increasingly had largely Christian populations. When the Disciple's text talks of episcopal reconciliation not being the norm 'in this province', there are difficulties in determining what 'this province' may be, but it is very likely that the same could have been said of all ecclesiastical provinces to the north of the Massif Centrale.

To judge by the texts, Insular penance had from the start a prominent monastic strand. The *Praefatio Gildae* and the Synod of North Britain are addressed to monastic and clerical sins, not those of the laity; the *Excerpta de libro Davidis* are addressed to the clergy and the Penitential of Vinnian to the clergy and the laity. While authority over the penance of the clergy, and at least some laity, might be claimed by the bishop as late as the eighth century in Ireland, the abbot would naturally exercise authority over the moral failings of his monks.[85] It is not surprising, therefore, that the clearest survivals of the ancient public penance, with its distinct stages

[85] *Ragail Phátraic*, ed. and trans. J. G. O'Keeffe, 'The Rule of Patrick', *Ériu* 1 (1904), 216–24 (§§ 1, 4 and 6).

and its episcopal control, appear when heresy is the issue. The preservation of orthodoxy was admittedly the business of the bishop. The monastic element in Insular penance, however, encouraged its extension to lesser sins, and it thus inevitably became repeatable.[86] The *Praefatio Gildae* moves from fornication and sodomy at one end of the scale to failure to complete a task ordered by the abbot or breaking a hoe at the other.[87] Whereas the laity were expected to expiate lesser sins by almsgiving, monks, lacking property, were compelled to make further use of the penitential system of fasting and abstinence.

When we turn to the publicity of confession, that is to say, to the public acknowledgement of sins, even those committed in secret, the position is still not clear-cut.[88] The usual contrast is between public confession in the early church as against private confession to a 'soul-friend' among the Irish. This is then extended to the entire Insular tradition of penance. The contrast, however, is too simple. First, there is the tendency to require monks to confess their sins openly. This is especially marked when the sin is one of anger: even the mildest grievance should be brought

---

86 Repeatable penance was known on the Continent, before Columbanus's *peregrinatio*, and therefore before the Celtic tradition of 'private penance' could have had any effect, as shown by Toledo III, c. 11 (ed. J. Vives, *Concilios Visigóticos e Hispano-Romanos* (Barcelona and Madrid, 1963)), 12. 22: 'Quoniam conperimus per quasdam Spaniarum ecclesias non secundum canones sed foedissime pro suis peccatis homines agere poenitentiam, ut quotiens que [= quisque] peccare voluerit totiens a presbytero se reconciliari expostulent; et ideo pro coercenda tam execrabili praesumtione id a sancto concilio iubetur, et [= ut] secundum formam canonicam antiquorum detur poenitentiam [= poenitentia], hoc est ut prius eum quem sui poenitet facti a comunione suspensum faciat inter reliquos poenitentes ad manus inpositionem crebro recurrere; expleto autem satisfactionis tempore, sicuti sacerdotalis contemplatio probaverit eum conmunioni restituat. Hii vero qui ad priora vitia vel infra poenitentiae tempus vel post reconciliationem relabuntur, secundum priorum canonum severitatem damnentur.' Vogel (*Les 'Libri paenitentiales'*, pp. 35–6), claims that this passage is evidence for the influence of the Celtic type of penance on the Continent. The difficulties are both chronological and geographical: Columbanus arrived in Gaul *c.* 591 and is held to have been responsible for the first introduction of Celtic penance; further Vogel himself makes the odd claim that 'Le Sud de la Loire ne semble avoir été touché [*scil.* by penance of the Celtic type], exception faite pour les terres relevant de l'Eglise d'Espagne.' There were important links between Ireland and Spain in the seventh century, but they hardly explain so early an attestation of repeatable penance.

87 *Praefatio Gildae*, cc. 1, 15 and 26.

88 Gaudemet (*L'Eglise dans l'empire romain*, p. 675 and n. 7) inclines to the view that confession was normally secret.

out into the open.[89] Secondly, for Theodore, one of the most useful parts of Basil's letters 'On the Canons' will have been the observation that the adulteries of women should not be openly confessed, lest such publicity should bring vengeance on the penitent.[90] Even if kinsmen knew the truth, they might not feel impelled to avenge a sin known only to themselves and repented, whereas if all knew their shame vengeance might be inescapable.[91] In a feuding society, therefore, public confession would often be impossible – a truth no doubt just as apparent to Theodore in Canterbury as to Basil in Cappadocia.

The early Celtic penitential which concerns itself with the sins of the laity, that of Vinnian, places their characteristic sins under two headings: violence, especially homicide, and *fornicatio* (which includes adultery).[92] The typical layman bears arms and is sexually active; it is not surprising, therefore, that his principal sins have to do with wrongful forms of these aspects of lay life. In perceiving lay sin in this way, Vinnian was following faithfully the ancient customs of penance which required the sinner to lay aside arms and to refrain from sexual intercourse for the duration of his penance. We may then follow Vinnian's lead and ask what form of publicity would follow such characteristic lay sins. For adultery, as we have seen, Basil himself counselled secrecy. For homicide, on the other hand, it was a universal early medieval requirement that the deed be made public: secret homicide – murder in its original sense – was a much more serious offence than acknowledged killing. If, then, we consider the peculiarity of Celtic penance to consist in a cloak of secrecy laid over the sin, we are merely confused: the issue was already settled by the most urgent imperatives of lay society throughout the Christian world.

Cummian's treatment of homicide is in the same tradition as Vinnian's: the person who plans homicide must relinquish arms for the rest of his life.[93] This is one of the clauses in Cummian's Penitential used by the Disciple.[94] The statement of the case uses the same phrase, *odii meditatione*, employed by Cummian. Yet the judgement is very different: 'if he does

---

[89] Cummian, IV.14–16; Old Irish Penitential, V.14–15.

[90] St Basil, *Lettres*, ed. Courtonne, no. cxcix.34.

[91] Cf. the events related by Gregory of Tours, *Decem Libri Historiarum* V.32 (ed. Krusch and Levison, MGH, SRM I.i, p. 237).

[92] Vinnian, c. 35 (ed. Bieler, *The Irish Penitentials*, p. 86).   [93] Cummian, IV.5.

[94] Disciple, I.iv.4.

not wish to relinquish arms, let him do penance (on bread and water) for seven years, without meat and wine for (a further) three years'. The Anglo-Saxon male, as wedded to his weapons in life as he sometimes still was in the grave, could not be expected to follow his Irish counterpart in following the ancient customs of penance. In this respect, Theodore was further from the penance of the early church than were his Irish contemporaries – not out of ignorance of traditional rules but merely because pragmatic compromise with the values of lay society was inescapable, just as it was for Basil over the different treatments meted out to the man and the woman who committed adultery.

Theodore's Penitential is not, therefore, to be summed up in terms of Theodore going Celtic. The contrast between Insular and continental systems of penance has been exaggerated, and this exaggeration has created the problem. Theodore may be seen, in his penitential teaching, applying rules he had inherited from Basil, and applying them, moreover, to the conditions of a country in which feud was part of the fabric of society. Inevitably this meant that his approach came close to that of the Irish, for they faced a similar situation.[95] Theodore could thus make use of an Irish text, the *libellus Scottorum*.

---

[95] In the Old Irish Penitential, V. 2, this concern for circumstances giving rise to feud even encompasses *fingal*, 'kin-slaying'. On the other hand, Theodore, unlike the Irish, cannot insist on the penitent, even for homicide, relinquishing the use of weapons: cf. U I.iv.4 with Cummian, IV.5.

APPENDIX I

Theodore and Cummian[96]

Cummian	U
II.10 (?+ X.14)	I.ii.8
II.11	I.ii.10
II.7	I.ii.16
III.5	I.iii.2
III.6	I.iii.3
III.3	I.iii.4
III.7	I.iii.5
IV.5	I.iv.4
IV.7	I.iv.7
IV.8	I.iv.7
VIII.25	I.vii.5
IX.1[97]	I.xii.8
II.23[98]	I.xiv.9
	I.xiv.10
II.24[99]	I.xiv.11
II.26	I.xiv.12
II.29[100]	I.xiv.13
II.32[101]	I.xiv.29

[96] This table is a revised version of that given by Finsterwalder, *Die Canones Theodori*, pp. 229–31 (Anhang III).
[97] From Gildas, 9.
[98] From Vinnian, 36.
[99] From Vinnian, 37 and 38.
[100] From Vinnian, 44 and 45.
[101] From Vinnian, 47.

APPENDIX II

The *Hibernensis* and the Penitentials of Theodore

Hibernensis I.22.*b*. Qui
autem episcopum uel
presbyterum occiderit ad
iudicandum remittendus
est.

D 79. Qui autem
episcopum uel
presbiterum occiderit,
regi dimittendus est ad
iudicandum.

U I.iv.5. Qui autem
episcopum uel
presbiterum occiderit,
regis iudicium est de eo.

I.22.*c*. Episcopus non
exeat ad aliam parochiam
et suam relinquat, nisi
multorum episcoporum
iudicio et maxime
supplicatione perficiat.

D 136. Episcopus non
exeat ad aliam parochiam
et suam relinquat nisi
multorum episcoporum
iudicio et maxime
supplicatione perficiat.

XLVI.32.*c*. *In alia uero
sinodo*: Septem annis
peniteat, tribus quidem
districte, quatuor uero
remisse. Similiter de uiro
intelligenda, si et ipse

U I.xiv.4. Mulier
adultera .vii. annos
peniteat. Et de hoc in
canone eodem modo
dicitur.
Cf. *Conc. Ancyr.* xx
(xviii), *Interpr.*
Gall., ed. Turner II, 10:
'Si alicuius uxor
moechata fuerit aut ipse
moechatus fuerit, .vii.
annos peneteat'.

LIV.12.*a*. *Theodorus ait*:
Porci qui sanguinem
gustantes tetigerint
manducentur, sed si
cadauera mortuorum
lacerantes manducent,
carnes eorum non licet
comedi usquequo
macerentur.

D 23. Porci qui
sanguinem gustantes
tetigerint manducentur.
Sed qui cadauera
mortuorum lacerantes
manducent, carnes eorum
non licet commedere
usquequo macerentur.

U II.xi.7–8. Ergo porci
qui sanguinem hominis
gustant, manducentur.
Sed qui cadauera
mortuorum lacerantes
manducauerunt carnem
eorum manducare non
licet, usque dum
macerentur, et post anni
circulum.

b. Item. Si porcus sanguinem biberit, licet; si tantum gustauerit, nihil est.

LIV.13.*b. Theodorus* episcopus. Equum non prohibent, tamen consuetudo non est comedi.

D 22. Equum non prohibent; tamen consuetudo est non commedere.

U II.xi.4. Equum non prohibent, tamen consuetudo non est comedere.

LIV.14. *Theodorus episcopus* dicit: Greci carnem morticinam non dant porcis suis; pelles uero morticinorum ad calciamenta licet accipi, sed non in sanctum aliquid.

D 19. Greci carnem morticinam non dant porcis suis; pelles autem eorum ad calciamentum et lana et cornua licent accipi, sed non in sanctum aliquid.

U II.vii.7. Greci carnem morticinorum non dant porcis, pelles tamen uel coria ad calciamenta licent, et lana et cornua accipere licet; non in aliquod sanctum.

Si porci comedant carnem morticinorum, aut sanguinem hominis, non abiciendos credimus, nec gallinas equali modo. Animalia quae a lupis siue canibus consumantur, non comedenda, nisi porcis proiciantur et canibus, nec ceruus, nec caper si mortui inuenti fuerint.

D 20. Tamen si casu porci commederint carnem morticinorum aut sanguinem hominis non abitiendos credimus nec gallinas eodem modo.
D 21. Animalia quae a lupis uel a canibus consummantur non sunt commedenda nisi porcis et canibus; nec ceruus aut caprus si mortui inuenti sunt.

U II.xi.7. Si casu porci comedent carnem morticinam aut sanguinem hominis, non abiciendos credimus, nec

U II.xi.1. Animalia quae a lupis seu canibus lacerantur non sunt comedenda, nec ceruus nec capra, si mortui inuenti fuerint, nisi forte ab homine adhuc uiua occidentur prius, sed porcis et canibus dentur.

Pisces licent, quia alterius naturae sunt.

Pisces autem licent quia alterius naturae sunt.

U II.xi.3. Pisces autem licet comedere, quia alterius naturae sunt.

Aues et animalia cetera, si in retibus strangulentur, non sunt comedenda. Paulus enim ait: Abstinete uos a suffocato sanguine et ab idulatria. Similiter ab accipitre mortificanda.

D 168. Aues et animalia cetera si in retibus strangulentur non non sunt commedenda. Similiter accipitre mortua. Apostolus ait: Abstinete uos a a suffocato sanguine et ab idolatria.

U II.xi.2. Aues uero et animalia cetera si in retibus strangulantur, non sunt comedenda hominibus; nec si acci piter oppresserit, si mortua inueniuntur, quia in quar to capitulo Actus Apostolorum precipitur abstinere a fornicatione a sanguine soffocato et idolatria.

Equum non prohibet, tamen consuetudo non est comedere.

D 22. Equum non prohibent, tamen consuetudo est non commedere.

U II.xi.4. Equum non prohibent, tamen consuetudo non est commedere.

LXIV.5. *Sinodus An chiritana*: Qui diuinationes expetunt more gentilium, quinque annos peniteant.

U I.xv.4. De hoc in canone dicitur: qui auguria, auspicia siue somnia uel diuinationes quaslibet secundum mores gentilium obseruant, aut in domus suas huiusmodi homines introducunt, in exquirendis aliquam artem maleficiorum, penitentes isti, si de clero sunt, abiciantur; si uero seculares, quinquennio peniteant.

9

Theodore and the *Passio S. Anastasii*

CARMELA VIRCILLO FRANKLIN

The life and cult of the Persian soldier turned Christian martyr, Magundat-Anastasius, intersect at several points with what we know of the biography of Theodore of Tarsus.[1] Magundat-Anastasius, the older of the two, was a Persian soldier who took part in the siege of Chalcedon in 614–15. Tarsus in Cilicia, Theodore's city, had been abandoned to the advancing Persians by the emperor Heraclius only three years before, when Theodore was a young boy. The cult of Anastasius spread soon after his death in 628 to Constantinople, and perhaps even Cilicia, regions closely connected with Theodore's life. By 650 at the latest, and perhaps somewhat earlier, the relic of the head of Anastasius had been brought to the Cilician monastery *ad Aquas Salvias* in Rome where Theodore most likely had been living as a monk before being sent to Canterbury in 668. The cult of Anastasius also reached England between the middle of the seventh century and Bede's lifetime. My purpose here is to show that it was the Greek-speaking Theodore who was responsible for introducing the cult of the Persian convert to England.[2] New evidence suggests in fact that a Latin interlinear translation of the Greek *Acta* of Anastasius was found at Canterbury. It was most likely brought there by Theodore, perhaps as a gloss over the Greek. The technique of this translation and its linguistic

---

[1] For a brief overview of Anastasius and relevant bibliography, see *Bibliotheca Sanctorum* I (1961), 1055–6. I am preparing editions of all the Latin texts relating to St Anastasius. For what we can know of Theodore's career, see the remarks of Michael Lapidge, above, pp. 1–29, as well as fuller discussion in *Biblical Commentaries*, ed. Bischoff and Lapidge, pp. 5–81.

[2] W. Berschin, *Biographie und Epochenstil im lateinischen Mittelalter*, 3 vols. (Stuttgart, 1986–; in progress) I, 292, mentions but does not discuss the possibility that the cult of St Anastasius was brought to England from Rome by Theodore.

similarities to other works only recently attributed to Theodore suggest further that this Latin version may have been executed by the future archbishop of Canterbury himself.

The story of the life and martyrdom of Anastasius unfolds against the background of Persian advances and the occupation of the holy places in Palestine. In the opening years of the seventh century, the armies of Sasanian Persia under Chosroes II began a mighty offensive against the empire of Byzantium. Crossing the Euphrates, the Persians moved against Asia Minor in the west, Armenia to the north, and then swept south overwhelming Palestine. Jerusalem was captured in the spring of 614 after a brief siege; Palestine would remain under Persian occupation until 628. Thousands were massacred; many others, among whom was the patriarch Zacharias, were taken to Persia; the relic of the True Cross was sent to Ctesiphon as a trophy to the Persian (self-styled) 'King of Kings'.

Magundat,[3] the future Anastasius, was present as a *kaballarios* (καβαλλάριος) in the army led by Sayn when the True Cross arrived at Ctesiphon. Although the son of a *magus* (μάγου) and himself trained in 'the magical arts' (τῶν μαγικῶν μαθημάτων) of Zoroastrianism, the Persian soldier became curious about the religion of the Cross. After the siege of Chalcedon of 614/615, he deserted and began a series of travels which led him to Jerusalem, where he was baptized by Modestus, the vicar of the exiled patriarch of Jerusalem, and then he joined the monastery 'of Abbot Anastasius' outside the Holy City. Enflamed with a desire to emulate the example of the martyrs whose exploits he saw represented on the walls of the church, after seven years of settled monastic life Anastasius left his community and embarked on wanderings that culminated with his capture by the Persians in Caesarea and his trial and execution by strangulation at *Bethsaloe* (Kirkuk in modern Iraq) on 22 January 628. His head was then severed so that the seal which had been placed around his neck could be brought unbroken to the Persian king.

The Greek *Acta* (*BHG*, no. 84)[4] of the Persian soldier turned Christian

---

[3] The following details of the life of St Anastasius are taken from the Greek *Acta*, discussed below (and n. 4).

[4] *BHG*, no. 84 was published in two earlier editions: H. Usener, *Acta Martyris Anastasii Persae* (Bonn, 1894), pp. 1–12, and A. Papadopoulos-Kerameus, Ἀνάλεκτα Ἱεροσολυμιτικῆς σταχυολογίας IV (St Petersburg, 1897), pp. 126–48. More recently Bernard Flusin has produced new editions of all the Greek texts relevant to St Anastasius: *Saint Anastase le Perse et l'histoire de la Palestine au début du VIIe siècle*, 2 vols. (Paris, 1992); the

monk were written between March and 17 December 630 by a monastic confrere, based on the oral account provided by the companion whom the Abbot Justinus had assigned to comfort Anastasius and to witness his trials.[5] The main thrust of the *Acta* is to rejoice in God's choice of a martyr 'even from among the Persians'.[6] Together with the relics of the martyr's body, the *Acta* served as powerful instruments for the spread of the cult of the saint. Anastasius's body and severed head had at first been buried in the monastery of St Sergius near the place of his execution in northern Iraq. The account of how the relics were transferred – they were actually stolen – to Palestine, first to Caesarea and then to his monastery near Jerusalem, is provided by the Greek *Translatio* (*BHG*, no. 88), written soon after their arrival on 2 November 631, probably by the same monk who had composed the *Acta*.[7] But the Arab invasion of Palestine and the fall of Jerusalem in 638 forced the monks of 'Abbot Anastasius' to abandon their monastery and carry their relics with them.

THE CULT OF ST ANASTASIUS AT ROME

Before *c.* 650, the head of the Persian martyr, a copy of the Greek *Acta* and probably a miraculous icon, had been deposited at the Cilician monastery *ad Aquas Salvias* outside the walls of Rome.[8] This was one of the two

text of *BHG*, no. 84 is ed. *ibid.* I, 15–91. I am grateful to M. Flusin for the courtesy of making the typescript of his book available to me before publication. In what follows I give page and line numbers both to the edition of Usener (designated U) and that of Flusin (designated F). Chapter numbers, where given, refer to the edition of Flusin (Usener's text is continuous, and has no chapter-divisions).

[5] C. Vircillo Franklin and P. Meyvaert, 'Has Bede's Version of the *Passio S. Anastasii* come down to us in *BHL* 408?', *AB* 100 (1982), 373–400, at 399.

[6] *Acta*, ch. 5 (U, p. 2 = F, p. 45).

[7] Also ed. Usener, *Acta*, pp. 12–14, and Flusin, *Saint Anastase* I, 95–115. The account was written before 1 September 632, since the author says, μηνὶ νοεμβρίῳ δευτέρᾳ τῆς ἐνεστώσης πέμπτης ἰνδικτιῶνος (U, p. 14 = F, p. 105).

[8] For a survey of the texts concerning this monastery, see G. Ferrari, *Early Roman Monasteries* (Vatican City, 1957), pp. 33–48, and, correcting some of Ferrari's statements, J.-M. Sansterre, *Les Moines grecs et orientaux à Rome aux époques byzantine et carolingienne*, 2 vols. (Brussels, 1983), *passim*, but esp. ch. 1. Sansterre rejects the contention of U. Broccoli (*L'abbazia delle Tre Fontane. Fasi paleocristiane e altomedievali del complesso "ad Aquas Salvias" in Roma* (Rome, 1980), pp. 21–2) that the Cilician monastery existed already in the sixth century. Rather, Sansterre sees 604, the date of a letter by Pope Gregory I relative to the 'massa quae Aquae Salvias nuncupatur' (*Gregorii I*

Greek monastic communities whose early establishment in the eternal city is attested in the minutes of the second session of the Lateran Council of October 649.[9] The *terminus ante quem* for the arrival of the relic in Rome is provided by the addition of a gospel pericope (Mark V.21–34) noting the feast of St Anastasius in the archetype of the ancient Roman evangeliary which is dated *c*. 645.[10] The *terminus post quem* must remain the translation of the relics to Jerusalem at the beginning of November 631. It would seem tempting to conclude that the arrival took place under Pope Theodore (642–9), who was either himself a Greek from Jerusalem and/or whose father came from Jerusalem.[11]

It has been suggested that the founding of the Cilicians' monastery in Rome might be connected with the capture of Tarsus by the Persian general Shahrbaraz around 611, since the monastery was built on the location where tradition placed the beheading of Paul, the apostle venerated at Tarsus.[12] The monastery, called by different names at

---

Papae Registrum Epistolarum, ed. P. Ewald and L. M. Hartmann, 2 vols. (Berlin, 1899) II, 433–4) and which does not mention any sanctuary in this place, as a *terminus post quem* for the establishment of the Cilician monastery. Sansterre also maintains that it was a new foundation (I, 13–14 and II, 229). For a shorter treatment of his main conclusions, see also J.-M. Sansterre, 'Le Monachisme byzantin à Rome', *SettSpol* 34 (1988), 701–46.

[9] Mansi, *Concilia* 10, 904A [= 903A]. For full discussion, see Sansterre, *Les Moines grecs* I, 9–10. The other Greek house in existence at Rome in this period was the Armenians' 'Monasterium Renati' on the Esquiline: see Sansterre, *ibid.* I, 12–13.

[10] T. Klauser, *Das römische Capitulare evangeliorum. Texte und Untersuchungen zu seiner ältesten Geschichte: I. Typen* (Münster, 1935), p. 16, and discussion and further bibliography in Sansterre, *Les Moines grecs* I, 15 and n. 60. The itinerary *De locis sanctis martyrum quae sunt foris Romae* mentions the monastery 'Aquae Salviae, ubi caput sancti Anastasi est, et locus ubi decollatus est Paulus' (R. Valentini and G. Zucchetti, *Codice topografico della città di Roma*, 4 vols. (Rome, 1942) II, 109). This text, however, can no longer be considered the *terminus ante quem* since it has now been dated between 650 and 682–3 (H. Geertman, *More Veterum. Il 'Liber pontificalis' e gli edifici ecclesiastici di Roma nella tarda antichità e nell'alto medioevo* (Groningen, 1975), pp. 200–2). For further discussion of previous datings of the arrival of the relic of St Anastasius's head in Rome, see Sansterre, *Les Moines grecs* I, 14–17.

[11] Sansterre, *Les Moines grecs* I, 15.

[12] Flusin, *Saint Anastase* II, 372. This place was on the ancient road which went from the via Ostiensis to the via Ardeatina or, according to others, to the via Laurentina (Sansterre, *Les Moines grecs* I, 13). The ancient tradition that placed the decapitation of St Paul on this spot, and not on the via Ostiensis, was established already by the time of Gregory I.

first,[13] eventually came to be known generally as 'S. Anastasius ad Aquas Salvias', as it was at the end of the eighth century[14] when it was one of the principal monastic establishments of the city.[15] It became a regular stop on pilgrims' tours of the eternal city.[16] The power of the relic of the head of the saint venerated there is illustrated most spectacularly by the miraculous exorcism it performed in 713 on the daughter of a wealthy Syrian bishop and described in the so-called 'Roman Miracle', written in Greek in Rome but soon translated into Latin.[17] Both the Greek *Acta* and the account of a miracle performed by the icon at Caesarea soon after the martyr's death were quoted at the Seventh Oecumenical Council of 787 (= Nicaea II) to buttress the legitimacy of the cult of images.[18] But the discussions at Nicaea II testify that the centre of the cult of St Anastasius had moved to Rome, where both the relic and the icon were found.

[13] In the *acta* or 'minutes' of the Lateran Council, it is called 'de Cilicia qui ponitur ad Aquas Salvias'; it was also known as the monastery 'sanctae Dei genitricis semperque virginis Mariae ubi sanctus ac beatus Paulus apostolus decollatus est in loco qui appellatur Aqua Salvia ubi requiescunt venerabiles reliquiae beati martyris Anastasii' (as in the *Roman Miracle* (*BHG*, no. 89, ch. 4: U, p. 15 = F, p. 171)). The *Miracle* makes it clear that this is the monastery itself and not an oratory – a Latin oratory – dependent on the Greek monastery. Bede's entry in his *Chronica maiora*, 'monasterio beati Pauli apostoli, quod dicitur ad Aquas Salvias' (ed. T. Mommsen, *Chronica Minora III*, MGH, Auct. Antiq. 13 (Berlin, 1898), 310–11), clearly is tied to the martyrdom of St Paul which tradition placed here.

[14] In the *acta* of Nicaea II and in the *Liber pontificalis*, under Hadrian I: see Ferrari, *Monasteries*, p. 34, and Flusin, *Saint Anastase* II, 389–92.

[15] Sansterre (*Les Moines grecs* I, 108 and 149–50) discusses the role which the monastery might have played in the cure of souls in the surrounding countryside, and in developing the cult of St Anastasius as a thaumaturge. It was one of the longest-lived Greek monasteries in Rome. It appears still in the possession of 'Greek' monks around the first quarter of the eleventh century, when the biography of St Nilus (d. 1004) was being written. It is still in existence today, known as the Tre Fontane, having passed into the Cistercians' possession around 1140.

[16] For example, S. Anastasius was included in *De locis sanctis* and in the 'Malmesbury Catalogue'; King Liutprand of the Lombards visited it in 729 and kissed the relic. See Ferrari, *Monasteries*, p. 34, and Sansterre, *Les Moines grecs* I, 149.

[17] See above, n. 7. I am preparing a new edition of the Latin translation (*BHL*, no. 412). This text, an important document for our understanding of the Greek lay as well as monastic communities of the city, must be numbered among the original Greek works produced in Rome in the eighth century.

[18] At this council, legates of the Roman church cited how the Persian was led to martyrdom by images, and noted the existence of the icon in Rome; the bishop of

How and by whom the relic, the icon and the *Acta* of Anastasius the Persian monk were brought to Rome and deposited at the monastery 'ad aquas Salvias' remains unclear. It is possible that it was Palestinian monks from the Jerusalem area who carried them as they fled their homeland in the face of Arab invasion.[19] But there is some evidence, although very tentative, that suggests that it may have been Cilician monks themselves who brought the relic, the icon and the *Acta* to Rome and deposited them in their new monastery outside the Roman walls.[20]

Attached to the Greek *Acta* is a collection of miracles, written in Greek.[21] The story of the first fourteen follows the itinerary of the translation of the relics from Persia to Jerusalem in 631. The last three, however, are due to a continuator. They tell how a monk of Jerusalem (probably 'of Abbot Anastasius') went to Constantinople with the body and the icon of the saint, after passing through Syria, Cilicia and Cappadocia. While the factual narrative is a pretext for the telling of miracles, there may be a layer of truth in the account of the movements of the monk carrying his precious cargo toward Constantinople.[22]

The cult of St Anastasius is attested early on in Constantinople. Between 631 and 638 George of Pisidia, the famous court poet and deacon of Hagia Sophia, wrote an *Encomium* of the Persian monk which he recited before a gathering which included the patriarch Sergius and Anastasius's former teacher Pyrrhus, the future patriarch of Constantinople.[23] George's *Encomium* clearly presupposes the *Acta*, indicating that they were available

---

Taormina spoke of an exorcism performed in Rome: Mansi, *Concilia* 13, 24C-D. See also Sansterre, *Les Moines grecs* I, 149 and nn.

[19] Sansterre (*Les Moines grecs* I, 18–19) discounts earlier theories that proposed monothelism as the principal cause for the establishment of the oldest Greek monasteries in the eternal city.

[20] Sansterre, *Les Moines grecs* I, 16–17.

[21] Ed. Usener, *Acta*, pp. 20–8, and Flusin, *Saint Anastase* I, 111–53.

[22] It was because of this account that Usener thought that the cult of St Anastasius came from Rome to Constantinople, and not directly from Jerusalem (*Acta*, p. v). See also Sansterre, *Les Moines grecs* II, 72, n. 72.

[23] A. Pertusi, 'L'encomio di S. Anastasio, martire persiano', *AB* 76 (1958), 5–63. Pertusi provides convincing arguments for assigning this work to George of Pisidia rather than Sophronius; Pyrrhus, who is here identified as Anastasius's nameless teacher in the *Acta*, was to succeed Sergius on the patriarchal throne of Constantinople. Both of them were condemned for their adherence to monothelism and monoenergism at the Sixth Oecumenical Council. Pertusi's arguments and conclusions are accepted by Flusin, *Saint Anastase* II, 381–9.

at Constantinople within a few years of their composition;[24] but is silent on the relic and icon of the saint. However, in 1200 a visitor to the church of St Luke to the west of Constantinople reports the presence of the relic of 'St Anastasius, who is without head, because his head has been stolen'.[25] If Anastasius's body was in fact in Constantinople at this time, its arrival would have to be dated before the end of the eighth century, when the empress Irene and her son Constantine VI dedicated a church to him.[26]

There is finally the evidence that it was at the Cilicians' monastery in Rome that the relic and the icon were taken. But this can carry little weight, since the monastery of St Saba on the Aventine, the earliest Roman community of Palestinian monks, may not have existed by the time the cult of Anastasius reached Rome.[27] In sum, it seems at least plausible to suggest that after the Arab invasion of Palestine beginning in 633–4, the relics, the icon and the *Acta* of the Persian saint may have been carried away from Jerusalem as the monks of Palestine were forced to abandon their communities. All of the relics, or the body alone, may have gone to Constantinople. It was during these peregrinations that perhaps the head and icon of the saint came into the possession of Cilician monks who brought them to Rome when the Arabs first entered Cilicia in 640–1, or even earlier when Heraclius evacuated the province after the defeat of Yarmuk in 636 to prevent the provisioning of the Arabs in case of attack against Asia Minor.[28] The body was kept at Constantinople.

THE LATIN TRANSLATION OF THE GREEK *ACTA*
(*BHL*, NO. 410B)

When Albert Poncelet described the hagiographical manuscripts of

---

[24] Pertusi ('L'encomio', p. 23, n. 5) suggests that perhaps knowledge of the saint and an early draft of the *Acta* were brought to Constantinople by the armies of Heraclius.

[25] Anthony, archbishop of Novgorod; see B. de Khitrowo, *Itinéraires russes in Orient* I.1 (Geneva, 1889), 103 (G. P. Majeska has in preparation a new edition of this important work). See also Sansterre, *Les Moines grecs* I, 15 and n. 58.

[26] R. Janin, *La Géographie ecclésiastique de l'empire byzantin III. Les Eglises et les monastères*, 2nd ed. (Paris, 1969), p. 27.

[27] Sansterre, *Les Moines grecs* I, 28, basing himself on the Syriac life of Maximus the Confessor recently discovered by Sebastian Brock (see above, p. 50), dates the founding of St Saba between 647 and 653, but 'sans doute près de la première date que de la seconde'.

[28] Sansterre, *ibid.* I, 16–17.

Turin's Biblioteca Nazionale in 1909, he assigned the number 410b to an unpublished *Passio S. Anastasii*, adding, 'cf. *BHL* 408'.[29] He was thus summarizing his conclusions that the Turin text shared similarities with two of the lives of the Persian monk which were then known, the one numbered *BHL*, no. 408 and already published in the *Acta Sanctorum*,[30] and the other, *BHL*, no. 410, included in the collection known as the 'Magnum Legendarium Austriacum'.[31] A comparison of these three texts with the original Greek *passio*, however, exposed their true relationships. It revealed first of all that the Turin text (*BHL*, no. 410b) is the only surviving witness to an original Latin translation of the Greek *Acta*, and that *BHL*, nos. 408 and 410, are later, independent reworkings of this first Latin version.[32] Furthermore, the technique used by the editor of *BHL*, no. 408 and the history of the transmission of that text, indicate that this text was Bede's own revision of the *passio* of St Anastasius which he listed among his writings at the end of his *Historia ecclesiastica*, and that the text on which Bede's version was based is the original Latin translation, surviving as *BHL*, no. 410b, in the Turin manuscript.[33]

How did this early Latin version, a text clearly connected with the Greek community of seventh-century Rome, reach England and Bede? Benedict Biscop, the founder of Bede's monastery, who made several trips to Rome, and whose activity as a book collector for his foundation is well known, immediately comes to mind.[34] But a much stronger case can be made from the material discussed above, namely that it was Theodore who brought the knowledge of St Anastasius to England. There are, first of all, the historical connections which tie him to this saint, as discussed above. They both lived through the momentous events that shook the Middle East in the early seventh century. The Cilician monks who inhabited the monastery 'ad Aquas Salvias' may have been the ones to bring the relic, the icon and the *Acta* of the Persian martyr to Rome. And Theodore, a Cilician from Tarsus, was most likely a monk of this community before his departure for Canterbury in 668. This was first suggested in 1952 by

---

[29] A. Poncelet, 'Catalogus codicum hagiographicorum latinorum Bibliothecae Nationalis Taurinensis', *AB* 28 (1909), 417–75, at 431.

[30] *Acta SS*, Ian. II, 426–31.   [31] This version has not yet been published.

[32] Franklin and Meyvaert, 'Bede's Version', pp. 376–8.

[33] *HE* V.24 (pp. 568–70); Franklin and Meyvaert, 'Bede's Version', pp. 384–96.

[34] For Benedict Biscop's several trips to Rome to acquire books, see particularly Bede's *Historia abbatum*, chs. 4–6.

Anton Michel, who stated that Theodore was a monk at the monastery built on the spot associated with the decapitation of his compatriot, the apostle Paul of Tarsus.[35] Guy Ferrari, in his survey of Roman monasteries, pointed out that the only fact connecting Theodore with the monastery of S. Anastasius was their common origin in Cilicia; he concluded that while it is possible that Theodore was a monk there, and in fact might even have had a share in the actual establishment of the monastery 'de Cilicia', it is not certain that he was so. He might have been a member of one of the other monastic houses inhabited by Greek monks, such as St Saba or the *monasterium Renati*.[36] My argument that the *Passio S. Anastasii* was almost certainly brought to England by Theodore, and Michel's contention that Theodore was living at the monastery 'ad Aquas Salvias' when he was appointed by Pope Vitalian to the archbishopric of Canterbury, strengthen each other.

My argument is based first of all on a new piece of evidence which ties the *Passio S. Anastasii* (*BHL*, no. 410b) to Theodore and Canterbury. This text is linked in its transmission to the version of the *Passio SS Victoriae et Anatholiae* which Aldhelm, the most famous of the pupils at the school of Canterbury under Theodore and Hadrian, used in the composition of his *De uirginitate*. This would suggest that the point of arrival of *BHL*, no. 410b in England was Canterbury at the time of Theodore. Secondly, a study of the technique used by the translator of *BHL*, no. 410b reveals that this text began as an interlinear gloss. It is very possible, then, that *BHL*, no. 410b did not come to England as an independent Latin work, but as a gloss over the Greek text. The Greek-speaking Theodore, therefore, far better than Benedict Biscop, would have had reason to bring this work to England.[37] The language, finally, and particularly the approach to Latin exhibited in this translation are strongly reminiscent of those found in the Canterbury biblical commentaries discussed by Michael Lapidge as well as in Theodore's *Laterculus Malalianus* as discussed by Jane

[35] A. Michel, 'Die griechische Klostersiedlungen zu Rom bis zur Mitte des 11. Jahrhunderts', *Ostkirchliche Studien* 1 (1952), 32–45, at 41.

[36] Ferrari, *Monasteries*, pp. 39–40.

[37] A copy of *BHL*, no. 410b, could easily have reached Bede's monastery from Canterbury, for example through Benedict Biscop or through Albinus, Hadrian's successor as abbot of SS Peter and Paul in Canterbury; see discussion by Jane Stevenson, below, p. 218, who also points out (p. 210) that very few Anglo-Saxons are known to have visited Rome between 650 and 680.

Stevenson,[38] making it possible to advance the hypothesis that this early translation of the Greek *Acta* was the work of Theodore himself.

The evidence from Aldhelm

BHL, no. 410b is preserved in only one witness, Turin, Biblioteca Nazionale, F. III. 16 (Ottino, no. 24), a tenth-century collection of saints' lives from Bobbio.[39] As the abbey's saints are not included in this manuscript, however, the origins of the collection must be sought outside Bobbio. The first part of the manuscript, up to fol. 95, in which the *Passio S. Anastasii* is included, is a homogenous series of passions of martyrs, nearly all of whom are of eastern (particularly Palestinian) or Roman origins.[40] It does not include, however, the saints prominent in the sanctoral of the Roman church. The rest of the manuscript contains more texts of the same type plus a small number of hagiographical works related to monastic houses, especially continental Irish foundations. A large number of the *vitae* in this manuscript are translations from the Greek.[41] The nucleus of this collection, then, may have been a group of *passiones* originating from the Greek milieu of Rome. Many of these saints were also known in England. Out of thirty-three,[42] ten, for example, are included

---

[38] Stevenson, below, pp. 204–21; M. Lapidge, 'The School of Theodore and Hadrian', *ASE* 15 (1986), 45–72; *idem*, 'The Study of Greek at the School of Canterbury in the Seventh Century', *The Sacred Nectar of the Greeks: the Study of Greek in the West in the Early Middle Ages*, ed. M. W. Herren (London, 1988), pp. 169–94; and esp. *Biblical Commentaries*, ed. Bischoff and Lapidge, pp. 269–74.

[39] On the manuscript, see (in addition to Poncelet, cited above, n. 29), C. Cipolla, *Codici bobbiesi della Biblioteca nazionale universitaria di Torino con illustrazioni* (Milan, 1907), p. 154; G. Ottino, *I Codici bobbiesi nella Biblioteca nazionale di Torino* (Turin, 1890), pp. 20–2; A. Siegmund, *Die Überlieferung der griechischen christlichen Literatur in der lateinischen Kirche bis zum zwölften Jahrhundert* (Munich and Pasing, 1949), *passim*; and G. Philippart, *Les Légendiers latins et autres manuscrits hagiographiques*, Typologie des sources du moyen âge occidental 24–5 (Turnhout, 1977), 33, n. 31.

[40] The manuscript seems to be divided into parts by the handwriting, but also by the fact that, beginning on 95v, the arrangement of the texts *per circulum anni* is abandoned. In addition, the contents of the first part are much more homogeneous. I intend to present a thorough codicological study of this manuscript in a forthcoming publication.

[41] As already noted by H. Delehaye, 'Les Martyrs d'Egypte', *AB* 40 (1922), 5–154, at 126, n. 1; see also above, n. 37.

[42] I exclude from this list saints of the Irish foundations, and the very first work, a fragment of Ado's life of Augustine, because it was not part of the original manuscript.

in Bede's *Martyrologium*, and about fifteen in the Old English Martyrology.[43] This might mean that the Turin manuscript preserves in part a hagiographical collection which travelled from Rome to England and then back to the Continent.[44] For the present purposes, however, I wish to present a most significant connection between two texts preserved in the Turin manuscript and the *opus geminatum* on virginity written by Aldhelm, who belonged to the first generation of students educated at Canterbury after the arrival of Theodore and Hadrian.[45]

Among the numerous sources which Aldhelm used in the composition of the *De uirginitate* are found three hagiographical works that are also contained in the Turin manuscript. One is *BHL*, no. 1787, the *passio* of the virgin couple Chrysanthus and Daria, a fairy-tale concoction that circulated in both Latin and Greek redactions already in the sixth century. Their tomb on the via Salaria Nuova appears as a cult centre in the pilgrims' itineraries of the seventh century. The second is the story of the sisters Chionia, Irene and Agape (*BHL*, no. 118), preserved as part of a composite text treating the *passio* of Anastasia and the martyrs associated

---

[43] Included in Bede's *Martyrologium* are: SS Anastasia, Anastasius, Anatholia, Victoria, Eusebius (of Vercelli), Euphemia, Fausta, Ambrose, Felicitas and the Forty Martyrs of Sebaste: see J. Dubois and G. Renaud, *Edition pratique des martyrologes de Bède, de l'Anonyme lyonnais et de Florus* (Paris, 1976) as well as H. Quentin, *Les Martyrologes historiques du moyen âge* (Paris, 1908), pp. 17–119. Included in the Old English Martyrology are: SS Anastasia, Anastasius, Eleutherius, Anatholia, Symphorosa, Eusebius (of Vercelli), Afra, Mames, Euphemia, Fausta, Chrysanthus and Daria, Dionysius, Felicitas and the Forty Martyrs of Sebaste: see *Das altenglische Martyrologium*, ed. G. Kotzor, 2 vols., Bayerische Akademie der Wissenschaften, phil.-hist. Klasse: Abhandlungen n.s. 88 (Munich, 1981). Only textual comparisons can determine whether Bede and the Old English Martyrologist used the versions of the Bobbio manuscript. However, Quentin's and Kotzor's *BHL* identifications agree by and large with those of the manuscript.

[44] I hope to examine this issue at length in the near future.

[45] Aldhelm's *De virginitate* is ed. R. Ehwald, *Aldhelmi Opera*, MGH, Auct. Antiq. 15 (Berlin, 1919), 209–323 (prose) and 325–471 (verse). For a translation of the prose, see M. Lapidge and M. Herren, *Aldhelm: the Prose Works* (Cambridge, 1979), pp. 51–132; for the verse, see M. Lapidge and J. R. Rosier, *Aldhelm: the Poetic Works* (Cambridge, 1985), pp. 97–167. For a survey of Aldhelm's life and writings, see *Prose Works*, pp. 5–19. Scholars have not been able to date the *De virginitate* with any certainty. A recent dating of the prose work to 685–8 (F. Clark, *The pseudo-Gregorian Dialogues*, 2 vols. (Leiden, 1987) I, 163–4) is based on arguments already questioned in Lapidge and Herren, *Aldhelm: the Prose Works*, p. 14.

with her.[46] As these works do not at the moment appear to have existed in different versions,[47] no special relationship can be established at this point between the texts as transmitted in the Turin manuscript and the ones available to Aldhelm.

The case for the other hagiographical text common to Aldhelm's *De uirginitate* and the Turin manuscript is quite different. Both in the prose *De uirginitate* and in the corresponding poetic counterpart, Aldhelm had treated the two virgin saints Victoria and Anatholia together, their sisterly fate intertwined even though their exile, and then martyrdom, separated them.[48] Bede, however, commemorates these saints separately, Victoria on 23 December, Anatholia on 9 July, and seems unaware of any connection between the two virgins.[49] The Old English Martyrology commemorates Anatholia alone on 10 July.[50] This tradition, which probably originated from their different feast days resulting from their separate deaths, is reflected in the early known texts.[51] These are:

(1) *BHL*, no. 8591, a life of Victoria, published by the Bollandists in both a longer and shorter version from two thirteenth-century manuscripts;[52]

---

[46] For these saints, see *Bibliotheca Sanctorum* I (1961), 303–4, and IV (1964), 300–5, with bibliography. For the legends, see *BHL*; for Aldhelm's texts, see *De virginitate* (prose), chs. 35 and 50 (ed. Ehwald, pp. 276–80 and 305–7 respectively) and (verse) lines 1123–50 and 2194–278 (ed. Ehwald, pp. 404–5 and 443–6, respectively).

[47] The Bobbio texts appear to have only minor textual variants from the ones published, but I plan to undertake a full collation of the manuscripts.

[48] *De virginitate* (prose), ch. 52 (ed. Ehwald, pp. 308–10); (verse), lines 2350–445 (pp. 449–52).

[49] Dubois and Renaud, *Edition pratique*, pp. 228 and 122, respectively.

[50] *Das altenglische Martyrologium*, ed. Kotzor, pp. 145–6. Both saints are commemorated on this date in the *Martyrologium Hieronymianum*. There is no entry for 23 December in the Old English Martyrology. On the two saints, see *Bibliotheca Sanctorum* I (1961), 1076–82, and M. Grazia Mara, *I martiri della Via Salaria* (Rome, 1964), pp. 149–201, who provides a new edition of the *passio* (without, however, reference to *BHL*).

[51] Other texts not relevant are not discussed here. For a survey of all the texts concerning these two saints, see *BHL*. I should emphasize that the more important text in this regard is *BHL*, no. 8591 (rather than 418), because it is the one which underwent drastic revision.

[52] Ptd from Namur, Bibl. munic., 15, and Brussels, Bibl. royale, 206 in *AB* 2 (1881), 157–60 ('De S. Victoria'); the longer version is ptd *Catalogus Codicum Hagiographicorum Bibliothecae Regiae Bruxellensis* I (Brussels, 1886), 117–18. The text listed *BHL*, no. 8591, also contains at its beginning some indications about Anatholia's early life. Mara (*I martiri*) seems unaware of the Bollandists' publication of the longer text.

(2) *BHL*, no. 418, a fragmentary, clearly acephalous life of Anatholia's exile, conversion of her persecutor Audax, and death, published in the *Acta Sanctorum*;[53]

(3) *BHL*, nos. 8591a-d and 418a-c, described as a text in which the *passio* of Victoria is conjoined to that of Anatholia. A version of this text has been published based on a Beneventan manuscript of the late eleventh century (now Vatican City, Biblioteca Apostolica Vaticana, lat. 1197) as well as the aforementioned Bobbio codex now in Turin, BN, F. III. 16.[54] It is clear that this is the original text from which *BHL*, nos. 8591 and 418 are derived.

Students of the hagiographical dossier of the two saints had long speculated that the *passiones* of these two virgins must have been conjoined originally, and as the principal proof of their assertion they presented Aldhelm's treatment based on the presumed 'acta maiora' available to him but considered lost,[55] until the publication of the conjoint text (no. 3 above). This version follows the outlines of the story of the two virgins as told in Aldhelm's work. It begins with the courting of the two sisters by the suitors Eugenius and Aurelius, then describes their resistance, their separate exile, tribulations and death. As with many hagiographic legends, this *passio* was edited when it was copied into the legendaries which now preserve it. The published edition, however, frequently does not report important variant readings, and ignores three witnesses: Naples, Biblioteca Nazionale, XV. AA. 12 (s. x/xi); Florence, Biblioteca Laurenziana, Amiatino 2 (s. xi); and Florence, Biblioteca Nazionale, II. I. 412 (s. xiii).[56] The manuscripts themselves must then be consulted to

[53] *Acta SS*, Iul. II, 672–3.

[54] Mara, *I martiri*, pp. 172–201 (with facing Italian translation). On Vatican City, BAV, lat. 1197, see: *BHL, Supplementum* (1911), pp. 20 and 305; *Catalogus Codicum Hagiographicorum Latinorum Bibliothecae Vaticanae* (Brussels, 1910), pp. 63–4; M.-H. Laurent, *Codices 1135–1266* (Vatican City, 1958), pp. 119–23. For the Bobbio manuscript, see above, nn. 29 and 39.

[55] *Acta SS*, Iul. II, 671; *Aldhelmi Opera*, ed. Ehwald, p. 308, n. 3; Quentin, *Les Martyrologes*, pp. 95–6.

[56] For example, Mara's edition (p. 174, lines 17–18) reads 'vince diabolum et esto vera Victoria', while the Turin manuscript reads 'vince diabolo et esto vera Christi Victoria' which, however, is not recorded in the apparatus criticus; and elsewhere (p. 182, line 79), Mara's edition does not note the reading of the Turin manuscript 'sed et (*add.*) aliter'. Mara considers the Turin manuscript to be the archetype – which may very well be the case – but no cogent proof is offered. For the Naples manuscript, see A. Poncelet, 'Catalogus codicum hagiographicorum latinorum bibliothecarum neapolitanarum', *AB*

identify which tradition of the text was known to Aldhelm. The agreement in language of the Turin *passio* with Aldhelm's work, as against the other manuscripts, proves that this text is closely related to the version of the *passio* of the two virgins that Aldhelm used. A few examples will suffice to illustrate this point:

(1)   Aldhelm, *De uirginitate*, ch. 52 (ed. Ehwald, p. 308): '... beata Victoria praesago vocabulo vere *Christi victoria* ...'

Turin, BN, F. III. 16, 55r: '... Audi me sancta virgo Victoria et nomini tuo respondens vince diabulo et esto vera *Christi victoria* ...'

Vatican City, BAV, Vat. lat. 1197, 54r: '... Audi me sancta virgo Victoria et nomini tuo respondeo [*sic*] vince diabolum et esto *vera Victoria*.'

Naples, BN, XV. AA. 12, 23r: '... Audi me sancta Victoria et nomini tuo respondens vince diabolum et esto *vera Victoria*.'

(2)   Aldhelm, *De uirginitate*, ch. 52 (ed. Ehwald, p. 309): '... mancus manu arida et *elefantina* cutis callositate purulentus et *vermibus* scaturiens putidum exalavit spiritum'.

Turin, BN, F. III. 16, 57r: '... *helefantiosus* factus a *vermibus* expiravit'.

Vatican City, BAV, Vat. lat. 1197, 55v: '... *elefantiosus* factus exspiravit'.

Naples, BN, XV. AA. 12, 24r: '... *helefantiosus* factus in *vermibus* expiravit'.

Aldhelm used this hagiographical text beyond the immediate confines of his treatment of Victoria and Anatholia. It was a striking passage from this

---

30 (1911), 137–251, at 200–5 (nos. 7–8). For Amiatinus 2, see A. M. Bandinius, *Bibliotheca Leopoldina Laurentiana seu Catalogus manuscriptorum qui iussu Petri Leopoldi ... in Laurentianam translati sunt* I (Florence, 1791), p. 625. For Florence, Biblioteca Nazionale, II.1.412, see G. Mazzatinti, *Inventari dei manoscritti delle biblioteche d'Italia* VIII (Forli, 1989), p. 123. For present purposes, I am leaving aside both the Amiatinus manuscript, which contains a slightly abbreviated text, and Florence, BN, II.1.412, which is later. Both these manuscripts include, with the Naples manuscript, the phrase of passage 3 (discussed below) omitted by Aldhelm, the Bobbio manuscript and Vat. lat. 1197. F. Dolbeau, 'Recherches sur les oeuvres littéraires du pape Gelase II. B. Subsiste-t-il d'autres travaux de Jean de Gaète?', *AB* 107 (1989), 347–83, at 358, n. 43, as well as B. de Gaiffier in his review of Mara's book (*AB* 89 (1966), 270–2) point out the existence of numerous other manuscripts of the separated *passiones*, all of which would have to be consulted for a critical edition. It already seems clear that *BHL*, no. 8591, underwent drastic revision to make it conform to liturgical requirements.

passio that provided him with the tripartite definition of chastity as *virginitas*, *castitas* and *iugalitas* which he presents to the nuns at Barking, to whom his work is dedicated:[57]

(3) Aldhelm, *De uirginitate*, ch. 19 (ed. Ehwald, pp. 248–9):

Porro tripertitam humani generis distantiam orthodoxae fidei cultricem catholica recipit ecclesia, sicut in quodam volumine angelica relatione refertur ... ut sit virginitas divitiae, castitas mediocritas, iugalitas paupertas; ut sit virginitas pax, castitas redemptio, iugalitas captivitas; ut sit virginitas sol, castitas lucerna, iugalitas tenebrae; ut sit virginitas dies, castitas aurora, iugalitas nox; ut sit virginitas regina, castitas domina, iugalitas ancilla; ut sit virginitas patria, castitas portus, iugalitas pelagus; ut sit virginitas homo, castitas semivivus, iugalitas corpus; ut sit virginitas purpura, castitas rediviva, iugalitas lana. Omnia haec non sunt extra palatium; sed aliter sedet in carruca praefecturae dignitas, aliter mulionis vilitas, aliter qui pedibus continet mulas, et tamen sub uno imperatore militare noscuntur, et reliqua.

Turin, BN, F. III. 16, 56r:

Ut sit virginitas divitae [cf. Naples: divitia], castitas mediocritas, iugalitas paupertas; ut sit virginitas pax, castitas redemptio, iugalitas captivitas; ut sit virginitas sol, castitas lucerna, iugalitas tenebrae; ut sit virginitas dies, castitas aurora, iugalitas nox; ut sit virginitas regina, castitas domina, iugalitas ancilla; ut sit virginitas patria, castitas portus, iugalitas pelagus [Naples adds: ut sit virginitas caro sana, castitas cicatrix, iugalitas vulnus]; ut sit virginitas nova purpura, castitas rediviva, iugalitas lana; ut sit virginitas novus homo, castitas anima, iugalitas corpus. Omnia haec non sunt extra palatium; sed et aliter sedet in carruca sua praefecturae dignitatis [cf. Vat. and Naples: dignitas], aliter in carrucam [cf. Vat. and Naples: in eadem carruca] mulionis vilitas, aliter qui pedibus ambulans continet mulas; et cum praefectus et mulio et continens mulas [cf. Vat. *om.* et cum ... mulas; and Naples *om.* praefectus ... mulas] sub uno imperatore militare noscuntur. Habent tamen de suis gradibus unus magnitudinem, alius mediocritatem, tertius vero ultimae vilitatis [cf. Vat. and Naples: vilitati] occumbit [cf. Naples: subcumbit].

---

[57] Ehwald (*Aldhelmi Opera*, p. 248, n. 2) had noted the striking similarity, as well as the linguistic differences, between Aldhelm's passage and the longer version of *BHL*, no. 8591, published by the Bollandists from the Brussels manuscript. Lapidge and Herren (*Aldhelm: the Prose Works*, pp. 192–3, n. 19 and 194, n. 10) compared Aldhelm's text to the shorter version. Aldhelm acknowledges his use of a source when he introduces this discussion of virginity with the words, 'sicut in quodam volumine angelica relatione refertur', and he ends it with 'et reliqua' (ed. Ehwald, pp. 248 and 249).

Vatican City, BAV, Vat. lat. 1197, 54v:

Ut sit virginitas divitiae, castitas mediocritas, iugalitas paupertas; ut sit virginitas pax, castitas redemptio, iugalitas captivitas; ut sit virginitas sol, castitas lucerna, iugalitas tenebrae; ut sit virginitas dies, castitas aurora, iugalitas nox; ut sit virginitas regina, castitas domina, iugalitas ancilla; ut sit virginitas patria, castitas portus, iugalitas pelagus; ut sit virginitas nova purpura, castitas rediviva, iugalitas lana; ut sit virginitas novus homo, castitas anima, iugalitas corpus. Omnia haec non sunt extra palatium; sed aliter sedet in carruca sua praefecturae dignitas, aliter in eadem carruca mulionis vilitas, aliter qui pedibus ambulat et continet mulas; sub uno imperatore militare noscuntur. Habent tamen de suis gradibus unus magnitudinem, alius mediocritatem, tertius vero ultimae vilitati occumbit.

Naples, BN, XV. AA. 12, 23v:

Ut sit virginitas divitia, castitas mediocritas, iugalitas paupertas; ut sit virginitas pax, castitas redemptio, iugalitas captivitas; ut sit virginitas sol, castitas lucerna, iugalitas tenebrae; ut sit virginitas dies, castitas aurora, iugalitas nox; ut sit virginitas regina, castitas domina, iugalitas ancilla; ut sit virginitas patria, castitas portus, iugalitas pelagus; *ut sit virginitas caro sana, castitas cicatrix, iugalitas vulnus*; ut sit virginitas nova purpura, castitas rediviva, iugalitas lana; ut sit virginitas novus homo, castitas anima, iugalitas corpus. Omnia haec non sunt extra palatium; sed et aliter sedet in carruca sua praefecturae dignitas, aliter in eadem carruca mulionis vilitas, aliter qui pedibus ambulans continet mulas; et cum sub uno imperatore militare noscuntur, habent tamen de suis gradibus unus magnitudinem, alius mediocritatem, tertius vero ultimae vilitati subcumbit.

A more detailed discussion of the exact textual relationship between the Turin *Passio SS Victoriae et Anatholiae* and Aldhelm's work must wait until the complete history of the text of this legend can be unravelled.[58] For the present purposes, however, we can conclude from the above passages that Aldhelm's work agrees most consistently with the version of the *passio*

---

[58] Hagiographical legends, as is well known, are very fluid texts, and until all known manuscript witnesses are surveyed, the story of their full development remains incomplete. However, there is no question that Aldhelm mined this text thoroughly. As a further example, Aldhelm used (and expanded) the same biblical quotations as in the *passio* in his treatment of Elijah (*De virginitate*, ch. 20; ed. Ehwald, pp. 249–50). But Aldhelm characteristically made the material his own, by elevating the simple and unadorned language of his source, and by adding his own favourite authorities. In this passage, for example, he quotes Caelius Sedulius's *Carmen paschale* (I.179–80 and 182) to expand the biblical reference (IV Kings I.9–14) provided by his source.

preserved in the Turin manuscript. In passage (1), only the Turin manuscript's reading matches Aldhelm's *Christi victoria*. In passage (2), both the Turin and Naples manuscripts match the details given in the *De uirginitate*. But in passage (3), the Turin and Vatican manuscripts share the omission of one phrase with Aldhelm's work. Aldhelm's copy of the *passio* of the two virgins may very well be an ancestor of that preserved in the Turin manuscript. Thus we find more circumstantial evidence to support the view that Theodore brought the *Passio S. Anastasii* to England. For it is likely that *BHL*, no. 410b, joined to the *Passio SS Victoriae et Anatholiae* in this unique exemplar, may also have been present with it at Canterbury. For it must have been there that Aldhelm read the passion of the two virgins and then used it as one of his sources. Although little of Aldhelm's early life is certain, we know that he studied at Canterbury on two separate occasions.[59] The fuller picture that is emerging of this school under the tutelage of Theodore and Hadrian certainly indicates that a significant part of Aldhelm's prodigious learning must have been acquired there.[60]

Language and translation technique

A comparison of any passage of *BHL*, no. 410b, with the corresponding Greek text will immediately reveal how closely the translator followed his model.[61] The Latin translates the Greek word for word, line after line, brutishly following the word order of the Greek, and even transposing idioms and grammatical constructions, peculiar to Greek, into Latin. Syntactical and lexical choices are determined in this text by the wish, or

---

[59] Lapidge and Herren, *Aldhelm: the Prose Works*, pp. 7–8.

[60] It seems possible to me at this point that the *Passio SS Victoriae et Anatholiae* also was carried to Canterbury by Theodore from Rome, as part of the passionary nucleus of Turin F. III. 16. This text, however, unlike the stories of Chrysanthus and Daria and of Anastasius, does not seem to rest on a Greek original. I do not think it likely that Aldhelm himself obtained this work from Rome. Although a letter from one of his students refers to a trip to Rome (*Aldhelmi Opera*, ed. Ehwald, p. 494), this voyage cannot be dated, nor is there any evidence that Aldhelm brought back books. He died in 709. In this connection, I should again like to repeat Jane Stevenson's observation (cited above, n. 37) that very few Anglo-Saxons visited Rome in the seventh century. Another Latin text translated from the Greek, perhaps in Rome, and available in Anglo-Saxon England, is the *Passio S. Marci Evangelistae* (*BHL*, no. 5276), as was suggested to me by Paul Meyvaert, whom I thank. Both its Latin and Greek tradition are deserving of study.

[61] For extensive comparisons, see Franklin and Meyvaert, 'Bede's Version', pp. 379–80.

need, of the translator to remain faithful to the original. The Latin text in effect becomes a servile duplication of the Greek. Every Greek particle is translated, δέ being the most common, which is generally translated as *autem*, occasionally as *vero* and rarely as *at*. The particle μήν on the other hand is generally translated as *quidem*. The greatest problem resulting from the brutal servility is exemplified by the translation of the Greek article followed by a verbal noun, a participle or another phrase, with a Latin relative pronoun without, however, the use of a verb for the resulting Latin relative clause,[62] as in the phrase *quae flammam alentem desiderii illius* (16v) translating the Greek τὰ τὴν φλόγα τρέφοντα τῆς ἐπιθυμίας ἐκείνης (U, p. 4.25–6 = F, p. 55 (ch. 12.13–14)).

This desire to be faithful to the Greek is coupled with ignorance of, or indifference to, Latin grammar and usage. One major source of confusion is the translator's misuse of the syntax and endings of the Latin cases.[63] The genitive, dative and ablative are frequently used in each other's place; in many instances, furthermore, one declension's case ending is used for another. As a result, the source of the problem frequently is not clear. Consider the Latin sentence:

Sanctae autem civitati excidioni factae, et venerandorum atque adorandorum locorum igni combustis in praedicto irae propter peccata nostra, sumpta sunt et onoranda ligna (15v).

This sentence renders the following passage of Greek:

τῆς δὲ ἁγίας τοῦ θεοῦ πόλεως ἁλούσης καὶ τῶν σεβασμίων καὶ προσκυνουμένων τόπων πυρικαύστων γενομένων ἐν τῇ προειρημένῃ ὀργῇ διὰ τὰς ἁμαρτίας ἡμῶν, ἐλήφθη καὶ τὰ τίμια ξύλα (U, p. 2.13–16 = F, p. 47 (ch. 6.6–8)).

Did the translator think of *civitati* as a second declension genitive? Or that the genitive of the third declension was the same as the dative by analogy with the first declension feminine adjective *sanctae*? Just as unclear is also the intent of the translator in the phrase *excidioni factae*. Was this an attempt to parallel the Greek genitive absolute in Latin, in which *excidioni* fell victim to a similar case confusion as above, or was this actually an attempted Latin ablative absolute in which both noun and adjective were

---

[62] This construction, employed by the early translators of the Bible, also occurs in the *Aratus Latinus*, which was translated from Greek in Merovingian Gaul. See H. Le Bourdellès, *L'Aratus Latinus. Etude sur la culture et la langue latines dans le Nord de la France au VIIIe siècle* (Lille, 1985), esp. pp. 198–9.

[63] Stevenson (below, pp. 217–18) points out similar occurrences in the *Laterculus*.

given the wrong ending? The same wavering between Greek and Latin usage is found in the final phrase of this unhappy passage, where after *venerandorum atque adorandorum locorum* (to parallel the Greek genitive absolute) there is an inexplicable switch to the ablative *combustis*.

In other contexts, however, the source for the wrong case is easily discerned. Often, for example, the genitive singular and the nominative/ accusative ending of the third declension are interchanged, suggesting that the translator's knowledge of Latin was being acquired orally.[64] Most frequently, Latin usage imitates Greek usage. The 'genitive' *missas factas* (17r) derives from the s-ending of the corresponding Greek phrase (U, p. 4.33 = F, p. 57 (ch. 15.2): συνάξεως γενομένης). Prepositions are followed by the wrong Latin case, by analogy with the Greek.[65] Thus Latin *cum* is frequently followed by the genitive,[66] and *de* too is followed by the genitive.[67] In some cases, the translator neglected to decline nouns altogether, leaving them in the nominative.[68] Frequently, the wrong case can be explained by ignorance of the correct gender of nouns and adjectives, as in *mares* (14r) rather than *maria*, or *captiuus ... crux* (15r).[69]

Verbal usage also betrays a poor grasp of, or indifference toward, Latin, particularly in the use of voice. Often the Latin passive is used as though it were a middle, as in *suscepta pluviam* (15v) to translate δεξαμένη (U, p. 2.31 = F, p. 47 (ch. 7.7)).[70] Some intransitive Latin verbs are used transitively, such as (for example) *adquiesco*, which appears correctly in its intransitive meaning,[71] but also as a transitive verb, as in *adquieuerunt eos separatim ponere corpus eius* (22r), translating word for word ἔπεισαν αὐτοὺς

---

[64] As in the phrase *secte existentes* (16r), where *existentes* is used instead of *existentis*. Stevenson points out that frequently the 'mistake' reflects actual pronunciation. By the same token, *per auditu* (15r) might reflect the dropping of final *-m* in spoken Latin.

[65] My examples have numerous parallels in the *Laterculus*: see Stevenson's introduction to her forthcoming edition of that text.

[66] E.g. 'cum eorum ... captivorum' (20v).

[67] The phrase 'de quoquine quam etiam de horti' (16r). Note also mixed cases, such as 'inter me et aliis duobus sellariis' (19v).

[68] As in 'Sellarius ... christiano existenti' (21r). For parallels, see Stevenson's introduction to her forthcoming edition of the *Laterculus*.

[69] But 'honoranda atque uiuifica crux' on 14v! Again, Stevenson lists similar examples from the *Laterculus*.

[70] But in the following sentence δεξάμενος (U, p. 2.32 = F, p. 47 (ch. 7.8)) is translated better as *suscipiens*. Another example of a middle Greek form translated as a passive is *suspectus* (15v), translating the middle ὑφορώμενος.

[71] E.g. 'Adquiesce mihi' (18v) or 'Nec donis imperatoris tui adquiesco' (21r).

(U, p. 11.13 = F, p. 85 (ch. 39.6)). The word *quia* is used instead of the indirect discourse, as in *Scio quia confunderis propter congentiles tuos* (19v).[72] The construction *ut* with the subjunctive is occasionally used instead of a verbal noun, as in *amor ut inluminaretur* (15v) to translate ὁ πόθος τοῦ φωτισθῆναι (U, p. 3.24 = F, p. 51 (ch. 9.1)).

In addition to poor grammar, this text also betrays confusion and ignorance in the choice of words. In the phrase *quorum a suo patre edocuerat* (16v) which translates ὧνπερ παρὰ τοῦ ἰδίου πατρὸς μεμάθηκεν (U, p. 4.31–2 = F, p. 55 (ch. 13.3–4)), the word *doceo* is confused with *disco*. In the same passage, ἠξίου εὔχεσθαι (U, p. 4.1–2 = F, p. 55 (ch. 13.7)) is translated as *dignabat orare*, which probably stems from confusing the translation for ἀξιοῦμαι/ἄξιος with that for ἀξιόω.[73] Most frequently, however, the mechanical use of a glossary determines the choice of the Latin word used to translate a Greek word. Thus, for example, in this same passage we find the verb *submisit* (in the phrase *submisit ei cogitationes malignas*) used to translate ὑπέβαλλεν (U, p. 4.30 = F, p. 55 (ch. 13.2)). And in fact the most extensive Greek-Latin glossary to have survived, the pseudo-Cyril glossary, reads ὑποβαλλῶ. *subicio suggero submitto subdo.*[74] The choice available to the translator may very well have been similar to the one provided by the pseudo-Cyril glossary. Examples of words having the wrong connotations for a particular passage are extremely numerous. Sometimes these are quite common words, such as *amor* above used to translate πόθος.

The translation of a text such as *BHG*, no. 84, in fact required a comprehensive Greek-Latin dictionary. If one compares the vocabulary of *BHL*, no. 410b, with the two Greek-Latin general dictionaries that have survived, the fragment *Folium Wallraffianum* and the pseudo-Cyril, it becomes clear that there are connections between the *Passio S. Anastasii* and these glossaries.[75] But the conclusion that the translator used either of

---

72 Stevenson, in the introduction to her forthcoming edition of the *Laterculus*, has several similar examples.

73 A similar confusion results in translating ἀξιωθῆναι (U, p. 3.25–6 = F, p. 51 (ch. 9.2)) as *dignaretur* (15v).

74 'Glossae Graeco-Latinae', in *Corpus Glossariorum Latinorum*, ed. G. Goetz, 7 vols. (Leipzig, 1888–1923) II, 465.

75 For the background of what follows, see the excellent discussion by Carlotta Dionisotti, 'Greek Grammars and Dictionaries in Carolingian Europe', in *The Sacred Nectar of the Greeks*, ed. Herren, pp. 1–56, esp. 6–15. The *Folium Wallraffianum* is ed. J. Kramer, *Glossaria bilinguia in papyris et membranis reperta* (Bonn, 1983), pp. 51–9.

them cannot be reached. This would be impossible to do in any case for the *Folium Wallraffianum*, which is a single leaf from a papyrus codex written in Constantinople in the sixth century. It consists of only eighty entries, arranged alphabetically, from [πα]ραχειμάζει. *hibernat hiemat* to παροι-μία. Only three words used in *BHG*, no. 84, are found in the *Folium*. Two of these are translated by *BHL*, no. 410b, with the same word as in the *Folium*. One of these two words, furthermore, occurs three times in the Greek *Acta* and is translated with two different words in *BHL*, no. 410b; both of these Latin terms are found in the *Folium* entry.[76] The third word, however, is translated in a slightly different way in *BHL*, no. 410b.[77]

Much more evidence is available to evaluate the relationship between *BHL*, no. 410b, and the pseudo-Cyril glossary, the most extensive Greek-Latin dictionary to have survived from late antiquity, a dictionary with a multiplicity of sources, and by far the most complex and sophisticated such tool compiled in the Middle Ages. While its original purpose was to help Greek speakers understand Latin, in its final form it may have been compiled in Byzantine Italy for western users. Its compiler was not a Latin speaker, since his numerous mistakes betray a lack of mastery of Latin grammar and idiom.[78] A sporadic check for similarities between pseudo-Cyril and *BHL*, no. 410b, reveals that the glossary and the text agree more than 60 per cent of the time in the way they translate Greek words.[79]

This degree of agreement suggests that while the translator of *BHL*, no.

---

[76] These words are: (1) παρρησία (U, pp. 5.15, 6.21 and 10.13 = F, pp. 57 (ch. 16.5), 65 (ch. 22.8) and 83 (ch. 37.17), respectively) translated as *fiduciam* (18v and 21v) and *constantiam* (17r); cf. *Folium*, ed. Kramer, p. 53: 'παρρησία κατὰ χάριν fiducia constantiam', and pseudo-Cyril, p. 399: 'παρρησία licentia fiducia confidentia'; (2) παρέ-χομέν σοι (U, p. 5.25 = F, p. 61 (ch. 19.7–8)) translated as *prebemus tibi* (17v); cf. *Folium*, ed. Kramer, p. 52: 'παρέχει praestat praebet' and pseudo-Cyril, p. 398: 'παρέχω adhib[eo pre]beo tribuo' (with my reconstruction of a five-letter lacuna).

[77] This is παρερχόμενος (U, p. 5.11 = F, p. 57 (ch. 16.2)), translated as *pertransiens* (17r). Cf. *Folium*, ed. Kramer, p. 52, line 46: 'παρερχεται transit', but also pseudo-Cyril, p. 398: 'παρερχομαι pretereo transeo transgredio'.

[78] Dionisotti, 'Greek Grammars', p. 11, points out, for example, that the compiler reproduced the mistakes of his source in the gender of many Latin nouns, and that he created forms such as *sprevo, pepero* and *censuo* from his source's *sprevi, peperi* and *censuit*.

[79] I have checked several passages, eliminating the most common words which, if included, would increase the rate of agreement. Furthermore, actual agreement is even higher because I counted words not found in pseudo-Cyril among the non-agreements, rather than eliminating them from the sample.

410b, did not use pseudo-Cyril, at least as we now have it,[80] he very likely must have used something quite similar to it, perhaps a source used by the compiler of pseudo-Cyril, or another glossary that shared a common source with pseudo-Cyril. It is interesting to note, for example, that in some cases when the translation of a Greek word in *BHL*, no. 410b, does not occur in pseudo-Cyril, it is found in pseudo-Philoxenus, the most comprehensive Latin-Greek glossary to have survived and which, it is believed, must have shared at least one common source with pseudo-Cyril.[81] For example, the word μαθημάτων (U, p. 2.9 = F, p. 47 (ch. 6.3)) is translated quite well as *discipline* in *BHL*, no. 410b (15r). While pseudo-Cyril (p. 363) translates this word as *documentum studium*, pseudo-Philoxenus (p. 51) reads *disciplina* ἀγωγή ἐπιστήμη μάθησις. Carlotta Dionisotti has suggested that the similarities between the two glossaries are best attributed to a common, shared source rather than to a proto-glossary from which both derive; and perhaps this glossary, or one closely related to it, was available to the translator of *BHL*, no. 410b.[82]

Interlinear glossing

The mechanical, literal nature of this translation provides some indications about the material conditions under which it was executed. The 'barbarity' of the language suggests that this text in Latin was not intended to be read independently of the Greek. It does not seem likely, in other words, that the original translation with its utter disregard for the rules of Latin grammar and diction was meant as a substitute for the Greek text for Latin readers. Rather, such servile rendering of the Greek suggests another purpose. This translation could have been a first draft, to be reworked later

---

80 For one thing, pseudo-Cyril may not yet have been available. Dionisotti ('Greek Grammars') has not suggested a date for its compilation; the earliest surviving manuscript, London, BL, Harley 5792, was written in Italy *c.* 800.

81 Dionisotti, 'Greek Grammars', pp. 6–11. It is ptd *Corpus Glossariorum Latinorum*, ed. Goetz II, 1–212.

82 Dionisotti, 'Greek Grammars', p. 36, n. 23. On some occasions, *BHL*, no. 410b, uses translations which find echoes in each glossary. Thus ὑπομονὴν (U, pp. 3.34, 4.23, 7.15 and 8.8 = F, pp. 51 (ch. 9.7), 55 (ch. 12.13), 67 (ch. 24.3) and 73 (ch. 30.2), respectively) is translated as *tollerantiam* (16r) as in pseudo-Cyril, and as *perseverantiam* (16v, 18v and 20r) as in pseudo-Philoxenus. But it should also be noted that not every word which occurs in *BHG* no. 84/*BHL* no. 410b is found in either pseudo-Cyril or pseudo-Philoxenus.

by somebody better skilled in Latin. There are numerous examples of such two-step translations in the West, the most famous being perhaps Gregory of Tours's version of the *Legend of the Seven Sleepers of Ephesus* based on John the Syrian's literal translation into Latin.[83] We also have several examples of such two-step translations from Naples.[84] Or it may have been prepared as an aid to the comprehension of the Greek text for Latin readers, and it may not have been meant ever to stand on its own, as was the case, for example, with the *Aratus Latinus*.[85] It could also have been an exercise executed by someone beginning to learn Latin. One needs to ask the question, therefore, whether this translation of the Greek *Acta* of St Anastasius could have been executed as an interlinear gloss, rather than as an independent text written separately from the Greek. The method of the translation as an interlinear gloss would be consistent with any of the above purposes.

As *BHL*, no. 410b, has survived only as an independent text and not as an interlinear gloss, what evidence can be adduced that it may have begun its existence as a translation over the Greek source? There is first of all the fidelity to the Greek word order in the Latin text. Such close adherence would easily be explained if one assumes that the translator was writing the translation directly on top of the Greek and that later, when the Latin text was copied out as an independent work, the same word order was kept.[86]

Another piece of evidence in support of the theory that the original translation was done as an interlinear gloss is the fact that the original translator had left at least two phrases untranslated, that he had, in other words, left *visible blanks*. When Marzabanas is trying to convince Anastasius to return to his former life, he promises him ἄλογα καὶ μιλιαρίσια καὶ συγκρότησιν (U, p. 5.25–6 = F, p. 61 (ch. 19.8)). In the Turin manu-

---

83 *De gloria martyrum*, ch. 95: 'passio eorum, quam Siro quodam interpretante in Latino transtulimus' (ed. B. Krusch, MGH, SRM I, 109).

84 Some of these have been discussed by F. Dolbeau, 'Le Rôle des interprètes dans les traductions hagiographiques d'Italie du Sud', *Traduction et traducteurs au moyen âge* (Paris, 1989), pp. 145–62.

85 See above, n. 62.

86 As I shall suggest in my edition of *BHL*, no. 410b, there is clear evidence that the original translation has undergone some revision before or while being copied into the Bobbio manuscript. This transitional stage would explain the few cases in which the Latin word order is different in very minor ways from the Greek.

script (17v), this phrase appears as *iumenta ut scis militaris et continentiam*. If we assume that the translator had written as follows over the line:

iumenta et   et   continentiam
ἄλογα καὶ μιλιαρίσια καὶ συγκρότησιν

leaving a blank for μιλιαρίσια, then we can explain *scis militaris* as a clumsy transliteration of καὶ μιλιαρίσια. The scribe who copied the over-the-line gloss, in other words, saw the blank and transliterated the Greek letters as best he could, which would eventually lead to the reading *ut scis militaris* of *BHL*, no. 410b.

One might argue that the translator was writing the text independently to begin with and that, not knowing how to translate καὶ μιλιαρίσια, he transliterated these words in Latin or wrote them out in their proper alphabet, and that this is the source of the reading *ut scis militaris*. This explanation, however, does not account for the word *ut*. If we assume an interlinear translation, on the other hand, we can reason that the original translator wrote *et* (thus translating καὶ) and then left a blank. But the later scribe – ignorant of Greek – did not realize that and filled in the blank with καὶ μιλιαρίσια, thus explaining the presence of both *ut* and *scis* where *ut* may represent a later feeble attempt to make sense out of the Latin (*ut sis militaris*).[87] In other words, the double translation of καὶ is more easily explained by an interlinear blank left by the translator and noted by the scribe of the ancestor of our current text.

Another passage left untranslated originally occurs in the phrase ἠρώτα τὸν ἑαυτοῦ ἐπιστάτην (U, p. 4.12–13 = F, p. 53 (ch. 12.6)), which should be translated as *interrogabat suum magistrum*.[88] The Turin text (16v) instead reads *interrogabat super his tam*. This must be explained again by assuming that, for some reason, the words τὸν ἑαυτοῦ ἐπιστάτην had not been translated; the wording *super his tam* results from *super* = ἐπι; *his* = -ισ-; and *tam* = τάτην.[89] In other words, the scribe of Turin's

---

87 The scribe of the copy at the head of the tradition which resulted in *BHL*, nos. 408 and 410 knew Greek, since these texts read *pecuniam* and *argenteos et aureos*, respectively. Theodore had precise interests in weights and measures, esp. coinage: see Lapidge, 'The School', p. 61, and *Biblical Commentaries*, ed. Bischoff and Lapidge, pp. 262–3.

88 Which is exactly the text as it is preserved in *BHL*, no. 408; *BHL*, no. 410, a highly shortened text, skips *suum magistrum*.

89 Admittedly, *tam* could be a later attempt to make sense of the Latin. Or could this be an attempt to suppress the name of the monothelete Pyrrhus? See above, n. 23.

ancestor attempted in this way to complete the translation.[90]

There is finally a third category of evidence to support the contention that the original translation was written first over the Greek text. *BHL*, no. 410b contains two phrases incorporated into the regular text that clearly must have originated as glosses written in the margin of the Greek manuscript used by the translator. The first of these phrases occurs in the preface, and has already been discussed.[91] It is the statement, 'ego Modestus indignus archiepiscopus Hierusolimae sanctae Dei ciuitatis', which can be adduced as evidence that the original Greek *Acta* were commissioned by Modestus, patriarch of Jerusalem. At the point in the text where the author says that he has been commanded to write the life of Anastasius, Modestus indicated his role in the composition of the work in his own copy of the *Acta*. This note was then translated as a marginal note.

The second marginal note is the phrase 'et ille quidem compatiebatur ei', which is also found only in the Turin manuscript incorporated in the following passage (16v):

Abbati uero	τῷ ἀββᾷ δὲ
quae cordis eius erant	τὰ τῆς ἑαυτοῦ καρδίας
denudans cum multarum	ἀπογυμνώσας μετὰ πολλῶν
lacrimarum	δακρύων
et ille quidem compatiebatur ei	
dignabat orare pro eo.	ἠξίου εὔχεσθαι ὑπὲρ αὐτοῦ
	(U, p. 4.35 = F, p. 55 (ch. 13.6))

There is nothing to correspond to this phrase in any of the surviving Greek manuscripts or later Latin texts. In fact, this phrase does not fit the syntax of the Greek passage in which it would have to be situated; nor does it fit into the Latin text which preserves it. But as is also the case with the first marginal note discussed above, this phrase makes perfect sense if one thinks of it in relation to the context of the story. Just as the note about

---

[90] The scribe of the ancestor of the two Latin revisions, on the other hand, understood and correctly translated *suum magistrum*. A very similar occurrence took place in the transmission of the *Aratus Latinus*, which originated as an interlinear gloss over the Greek text in *scriptura continua*, where ὡράων, ὄφρ' ἔμπεδα was translated as 'horas *quae hon*ophrem puerum' by the original translator, where ων is translated both as *quae* and then incorporated as '*hon*ophrem' by the scribe who filled the blank. Another parallel – this time of the later scribe trying to make Latin sense of the Greek – is *dat et arphiae*, which corresponds to δ' ὅτε ταρφεῖαι. See Le Bourdellès, *L'Aratus Latinus*, pp. 47–8.

[91] Franklin and Meyvaert, 'Bede's Version', pp. 396–9.

Modestus could not possibly have been added by a Latin scribe, but was added by the archbishop himself, this phrase also originated in the historical context in which the *passio* was originally composed. It harks back to the monastery in which Anastasius spent those seven years before striking out in search of martyrdom. At this point in the story, Anastasius is telling the abbot his premonitions of early death, and shedding copious tears, begs him to pray for him. The note is a marginal addition made by someone who knew the details of that interview in the back of the church, perhaps Abbot Justinus himself, or perhaps another monk of the monastery of Abbot Anastasius. Or perhaps it may have been Modestus, whose connection with the events of Anastasius's life is narrated in this *passio*. Perhaps this note was meant as a correction to or amplification of the text and not purely as a marginal annotation. In any case, it cannot have been an integral part of the text, or its survival only in the Turin manuscript could not be explained. If we assume that the original translation was written as an interlinear gloss, and that the translator also translated these marginal notes, the result would not be very neat; occasionally it would run over the line. In such a case, the Latin translation of the marginal notes and of the text could easily have been confused, as they were in the textual transmission of the Turin manuscript.[92]

The evidence proves conclusively, I believe, that *BHL*, no. 410b, originated as an interlinear gloss rather than as an independent Latin text. It could, therefore, have been brought to England as such over the Greek text. The Canterbury biblical commentaries which reflect the teaching of Theodore are saturated with learning derived from Greek patristic texts.[93] The question of whether Theodore was quoting from memory, or whether in fact he carried the writings of the Greek fathers to Canterbury with him can now be answered, although not completely. Some Greek patristic works were certainly available at Canterbury, as was the Chronicle of John Malalas.[94] In addition, other Greek texts, such as Epiphanius's rare work *De .xii. gemmis*, and a Greek acrostic poem on the Day of Judgement, are

---

[92] Another copy, however, was made of the interlinear translation. This one did not include the marginal notes, and it was the ancestor of the models used by the authors of *BHL*, nos. 408 and 410.

[93] See *Biblical Commentaries*, ed. Bischoff and Lapidge, pp. 205–33, as well as Lapidge, 'The Study of Greek', p. 178.

[94] See discussion by Jane Stevenson, below, p. 212.

also attested in late seventh-century England.[95] We should at least allow the possibility that Theodore brought to England the Greek *passio* of St Anastasius with its accompanying interlinear Latin gloss. Of all the saints in the calendar, none had such close personal ties to the archbishop.[96]

CONCLUSIONS

The translator's latinity allows these conclusions to be carried even further. It is consistent with Theodore's approach to that language, as illustrated both by the Canterbury biblical commentaries edited by Bischoff and Lapidge as well as by the *Laterculus Malalianus* discussed by Jane Stevenson. *BHL*, no. 410b, is replete with Greek words used as if they were Latin, such as *schema* (17v), or latinized, such as *humanari* (20v) – which is also used in the *Laterculus*, ch. 4 – or *convalescebat* (17r), which is used not in its usual Latin meaning but rather as a calque on Greek διισχυρίζομαι. One correspondence between the Canterbury biblical commentaries and the *Passio S. Anastasii* stands out. In the commentaries the opinion was expressed that *praetorium* was a Greek word: 'Praetorium grece, latine curia dicitur.'[97] In the Greek *Acta* this word is used as if it were in fact a Greek word to explain the Persian term *derbas*: ἔμπροσθεν τοῦ δερβᾶς, ὅ ἐστιν πραιτώριον τοῦ σελλαρίου (U, p. 5.22–3 = F, p. 59 (ch. 17.2)); cf. the Turin text, 'ante derbas quod est praetorium sellarii' (17r). Theodore's

---

95 The evidence is summarized by M. Lapidge, 'The Present State of Anglo-Latin Studies', *Insular Latin Studies*, ed. M. W. Herren (Toronto, 1981), pp. 45–82, at 47–8; see also *Biblical Commentaries*, ed. Bischoff and Lapidge, pp. 185–6 and 213–14.

96 This of course raises the possibility that it was Modestus's own copy which came into Theodore's possession (Franklin and Meyvaert, 'Bede's Version', pp. 396–9). That is not impossible. Theodore could have gotten this copy either in Rome or in Constantinople, or even in Cilicia. The possibility that the marginal notes in the Greek manuscript might also have been copied from Modestus's copy cannot, furthermore, be completely rejected. Since *BHL*, nos. 408 and 410, clearly depend from a copy of *BHL*, no. 410b, which did not incorporate the marginal notes, and since it now seems likely that the Bobbio copy ultimately derived from England, one can only conclude that the Latin text which travelled to England either had the marginal notes as marginal notes, or that it was in fact a gloss over a copy of the Greek text which contained the marginal note. Theodore is also thought to have introduced the cult of St Milus, bishop of Susa (Persia), into his diocese; see discussion by Christopher Hohler, below, pp. 225–6, and Lapidge, 'The School', p. 49, n. 27.

97 EvII 85 (*Biblical Commentaries*, ed. Bischoff and Lapidge, p. 412); see also Lapidge, 'The Study of Greek', p. 183.

discussion in the biblical commentaries of this word as if it were a Greek term is reflected precisely in the way the word is used in the Greek *Acta*.[98]

In the treatment of biblical quotations, as well, the translator of *BHL*, no. 410b, follows a practice consistent with that of the *Laterculus* and the Canterbury biblical commentaries.[99] By and large, he quotes the Vulgate verbatim, departing in this respect from the Greek Bible as it is cited in the *Acta*.[100] At other times, however, he modifies the biblical quotation so as to remain faithful to the Greek *Acta*.[101] But, clearly, the translator of *BHL*, no. 410b, must have known the Latin Bible to some considerable extent, because his choice of words – even in cases where he is more faithful to the Greek *passio* – reveals familiarity with the Vulgate.[102]

Bede characterized the text now numbered *BHL*, no. 410b, as 'male de greco translatum'.[103] This judgement of a work which now is perhaps to be attributed to Theodore himself contrasts sharply with the praise which the historian lavished on the archbishop, whose scholarship, along with

---

[98] Pertusi ('L'encomio', p. 28, n. 2) points out that *derbas* and *sellarios* are hellenized middle Persian words.

[99] See *Biblical Commentaries*, ed. Bischoff and Lapidge, pp. 190–9, as well as Lapidge, 'The Study of Greek', pp. 171–3.

[100] For example, where the author of *BHL*, no. 410b, quotes Luke XXI.15 exactly as in the Vulgate text (18v), which adds *et contradicere* to the Greek New Testament as quoted in the Greek *Acta* (U, p. 7.2 = F, p. 67 (ch. 23.11–12)).

[101] As, for example, at 22r. Here, in writing the words 'et custodit dominus omnia ossa eorum unum ex eis conterere *non permittens*' (Ps. XXXIII.21), the translator translates the Greek *Acta* verbatim, where the words μὴ συγχωρῶν (U, p. 11.21 = F, p. 87 (ch. 39.11–12)) are added to the LXX text. The Latin translation 'iuxta LXX' also reads *non conteretur*.

[102] In the above quotation, for example, his use of *conteretur* echoes the Psalm version 'iuxta LXX'. As one would normally expect, it was the psalter 'iuxta LXX', then in use in Rome, which the translator used. The psalter 'iuxta Hebraeos' here reads *confringetur*. There is one case where the translator of *BHL*, no. 410b, missed a biblical reference. The Greek *Acta* (U, p. 11.11 = F, p. 85 (ch. 39.5)), in describing the support provided for Anastasius by the family of Yesdin, refer to Ex. XVII.12, where Aaron and Hur *held up* Moses's weary arms during battle. In rendering ὑπερείδοντες as *superdespicientes*, the translator reveals that he did not catch the biblical allusion. It should be noted that the author of a later translation, *BHL*, no. 411, also failed to notice this reference, as did two modern editors of the Greek *Acta*. The allusion was kindly pointed out to me by Bernard Flusin.

[103] *HE* V.24 (pp. 568–70): 'et peius a quodam imperito emendatum'. It is not absolutely clear how Bede knew that this was a translation from the Greek. I will treat this issue, and the question of emendations, in my forthcoming study of the Latin *passiones*.

Hadrian's, 'attracted a crowd of students into whose minds they daily poured the streams of wholesome learning', and Bede goes on to remark that some of these pupils knew Latin and Greek as well as their native tongue.[104] It would seem that such a learned man could not have been responsible for a work for which Bede shows such disdain. Yet although he was writing only a generation after Theodore's death, Bede provides surprisingly few details concerning the exact nature of Theodore's scholarship. He ascribes no works to him. He tells almost nothing of Theodore's life and education before he came to England as an old man. Clearly, Bede did not know the name of Theodore's Roman monastery, or he would have mentioned it either in his *Historia ecclesiastica* or in his *Chronica maiora*, where he discusses the monastery 'ad Aquas Salvias'.[105] Theodore's early life, education and scholarly activity are only now coming to light. Recent studies have emphasized his Greek intellectual orientation, and his disregard – even ignorance – of Latin in fact confirms Bede's own emphasis on Theodore's Greek learning, that until now could be dismissed as an exaggeration. The *Passio S. Anastasii*, 'poorly translated from the Greek', reveals ignorance of Latin, not of Greek. When compared to the *Laterculus* and the Canterbury biblical commentaries and glosses, it illustrates to a much greater extent the characteristics present in these works. If indeed it is the work of Theodore, this translation of the Greek *Acta* of Anastasius must have been done much earlier. Perhaps this version was composed as an exercise when Theodore was learning Latin in Rome, rather than during his old age in England, by which time his acquired Latin would naturally have improved.[106]

---

[104] *HE* IV.2 (pp. 333–4).   [105] *Chronica Minora III*, ed. Mommsen, pp. 310–11.

[106] This would also help to explain the systematic use of a glossary and the inconsistent, almost tentative, way terms are translated. For example, ἀργυροκόπον τὴν τέχνην (U, pp. 3.22 and 36.6 = F, pp. 49 (ch. 8.7) and 51 (ch. 10.2)) is translated as *argentariae artis* (15v) and better as *argentarium arte* (16r). It is possible of course that these are later corrections, which a scribe then incorporated into the text. But if so, one would have to explain why the 'corrector' did not correct more thoroughly. If Theodore followed the norm of his contemporaries, he did not know any Latin before he came west. Even in Constantinople, which had been partly latinized under Justinian, Latin had ceased to be used by the time of Heraclius (610–41). Pope Martin I was interrogated in Greek in Constantinople in 653. There is no trace of any Latin grammarian there after the seventh century. Palestinian and other Greek-speaking monks must have kept to their own language even when they moved to Rome. Maximus the Confessor's Latin, for example, was by his own admission insufficient (on all this, see Sansterre, *Les Moines grecs* I, 62–4 and 74). And at the monastery of S. Anastasio in the early eighth century the *Roman Miracle* was written in Greek, not Latin.

10

Theodore and the *Laterculus Malalianus*

JANE BARBARA STEVENSON

The Latin text known as *Laterculus Malalianus* is preserved in two manuscripts, Vatican City, Biblioteca Apostolica Vaticana, Pal. lat. 277, written probably in Rome in the early eighth century,[1] and a ninth-century copy made from it, now Leiden, Bibliotheek der Rijksuniversiteit, Voss. misc. 11.[2] It is very badly named, since the chronographer Malalas is only one of the author's sources, though admittedly a very important one, and it is not, even in the loosest sense, a *laterculus*. The attribution to Theodore of Canterbury which I propose to argue gives it an interest and importance out of all proportion to its modest length, since Canterbury was the first school of Christianity and Latin literacy in Anglo-Saxon England: first in time, and in importance second only to Wearmouth–Jarrow.[3] Specific dating and localizing criteria are circumstantial, but

---

[1] *Chronica Minora III*, ed. T. Mommsen, MGH, AA13 (Berlin, 1898), 424–37. There is also an earlier edition of *Laterculus* (under the name *Chronicon Palatinum*) by Cardinal Angelo Mai, repr. in PL 94, 1161–74; see also the important article on *Laterculus* by Ludwig Traube, 'Chronicon Palatinum', *BZ* 4 (1895), 489–92, repr. with additions in his *Vorlesungen und Abhandlungen*, ed. F. Boll, 3 vols. (Munich, 1909–20) III, 201–4. Both previous editors knew only the Vatican manuscript; the Leiden manuscript has in fact nothing independent to contribute.

[2] K. A. de Meyier, *Codices Vossiani Graeci et Miscellanei*, Bibliotheca Uniuersitatis Leidensis Codices Manuscripti 6 (Leiden, 1955), 245–6. Pt III of this composite manuscript, written in early Caroline minuscule, possibly at Weissenburg, includes a copy of *Laterculus*, together with a short computistical text on epacts, beginning 'Era inuenta est a Iulio caesare'.

[3] This is not exclusively a modern perception. A tenth- or eleventh-century German monk called Gausbertus placed Theodore and Hadrian at the head of the entire Insular contribution to continental learning and literature; see L. Delisle, 'Notices sur les manuscrits originaux d'Adémar de Chabannes', *Notices et extraits des manuscrits de la Bibliothèque Nationale et autres bibliothèques* 35 (Paris, 1890), 241–357, at 311–12.

various: they include two references to Irish scholarship, and one to the recent erection of a basilica to the Virgin in Rome.[4] *Laterculus* was edited by Theodor Mommsen, for the Monumenta Germaniae Historia, as a 'minor chronicle'; and it is certainly based in part on the *Chronographia* of John Malalas, written in Greek in Constantinople or Antioch in the later sixth century. But some two-thirds of its length is completely independent of Malalas, and although its Malalaian structure is a correlation of the gospels and Roman imperial history, its independent content is basically exegetical. If it is a chronicle at all, it is an extremely poor one. I hope to show that the historical element is merely an aspect of its real identity as a work of exegesis following the traditions of Antioch. Its manuscript context certainly supports this theory, since the only surviving text was placed among exegetical and computistical writings.[5]

The nature of the material with which it is associated in the primary

---

[4] This is argued at length in my book, *The 'Laterculus Malalianus' and the School of Archbishop Theodore*, CSASE (forthcoming). The text of *Laterculus*, and its references to Rome and to the Irish, have been noticed by a number of writers. Its existence was noted by J. F. Kenney, *The Sources for the Ecclesiastical History of Ireland I: Ecclesiastical* (New York, 1929), p. 518, n. 71; by R. E. McNally, 'Isidorean Pseudepigrapha in the Early Middle Ages', *Isidoriana*, ed. M. C. Díaz y Díaz (Leon, 1961), pp. 305–16, at 309; in *Scriptores Hiberniae Minores* I, ed. R. E. McNally, CCSL 108B (Turnhout, 1973), 189: and in *Bedae Opera Didascalica* I, ed. C. W. Jones, CCSL 123A (Turnhout, 1975), xiv. None of these writers gave the work much thought, and all of them assumed that its origins were in Rome itself.

[5] I have dated *Laterculus* somewhat earlier than Mommsen, whose MGH edition has set the terms for all subsequent discussion of this text. This is not an arbitrary decision. The heroic scale of Mommsen's editorial labours meant that he rarely spent very long on any one text – certainly not one so short and apparently straightforward as *Laterculus*. Having transcribed the single manuscript known to him with exemplary fidelity, he quite clearly considered and analysed the resulting edition in the light of his near-encyclopedic knowledge of early medieval Latin, and voiced his conclusions about it in the two-page essay which has since done duty as the basis for all discussion. He noted the important Proba parallel, but his Vergil parallels are so slight as to denote nothing more than his sensitivity to an unexpectedly literary flavour in the writer's vocabulary – they mostly consist of a single common word. His reason for assigning the text to such a late date lies in the combination of the apparently Insular connections of the writer, evidenced by his antipathy to the Irish, and the presence among the early works of the Venerable Bede, datable to the early 700s, of a recalculation of the date of Creation which put the age of the world in the fourth millennium rather than the sixth. So his date is therefore fixed by reference to Bede, the author of the only surviving Insular work to engage in this sort of chronographic revisionism, even though, obviously, Bede was not an Irishman.

(Vatican) manuscript, which includes two Insular computistical works and some texts of Isidore (who was much admired in the British Isles as early as the second half of the seventh century), gives a strong impression of having been put together by an Insular scholar, whom one would not expect to find writing swift and workmanlike, though not particularly elegant, Italian Uncial script, of a type which is particularly associable with Rome.[6]

Pal. lat. 277 contains two short works by Isidore, *Liber praefationum ueteris nouique testamenti* and *De ortu et obitu sanctorum patrum*, the *Laterculus* itself, the Hiberno-Latin pseudo-Isidorean *Quaestiones tam de nouo quam de uetere testamento*, a brief, unidentifiable computistical fragment, the Hiberno-Latin 'Acta [suppositi] concilii Caesareae' (also a computistical text), and Pope Leo the Great's *Sententiae de apocryphis scripturis*. This odd mixture of texts suggests the possibility that the original compiler was one of the several Southumbrians known to have been educated both at Canterbury and in Ireland (of whom Heahfrith was apparently an example), or that he belonged to one of the Anglo-Irish missionary groups working on the Continent.

The reading *suminantur* for *ruminantur* in ch. 4[7] is a further corroboration of the thesis that *Laterculus* was copied, rather than surviving as an authorial autograph, and further, that the exemplar from which it was copied was written in England or Ireland. The considerable similarity of s and r in Insular minuscule hands suggests that the exemplar from which this text was copied was of Insular origin; and since the manuscript cannot be very far removed in time from the original text, that this original may itself have been written in the British Isles.[8] Thus, the *termini* provided by the original writing of Malalas's Greek chronicle in the late sixth century

---

[6] Two out of the seven works included in Pal. lat. 277 are almost certainly Irish in origin; a further indication that the collection was put together in an Insular milieu. But the dating of this text so late as the mid-eighth century is problematic on a number of grounds, not the least of which is the date of the surviving manuscript. The affinities of this script, and even more, the style of its decorative capitals, suggest that it may have been written in the *early* eighth century.

[7] Ed. Mommsen, p. 427.

[8] *Palaeographia Latina* I, ed. W. M. Lindsay (Oxford, 1922), p. 43: '... by so doing [Continental] scribes courted another danger, the confusion of [r] with [s]; for Insular [s] falls below the line ... the confusion of these two letters usually points to an Insular minuscule exemplar'.

and the transcription of the unique manuscript of the Latin *Laterculus* from an apparently Insular exemplar in the early eighth combine to place *Laterculus* solidly in the seventh century, and its polemically anti-Irish statements place it in Anglo-Saxon England.

When seeking to localize a conspicuously scholarly text in early Anglo-Saxon England, most modern scholars would naturally think of Bede's school at Wearmouth–Jarrow. But even Wearmouth–Jarrow itself lay in Canterbury's debt. Benedict Biscop, who was later to found Wearmouth and Jarrow, was on his third visit to Rome when he was entrusted by Pope Vitalian in 668 with the task of conveying the elderly monk Theodore of Tarsus, the newly created archbishop of Canterbury, together with his companion Hadrian, from Rome to England, where they arrived in 669. Benedict lived with Theodore and Hadrian in Canterbury for two years, as abbot of SS Peter and Paul (later St Augustine's), before Hadrian was ready to take over this responsibility. Biscop then returned to his native Northumbria and founded there a school which was, briefly, the light of the West. And Bede, its chief glory, spoke in the highest terms of the education which Theodore and Hadrian offered at Canterbury. He said of Albinus, Hadrian's successor, 'in tantum studiis scripturarum institutus est, ut Grecam quidem linguam non parua uero parte, Latinam uero non minus quam Anglorum, quae sibi naturalis est, nouerit'.[9] Bishop Tobias of Rochester, another Canterbury alumnus, is also described by Bede as knowing both Greek and Latin.[10] And although Aldhelm, our main surviving witness to the school of Canterbury, does not seem ever to have learned Greek, his extraordinary learning stretched far and wide across the field of Latin literature, classical and Christian, in a way which even Bede himself could not match, and he is witness to the existence of a remarkable library in southern England. It is also worth noting that the Canterbury archives appear to have been one of Bede's most significant historical resources. Abbot Albinus of Canterbury was both the instigator of Bede's *Historia ecclesiastica*, and one of Bede's chief informants, as Bede's Preface bears witness. But the achievement of Theodore and Hadrian was only a matter of reportage until Bernhard Bischoff and Michael Lapidge began to

---

[9] *HE* V.20 (p. 530): 'was so well trained in scriptural studies that he had no small knowledge of the Greek language and that he knew Latin as well as English, his native tongue'.

[10] *HE* V.8 (p. 474).

uncover the Canterbury origins of parts of the early medieval glossary tradition.[11]

The authors cited by name in the Canterbury biblical commentaries include Epiphanius of Cyprus, John Chrysostom, Gregory of Nazianzus, Theophilus (of Alexandria?) and Josephus. Far more Greek than Latin writers are so honoured.[12] Our *Laterculus Malalianus*, which is a historical exegesis of the life of Christ, is the sole surviving complete scholarly work[13] from seventh-century Canterbury, and its characteristics are therefore of the highest significance.

The first thing to be said about the *Laterculus* is that it gives some support to Bede's claim that Greek was taught at Canterbury to that first generation of students.[14] It certainly provides further evidence, corroborating that of the Canterbury biblical commentaries, that Greek texts were available, and used, in Anglo-Saxon England. And it also shows that Canterbury was almost the only western school in the seventh century to teach the exegetical methods of the school of Antioch.[15] *Laterculus* demands a thorough re-examination of the entire question of the relationship between Insular Latin culture and the East and calls into question fundamental assumptions about what is Irish and what is English.

My reasons for deducing that *Laterculus* was written by Archbishop

---

[11] The full results of their work are found in *Biblical Commentaries*, ed. Bischoff and Lapidge; see also their preliminary remarks, in Bischoff, 'Wendepunkte in der Geschichte der lateinischen Exegese im Frühmittelalter', *Mittelalterliche Studien. Aufsätze zur Schriftkunde und Literaturgeschichte*, 3 vols. (Stuttgart, 1966–81) I, 205–73, esp. 206–9, and in Lapidge, 'The School of Theodore and Hadrian', *ASE* 15 (1986), 45–72.

[12] For a full account of the Greek and Latin sources, see *Biblical Commentaries*, ed. Bischoff and Lapidge, pp. 190–233. I am grateful to Michael Lapidge for the privilege of seeing parts of their text in typescript.

[13] As distinct from the incompletely preserved biblical commentaries and glossaries, the Penitential (all of which give us Theodore's thought at second hand), Theodore's octosyllabic poetry and some official correspondence.

[14] See, for example, Bede, *HE* V.8 and 20 (pp. 474 and 530).

[15] What I imply by describing *Laterculus* and the Theodoran tradition of biblical glossing as 'Antiochene' is that they rigorously eschew allegory and devote themselves to issues of literal and historical truth (the identification of Middle Eastern birds and beasts named in the Bible, for instance), while exhibiting a marked interest in Old Testament typology. It can hardly be too strongly stressed that in a seventh-century western context, this avoidance of the allegorical methods of exegesis hallowed by Augustine and Gregory was deviant to the point of being practically unique.

Theodore are mainly circumstantial. To begin with, this is a seventh-century text, written in Latin by a man whose education in the Greek patristic tradition was both wide and deep, and whose knowledge of Latin was relatively superficial. This is negatively supported by the fact that I have been quite unable to trace any influence from the thought of Augustine or Gregory in *Laterculus*, which forms an absolute contrast with every other piece of seventh- to eighth-century Latin exegesis, Insular or continental, known to me. It is completely extraordinary to find a western treatment of the life of Christ which stands independent of the Latin patristic tradition, and draws only on the Greek. On the other hand, there are two Latin poets who have provably impressed the author of *Laterculus*, Caelius Sedulius (whom he draws on at least ten times), and Proba. Vergil, *pace* Mommsen, is a more difficult influence to assess: Mommsen's parallels are superficial in the extreme, and if relevant at all, could equally well have come through Proba. Proba's *Cento* was very little read in the early Middle Ages, but it *was* known to Aldhelm, who had received part of his training in the school at Canterbury. Furthermore, Caelius Sedulius was one of Aldhelm's favourite authors. I also found two passages which suggest that the author of *Laterculus* had read Gildas. Gildas was very well known to Aldhelm, but on the other hand, there is little or no indication that he was read at all outside the Celtic West (Ireland, Wales and Brittany) and England. Another fact which can be deduced about the author of *Laterculus* is that he was familiar with the city of Rome, because he refers to a great church dedicated to the Virgin, which had just been built on the Capitol. This must refer to Aracoeli, dedicated to the Virgin, and built on the Capitol some time in the second half of the seventh century.[16] This Roman reference in *Laterculus* is particularly interesting, given that there are strong grounds for associating its composition with seventh-century England. The well-known Anglo-Saxon fondness for going on pilgrimage to Rome took some time to get started. Only a very few Anglo-Saxons, notably Benedict Biscop, Wilfrid, King Cædwalla and possibly

---

[16] R. Krautheimer, *Rome: Profile of a City, 312–1308* (Princeton, NJ, 1980), p. 285: 'to the North, perhaps using the ruins of the Temple of Juno, the monastery and church of S. Maria in Capitolio had been set up by the eighth century or earlier'. No remains of this church survive to clarify the question of its date, because it was rebuilt in the twelfth century, and rebuilt yet again in the thirteenth, each time in a larger and more impressive form, thus obliterating the original basilica (*ibid.*, pp. 286–7).

Aldhelm,[17] are said to have been visiting Rome in the period from 650 to 680.[18] Although the unique manuscript of *Laterculus* is of Roman origin, and there was a plethora of Greek and Greek-trained monks in later seventh-century Rome, there are several reasons for insisting that *Laterculus* must be Insular in origin. One small but interesting pointer is in the manuscript itself: the reading *suminantur* for *ruminantur*, mentioned above. I have already mentioned the significance of the author's possible use of Gildas, suggesting as it does that the text was composed, not just copied, in an Insular milieu. But a far stronger piece of evidence for an English origin is that the author goes out of his way, on two separate occasions, to be rude about the Irish, saying in his preface, 'iam ne nos fallant multiloquio suo Scottorum scolaces',[19] and in ch. 4, 'In sex milia autem annorum concordant omnes apparuisse Dominum; quamuis Scotti concordare nolunt, qui sapientia se existimant habere, et scientiam perdederunt.' The peevish tone of these comments is interestingly comparable with Aldhelm's gibes at Irish scholarship – see, in particular, his letter to Wihtfrith. The point here is that *Laterculus* was written in the later seventh century, at which time nobody but the English saw enough of the Irish to be particularly bothered about them. Certainly, we find some conspicuous Hibernophobia in continental circles in the later eighth and

---

[17] *Aldhelmi Opera*, ed. R. Ehwald, MGH, Auct. Antiq. 15 (Berlin, 1919), 494: the letter of an anonymous student to Aldhelm includes the phrase 'quia tu Romae aduena fuisti', but there is no way of placing this statement relative to the chronology of Aldhelm's life, which ended in 709.

[18] The pilgrimage was a dramatically distinctive feature of Anglo-papal relations in the eighth century, on the witness of both Bede and Boniface. See, for instance, Bede's comment on the year 725 in his *Chronica Maiora* (*Chronica Minora III*, ed. Mommsen, pp. 223–333, at 320): 'his temporibus multi Anglorum gentis, nobiles et ignobiles, uiri et feminae, duces et priuati, diuini amoris instinctu de Britannia Romam uenire consueuerant'. See also W. Levison, *England and the Continent in the Eighth Century* (Oxford, 1946), pp. 34–44. But this flood of eager pilgrims seems very much a feature of the confident and consolidated church of the mid and late eighth century. Venturesome Anglo-Saxon Christians of the seventh century were more likely to cross the sea to Ireland, like Wihtfrith and Heahfrith, or to the monasteries of Gaul, like the future abbess Hild, than to go as far as Rome.

[19] The last word is probably a word-play on *scholares*, which one might have expected, and Greek σκύλαξ, a 'puppy-dog'. I am reminded of Aldhelm's well-known metaphor, in his letter to Heahfrith, of Theodore as a great boar, surrounded by a yelling pack of Irish hounds: to Theodore, the Irish are not even as dignified as *molossi*: they are merely yapping puppies.

ninth centuries,[20] but in the seventh, there were not enough *peregrini*[21] about to have excited any particular reaction. And there is only one testimony of an expedition to Rome from seventh-century Ireland that I know of, namely Cummian's dispatch of three monks to go to Rome and find out how they calculated Easter.

To sum up, the author of *Laterculus* was educated in the Greek tradition, familiar with Rome, disliked the Irish, and flourished in the later seventh century. This seems to point straight to Theodore of Tarsus, who was certainly educated in the eastern empire, was living at Rome in the 660s, and is pictured by Aldhelm in his letter to Heahfrith as locked in battle with Irish students, like an old boar surrounded by hounds, suggesting with some force that he was well aware of contemporary controversies between Irish and English scholars.[22] Furthermore, the Latin sources of *Laterculus*, such as they are, were all known to Aldhelm; and the biblical commentaries known to originate in seventh-century Canterbury show a very considerable overlap in the Greek authorities used. Whenever *Laterculus* and the Theodoran biblical commentaries happen to coincide in their comments,[23] they are in agreement.

It has been assumed for a very long time that any eastern influence on Insular thought and letters was the result of a mysterious spiritual affinity between Celts and Asiatics, who are to be contrasted with the unimagin-

---

[20] See for example B. Bischoff, 'Theodulf und der Ire Cadac-Andreas', in his *Mittelalterliche Studien* II, 19–25, and also Theodulf's poem *Ad Carolum regem*, ed. E. Dümmler, MGH, PLAC 1 (Berlin, 1881), 483–9, which describes at some length (lines 214–34, at pp. 488–9) an Irishman 'quae tamen ignorat, omnia nosse putat'.

[21] The Christian Irish presence on the Continent (leaving aside isolated individuals like Pelagius's supporter Caelestius, and occasional Irishmen mentioned by writers such as Sidonius Apollinaris) began towards the end of the sixth century with the foundation of Annegray, Fontaines, Luxeuil and Bobbio by Columbanus, and of Péronne by Fursa. In all these cases, a small core of Irish monks was balanced by much larger numbers of continental recruits. Apart from the perennial battle over the calculation of the date of Easter, on which Columbanus has left us two important epistles (*Epistolae* I and III, ed. G. S. M. Walker, *Sancti Columbani Opera* (Dublin, 1957), pp. 1–13 and 22–5), there is no evidence that the eccentricities of Irish scholarship attracted the attention of their continental neighbours at this time. It was the Carolingian era which saw the influx of a larger number of Irish scholars than the market could easily bear, which led to the development of pronounced anti-Irish sentiments in some Frankish quarters.

[22] Aldhelm, *Epistola ad Ehfridum*, ed. Ehwald, *Opera*, p. 493.

[23] For example, that all human beings will be resurrected at the age of thirty (ch. 16), and that the Magi arrived two years after Christ's birth (ch. 6).

ative, practically minded Romans and Anglo-Saxons. This type of racial mythography is notoriously counterproductive; but the extent of its speciousness in an early Insular context is thrown into a sharp, new relief by this unexpected evidence for the nature of the teaching at Canterbury.

The decades of Theodore's active life saw the movement of Greek monks westwards as refugees from the Moslem conquests, and from the politico-theological conflict between the emperors in Constantinople and the papacy. The wider world within which this apparently quixotic appointment of an elderly Greek monk to the see of Canterbury was made and the importance of the English church to the papacy are also relevant to my localization of this piece of writing. The synod of Hatfield, in which Theodore played the leading role, was one of three provincial synods which, taken together, presented a united western position on a number of extremely controversial issues and enabled Agatho, the then pope, to speak with confidence as the head of the western church as he negotiated a mutually agreeable resolution of the schism between East and West. Seventh- and eighth-century popes seem to have perceived it as very much in their interest to maintain and foster a special relationship between Rome and the English church. Pope Vitalian, Bede tells us, was initially extremely anxious that his chosen candidate for Canterbury should be a staunch supporter of the Roman point of view, and not introduce Greek ideas into the English church; hence his sending of the African Hadrian as a companion to Theodore and as abbot of the monastery of SS Peter and Paul. It is interesting in this context to observe that *Laterculus* consistently defends the Roman viewpoint wherever it touches on a subject of contention between East and West – including what would later be known as the *filioque* clause – despite its overwhelmingly Greek intellectual background.

THE CONTENTS OF *LATERCULUS MALALIANUS*

The ideas put forward in *Laterculus* include numerology, the seven ages of the world, embryology, the historical context of Christ's life on earth, the typological significance of the Red Sea, the theology of circumcision, and many other historical and theological points. But the first half of *Laterculus* (chs. 2–11) follows the *Chronographia* of John Malalas almost exactly, with one or two minor additions, and an introduction. This is what they contain.

We begin with the Annunciation, and a discussion of the various important events which have fallen on this date (25 March), most of which is additional to Malalas. Then we return to straight translation for an account of the division of historical time: we are told that there were 3,000 years between Adam and Phalech, and 2,967 years from Phalech to the birth of Christ, which of course makes 6,000 years from the creation of Adam to the Crucifixion, when Christ was thirty-three. Most of this is straight from Malalas – indeed, the dating of the Crucifixion to *Anno Mundi* 6,000 is unique to Malalas and texts associable with him – the only addition is a gratuitous, parenthetic remark about the stupidity of the Irish. The next event mentioned in *Laterculus* is the visit of the Magi, first to Herod, and then to Christ at Bethlehem, followed by the flight into Egypt. Here again, the writer inserts additional material, which he claims to have derived from Epiphanius, the fourth-century iconoclast bishop of Constantia in Cyprus.[24] The author, following Malalas once more, then treats of the return to Jerusalem, Augustus's dream of an unknown Jewish divinity, the succession of Tiberius, the baptism of Christ, the death of John the Baptist, the Crucifixion and the Resurrection. His account follows the chronology of the biblical narrative in sequence. Each of these significant events is given its date, often very elaborately. Here is an example of the writer's technique:[25]

[24] I argue at some length in my book (cited above, n. 4) that Mommsen was wrong to attribute this passage, in direct contradiction to its author, to Epiphanius Scholasticus, the Latin translator of Sozomen's *Historia tripertita*. The apocryphal episode in question is a *locus classicus* for the iconoclast position (unfortunately, only a handful of quotations remain to us of Epiphanius's iconoclast works, since the verdict of history went against him on this issue). Moreover, there is considerable evidence that various works by Epiphanius, including his treatises on precious stones, and on weights and measures, were used at Canterbury; and, as M. L. W. Laistner says, '[the *Historia tripertita*] does not appear to have been much consulted by continental authors of the eighth century, and in England it seems to have been unknown at that period' (*The Intellectual Heritage of the Early Middle Ages*, ed. C. G. Starr (New York, 1957), p. 30). So, despite the superficial attractiveness of preferring a Latin source for a Latin text, the *Historia* appears to be the less likely of the alternative sources for this episode. There is certainly no direct correspondence of vocabulary, detail, or expression.

[25] Interestingly, the *Canones Theodori*, ch. 143, based on Archbishop Theodore's verbal *iudicia*, use a double date, giving both the Greek and the Roman month, in the same way: 'Bis in uno anno concilia episcopi fiant id est quarta septimana post pentecosten. Secundo .xii. die mensis Hyperberethei id est .iiii. idus .viii.bris iuxta Romanos' (ed. P. W. Finsterwalder, *Die Canones Theodori Cantuariensis und ihre Überlieferungsformen* (Weimar, 1929), p. 250). It is not common for seventh-century Latin works to include Greek dates.

in the sixth month of the forty-first year of that Caesar, in the month of Distrus (that is, according to the Latins, March), on the twenty-fifth day of the month (which is the eighth of the Kalends of April, which is called Xanthicus according to the Greeks) . . . the archangel Gabriel was sent to bear witness to blessed Mary.

The second half of *Laterculus*, which is original prose rather than translation or paraphrase of Malalas, is rather different in its contents. Ch. 12 goes back to Christ's birth, and begins a recapitulation of the life of Christ treated typologically rather than historically, and displaying a marked Antiochene bias. *Laterculus* in fact is written in the form of two parallel structures of historical fact and spiritual significance. Although it is not very long, it is a work of considerable learning. The bipartite structure, odd though it may seem, can be paralleled quite easily in the Antiochene exegetical tradition, with its avoidance of undue dependence on allegory, and its concern with both literal and historical truth and typological significance. The most specific model for the plan of the work as a whole which I have found is Theodore of Mopsuestia's commentary on the minor epistles of St Paul, which similarly begins its discussion of each epistle by setting it in its political and temporal context.[26] The only two sources mentioned by name in *Laterculus*, apart from books of the Bible, are eastern. Epiphanius of Cyprus is cited in ch. 7, and Ephrem Syrus in ch. 19. I have been able to find a parallel, though one cannot be sure that it is a source, for every single theme in *Laterculus*. Theodore of Mopsuestia, the great Antiochene, was particularly helpful, as indeed was Epiphanius. The Syrian doctors, Ephrem, Narsai and Jacob of Serugh, who were trained in the Antiochene tradition, also afforded several useful parallels. John Chrysostom and Irenaeus were other theologians I found particularly relevant, though Theodoret, Cyril of Alexandria, Theophilus, Hippolytus and others were helpful on particular points. Every one of these writers was eastern, and wrote either in Greek or in Syriac;[27] most of them were Antiochene in tendency.

---

[26] His Commentary on Ephesians opens by collating the evidence of Acts, the traditions about John, and the history of the imperial reigns of Nero and Trajan before moving on to an exegesis of its contents: *Theodori Episcopi Mopsuesteni in Epistolas B. Pauli Commentarii: The Latin Version with the Greek Fragments*, ed. H. B. Swete, 2 vols. (Cambridge, 1880) I, 112–96, at 112–18. See further R. A. Greer, *Theodore of Mopsuestia, Exegete and Theologian* (London, 1961), pp. 104–5.

[27] The works of the great Syrian doctors were rapidly translated into Greek, and similarly, much Greek literature, theological and otherwise, was translated into Syriac. See

Outside of exegesis, the author of *Laterculus* also drew on the historians Josephus and Eusebius, and the medical writers Galen and Oribasius.[28] In short, the content of this author's thought seems to be entirely formed by Greek writers of one kind or another.[29] Note further that there is considerable overlap between the sources for the ideas in *Laterculus* and the authorities cited by the Canterbury biblical commentaries and glosses attributed to Theodore and Hadrian – John Chrysostom, Epiphanius, Josephus and many others.

The important point here is that *Laterculus* is unique in the records of post-patristic Latin exegesis in apparently owing nothing to the fathers of the western church. Thus, the peculiarities of *Laterculus* are both positive and negative. We find the total absence of the expected frame of reference; but the presence of a way of thinking about the New Testament which is not only internally consistent in its approach, but comparable both in outline and in detail with Greek exegetical traditions, particularly the work of Theodore of Mopsuestia. There is not a single idea or statement in *Laterculus* for which I have failed to find a Greek or Syriac parallel, and this is combined with a total absence of any concepts or turns of phrase which can be shown to echo the words of one of the Latin fathers.

The author was not, however, entirely ignorant of Latin literature. I have already mentioned his acquaintance with Christian Latin poets, Proba and Caelius Sedulius. Sedulius in particular is echoed, sometimes very closely, at least ten times. The author's phraseology is sometimes apparently influenced by Latin Bible-texts, even though he seems at other times

S. Brock, 'Greek into Syriac and Syriac into Greek', *Journal of the Syriac Academy* 3 (1977), 1–17 [= 422–35], as well as his discussion above, pp. 36–45.

[28] The *Synopsis* and *Euporistes* of Oribasius were certainly in England by the end of the ninth century because they were known to the compiler of 'Bald's Leechbook' (*c.* 900): see M. L. Cameron, 'The Sources of Medical Knowledge in Anglo-Saxon England', *ASE* 11 (1983), 135–55, at 147–8.

[29] A considerable number of Greek texts was translated into Latin between the fourth and seventh centuries. Bede, a useful *comparandum* since he is our major early Anglo-Saxon exegete, knew of some of Rufinus's translations of Origen and Gregory of Nazianzus, Eustathius's translation of Basil's *Hexaemeron* and some of John Chrysostom's works. There were almost certainly more translations of Greek exegesis made than we are now aware of. But it would be extraordinarily perverse of a Latin scholar from some Hibernophobic milieu (i.e. England or just possibly, Francia) to reject the influence of the Latin fathers and place his trust entirely in a battery of translations. This would require a combination of dependence on, and independence from, *auctoritas* unlikely in any period, but particularly implausible in the early Middle Ages.

to have been translating directly from the Septuagint. The only non-biblical Latin prose writer to influence the expression of *Laterculus* is Gildas, who seems to have contributed two phrases, though it should be said that a phrase in ch. 2 suggests that the writer knew Rufinus's Latin translation of Eusebius's *Ecclesiastical History* as well as (or instead of) the Greek original. The only point at which the actual content may be dependent on a Latin text is the author's reference to the legal ceremony of manumission in ch. 20, but this could perfectly well be based on Sedulius, who made the same point, in the same context.

The Bible-text of *Laterculus* is interesting and problematic. It appears to be separable into several layers. Some of its readings are pure Vulgate, as we now know it. Some are Vetus Latina, or possibly assignable to an early stage of the development of the Vulgate, and agree with readings found in such writers as Augustine and Cassiodorus. A few of the citations are quite startlingly anomalous, in ways that suggest that the writer was para-phrasing from memory. The Psalm-text is 'iuxta LXX' (i.e. Gallican), again as one might expect, since it was the text used at Rome. This is demonstrable from, for example, the reference to 'sicut gigas in uiam', which is a near-quotation from Ps. XVIII.6, which reads 'exsultauit ut gigans ad currendam uiam suam' in the 'iuxta LXX' version and is quite different in the 'iuxta Hebraeos'. Of the several references to Psalms in this text, all are either common to the two versions, or where they vary, close to the Septuagint. The Vetus Latina was often closer to the Septuagint than the Vulgate and this normally obscures the question of whether the writer was actually translating from the LXX at times. There is, however, one instance where he was almost certainly translating from Greek: his treatment of Exodus IV.21–6. *Laterculus* summarizes this story in a way which demonstrates influence from Jewish exegesis of this difficult passage. Verses 24–5 of the Vulgate Exodus read 'occurrit ei Dominus et uolebat occidere eum. Tulit ilico Seffora acutissimam petram et circumci-dit praeputium filii sui ... et dimisit eum postquam dixerat sponsus sanguinem ob circumcisionem.' The earliest Jewish exegesis of this passage was written in Palestine before 200 BC and established the following points: the object of the assault is Moses; the assailant is not Jahweh but an angel of the Lord; it is to the angel that Zipporah speaks in IV.25; and Moses's life is saved because of the sacrificial atoning value of the blood that is shed.[30] This ancient Jewish reading of the text affected

---

[30] G. Vermes, 'Baptism and Jewish Exegesis: New Light from Ancient Sources', *New Testament Studies* 4 (1957–8), 308–19, at 313.

the Septuagint, Vulgate and Peshitta.[31] *Laterculus* is very much in this Jewish tradition, as the writer gives the non-biblical *angelus* rather than *Dominus*; and it is Moses whom the angel attempts to kill and the sacramental, redemptive power of the blood shed in circumcision is stressed, with its obvious typological value as a prefiguration both of the blood shed in the circumcision of Christ, and the blood shed by Christ on the cross.

The LXX reading, which is unsupported by any known Hebrew text, refers, like *Laterculus*, to the *angel* of the Lord rather than the Lord himself. This suggests quite strongly that the writer is thinking in terms of the Septuagint. The Vetus Latina, very different from the Vulgate at this point, reads 'et factum est in uia, ad refectionem obuiant ei angelus, et quaerebat eum occidere';[32] clearly a translation from the Septuagint. But the vocabulary is completely different from that of *Laterculus* – note *occidere* rather than *interficere*, *obuiare* not *occurrere*, and that Zipporah seizes a *calculus* rather than a *lapis* – so that it seems very unlikely that *Laterculus* drew on any known Vetus Latina version.

All this greatly complicates any attempt to reconstruct the writer's Bible-text. But even when a writer is paraphrasing from memory, he is quite likely to retain words and structures from the version he knows most intimately, even if he elides or inverts parts of the original sentence. It may therefore be significant that non-Vulgate phrases, even in loose quotation or paraphrase, may be found to be shared with Vetus Latina or early 'mixed' Bible-texts, though the sentence in *Laterculus* has been so thoroughly recast that it resembles no one version in detail. The sections of Malalas which are used in *Laterculus* are translated so closely as to form what is practically a 'crib', to the extent of reproducing the Greek syntax. The genitive absolute 'sanctorum apostolorum uidentium' precisely matches τῶν ἁγίων ἀπόστολων ὁρώντων and, similarly, *ex consolibus* rather than *exconsule* is a Latin calque on ἀπὸ ὑπάτων. Some further examples are found in ch. 3: ἀπὸ Ἀδὰμ ἕως τοῦ Φαλεκ, υἱοῦ Ἐβερ, corresponding to 'ab Adam usque a Phalech, fili Eber', and καὶ ὑπέπεσε τῇ ἁμαρτίᾳ ὁ ἄνθρωπος, corresponding to 'et cecidit sub peccato homo'. However, it must be noted that this absolutely literal translation is not followed through the Malalian sections of *Laterculus* as a consistent principle; some

---

[31] B. P. Robinson, 'Zipporah to the Rescue: a Contextual Study of Exodus IV.24–6', *Vetus Testamentum* 36 (1986), 447–61, at 456.

[32] *Bibliorum sacrorum latinae versiones antiquae*, ed. P. Sabatier, 3 vols. (Rheims, 1743) II, 97–8.

sentences are more Latinate than others, though it is fair to say that the translation is always close.

The translation techniques used in *Laterculus* must be viewed in their appropriate context. There were many Greek monks in Rome, and furthermore, there was a fair amount of translation taking place. The minutes of the Lateran Council of 649, for example, were produced simultaneously in Greek and Latin. But the centre I want to focus specific attention on is not the Vatican secretariat, but the monastery of Tre Fontane, or St Anastasius *ad Aquas Saluias*, one of the three important Greek monasteries in seventh-century Rome.[33] This is of interest for a number of reasons. It housed a community of Cilicians under their abbot, George, who put their weight behind the pope and against the emperor in the politico-theological battle known as the monothelete controversy. Theodore was, of course, from Tarsus in Cilicia, and it is not only possible, but probable, that Tre Fontane was his monastery.[34] The monks of Tre Fontane brought with them to Rome the head of their patron saint, Anastasius, who was martyred by the Persians in 628, and quite quickly set about the delicate business of transferring the cult of this saint to Rome, a city which of course was absolutely crammed with home-grown saints of its own. An immediate result of this was, naturally enough, a flurry of literary activity. These Greek monks produced a translation of the *Passio S. Anastasii*,[35] which was originally written (in Greek) in 630; and this is how it is described by Paul Meyvaert and Carmela Franklin:

The Latin follows the Greek word order, line after line. The translation is replete with shortcomings: choice of the wrong word to render the Greek meaning, and an almost total neglect of Latin grammar, syntax and idiom, resulting here and there in statements that remain unintelligible to anyone who is unable to refer back to the original Greek.[36]

[33] Discussed by G. Ferrari, *Early Roman Monasteries. Notes for the History of the Monasteries and Convents at Rome from the V through the X Century* (Vatican City, 1957), pp. 33–48.

[34] There seems to have been a definite, and humanly comprehensible, tendency for monks from a particular region to form a separate community. For instance, as late as the pontificate of Donus (676–8), a Nestorian community was discovered living undisturbed 'in Monasterio quod appelatur *Boetiana*', in Rome (*Liber Pontificalis*, ed. L. Duchesne, 3 vols. (Paris, 1886–1957) I, 348).

[35] Preserved in Turin, Biblioteca Nazionale, F.III.16, fols. 14–23, a former Bobbio manuscript of the tenth century.

[36] See P. Meyvaert and C. Vircillo Franklin, 'Has Bede's Version of the *Passio S. Anastasii* come down to us in *BHL* 408?', *AB* 100 (1982), 372–400, at 380; and see now the

218

Meyvaert and Franklin further noted that this version of the *passio* was in Northumbria by the beginning of the eighth century, because it was rewritten into more correct Latin by Bede, who described it trenchantly as 'librum uitae et passionis sancti Anastasii, male de greco translatum et peius a quodam inperito emendatum'.[37] This original version of the *passio* at least shows that it was possible for a seventh-century Greek-speaking Cilician active in Rome to be satisfied with producing 'translations' from Greek to Latin which made only the most minimal concessions to the characteristics of the latter language.

Moreover, the cult of Anastasius, supported by the important relic of his head, was successfully established in Rome. As Meyvaert and Franklin say, 'the veneration of this relic by pilgrims coming from all over the West must have prompted the desire to provide a Latin version which would tell the story of the Persian monk's conversion and death'.[38] It seems to me interesting that the obviously inadequate Latin text of the *passio*, for all the shudders it evoked in Bede's refined consciousness, seems to have been thoroughly successful in its avowed intention of putting St Anastasius and his monastery firmly on the pilgrim's map of important holy sites in Rome, since the monastery is mentioned in *De locis sanctis martyrum quae sunt foris ciuitatis Romae*, probably written between 635 and 645.[39] I have suggested that the monastery of St Anastasius at Tre Fontane in Rome must be at the very least very close to the milieu in which Theodore of Tarsus lived and worked before he came to Canterbury. Meyvaert's discussion of the *passio* shows that a contemporary monk at Tre Fontane took the same approach to the translation of Greek that we find in *Laterculus*. We can add to this a further insight into the culture of Tre Fontane, a text called *Miracula S. Anastasii*, also written by a monk of St Anastasius,[40] in 712, but an original composition in Latin. It is interesting to observe that its latinity has the same un-Classical characteristics as *Laterculus*, though the style is considerably more flowery, with *dum* used for *cum* (ch. 2), nominative absolutes (ch. 2) and occasional errors of syntax[41] as well

---

discussion of Carmela Vircillo Franklin (above, pp. 175–203), who gives even more persuasive reasons for associating the *Passio S. Anastasii* with Archbishop Theodore himself.

[37] *HE* V.24 (pp. 568–70).   [38] 'Bede's Version', pp. 383–4.

[39] *Itineraria et alia geographica*, ed. P. Geyer *et al.*, CCSL 175 (Turnhout, 1965), 316, n. 6.

[40] 'Miracula S. Anastasii' [anon. ed.], *AB* 11 (1892), 233–41.

[41] For example, 'et assumens filiam suam *habens* spiritum immundum'.

219

as a similar tendency to use markedly anomalous versions of Latin Bible-texts.[42]

We are used, thinking about translation, to accepting the dictum of Jerome, so often quoted, that one ought to translate sense by sense, not word by word; and of course many late antique and early medieval texts, such as Jerome's Vulgate itself and Rufinus's translation of Eusebius's *Historia ecclesiastica*, do just that. But there is an alternative trend in early medieval translation, though we tend not to think of it as such, which is glossing: that is, writing word-by-word equivalents over the words of the original texts, as a tenth-century Northumbrian vandal called Aldred did, for instance, in the 'Lindisfarne Gospels' (in *c.* 960).[43] This approach to the text seems more closely related to the translation-technique used in the *passio* and, though less extremely, in *Laterculus*. It is an indirect but powerful statement of the primacy of the original text over the independence of the version.

The monastery of St Anastasius was by no means unique in taking this approach to the translation of Greek. For instance, the original Latin translation of the *vita* of Pelagia the Harlot (or: Penitent) follows the Greek word by word.[44] In short, the evidence that I have seen so far suggests that the translation from Malalas in the *Laterculus* appears to be of a standard acceptable to the majority of the writer's contemporaries, however much it might wound the sensibilities of an accomplished Latinist, whether in the seventh century, or the twentieth.

There is also a useful indication in the works of Gregory of Tours that translation was sometimes a two-stage process. In his *De gloria martyrum*, he informs us that he was assisted by a Syrian called John in translating the *passio* of the Seven Sleepers of Ephesus (whether from Greek or Syriac, he

---

[42] For example, 'quaerite et inuenietis, petite *et accipietis*,' (Luke IX.3; 7) for 'petite et dabitur uobis, quaerite et inuenietis'. This writer, like the author of *Laterculus*, uses Psalms 'iuxta LXX'.

[43] A. S. C. Ross, 'A Connection between Bede and the Anglo-Saxon Gloss to the Lindisfarne Gospels?', *JTS* ns 20 (1969), 482–94, at 493, says, 'surely then what Bede was doing when he was translating was making a word-for-word gloss'. He notes also that the 'translation' was achieved, as the *Epistola* tells us, by dictating to a second party, who wrote down Bede's words.

[44] *Pélagie la Pénitente: metamorphoses d'une légende, I. Les textes et leur histoire*, ed. P. Petitmengin *et al.* (Paris, 1981). The original Latin translation is edited by François Dolbeau, at pp. 161–249, and is a word-for-word rendering of the original. Dolbeau thinks it pre-Carolingian, though he does not commit himself to greater precision.

does not say): 'quod passio eorum, quam Siro quodam interpretante in Latino transtulimus, plenius prodit'.[45] We have here a dual activity. First *interpretatio*: which probably means that John the Syrian turned the original text word-by-word into Latin, without bothering about the literary qualities of this 'crib'; then *translatio*, performed by Gregory on this rough version, in which, having grasped the sense, he turned it into intelligible Latin.[46] It is clear from the context of Greek activity at Rome, notably the *Passio S. Anastasii*, that *interpretatio*, or word-by-word translation, could and sometimes did stand on its own. But there is also the possibility, in such cases, that the *interpretatio* was *intended* to provide the basis for reworking by an accomplished Latinist such as this text ultimately received at the hands of Bede. All I would argue for in the case of *Laterculus* is that there is reason to suggest that, in a classroom context, *interpretatio* might be held to be sufficient by a fundamentally Hellenophone scholar, forming as it did an adequate basis for analysis and discussion of the meaning of the text. *Laterculus*, it seems to me, consists of a rough *interpretatio* of Malalas's useful summary of the position of Christ in history, expanded, in true Antiochene style, by a series of typological meditations on the events described.

---

[45] Gregory of Tours, *De gloria martyrum*, ch. 94 (*Opera*, ed. W. Arndt and B. Krusch, MGH, SRM 1 (Hanover, 1884), 550–2).

[46] See H. Le Bordellès , *L'Aratus Latinus: Etude sur la culture et la langue latine dans le Nord de la France au VIIe siècle* (Lille, 1985), p. 125.

11

Theodore and the liturgy

CHRISTOPHER HOHLER

Given the specific subject implied by the title of this paper, a moment's thought will indicate that there are three different fields for enquiry. The first is: what form of liturgy was Theodore familiar with before his consecration to Canterbury? The second is: what liturgy did he find in Britain when he arrived? The third is: did he make any modifications to what he found? For the second and third questions, the preliminary answers must be that he will have found the Roman rite in use for mass and Office,[1] with St Benedict's variant of the Office being used by monks;[2] and that, as he was in a sense a 'front man' for Hadrian (who of the two will have had the most intimate knowledge of services in Latin), he is unlikely to have contributed anything novel himself, unless he had a devotion to particular saints, and introduced their feasts into the liturgical calendar at Canterbury.

---

[1] The question of the liturgical practices introduced into England by Augustine and his Roman monks is vitiated by the fact that there are no surviving liturgical manuscripts from this period; see H. A. Wilson, 'Notes on Some Liturgical Questions relating to the Mission of St Augustine', in *The Mission of St Augustine to England according to the Original Documents, being a Handbook for the Thirteenth Centenary*, ed. A. J. Mason (Cambridge, 1897), pp. 235–52; H. Ashworth, 'Did St Augustine bring the *Gregorianum* to England?', *Ephemerides Liturgicae* 72 (1958), 39–43; G. G. Willis, *Further Essays in Early Roman Liturgy* (London, 1968), pp. 191–206; and H. Mayr-Harting, *The Coming of Christianity to Anglo-Saxon England*, 3rd ed. (London, 1991), pp. 168–74. It has also been suggested that the *Martyrologium Hieronymianum* was first brought to England by Augustine: see J. Chapman, 'A propos des martyrologes', *RB* 20 (1903), 185–313, at 293.

[2] The evidence is that use of a distinctive form of the so-called 'Old Hymnal', which is closely associated with Benedict and Benedictine monasticism, is attested in England, and specifically in Canterbury, no later than the earlier eighth century: see H. Gneuss, *Hymnar und Hymnen im englischen Mittelalter* (Tübingen, 1968), pp. 28–36.

Answers to all these questions lie outside my own expertise; but for the third this is perhaps least true, and I begin with it. In the absence of any surviving calendar or martyrology from late seventh-century Canterbury, the texts which we must explore for evidence of saints' feasts introduced to England by Theodore are the following: Bede's *Martyrologium*;[3] a group of early Anglo-Saxon calendars of which the best known is the 'Calendar of St Willibrord';[4] the Gelasian sacramentaries;[5] and the Old English Martyrology.[6] Our first task will be to see which, if any, saints from the vicinity of Tarsus in Cilicia (where Theodore was born in 602), and more generally from Antioch in Syria (in the patriarchate of which Tarsus lay), may be seen to figure in these Anglo-Saxon liturgical sources.

The obvious martyrs of Tarsus are SS Cirycus and Julitta (the original name of the first of these was presumably *Kerykos* (Κήρυκος) in Greek, rather than Kyriakos).[7] Both are commemorated in the *Martyrologium Hieronymianum*,[8] though they are wrongly said in that source to have been martyred at Antioch – rather than at Tarsus – on 16 June, and this error runs through Latin historical martyrologies until the place of their martyrdom was corrected in the sixteenth century by Baronius.[9] In the

---

[3] Best consulted in the (preliminary) edition of J. Dubois and G. Renaud, *Edition pratique des martyrologes de Bède, de l'Anonyme lyonnais et de Florus* (Paris, 1976); see also [Bollandists], 'Martyrologium e codice Basilicae Vaticanae nunc primum editum', *AB* 49 (1931), 51–97. The essential discussion is still that of H. Quentin, *Les Martyrologes historiques du moyen âge*, 2nd ed. (Paris, 1908), pp. 17–119.

[4] *The Calendar of St Willibrord*, ed. H. A. Wilson, HBS 55 (London, 1918); see also P. Siffrin, 'Das Walderdorffer Fragment saec. VIII', *Ephemerides Liturgicae* 47 (1933), 201–21.

[5] See *CPL*, nos. 1899–1900, and *CLitLA*, pp. 299–311 (nos. 610–35). The assumption is that Gelasians were used in earlier seventh-century England, and that reflexes of these are preserved in the later Gelasians from eighth-century Bavaria.

[6] *Das altenglische Martyrologium*, ed. G. Kotzor, Bayerische Akademie der Wissenschaften, phil.-hist. Klasse, Abhandlungen ns 88, 2 vols. (Munich, 1981).

[7] *BHG*, nos. 313y–318e; *BHL*, nos. 1801–14; cf. also *Bibliotheca Sanctorum* X (1968), 1324–8.

[8] *Martyrologium Hieronymianum*, ed. G. B. De Rossi and L. Duchesne, *Acta SS.*, Nou. II.1 (Brussels, 1894), 79: 'In Antiochia Cyrici et Iulittae'.

[9] *Martyrologium Romanum*, ed. C. Baronius (Rome, 1586), p. 267: 'De his [*scil*. Quiricus et Iulitta] Beda, Vsuardus, Ado, & caeteri Latinorum, Graeci autem in Menologio idibus Iulij, vbi Tarsi Ciliciæ eos occubuisse martyrio tradunt: quod verum esse, legitima eorundem acta testantur; ex his plerique Latinorum sunt corrigendi, qui Antiochiæ eos passos referunt.'

Martyrologium of Bede, the entry is one of the short ones entered against 15 July, in agreement with Greek martyrological sources, and no place of martyrdom is given.[10] Bede's entry is followed by Hrabanus Maurus in both respects.[11] The compiler of the Old English Martyrology gets both date and place right, in a lengthy entry, but – unluckily for our present purposes – one of those left by Günter Kotzor for eventual discussion by Professor J. E. Cross (which, to my knowledge, has not yet appeared).[12] A detailed study of the Old English Martyrologist's entry for SS Cirycus and Julitta is a great desideratum, for there were numerous versions of their passion in both Greek and Latin (not to mention Georgian, and presumably therefore Syriac, Armenian and Coptic); the task of determining the precise source of the Old English entry is likely to be a laborious one. In any event, the legend of their passion was well enough known in eighth-century Rome to be painted on the walls of a chapel in S. Maria Antiqua.[13] This raises the interesting question of the source used by Bede for the short entry in his *Martyrologium*. As Bede says elsewhere, his general intention was to name the judge under whom each martyr suffered, and the nature of his/her suffering.[14] These details, which in this case are omitted by Bede, would have been discoverable from any version of the passio of SS Cirycus and Julitta, and it looks therefore as if Bede took his short entry from some sort of calendar (rather than from an extensive *passio*), with the intention of undertaking further research which he never completed. His *Martyrologium* also includes, as a short entry, St Mary Magdalene, her first appearance outside the Bible in the West; significantly, she is entered in Bede on the day on which she is commemorated in Byzantine liturgical sources.[15] The compiler of the Old English Martyrology picked up this detail and expanded it by including an abstract

---

[10] *Edition pratique*, ed. Dubois and Renaud, p. 128; but cf. the longer entry for 16 June (p. 109): 'In Tarso Ciliciae, passio sanctorum Cyrici pueri et Iulittae matris eius. . .' Cf. Quentin, *Les Martyrologes historiques*, p. 52.

[11] *Rabani Mauri Martyrologium*, ed J. McCulloh, CCCM 44 (Turnhout, 1979), 68.

[12] *Das altenglische Martyrologium*, ed. Kotzor II, 148–51.

[13] See E. Kitzinger, *Römische Malerei vom Beginn des 7. bis zur Mitte des 8. Jahrhunderts* (Munich, 1935).

[14] *HE* V.24 (p. 570): 'Martyrologium de nataliciis sanctorum martyrum diebus, in quo omnes, quos inuenire potui, non solum qua die uerum etiam quo genere certaminis uel sub quo iudice mundum uicerint, diligenter adnotare studui.'

[15] *Edition pratique*, ed. Dubois and Renaud, p. 133.

drawn from the *Vita eremetica* of St Mary Magdalene;[16] and if this entry can be taken to have stood in the original form of the Old English Martyrology (which must have been in existence at the very latest by *c.* 900, since that is the date of the earliest surviving, but fragmentary, manuscript), then it is the earliest recorded indication of the existence of the *Vita eremetica*. Early copies of the work are not at all common; though it is perhaps worth noting that there is one – the second of two *vitae* of this saint – in the Bodleian manuscript (now Oxford, Bodleian Library, Bodley 535) which also preserves the *vita prima* of St Neot and Bili's *Vita S. Machuti*, so the manuscript is clearly the work of someone who was interested in rare hagiographical items.[17] I recently consulted Mgr Saxer – the author of the most comprehensive study to date on the medieval cult of St Mary Magdalene[18] – to find out whether he had made any progress in tracing the early history of the *Vita eremetica*; but his present duties appear to have taken him away from work of this nature. The task is a large one, and crucial to our understanding of Bede's sources for his *Martyrologium*: there are, for example, numerous entries for St Mary Magdalene in *Bibliotheca Hagiographica Graeca*.[19] But whether Bede could have known such a source in Greek, even through the agency of Archbishop Theodore, is as yet unclear.

The most eccentric of all entries in the Old English Martyrology is that of St Milus of Susa in Persia.[20] So far as I know, he appears in no medieval Latin book at all: certainly he is not included in Bede's *Martyrologium*. The Greek *vita* of the saint, of which the full text does not appear to survive, is

---

[16] *Das altenglische Martyrologium*, ed. Kotzor II, 156–7; cf. J. E. Cross, 'Mary Magdalen in the Old English Martyrology: the Earliest Extant "Narrat Josephus" Variant of her Legend', *Speculum* 53 (1978), 16–25.

[17] On the manuscript, see most recently M. Lapidge in *The Annals of St Neots with Vita Prima Sancti Neoti*, ed. D. Dumville and M. Lapidge (Cambridge, 1985), p. lxxix.

[18] V. Saxer, *Le Culte de Marie Madeleine en Occident des origines à la fin du moyen âge* (Auxerre, 1959) (to be supplemented by the remarks of B. de Gaiffier, 'Notes sur le culte du Sainte Marie-Madeleine', *AB* 78 (1960), 161–8, at 164, n. 1), as well as Saxer's entry in *Bibliotheca Sanctorum* VIII (1967), 1078–104, and his more recent study, 'Les Origines du culte de Sainte Marie Madeleine en Occident', in *Marie Madeleine dans la mystique, les arts et les lettres*, ed. E. Duperray (Paris, 1989), pp. 34–47, which contains discussion of Bede's notice at pp. 34–7, but makes no mention of the Old English Martyrology or the *Vita eremitica*.

[19] *BHG*, nos. 1161x–1162c.

[20] *Das altenglische Martyrologium*, ed. Kotzor II, 251–2 (with discussion at 370).

225

most easily accessible in standard Greek *menaia*;[21] but one of these could scarcely have been the source used by the compiler of the Old English Martyrology. In any case, the Old English Martyrologist gives the relevant place-names in corrupt Syriac forms, which are strikingly different from those found in Greek.[22] Again, one wonders whether the Old English Martyrologist had access to a text which had been brought to England by Archbishop Theodore: a hypothesis which takes on further interest in light of Theodore's apparent links with Syria and Syriac literature.[23]

It is clear from these examples that the saints commemorated in early Anglo-Saxon liturgical and martyrological books were drawn from a variety of sources, and that these sources may often be associated – hypothetically at least – with known churchmen such as Theodore. An association of this sort is extremely plausible in the case of a number of entries in the Old English Martyrology of which the compiler character-istically stated that such-and-such a saint 'has a mass-song [or something equivalent] in the older mass-books', but added nothing further.[24] The saints in question are: Priscus (1 June), Nicander (17 June), Magnus (19 August), Rufus (27 August), Priscus again (1 September), Quintus (5 September), Sinotus (7 September) and Lupulus (15 October). For Nicander, Quintus, Sinotus and Lupulus no proper mass, so far as I know, is transmitted in any surviving massbook whatsoever. Magnus, Rufus and Priscus (1 September) on the other hand are given propers in all complete copies of the Gelasian Sacramentary, and their propers have thence passed into a very high proportion of medieval missals. Nicander is a saint of Venafro, Magnus of Fabrateria; Priscus, Quintus, Sinotus and Lupulus are all of Capua. The commemoration of Priscus on 1 June is otherwise unknown; the date, however, is probably the dedication of the church of S. Prisco outside Capua, which appears to have been the burial place of early

---

21 For bibliography on *menaia*, see *ODB* II, 1338. On St Milus, see *BHG*, no. 2276. The Syriac *Life* of St Milus is listed *BHO*, no. 772, and ptd S. E. Assemani, *Acta Sanctorum Martyrum Orientalium et Occidentalium*, 2 vols. (Rome, 1748) I, 66–83.

22 Cf. the forms *Drasythio*, *Leila* and *Malhpar* with (for example) those given in the 'Synaxarion of Constantinople', ed. H. Delehaye, *Synaxarium ecclesiae Constantinopoli-tanae. Propylaeum ad Acta SS. Nouembris* (Brussels, 1902), cols. 220–1. Kotzor (*Das altenglische Martyrologium* II, 370) compares the Old English forms with the forms given in Assemani's Latin translation of the Syriac text.

23 See Bischoff and Lapidge, *Biblical Commentaries*, pp. 233–40, and discussion by Sebastian Brock, above, pp. 49–52.

24 See discussion by Kotzor, *Das altenglische Martyrologium* I, 258*-263*.

Capuan bishops. The church itself was destroyed in 1766, but its mosaics were recorded in reasonable detail, and they are our principal source for knowledge of this group of saints. Lupulus, Rufus and Priscus were shown both in the dome and the apse of the church, and Sinotus and Quintus in the apse only. There survives no known *passio* for SS Sinotus, Quintus and Lupulus. It is the presence of fantastic saints such as these in the Old English Martyrology – the implied feeling on the part of the compiler of the archetype that they had somehow to be mentioned – that makes it not really credible that that archetype was later than the eighth century. The type of mass-book in which they figure must have come from Capua, or from somewhere very near, and it must have been adopted in some fairly important church.[25] In the 'Calendar of St Willibrord' all these saints are present as additions, except for Priscus on 1 June (which is in the 'second main hand'), and the two saints of August (Magnus and Rufus), who were omitted conceivably by mistake.[26] The Walderdorff Calendar, which was used in Regensburg but is drawn from earlier Anglo-Saxon materials, has all the saints concerned for the months it covers (the manuscript is fragmentary), usually specifying that they are of Capua, with the specification *orationes et preces*, meaning that propers for them will follow.[27] But although we have a number of leaves from the manuscript, we still have not got the Sanctorale.

The evidence of these Capuan saints has been treated many times during the past century, and most scholars have agreed that it must have been Hadrian who brought the 'old mass-book' with its commemorations (and propers) of Capuan saints to England.[28] I find it unthinkable that Hadrian thought it was important that dwellers in the fens and wolds of Britain – or members of the religious community at Regensburg, for that matter – should celebrate with special solemnity on their several days the memory of SS Lupulus, Quintus and Sinotus; so I take it that the book concerned is

---

[25] For a full discussion of this various evidence, see *Biblical Commentaries*, ed. Bischoff and Lapidge, pp. 155–67, where the hypothetical 'old mass-book' from which these entries were ultimately drawn is associated with Theodore's companion, Abbot Hadrian; cf. also below, n. 28.

[26] See *The Calendar of St Willibrord*, ed. Wilson, pp. xx–xxi and 31.

[27] Siffrin, 'Das Walderdorffer Fragment'.

[28] See, in particular, H. A. Wilson, 'English Mass-Books of the Ninth Century', *JTS* 3 (1901–2), 429–33; J. Chapman, *Notes on the Early History of the Vulgate Gospels* (Oxford, 1908), pp. 146–9; W. H. Frere, *Studies in Early Roman Liturgy I. The Kalendar* (London, 1930), pp. 45–7; and Willis, *Further Essays*, pp. 216–19.

the one used at St Augustine's Canterbury, where the companions Hadrian is recorded to have brought with him[29] will have been disposed to go on doing what they had always done at home, and the book then simply got copied. And I have suggested elsewhere that the reason why SS Magnus and Rufus (and various other Italian saints who have nothing to do with Rome) have propers in the unique manuscript of the 'Old Gelasian' sacramentary, which was written at Chelles, that haunt of English princesses, is that the prototype at Chelles got there, not direct from Rome, but via England.[30] Chelles is in the Parisian diocese which Bishop Agilbert took over when he was expelled from Winchester. Agilbert was Theodore's host on his way to England:[31] we are not specifically told that he was in touch with Hadrian as well, but it is likely enough. There is no special reason making it less probable that a Roman book with Campanian additions reached Chelles from England and was then copied, than that a Campanian book which had reached Canterbury was copied in a Northumbrian hand and reached Regensburg; and about this last proposition, there can be no doubt.

It is noteworthy also that the 'Prague Sacramentary', a species of Gelasian from Regensburg, omits SS Magnus and Rufus, though it includes St Priscus.[32] Many reasons of an accidental kind can be advanced to explain this as an omission. But it is remarkable that precisely these two should be missing in the 'Calendar of St Willibrord', while St Priscus is entered by a main, not an adding, hand. The 'Prague Sacramentary' had some relationship to Verona – it has a mass for St Zeno – and it seems to me possible that there were Italian Gelasians in whose ancestry the two saints had never appeared.

There is no need to pursue this line of enquiry further, for there is no doubt that Hadrian's influence is somehow involved. Where it begins to look like Theodore's influence is in the entries in the *Martyrologium* of Bede where the saints concerned are not in the *Martyrologium Hieronymianum* but

---

[29] Bede, *HE* IV.1 (p. 332): 'Praeceperat enim Theodoro abeunti domnus apostolicus, ut in diocesi sua prouideret et daret ei [*scil.* Hadriano] locum, in quo *cum suis* apte degere potuisset' (my italics).

[30] 'Some Service-Books of the Later Saxon Church', in *Tenth-Century Studies*, ed. D. Parsons (London and Chichester, 1975), pp. 60–83 and 217–27, at 61–2.

[31] Bede, *HE* IV.1 (p. 330): 'Theodorus profectus est ad Agilberctum Parisiorum episcopum . . . et ab eo benigne susceptus et multo tempore habitus est.'

[32] *CLitLA*, no. 630; ed. A. Dold, *Das Prager Sakramentar*, 2 vols. (Beuron, 1944–9).

are in the 'Synaxarion of Constantinople'.[33] Of the latter we have no copy earlier than the ninth century and (so far as I know) no one has looked through synaxaria in languages other than Greek to see if any sort of pattern emerges which might point to an earlier (that is, pre-ninth-century) form; in any event, there is no particular reason to think that the forms we know in Greek were codified long before the ninth century.[34] For that reason, it is all the more striking that a number of saints should be commemorated both in the 'Synaxarion of Constantinople' and in Bede's *Martyrologium*. As listed by Dom Quentin, the saints in question are, besides St Mary Magdalene, the following: the Cilician martyr Andrew, I suppose of Tarsus (15 May); Gregory 'the Theologian' (i.e. Gregory of Nazianzus; 25 January); Timothy (24 January); Onesimus (16 February); Invention of the Baptist's Head (24 February); Jeremiah the prophet (1 May); Athanasius (2 May); Epiphanius (12 May); Barnabas (11 June); Elisha the prophet (14 June); Andrew the martyr (19 August); Samuel the prophet (20 August); Zacharias the prophet (6 September); Nativity of BVM (8 September); Gregory Thaumaturgos (17 November); Ephrem (1 February) and Daniel the prophet (21 July). These constitute three secondary apostles (Timothy, Onesimus and Barnabas); five prophets (Jeremiah, Elisha, Samuel, Zacharias and Daniel); the Invention of the Baptist's Head (24 February, when it was taken to Edessa in Syria); the Nativity of the Blessed Virgin Mary; and five fathers of the church, namely Gregory of Nazianzus, Athanasius, Epiphanius of Salamis, Gregory Thaumaturgos and Ephrem the Syrian. In respect of the last five, Bede in his *Martyrologium* announces the commemoration as being *Sancti patris nostri*, the equivalent of the opening words in the Synaxarion for a doctor of the church held in special esteem, as Dom Quentin pointed out.[35] And whereas most (with two differences of a single day) are entered at the same dates as in the Synaxarion, St Ephrem the Syrian is given by Bede as on 9 July, whereas the Constantinopolitan feast is 28 January. St Ephrem's feast is, however, entered in one of the Syrian calendars printed by Nau, and only one, on 9 July; and that comes from Qennesra, that is to say, from the

---

[33] *Synaxarium ecclesiae Constantinopolitanae*, ed. Delehaye.

[34] See Delehaye, *ibid.*, pp. iv–lxxvi, and *idem*, 'Les Ménologes grecs', *AB* 16 (1897), 311–29, repr. in his *Synaxaires byzantins, ménologes, typica* (London, 1977), no. III, as well as W. Vander Meiren, 'Précisions nouvelles sur la généalogie des synaxaires byzantins', *AB* 102 (1984), 397–301.

[35] *Les Martyrologes historiques*, p. 113.

famous Jacobite monastery on the Euphrates facing the well-known Christian site of Dura-Europus (rather than an apparently different monastery of the same name south of Aleppo).[36] The effect of this is marred by another calendar from the same place which puts Ephrem on 9 June, not to mention the fact that the same calendars say that the doctor is also to be commemorated on 1 February and, along with the other Syrian doctors Isaac and James, on 20 February, whereas no specification is made that the Ephrem to be commemorated on 9 July (or June) is the doctor of the church.[37] But no other source for Bede's date seems to be recoverable. The link is a striking one, therefore.

One should also note that there are some conspicuous omissions from the 'Synaxarion of Constantinople' in Bede's *Martyrologium*: note, for example, Dionysius the Areopagite as bishop of Athens; St John Chrysostom (a native of Antioch); and St Basil of Caesarea. Dionysius, bishop of Paris, is included by Bede, on 9 October; and in the Synaxarion, against 3 October, is identified with the Areopagite. But the two were still separate in Bede's day, in both East and West; and Florus of Lyon, taking his text from Eusebius, entered the Areopagite separately on 3 October, his *Greek* feast day.[38] Under the circumstances it seems certain that some Syrian – rather than Constantinopolitan or Athenian – document was drawn on by Bede, and I suspect that it included, as Bede does, St Babylas and the Three Children from Antioch, as well as St Simeon the Stylite, even if these were also included in the *Martyrologium Hieronymianum*, and could have provided Bede with a more immediate source in these cases. St Babylas is commemorated on 4 September in the Synaxarion, but on 24 January – as in Bede and the *Martyrologium Hieronymianum* – in the Syriac calendars. The main entry for St Symeon the Stylite in the Synaxarion is 1 September, but he has a secondary entry at 27 July in the Synaxarion, and this is the date which is found in the Syriac calendars, the *Martyrologium Hieronymianum* and Bede.

Of this group of oriental saints, none appears either in the early Anglo-Saxon calendars (such as the 'Calendar of St Willibrord') or in the Old English Martyrology – any more than St Milus of Susa is noticed by Bede. It seems thus that we have to accept that two Syrian documents were

---

[36] F. Nau, *Martyrologes et ménologes orientaux I-XIII. Un martyrologe et douze ménologes syriaques*, PO 10.1 (Paris and Freiburg, 1912), 43.

[37] *Ibid.*, pp. 51 (9 June), 38, 99 and 109 (1 February) and 38 (20 February), respectively.

[38] *Edition pratique*, ed. Dubois and Renaud, p. 181.

in England, one in Syriac and in the hands of someone who could put it into Latin (or Old English). As the oriental saints reach us by different channels, it is possible that they were brought by different men. But it is difficult not to conclude that one of these men must have been the archbishop, and the second, if different, a companion of his.

I now return to the remaining questions which I raised at the outset. About the services that Theodore knew and those he found on arrival, two difficulties arise at once. We know nothing about the length of time Theodore spent anywhere.[39] In 602 he was in Tarsus and in 667 he was a monk in Rome. But we do not know whether Tarsus, as St Paul's birthplace, was also given as his, to avoid tedious explanations, as the one place in Cilicia of which everyone would have heard; and, even if we accept that Tarsus means Tarsus and not a little village up country, we still do not know whether his father was native, and not an official on a tour of duty, nor, particularly in view of the disturbed state of that part of the world at that time, whether he or they did not rapidly move elsewhere. Nor, I think, do we know how far services for Chalcedonians (that is, orthodox, Greeks) at the time were in Syriac rather than in Greek, or how far his family background was either Greek or Syrian.[40] Nor do we know when, where or why he became a monk.

Our ignorance about the precise details of Theodore's life is matched by our ignorance, except in broad outline, of eastern liturgical services.[41] The general structure of the mass is the same everywhere; but when it comes to details – just what prayers are said at what point, when, and what chants are interposed at what point – then even among surviving Latin missals

[39] Cf. discussion by Lapidge, above, pp. 1–29, and more fully in *Biblical Commentaries*, ed. Bischoff and Lapidge, pp. 5–81.

[40] The point being that Syria, including Antioch and Edessa (which Theodore is known to have visited: see discussion by Lapidge, above, p. 7) was bilingual in Greek and Syriac at that time: see G. Haddad, *Aspects of Social Life in Antioch in the Hellenistic-Roman Period* (New York, n.d. [1952?]), pp. 104–21, and H. J. W. Drijvers, 'East of Antioch: Forces and Structures in the Development of Early Syriac Theology', in his *East of Antioch: Studies in Early Syriac Christianity* (London, 1984), no. I, together with discussion by Sebastian Brock, above, pp. 37–46.

[41] The starting-point for the study of Byzantine liturgy is *Liturgies Eastern and Western*, ed. F. E. Brightman and C. E. Hammond (Oxford, 1896); see also H.-J. Schulz, *The Byzantine Liturgy* (New York, 1986), and R. F. Taft, *Beyond East and West: Problems in Liturgical Understanding* (Washington, DC, 1984). On the liturgy of Antioch (in whose patriarchate Tarsus lay), see M. H. Shepherd, 'The Formation and Influence of the Antiochene Liturgy', *Dumbarton Oaks Papers* 15 (1961), 25–44.

there are obviously serious differences between, say, Mozarabic books and the rest, substantial ones between Ambrosian books and the rest, and noticeable ones – if one settles down to comparing in detail – between the missals of every Latin cathedral, Benedictine monastery and order. With the Office differences are much greater. *Mutatis mutandis* the situation is the same, if not worse, in the Greek East. The Greek liturgical books that are accessible represent effectively the consensus of Mount Athos and the patriarchal church of Constantinople in the sixteenth century. But it has relatively recently been shown that Nocturns and Vespers as sung at Hagia Sophia and in the cathedral of Thessalonica before 1453 were seriously different.[42] And surviving Greek books from southern Italy stem from a late eleventh-century reform of the Greek monasteries there, which lined them up more or less on Constantinopolitan use, and we do not know what was done before.[43] The Greek monastic *typika* are understood to stem from the model usages of the monastery of St Sabas in the Jordan Valley.[44] How far they differ from one another I do not know; if anyone has laid out their contents in sets of comparative tables, his work has not come my way. And a further joker has latterly been added to the pack by those who have pointed out that, until a reform in the eleventh century which brought it into line with Mount Athos, the church of Georgia followed the (Greek) usages of the Holy Sepulchre in Jerusalem. The point about all this is that we cannot simply assume that what was done in Greek in Constantinople or Rome in the seventh century differed as much from, or in the same way as, what was done in Latin (as would have been the case in either city in the first half of the twentieth).

It is therefore impossible to estimate what effect a lifetime's experience of Greek public liturgy might have had on the Latin liturgical practices of Archbishop Theodore. In matters of private liturgy, however, there is somewhat more evidence, although one must stress once again how tenuous this evidence is. It has recently been suggested that various traces can be found in early Anglo-Saxon written records of a (now lost) booklet

---

[42] O. Strunk, 'The Byzantine Office at Hagia Sophia', *Dumbarton Oaks Papers* 9–10 (1956), 175–202, repr. in his *Essays on Music in the Byzantine World* (New York, 1977), pp. 112–50.

[43] O. Strunk, 'S. Salvatore di Messina and the Musical Tradition of Magna Graecia', in his *Essays on Music in the Byzantine World*, pp. 45–54.

[44] On the so-called 'Sabaitic Typika', see *ODB* III, 2131–2, as well as E. Wellesz, *A History of Byzantine Music and Hymnography*, 2nd ed. (Oxford, 1961), p. 135.

of Greek prayers assembled somewhere in the patriarchate of Antioch in the seventh century.[45] This hypothetical booklet seems to have included copies, all in Greek, of a litany of the saints, the Lord's Prayer, the Apostles' Creed and the Trisagion (or 'Sanctus' in Latin), for transliterations into Latin of all of them are found in various manuscripts of the Anglo-Saxon period. In particular, copies were made of these four prayers in London, BL, Cotton Galba A. xviii (the so-called 'Athelstan Psalter') sometime in the second quarter of the tenth century, perhaps for the use and consultation of Israel the Grammarian, a well-known student of Greek who was in England at that time. That the Greek originals were in England no later than the later eighth century is proved by the fact that a translation of the Greek litany of the saints was made into Latin, which is preserved in a prayerbook of probable Worcester origin, now London, BL, Royal 2. A. XX.[46] Given the origin of these prayers in the patriarchate of Antioch (in which Tarsus was situated), the most reasonable explanation of their presence in England before the later eighth century is that they were brought by Archbishop Theodore. But the matter requires further investigation.

I turn finally to the fearsome question of liturgical music. There has in recent years been a lengthy debate over how the music in early noted Greek liturgical manuscripts (effectively starting around AD 1000, as in the Latin West) is to be read.[47] I confess that I am not a musician, I may have misunderstood much that I have read, and I may formulate things wrongly. But modern Greek church music takes its start with the activities of the archimandrite Chrysanthos, whose main work, the *Mega Theoretikon*, was published in Greek in Trieste in 1832. Drawing on the traditions of the patriarchal church in Constantinople, Chrysanthos said that two of the eight modes (the second and its plagal) used a chromatic

---

[45] See F. J. Badcock, 'A Portion of an Early Anatolian Prayerbook', *JTS* 33 (1931–2), 167–80, and esp. M. Lapidge, 'Israel the Grammarian in Anglo-Saxon England', in *From Athens to Chartres: Neoplatonism and Medieval Thought. Studies in Honour of Edouard Jeauneau*, ed. H. J. Westra (Leiden, New York and Cologne, 1992), pp. 97–114, at 112–13, repr. in his *Anglo-Latin Literature, 900–1066* (London and Rio Grande, OH, 1993), pp. 87–104, at 102–3; *idem, Anglo-Saxon Litanies of the Saints*, HBS 106 (London, 1991), 13–25; and *Biblical Commentaries*, ed. Bischoff and Lapidge, pp. 168–73.

[46] Lapidge, *Anglo-Saxon Litanies of the Saints*, pp. 212–13 (no. XXVI).

[47] For general orientation, see Wellesz, *A History of Byzantine Music and Hymnography*, pp. 246–324.

scale, and that the actual notation, ignoring miscellaneous interlinear signs, was meant always to be ornamented. He proposed a simplification of the notation (which was instantly adopted), reducing the number of interlinear signs, and he and two colleagues set to work to recopy the musical texts, showing every note that had to be sung, as opposed to having a mere skeleton which only lengthy training would qualify a singer to fill out. The resultant musical texts, many of which were printed, were mostly much too long for normal use; but I understand that the reaction of the Greek church to this was not to return to the old skeleton but to prepare new shortenings based on the extended texts. Greek notation does not use a staff. It tells a singer, say, to go up two and down one; but in order to know where you have got, you have to rehearse the whole thing (silently even) from the beginning. This means that comparing two versions of the same melody becomes diabolically difficult. And Greek scholars maintain that the music cannot properly be written on staves because of the chromatic scales and sundry glissandi, though of course a general representation is obviously possible. Western scholars, however, are liable to argue against the existence of such chromatic scales, and hence that those who used the early manuscripts sang what was written and no more. My instinct is to side with the Greek scholars, with suitable reservations about what the average monk might have been expected to achieve. Furthermore, I do not believe that liturgical music in the Roman empire differed in its principles according to whether you were a Latin or a Greek, because, in the higher reaches of the church, the Latins will have followed the Greeks. And I feel sure that singing in Latin at Rome, at all relevant dates one of the greatest cities of the empire, will have followed the same rules as anywhere else over such things as chromatic scales and ornamentation, for there is no obvious reason why the Greeks should have changed the principles of their music for Roman consumption. I suspect that it is the West which has diverged, owing to Charlemagne's sudden decision that everyone must sing as they did in Rome (which is likely to have involved numerous simplifications) and to the rise of polyphony, which plays no part in Greek church music and which also tends to simplification. So long as music is not written down, the tradition of anything elaborate is dependent on the existence of a quite limited number of teachers and pupils, and its survival is always a matter of great fragility.

Bede does not specifically say that Theodore had anything directly to do with music, but interposes a paragraph on the subject between two paragraphs discussing Theodore;[48] and the implication is that Theodore as well as Wilfrid was anxious to spread from Canterbury liturgical singing as practised in Rome. The possible relevance here of Theodore is the negative one, that there is no hint (that I know) that he had or was expected to have any problems with the music, which suggests to me that Latin music in Rome, and therefore at Canterbury, was a great deal more like modern Greek music than Latin music in general very soon became. No music survives from England from earlier than the tenth century; and when notation does begin to appear in liturgical manuscripts at that time, it derives from centres of reformed monasticism in France and Germany. Roman music, in the meantime, was out of step with that of northern Europe, and was suppressed in the thirteenth century (though the claim has recently been made that the earlier Roman music has been preserved in part in certain manuscripts, among them one from the church of S. Cecilia in Trastevere). Accordingly, it is now virtually impossible to form any impression of what the church music of seventh-century Rome may have sounded like; but if my hypothesis is correct, it will have differed very little if at all from that of the Greek church in which Archbishop Theodore was brought up. In this respect, as in so many others, the impact of Theodore on the English church was arguably profound; but the demonstration of that impact will require the continuing study of Greek (as well as Syriac) liturgical sources.

---

[48] *HE* IV.2 (p. 334): 'sed et sonos cantandi in ecclesia, quos eatenus in Cantia tantum nouerant, ab hoc tempore per omnes Anglorum ecclesias discere coeperunt'.

12

Theodore's Bible: the Pentateuch

RICHARD MARSDEN

The biblical commentaries preserved in Milan, Biblioteca Ambrosiana, M. 79 sup., are a treasury of information about Theodore's contribution to Anglo-Saxon learning in the late seventh century. For the historian of the Latin Bible, however, the *lemmata* which accompany the commentaries are a source of knowledge no less valuable. There are 465 distinct *lemmata* for the Pentateuch, a high proportion of them from Genesis or Exodus, including also sixteen from Jerome's preface to Genesis.[1] Varying in length from a single word to whole sentences, and totalling nearly 1,500 words, they provide us with our earliest clear evidence of a Pentateuch text in use in Anglo-Saxon England, predating by a generation the Northumbrian 'Codex Amiatinus'.[2] More than this, they may add to our general knowledge of Vulgate textual history in the period between Jerome's death and the Carolingian Bible revisions of the eighth and ninth centuries, a period from which, apart from the Codex Amiatinus, only two other Bible manuscripts containing the Pentateuch survive.[3] However fragmentary it

---

[1] The Milan manuscript has 474 glosses. Damage has removed two *lemmata*, while in seven more cases the glossator comments in general terms on a scriptural passage, highlighting no specific words. 196 *lemmata* are from Genesis, 111 from Exodus, sixty-nine from Leviticus, sixty from Numbers and thirteen from Deuteronomy.

[2] They are almost our earliest Anglo-Saxon evidence for any part of the Old Testament. The only other pre-Amiatinan witness is a sixth-century Italian uncial fragment of Maccabees, now Durham, Cathedral Library, B. IV. 6, fol. 169. Known Old Testament manuscripts of Anglo-Saxon origin or provenance are listed in an appendix to R. Marsden, 'The Old Testament in Late Anglo-Saxon England: Preliminary Observations on the Textual Evidence', in *The Early Medieval Bible: its Production, Decoration and Use*, ed. R. Gameson, Cambridge Studies in Palaeography and Codicology 2 (Cambridge, 1994), 101–24, at 123–4. On the Codex Amiatinus, see also below, p. 241.

[3] One of them lacks Deuteronomy. They are identified and described below.

236

may be, the evidence offered us by Theodore's *lemmata* thus demands the closest scrutiny.

Can such evidence, indirect as it is and surviving in an eleventh-century Italian copy, convey an accurate picture of the Pentateuch text in use at Canterbury in the 670s? There are compelling reasons for optimism. To begin with, the accuracy of a very large proportion of the text can be easily demonstrated. Textual differences between surviving Vulgate manuscripts at any period are comparatively few and a great proportion of their texts is universally shared.[4] Some eighty per cent of the 465 Theodore *lemmata* transmit this shared text, which has reached the Milan manuscript without alteration.[5] In a further eight *lemmata*, there is a total of eleven proper names, in the spelling of which in the Theodore versions there is minor variation from the forms most commonly found in early medieval Vulgate manuscripts, as in *Chebron* for *Hebron* in Gen. XIII.18 (PentI 93)[6] and *Ochozat* for *Ochozath* in Gen. XXVI.26 (PentI 155). Most of these variations have been ignored in my assessment of Theodore's Pentateuch, for proper names are notoriously misleading indicators of Vulgate textual origin and transmissional continuity.[7] More significant in the transmission of the Canterbury material is the fact that, whatever the form of a name adopted in our manuscript, it does not vary if it is repeated. This is illustrated by *Chananeus*, a name which occurs frequently and varies frequently in Vulgate manuscripts but which is used in the Theodore glosses to Num. XIII.30 (PentI 425 and 426) and XXIV.20 (PentI 445) with the same basic form in each case. This high standard of consistency is evident also in those cases where the wording of the *lemma* is repeated in

---

[4] Minor orthographical variations, such as *adf-* / *aff-*, or *ae* / *e*, are ignored in this assessment.

[5] I have included in this shared text nine single-word *lemmata* in which a noun is recorded in the nominative form, although in its scriptural context it is in an oblique case. Examples are Gen. XXIV.14 (PentI 143: see following note) *hydria* (in context, *hydriam*), Ex. XXV.4 (PentI 287) *purpura* (*purpuram*), Lev. XI.14 (PentI 356) *uultur* (*uulturem*) and Num. XI.32 (PentI 421) *chorus* (*c(h)oros*). Such simplification is not made in all such cases, however. A *lemma* from Lev. I.16 (PentI 333), for example, is given in its contextual accusative form, *uessiculam*.

[6] Numbers in brackets identify a *lemma* from PentI, ed. Bischoff and Lapidge, *Biblical Commentaries*.

[7] On the problems caused by proper names in the classifying of Vulgate texts, see R. Marsden, 'The Text of the Pentateuch in Late Anglo-Saxon England' (unpubl. PhD dissertation, Cambridge Univ., 1991), pp. 80–1.

the gloss, as may be seen in *lemmata* and *interpretamenta* to Ex. VI.23 (PentI 237), Lev. XI.35 (PentI 363), Num. XI.5 (PentI 413) and Num. XX.16 (PentI 434).[8]

The only example of inconsistency in Theodore's text is the use of *armilla* in the *interpretamentum* of the third of a series of glosses to Num. XXXI.50 (PentI 453), although *armell{a}* is the form of the word used in both the *lemma* and the *interpretamentum* to the second gloss of the series (PentI 452). The second form is in fact a commonly used variation of the first and may have been the original version in each case.[9] It is frequently difficult, however, to distinguish error from genuine variation in Theodore's text as it has reached us. The problem is particularly acute in respect of the many uncommon words, some of them describing exotic animals, which the glosses highlight. In a *lemma* from Lev. XI.18 (PentI 358), for instance, *onocratalum* for *onocrotalum* can almost certainly be ascribed to error (at whatever stage in transmission it occurred),[10] and also *pardulum* for *pardalum* in one of three *lemmata* from Deut. XIV.5 (PentI 473).[11] In a *lemma* from Gen. XLI.6 (PentI 204), however, *uridine* for *uredine* is paralleled sufficiently often in later Vulgate manuscripts, and elsewhere, to be classed as an orthographical variant. The same is true of *stilio* for *stelio* in Lev. XI.30 (PentI 361). However, some other variant word forms without parallel in other Vulgate sources are sufficiently distinctive to be classified as 'independent' readings, and they are dealt with as such below.

There are two obvious errors in the Theodore text. In the last *lemma* in the corpus, from Deut. XIV.28 (PentI 474), *separabit* occurs for *separabis*, although the content of the associated *interpretamentum* makes it plain that a verb in the second person is required. The error is to be ascribed probably

---

[8] I owe this observation to Michael Lapidge.

[9] Although *armilla* may be considered the correct form, *armella* was current also in late classical times and occurs in Vulgate manuscripts also. The variant is used twice, for instance, in the 'Codex Amiatinus' in seven occurrences of the word in Genesis and Exodus. It also is the form used in an eighth-century Latin–Anglo-Saxon gloss contained in Cambridge, Corpus Christi College, 144: see *The Corpus Glossary*, ed. W. M. Lindsay (Oxford, 1921), p. 18 (item A 722).

[10] The word is repeated in Deut. XIV.18 (which is not glossed by the Canterbury commentator), and here the same error was made in the Codex Ottobonianus (see below), but was later corrected. It occurred also, again before correction, in a Spanish manuscript.

[11] On the treatment of these *lemmata*, see further below, pp. 244–5. The erroneous spelling was repeated in two Paris Bibles of the early thirteenth century.

to a fairly late stage of copying. In a *lemma* from Num. XXIII.23 (PentI 440), *dicebatur* for *dicetur* is again clearly wrong when read in the context of an *interpretamentum* which specifically offers an explanation in terms of future, not past, events. To these might be added a *lemma* from Ex. XXV.4 (PentI 286), where *hiacincta*, apparently a feminine form of a second-declension masculine noun, was perhaps produced in error by analogy with *purpura*, which is from the same verse of Exodus and constitutes the following *lemma* (PentI 287).[12] In the case of a *lemma* from Gen. XXII.17 (PentI 137), *tuorum* for *suorum* is wrong, but it might be a deliberate emendation, for in this instance the text of the *lemma*, read in isolation, seems to demand the second person: *possidebit semen tuum portas inimicorum tuorum*.

If we ignore the many *lemmata* which transmit a universal Vulgate text, along with the few which contain errors or unimportant orthographical variations, we are left with eighty-eight *lemmata*, containing a total of ninety significant readings. In these resides the distinctive character of Theodore's Pentateuch text, when compared with that of surviving Vulgate manuscripts, early or later, of the medieval period. The readings may be divided into two main groups. The first comprises twenty-four, in which there is variation among the three Vulgate manuscripts which, as noted above, are the only substantial witnesses to the Pentateuch surviving from the pre-Carolingian period and which were more or less contemporary with the exemplar used at Canterbury in the seventh century. In these readings, the forms used in the Theodore text correspond with the forms in one or two of the Vulgate manuscripts but never in all three, so that it may be possible to establish something of the historical relationships between the various texts.[13] The second group contains sixty-six readings, from sixty-four *lemmata*, and may be divided for purposes of analysis into two sub-groups. In the first are nineteen Theodore variants which, although they do not occur in the three early Vulgate manuscripts, are witnessed in one or more later ones, from the eighth century onwards. The second

---

[12] See above, n. 5.

[13] In my analysis of the Theodore text in relation to surviving Vulgate manuscripts, I rely on the information available in the critical edition of the Old Testament prepared by the Benedictines in Rome: *Biblia Sacra iuxta Latinam Vulgatam Versionem ad Codicum Fidem*, ed. H. Quentin *et al.*, 18 vols. (Rome, 1926–94). The volumes used in this study are: I *Genesis* (1926), II *Exodus-Leviticus* (1929) and III *Numeri-Deuteronium* (1936), hereafter *Biblia Sacra* I, II and III, respectively.

sub-group consists of forty-seven readings in which 'independent' variation occurs; that is, in which the Theodore text has words or phrases whose forms are paralleled neither in the three surviving early Vulgate manuscripts nor in any of the later ones which have been collated. They may thus be a measure of the independence of the Canterbury textual tradition. The division between these two sub-groups will in some instances be more apparent than real, for it is obvious that the sharing of variants between the Theodore text and later Vulgate manuscripts may be entirely coincidental, especially when they are of a simple kind. Indeed, the historical value of the evidence offered by the variant readings in each of the groups varies greatly. Nevertheless, taken overall, it allows some tentative observations to be made about the transmission of Theodore's Pentateuch text and its place in Vulgate history.

It has been noted already that we rely on only three Vulgate manuscripts for direct evidence of the Pentateuch text in use in the seventh century or earlier.[14] These three, one a complete Bible and two part-Bibles, are in fact our earliest substantial witnesses to any part of the Old Testament, apart from a palimpsest, which preserves only Judges, a few verses of Ruth and fragments of Job.[15] The oldest of the three manuscripts is the illustrated 'Ashburnham Pentateuch', now Paris, Bibliothèque Nationale, nouv. acq. lat. 2334,[16] designated here by the siglum

---

[14] The remains of an Octateuch, now Paris, Bibliothèque Nationale, Nouv. acq. 1740 (siglum F in *Biblia Sacra* III), copied in France, have been ascribed by Lowe (*CLA* V, no. 691) simply to the first half of the eighth century; the earlier part of the period suggested by Gribomont ('700–730') seems unlikely ('Conscience philologique chez les scribes du haut moyen âge', *SettSpol* 10 (1963), 601–30, at 628). See also Fischer, *Bibelhandschriften* (cited below, n. 15), pp. 118–19. Of the Pentateuch, only Deuteronomy survives and, although I have used the manuscript in my comparisons of the text of the Theodore *lemmata* from that book with later Vulgate texts, no signifcant parallels or differences have been found.

[15] Vatican City, Biblioteca Apostolica Vaticana, lat. 5763 + Wolfenbüttel, Herzog August-Bibliothek, Weissenburg 64, fols. 282–97, 312, 317 and 328–33. The manuscript was written as early as the second half of the fifth century and re-used in the eighth century in northern Italy. See B. Fischer, *Lateinische Bibelhandschriften im frühen Mittelalter*, Vetus Latina: Aus der Geschichte der lateinischen Bibel 11 (Freiburg, 1985), pp. 119 and 350, and *CLA* I, nos. 40 and 41.

[16] *CLA* V, no. 693ab; S. Berger, *Histoire de la Vulgate pendant les premières siècles du moyen âge* (Paris, 1893), p. 11; H. Quentin, *Mémoire sur l'établissement du texte de la Vulgate. Première partie. Octateuque*, Collectanea Biblica Latina 6 (Rome and Paris, 1922), 414–32; *Biblia Sacra* I, xii-xiv; Fischer, *Bibelhandschriften*, pp. 163, 251 and 350.

G.[17] The manuscript was written during the first half of the seventh century, probably in northern Italy.[18] It was extensively emended and restored in the mid-eighth century in France and by the early ninth had reached Saint-Gatien, Tours, where there was further emendation of one folio. Although 129 of the original folios survive, there are many lacunae, and Deuteronomy is missing altogether. The second witness, the 'Codex Ottobonianus' (O), now Vatican City, Biblioteca Apostolica Vaticana, Ottobonianus lat. 66, seems to have been copied in northern Italy also, around 700 and probably in an Insular centre.[19] Although originally an Octateuch, it now lacks Ruth and parts of other books, and the later Genesis and sections of Exodus are complicated by substantial Old Latin interpolations.[20] Its text is very poor in places, with many errors. Third is the 'Codex Amiatinus' (A), Florence, Biblioteca Medicea Laurenziana, Amiatino 1, our only surviving complete pre-Carolingian Bible.[21] This magnificent volume was the last of three pandects prepared at Wearmouth–Jarrow under the direction of Abbot Ceolfrith and copied largely from good Italian exemplars. It was finished at some time before 716, the year in which it was taken to Italy to be presented to St Peter's in Rome. Fragments of III-IV Kings and Sirach from one of the two sister pandects, which were used in the two home churches at Wearmouth–Jarrow, survive in London, British Library, Add. 37777 + Add. 45025 + Loan 81.[22]

---

[17] The manuscript sigla used in this study are those of the Benedictine critical edition of the Old Testament (see above, n. 13).

[18] A gospelbook with a pre-Hieronymian text, surviving as Munich, Bayerische Staatsbibliothek, Clm. 6224, may have been copied at the same centre, according to Lowe (*CLA* IX, no. 1249).

[19] *CLA* I, no. 66; Quentin, *Mémoire*, pp. 432–8; *Biblia Sacra* I, xxxi-xxxii; and Fischer, *Bibelhandschriften*, p. 349.

[20] See *Vetus Latina: Die Reste der altlateinischen Bibel nach Petrus Sabatier neu gesammelt und herausgegeben von der Erzabtei Beuron* II. *Genesis*, ed. B. Fischer (Beuron, 1951–4), p. 10*, and Quentin, *Mémoire*, pp. 436–7. The readings are collected in C. Vercellone, *Variae Lectiones Vulgatae*, 2 vols. (Rome, 1860) I, 183–4 and 307–10.

[21] *CLA* III, no. 299; Fischer, *Bibelhandschriften*, pp. 9–34 and 67–9; Berger, *Histoire*, pp. 37–41; Quentin, *Mémoire*, pp. 438–52; *Biblia Sacra* I, xx-xxvi; M. B. Parkes, *The Scriptorium of Wearmouth–Jarrow*, Jarrow Lecture 1982 (Jarrow, [1983]); Marsden, *The Text of the Old Testament in Anglo-Saxon England*, CSASE forthcoming, chs. 3–5.

[22] *CLA* II, no. 177; Parkes, *Wearmouth–Jarrow*, p. 21; B. Bischoff and V. Brown, 'Addenda to *Codices Latini Antiquiores*', *MS* 47 (1985), 317–66, at 351–2; Fischer, *Bibelhandschriften*, pp. 19 and 21; Marsden, *The Text of the Old Testament*, chs. 3–5.

The difficulties of trying to understand three hundred years of Vulgate textual history from so few witnesses are evident.[23] Henri Quentin, one of the original collaborators in the Benedictine project to reconstruct Jerome's text of the Old Testament, gave each of them the status of sub-archetype, and the critical apparatus of the Rome *Biblia Sacra* was planned accordingly.[24] Quentin confidently assumed that G, O and A were derived directly from a single archetype, some way removed from Jerome's text, and were in turn the ancestors of three distinct families of the Vulgate, to one of which most subsequent manuscripts could be assigned. Thus, G was the putative head of the Spanish family, O of the Theodulfian and A of the Alcuinian. Decisive criticism of Quentin's methods and conclusions came from De Bruyne, Chapman, Burkitt and Rand, among others.[25] Chapman preferred to see G, O and A as 'close brothers in the most ancient group of an Italian family',[26] but there is no evidence to support his belief that the ancestry of this family lay in a Vulgate revision by Cassiodorus. Fischer has shown the extraordinary extent to which the three manuscripts in fact vary, both in the purity of their Vulgate text and in their reciprocal relationships, at least in the books of the Octateuch, where the only complete comparisons may be

There are twelve folios in all, plus three fragments of a thirteenth. The pandect may have been given to Worcester by Offa; see *ibid.*, ch. 3, and P. Sims-Williams, *Religion and Literature in Western England*, 600–800, CSASE 3 (Cambridge, 1990), 182.

23 Liturgical books, especially lectionaries, are another potential source of information about the early Pentateuch text, but their evidence is fragmentary and is often complicated by the persistence of pre-Hieronymian material. For a survey of this material, see P. Salmon, 'Le texte biblique des lectionnaires mérovingiens', *SettSpol* 10 (1963), 491–517. The usefulness of information supplied by direct quotations of scripture in contemporary works of exegesis and history is also very limited, for similar reasons; see Marsden, *The Text of the Old Testament*, esp. chs. 2 and 6.

24 The project, launched by a papal initiative in 1907, has only recently been completed; see above, n. 13. Quentin developed his 'archetype' theory in *Mémoire*, esp. pp. 453–6; and see also the prolegomena to *Biblia Sacra* I, esp. pp. xl–xlv.

25 See esp. F. C. Burkitt, 'The Text of the Vulgate' [review of Quentin's *Mémoire*], *JTS* 24 (1923), 406–14; E. K. Rand, 'Dom Quentin's Memoir on the Text of the Vulgate', *Harvard Theological Review* 17 (1924), 197–264; J. Chapman, 'The Families of Vulgate Manuscripts in the Pentateuch', *RB* 37 (1925), 5–46, 365–403; and D. De Bruyne, [review of *Mémoire*], *Bulletin d'ancienne littérature chrétienne latine* 1 (1929), 72–6. Quentin defended his methods and largely reaffirmed his views in *Essais de critique textuelle* (Paris, 1926). Cf. also Fischer, *Bibelhandschriften*, pp. 30–1.

26 'The Families of Vulgate Manuscripts', p. 397.

made.[27] We must conclude that the diverse texts which make up the three Bibles or part-Bibles, and which vary greatly in their quality, were in each case brought together quite arbitrarily. There is no evidence that any of the three was prepared as part of an authoritative recension, nor that any had an important influence on later Bibles.[28] All that may be said with any confidence is that, despite their idiosyncrasies, the three manuscripts collectively affirm the central importance of Italy in the transmission of the Vulgate in the early period, an importance which was to persist throughout the eighth century.[29]

Twenty-four of the 465 Pentateuch *lemmata* in the Theodore text, as has been noted, contain readings in which there is more or less variation among G, O and A and from which we might therefore hope to learn something of the place of the Canterbury exemplar in early Vulgate history. The correspondences between the three biblical manuscripts and our manuscript of the Theodore text (Theo) are summed up in the following table, in which the witnesses grouped to the left of the colons agree with each other against those to the right, in the number of readings indicated:[30]

Theo G A	: O	4
Theo G O	: A	7
Theo O A	: G	2

[27] See his discussion of the Alcuinian Bibles, *Bibelhandschriften*, pp. 203–403, at 354–5 and *passim*. In Genesis, for instance, A is the best witness, with G second and O far behind; but in Exodus, A is the worst and G the best.

[28] On the uncertainties of their relationship to the early Tours Bibles in the Octateuch, see *ibid.*, pp. 349–57. A useful brief survey of the Vulgate manuscript evidence by a recent participant in the Benedictine *Biblia Sacra* project is given in Gribomont, 'Conscience philologique', pp. 605–7 and 628–30.

[29] Fischer, *Bibelhandschriften*, p. 56. The importance of Italy is apparent from Fischer's tables of statistics for the pre-800 production and subsequent distribution of Bibles in Italy, England, Ireland, France and Germany: *ibid.*, pp. 97–100.

[30] A complete statistical analysis of the Theodore text and the three manuscripts produces another sixteen or seventeen cases of such variation, but these arise solely from obvious errors in O (such as *uita comedete* for *uita comite* in Gen. XVIII.10, a verse cited in PentI 111) and can serve no useful comparative purpose. Some of the O readings which I have retained could also be the result of error specific to that manuscript, but they may be genuine variants. Although O is by far the worst witness for a number of books, especially Genesis, this is not the case throughout the Octateuch. In Judges, for instance, it has a better text than either G or A; see *ibid.*, p. 357, and above, n. 27.

243

Theo G	:	OA	2
Theo O	:	GA	5
Theo A	:	GO	4

If the figures for individual manuscripts are isolated, it will be seen that Theodore's text agrees with G a total of thirteen times in the twenty-four readings, with O fourteen times and with A ten times. Although the measure of agreement with the texts of G and O is almost equal, only half the variants are shared by both manuscripts and the Theodore text. The latter appears to be furthest textually from the only Insular manuscript, A. The five Theodore readings for which O is the only other witness are *deus* for *dominus* (Gen. V.29; PentI 65), *erantque* for *eruntque* (Gen. VI.3; PentI 69),[31] *ei* om. (Gen. IX.24; PentI 85),[32] *in montem* for *in monte* (Gen. XIX.19; PentI 117) and *pustella* for *pustula* (Lev. XIII.2; PentI 364).[33] Only two readings, neither of them very positive for sourcing purposes, are exclusive to Theodore and G. They are *seres* (Lev. XIX.19; PentI 381), from which O and A (but no later manuscripts) vary with the present tense, *seris*, and *finitur* (Num. XXXIV.5; PentI 461), from which O, A and all later manuscripts vary with the future tense, *finietur*. One of the most distinctive readings apparently known to the Canterbury commentator is absent from G but is witnessed by both O and A. In the *lemmata* from Deut. XIV.5, *camelopardalum* ('giraffe'; cf. the Septuagint's καμηλοπάρδαλιν) has been treated as two separate words, describing two different animals, *cameleo* (PentI 472) and *pardulum* (PentI 473). These have consequently been given two separate *interpretamenta*. We may assume, therefore, that this separation had already been made in the commentator's Vulgate exemplar. There is nothing remarkable in this, for the *camelopardalus* is simply the last of an extended list of animals in Deut. XIV.5, some of which were no doubt quite unfamiliar to most copyists of, and commentators upon, the Vulgate.[34] The separation of the nouns occurs not only in O and A (in the latter case, after emendation by the original scribe), but

---

[31] Also in the 'Codex Gothicus' or 'Legionensis' (León, Real Colegiata de San Isidoro, 2; s. x) and Tours, Bibliothèque Municipale, 10 (*c.* 800), before correction.

[32] Also in Tours, Bibliothèque Municipale, 10 as an amendment by the copyist.

[33] The word *pustella*, although it occurs in no later Vulgate manuscripts, was current as an alternative for *pustula* (or *pusula*) in post-classical Latin.

[34] Deut. XIV.5: 'ceruum capream bubalum tragelaphum pygargon orygem camelopardalum' (Douai translation: 'The hart and the roe, the buffle, the chamois, the pygarg, the wild goat, the camelopardalus').

also in nine later manuscripts, including three Alcuinian. The apparent copying error in the Theodore text's *pardulum* for *pardalum* has been noted above, and the form *cameleo* is dealt with as an independent reading, below.

Despite its use of the variant just discussed, A's greater distance from Theodore's Pentateuch text overall than either G or O is apparent from the statistics. Ceolfrith's pandects were being copied in Northumbria not long after the period of Theodore's activities in Canterbury; but a shared source can be ruled out and there is no sign of any textual influence of the one Insular centre on the other. The four variants shared by Theodore's text and A, against G and O, do nothing to contradict this verdict. The concurrence in one of the *lemmata* from Gen. V.29 (PentI 64), for instance, where they share *ab operibus et laboribus*, results simply from the peculiarities of G and O, for the former prefaces *operibus* with *omnibus* and the latter omits *et laboribus*.[35] More important are the fourteen readings in which A differs from Theodore (compared with eleven differences from G and ten from O). These include readings from Gen. XI.7 (PentI 92), where A has *ergo* for *igitur*, a variation found in no collated Vulgate manuscript of any period, Gen. XXVI.10 (PentI 153), where A, again uniquely, adds *ei* to *dixitque* and Lev. XX.9 (PentI 385), where A's *aut* for *et* is unique in the earlier period but is found in the thirteenth-century Paris Bibles. Most notable is a *lemma* from Lev. XXIII.40 (PentI 395), where A's *stipulas* for *spatulas* is again unique. Despite the botanical eccentricity implied, the variant noun is not obviously out of place.[36] Study of the surviving fragments of the pandect which was an older sister to the Codex Amiatinus gives no reason to doubt that the latter is, on the whole, a faithful witness to what we may call Ceolfrith's Old Testament text, and thus to the exemplar used at Wearmouth–Jarrow.[37] It is likely that this had arrived in Northumbria directly from Italy, perhaps brought by Benedict Biscop or

---

[35] The other shared variants are in *lemmata* from Gen. I.2 (PentI 20), where A and Theodore (and a number of later manuscripts) have *erant* (absent from G and O), Gen. XXIII.16 (PentI 140), where they share *probate* (cf. *probati*; in A, the termination *-e* is in fact a correction, apparently made at Wearmouth–Jarrow) and Lev. XVII.5 (PentI 378), where A and Theodore share *et*, against *ut* in G and O (but no later manuscripts).

[36] The correct version is: 'sumetisque uobis die primo fructus arboris pulcherrimae spatulasque palmarum et ramos ligni densarum frondium'.

[37] See Marsden, *The Text of the Old Testament*, ch. 5.

by Ceolfrith himself in the 670s or 680s.[38] The text used by Theodore probably arrived at Canterbury from Italy more or less contemporaneously, but independently.

The second main division of notable readings in the *lemmata* of Theodore's Pentateuch contains sixty-six variants which occur in none of the three early witnesses. They are distributed fairly evenly throughout the collection, except that Genesis has proportionally rather fewer than Exodus. Forty-seven of them are completely independent, according to the available evidence, occurring in no later Vulgate manuscripts. Nineteen do have later parallels, however, and I shall deal with this sub-group first. It has already been suggested that some of the parallels are likely to be coincidental, a consequence of the same copying error (or even deliberate emendation) being made independently. This is likely to be the case, for instance, with a word-order change in Gen. X.8 (PentI 86), which is found otherwise only in an eleventh-century Bible belonging to the 'Codex Toletanus' group.[39] Variation in the naming of the deity is fairly frequent in Vulgate manuscripts (not surprisingly, in view of the similarity of the abbreviated forms of the two *nomina sacra*), and thus no significance need be attached to the Theodore text's *domino* for *deo* in a *lemma* from Gen. V.24 (PentI 62), to be found also in all the 'Toletanus' manuscripts, or *dominus* for *deus* in a *lemma* from Num. XXIII.23 (PentI 440), which is repeated in one Alcuinian and (before correction) in one Theodulfian Bible.[40] In a *lemma* from Lev. X.1 (PentI 351), *imposuerunt* occurs for *posuerunt* and is shared only with two Spanish manuscripts (s. viii/ix and s. x), but there is a number of other examples in the earlier manuscripts of

---

38 P. Meyvaert summarizes Benedict's many travels in 'Bede and the Church Paintings at Wearmouth–Jarrow', *ASE* 8 (1979), 63–77, at 63–7. On the books brought to England by Benedict and Ceolfrith, see Bede's *Historia abbatum*, chs. 6, 9 and 15 (*Venerabilis Baedae Opera Historica*, ed. C. Plummer, 2 vols. (Oxford, 1896) I, 369, 373 and 379) and *HE* IV. 18 (p. 388), and the anonymous *Vita Ceolfridi*, ch. 20 (*Baedae Opera*, ed Plummer I, 395). Our main evidence for Vulgate transmission in England at this time concerns the gospels; see esp. T. J. Brown in *Evangeliorum Quattuor Codex Lindisfarnenis. Musei Britannici Codex Cottonianus Nero D. iv*, ed. T. D. Kendrick *et al.*, 2 vols. (Olten and Lausanne, 1956–60) II, 31–58 and 89–92; P. Hunter Blair, *The World of Bede* (Cambridge, 1970), pp. 226–31, and Berger, *Histoire*, pp. 34–8.

39 In both, *potens esse* occurs for *esse potens*.

40 The Theodore glosses contain two other variations in the naming of the deity, one shared with O and noted above, p. 244, the other without parallel and noted below, p. 249. In the *lemma* from Num. XXIII.23 (PentI 440), the Theodore text also has the error *dicebatur* for *dicetur*, noted above.

the substitution of *impono* for *pono* (a verb much used in the Vulgate).[41] In other cases, the likelihood that a variant was part of an established textual tradition is perhaps greater, even though no early witnesses survive. In a *lemma* from Lev. VII.34 (PentI 345), the Canterbury text's *eleuationis* for *elationis* is also in the Codex Amiatinus, as a correction, added after the manuscript had arrived in Italy.[42] The variant appears as a correction in the 'Maurdramnus Bible' (772–81) and as an original reading in most of the Alcuinian Bibles and a few Italian Bibles of the eleventh and twelfth centuries, and later it became widely accepted through its adoption for the Paris Bibles. It may well have been established at an early period. In the *lemma* from Ex. XXV.36 (PentI 306), the Theodore text has *sperae* for *sp(h)erulae*, although in a *lemma* from Ex. XXV.33 (PentI 304) it uses *sperula*, which (as *sperula* or *spherula*) is the usual Vulgate form of the word in this verse. However, the former reading is not necessarily an error, for the use of the two forms – *sp(h)erae* in Ex. XXV.36 and the diminutive form in Ex. XXV.33 – is to be seen also in a number of ninth-century manuscripts, including Tours, Bibliothèque Municipale, 10 (*c.* 800), three of the Theodulfian Bibles and one late Alcuinian.[43] The use of *secundo* in a *lemma* from Gen. XLI.43 (PentI 205), *secundo clamante praecone*, seems unremarkable, for the word seems to function unremarkably as an adverb: 'secondly, the herald proclaiming'. In fact, however, it is a variation on *secundum*, used as an adjective, which properly belongs with the words which precede it in the Vulgate text. There it refers, not to the herald, but to Joseph, whom Pharaoh places in his 'second' chariot (confirming Joseph's position as second only to himself in Egypt): *fecitque ascendere super currum suum secundum clamante praecone ut omnes coram eo genuflecterent.* It seems that *secundo* was in the *lemma* from the start, for the Canterbury commentator gives an explanation relating specifically to its adverbial function: *ipse Ioseph primus erat post eum praeco.* This information is presumably true, but it is irrelevant and misses the point of the passage. Unless we assume that difficulty in understanding the correct Genesis version, despite its syntactical simplicity, prompted a deliberate emendation, we must admit the likelihood that the variant was in the Canterbury

---

[41] Thus, A has *inpones* for *pones* in Ex. XL.4 and G has *inposuit* for *posuit* in Num. XXIII.5.

[42] This is clear from an examination of the manuscript (91r).

[43] The same *lemma* contains also a radical change of syntax, which is unparalleled in other Vulgate manuscripts; see below, pp. 250 and 251.

exemplar of Genesis.[44] It did have some later currency, in Tours, Bibliothèque Municipale, 10, in a late Alcuinian Bible (but only as a correction) and in a few later Italian and Spanish Bibles. The variant, plausible as it is, may have been well-established at an early period, although this cannot be proved.

One of the most interesting of the paralleled readings in Theodore's text is *pendentes* for *ponentes* in one of the *lemmata* from Num. XV.38 (PentI 430). Although absent from any of the earliest witnesses, it occurs in a Pentateuch copied at St Gallen in about the third quarter of the eighth century, now part of St Gallen, Stiftsbibliothek, 2, pp. 3–294. According to Fischer, the text of this is unquestionably Italian in origin, despite some Spanish influence, but there are also many 'unique' readings,[45] and one of these is *pendentes* in Num. XV.38. It is tempting to see this as evidence that the same Italian tradition to which our Theodore text belongs influenced the exemplar of the St Gallen Pentateuch. At the very least, we are justified in accepting that *pendentes* in the Theodore *lemma* may represent a genuine alternative Vulgate reading, with further witnesses, not an accidental and isolated emendation. There are no other such parallels between our Theodore text and the St Gallen manuscript, but this is not surprising, for the latter now wants all of Genesis, Exodus and Leviticus, so that comparisons cannot be made with the first four hundred Theodore *lemmata*. No other contemporary St Gallen texts of the Pentateuch survive.

The nineteen Theodore readings with later parallels thus reveal no persistent pattern of correspondences, but the occurrence of a number of them in manuscripts associated with the Carolingian textual revisions, including those from Gen. XLI.43, Ex. XXV.33 and Lev. VII.34, discussed above, indicates that some at least may have been already established in the continental traditions which influenced those revisions, but of which no earlier trace remains.

No Vulgate manuscript is without a stratum of apparently unique

---

44 There is, however, evidence that Theodore's and Hadrian's knowledge of Latin was sometimes wanting; see M. Lapidge, 'The Study of Greek at the School of Canterbury in the Seventh Century', in *The Sacred Nectar of the Greeks: the Study of Greek in the West in the Early Middle Ages*, ed. M. Herren, King's College London Medieval Studies 2 (London, 1988), 169–94, at 181–9.

45 Fischer, *Bibelhandschriften*, p. 181; *CLA* VII, no. 893a (see also nos. 893b and 894); and Berger, *Histoire*, pp. 120 and 413. The manuscript includes *capitula* for Leviticus, Numbers and Deuteronomy but the text of only the latter two books.

variants, and the Canterbury exemplar will have been no exception. Some at least of the forty-seven independent variants which I have noted in the Theodore *lemmata* may thus genuinely reflect the independent element in the exemplar text. Others, however, may be the result of deliberate or accidental change by the commentator or a subsequent copyist. In a citation from Ex. XXXII.20 (PentI 327), deliberate abbreviation in extracting the *lemma* from the biblical text probably explains the loss of *ex eo* from *Et dedit ex eo potum filiis Israhel*. In another, from Gen. L.2 (PentI 215), we may assume that *condierunt eum* for *condirent patrem* was a deliberate summarizing paraphrase,[46] as also *panes super mensam* from *pones super mensam panes* in Ex. XXV.30 (PentI 301). This might be the explanation also for the *lemma* from Ex. XXIV.16 (PentI 285), *tegens nubes sex diebus* for *{et habitauit gloria Domini super Sinai} tegens illum nube sex diebus*.[47] Many of the independent variants involve minor additions, omissions or alterations. Such are *quia effusus es* for *effusus es* (Gen. XLIX.4; PentI 213), *fecerunt* for *fecerant* (Ex. XXXII.20; PentI 326), *et in gentes* for *et inter gentes* (Num. XXIII.9; PentI 439), *ad filiam* for *ad filiam eius* (Num. XXVII.8; PentI 448) and *holocausta* for *holocaustum* (Ex. XL.27; PentI 259). Enclitic *-que* is added or omitted four times, in *lemmata* from the preface to Genesis (PentI 4) and from Gen. I.3 (PentI 23), I.5 (PentI 24) and XXVIII.18 (PentI 164). There are four cases of variant word order, each involving the simple transposition of two words, in the *lemmata* from Gen. X.8 (PentI 86), XI.4 (PentI 91), XIV.13 (PentI 94) and XX.2 (PentI 124). Such variations are characteristic of Vulgate manuscripts and none affects sense significantly. All may well be the original readings of Theodore's Pentateuch, although their creation during transmission cannot of course be ruled out. There is variation in the name used for the deity in a *lemma* from Gen. XXII.14 (PentI 136), where *deus* appears for *dominus*.[48] In a *lemma* from Num. XV.19 (PentI 428), the Theodore text's genitive *domini* for the dative *domino* may well be deliberate, for the new syntax has a certain logic behind it.[49]

---

[46] Gen. L.2: 'praecepitque seruis suis medicis ut aromatibus condirent patrem'.

[47] I have classed the variant *nubes*, which occurs also in the 'Codex Cavensis' (Spain, s. ix[2]), as one of the nineteen paralleled readings, not a shared error, on the grounds that the nominative plural form of the noun is acceptable as the subject of the second part of the sentence.

[48] Two similar variations, paralleled in other manuscripts, have been noted above.

[49] 'Separabitis primitias Domini de cibis uestris'.

An interesting example of the use of an alternative form of a word occurs in the *lemma* from Lev. XI.5 (PentI 354), where *cyrogillum* has replaced the usual Vulgate form, *chyrogryllius*. These may be compared with the Greek χοιρόγρυλλιον, from which the word derives. The loss of the second *r* in the Theodore version is presumably a corruption, but the replacement of the aspirated velar stop by its voiceless equivalent could well be an example of the influence of seventh-century Greek pronunciation at the Canterbury school.[50] *Cyrogrillus* is in fact a widely attested Latin form of the name, but it occurs in no known Vulgate manuscript. In two of its *lemmata* from Deut. XIV.5, which have already attracted our attention for their treatment of *camelopardum* (καμηλοπάρδαλιν, 'giraffe') as two separate words, the Theodore text has *cameleo* for the first element (PentI 472). Interestingly, the same form was used (apparently through confusion with *chameleon*) by Hwætbert of Wearmouth–Jarrow in his *Enigmata*.[51]

The most significant of the remaining independent readings in Theodore's text are the following:

Preface (PentI 15)	*Domini* for *Christi*
Preface (PentI 16)	*doctorum modum* for *interpretes*
Gen. I.1 (PentI 17)	*fecit* for *creauit*
Gen. II.7 (PentI 32)	*spirauit* for *inspirauit*
Gen. III.24 (PentI 47)	*gladium autem flammeum ac uersatilem* for
	et flammeum gladium atque uersatilem
Gen. IX.20 (PentI 84)	*coepit . . . plantare uineam et exercere terram* for
	coepitque . . . exercere terram et plantauit uineam
Gen. XXXI.35 (PentI 181)	*mulierum* for *feminarum*
Ex. XXV.36 (PentI 306)	*sperae igitur et calami procedentes* for
	spherulae igitur et calami ex ipso erunt

There can be no certainty that all these alternative readings, none of which disrupts the sense in its respective passage, were already integrated in the Pentateuch text used at Canterbury and were not introduced, either at the time of compilation of the glosses, or during subsequent transmission. It is hard, however, to imagine that a variant such as that in the *lemma* to Gen. IX.20 (PentI 84), where the syntactical change is both radical but grammatically accurate, came about accidentally. In the *lemma*

---

[50] Such influence has been suggested by Lapidge in 'The Study of Greek', p. 180.

[51] *Enigm.* xlv: 'De cameleone' (CCSL 133, 255). This is the only early medieval Insular occurrence of *cameleo* recorded in *Dictionary of Medieval Latin from British Sources*, ed. R. E. Latham *et al.* (London, 1975–), s.v.

to Gen. XXXI.35 (PentI 182), *mulierum* for *feminarum* is more likely to have been written by the copyist of a large section of Genesis, and thus to have been in the exemplar, than by a copyist of the isolated *lemma*, for *mulier* occurs three times in the textual vicinity of XXXI.35 (in XXX.13, XXXIII.5 and XXXIV.1) and probably exerted its influence. The substitution occurs in no other Vulgate manuscript in this location, but a Spanish manuscript and two Paris Bibles have it in Lev. XXVII.5. In the *lemmata* from Jerome's Preface to Genesis, the variant *ante aduentum Domini* for *ante aduentum Christi* (PentI 15) may be assumed to have been introduced by analogy with *in domo Domini* a few words earlier, but *doctorum modum* for *interpretes* (PentI 16) has no such obvious explanation.[52]

The variant *spirauit* for *inspirauit*, in a *lemma* taken from the creation narrative in Gen. II.7 (PentI 32), might easily be dismissed as transmissional loss, if it were not that the same form of the verb appears in the *interpretamentum* to Gen. I.26 (PentI 31). This immediately precedes the Gen. II.7 *lemma* and explicitly anticipates the next stage of creation: *postea autem quando dicitur 'Spirauit'*. Both occurrences of *spirauit* are thus likely to be original, and to have been in the Canterbury exemplar, unless we are to assume that one occurred accidentally during transmission and this prompted emendation of the other also. In the case of the *lemma* for Ex. XXV.36 (PentI 306), which is part of an instruction to the Israelites about how to build the tabernacle and all its furniture, including the golden lampstand with its branches (*calami*), the otherwise invariable Vulgate version, *et calami ex ipso erunt* ('the branches shall be of one piece with [the lampstandard]'), has become *et calami procedentes* in the Theodore text. This variation must have been influenced by *procedentes* in the previous colon: *qui simul sex fiunt procedentes de hastili uno*. Plainly, it could only have been made by a commentator who still had this colon in front of him, before the *lemma* had been isolated and its form fixed.[53]

Whatever its idiosyncrasies, the place of Theodore's text in the main stream of Vulgate textual history is not in doubt. Even when a Theodore

---

[52] The otherwise invariable Vulgate version of the words used in the *lemma* is: 'in quibus ultimum paene gradum interpretes tenent'. In the *interpretamentum*, the 'doctors' are called *philosophi*.

[53] The possibility that the Canterbury teacher, reading from a complete Exodus text, made the emendation himself, perhaps in a paraphrasing process of the sort discussed above, cannot be ruled out, although it should be assessed in the light of reservations I make below about the competence of the Canterbury scholars in Latin.

reading departs radically from any known Vulgate reading in the 465
Pentateuch *lemmata*, in no case is authority for the departure to be found in
the pre-Hieronymian, Old Latin versions.[54] In no case, that is, except one.
In the first Genesis *lemma* (PentI 17), the opening words of Gen. I.1 are
cited in the form, *In principio fecit Deus caelum.* In all known Vulgate
versions of Gen. I.1, *creauit* is the verb used; in all known Old Latin
versions, it is *fecit.* In view of the consistent Vulgate character of the
Theodore text, it is improbable that such a prominent variant was in the
Pentateuch exemplar which was used at Canterbury. May the explanation
for its presence in the *lemma* be the influence, rather, of a familiar liturgical
text, in which the Old Latin forms had been preserved?[55] An Insular
example of such a text is to be found in the *Liber Commonei*, which forms
part of Oxford, Bodleian Library, Auctarium F. 4. 32, the so-called 'St
Dunstan's Classbook'.[56] Written in Wales in the early ninth century, and
in use at Glastonbury by the tenth, the *Liber* contains a section of lessons
and canticles for the Easter vigil, in a version which is thought to preserve
the forms in use at the time of Gregory the Great's reform of the liturgy.
The first lesson is Gen. I.1–II.3, and the text of this is Old Latin in form,
starting with *In principio fecit.*[57] The question remains open, however,
whether such influence would have occurred at the Canterbury school
itself, or at some later stage in transmission to the Milan manuscript. In
view of the apparent general accuracy of transmission that has been noted,
the former alternative seems more likely.

[54] Fischer has noted that England appears to have transmitted little in the way of Old Latin
texts, compared with other Insular areas and the Continent (*Bibelhandschriften*,
pp. 20–1). However, Old Latin or mixed texts were certainly known in England, as
Paul Remley's work on the poem *Genesis A* has shown ('The Latin Textual Basis of
Genesis A', *ASE* 17 (1988), 163–89). The source of such texts is likely to have been
Ireland or Wales.

[55] On the role of the liturgy in the preservation of Old Latin forms, see esp. Salmon, 'Le
Texte biblique', and J. Gribomont, 'L'Eglise et les versions bibliques', *La Maison-Dieu*
62 (1960), 41–68.

[56] The manuscript is edited in facsimile by R. W. Hunt, *St Dunstan's Classbook from
Glastonbury*, Umbrae Codicum Occidentalium 4 (Amsterdam, 1961). See also M.
Lapidge, 'Latin Learning in Dark Age Wales: some Prolegomena', in *Proceedings of the
Seventh International Congress of Celtic Studies*, ed. D. E. Evans, J. G. Griffith and E. M.
Jope (Oxford, 1986), pp. 91–107, at 92–4.

[57] The text is ptd B. Fischer, 'Die Lesungen der römischen Ostervigil unter Gregor den
Grossen', in *Colligere Fragmenta: Festschrift Alban Dold zum 70. Geburtstag am 7.7.1952*,
ed. B. Fischer and V. Fiala, Texte und Arbeiten I. 2 (Beuron, 1952), 144–59, at 145.

Another possible explanation for the Old Latin form of Theodore's Gen. I.1 would be the close acquaintance of the Canterbury teachers or pupils, not with a liturgical version, but with the Latin works of the fathers, who consistently and frequently use *fecit*. This seems highly unlikely, however, for there is persuasive evidence elsewhere in the glosses, as Michael Lapidge has shown, that the exegetical material in use in the Canterbury school was Greek, and we may consequently rule out mediation through Latin patristic texts. The competence of Theodore and Hadrian in Latin is also sometimes in question, as we have noted.[58] The treatment of Gen. IV.8 (PentI 51) is a case in point. The first colon of IV.8 is cited in its exact and invariable Vulgate form: *'Dixitque Cain ad Abel'* et *reliqua usque 'egrediamur foras'*.[59] The latter words are followed in all Vulgate versions by *cumque essent in agro*. This is not cited in the *lemma*, but the *interpretamentum*, in describing the second sin of Cain, makes use of the Vulgate vocabulary: *secundum dolus, ut est 'egrediamur foras in agrum'*. Lapidge has pointed out that the *interpretamentum* seems to be a fairly close rendering of the Greek of Basil, even down to a translation of Basil's εἰπών, Διέλθωμεν εἰς τὸ πεδίον.[60] In fact, the translation has been somewhat inflationary by the use of *foras*. The sense of διέλθωμεν εἰς would have been conveyed adequately and simply by *egrediamur ... in*. This may confirm that the commentator did indeed have Basil's Greek before him and that he was not totally confident in expressing himself in Latin. He seems to have used the Vulgate text of the passage he was glossing as a 'crib' in translating the Greek version, in effect combining the sense *egrediamur foras* and *in agr{um}* and perpetuating a partial tautology which the Greek did not demand. Whether this accurately describes the process of translation or not, there can be little question of a Latin patristic commentary on the passage being used by the commentator. On the available evidence, none of the Latin commentaries that might have been known at the Canterbury school uses *foras*, and all render πεδίον twice by *campus*, a more obvious choice than *ager*.[61]

---

[58] Cf. above, n. 53.

[59] The glossator's two words *et reliqua* cover the omission of only two words of the Genesis text: *fratrem suum*. The only variation in this passage in the early Vulgate witnesses is in O: *dixitque + autem*.

[60] 'The Study of Greek', p. 177.

[61] Thus, Ambrose, *De Cain et Abel* II. 26 (CSEL 32.1, 400): *eamus in campum*. Bede, citing Gen. IV.8 in his *Commentarius in Genesim* II (CCSL 118A, 76), appears to be alone in his

There is no reason to doubt that, in the Pentateuch *lemmata* of Milan, Biblioteca Ambrosiana, M. 79 sup., we have a reliable record of the Vulgate text (or at least one such text) used for teaching purposes at the school of Theodore and Hadrian in Canterbury during the 670s and 680s. Analysis of the Milan text has suggested that its history was separate from, but parallel with, that of the exemplar or exemplars used in Northumbria for Ceolfrith's three pandects, which included the Codex Amiatinus. It came, that is, as a good text directly from Italy, and there is thus a good chance that it arrived with Theodore himself or with Hadrian, either as an independent Pentateuch or as part of a Heptateuch or Octateuch; the practical needs of the classroom almost certainly rule out a pandect.

There are too few witnesses for us to be able to do more than make informed guesses about the Italian history of the Vulgate during the seventh century. The evidence of G, O and A indicates a pool of texts in circulation, more or less remote from Jerome's original text but never far removed and mostly of good quality, though this varied. Cousinship, rather than brotherhood, may be the most appropriate metaphor for the relationships between these manuscripts, and the exemplar for Theodore's text made one with them. Its exact relationship with the other texts is unclear; its apparent closeness to G and O, rather than A, may simply be a distortion resulting from the small range of statistics available. The interesting feature of Theodore's text is the comparatively high number of independent readings, although how high depends on how many of them we allow to be genuine readings, rather than emendations made at the Canterbury school or subsequently. An overwhelming majority of them occurs in Genesis. Certainly, in the passages chosen by the Canterbury commentator from this book, both G and A show far fewer idiosyncrasies. A comparison of each of the Theodore text's independent readings with the Hebrew (in its surviving Massoretic form) has revealed that none can be explained as closer translations – and thus possibly nearer to Jerome's version – than the versions of G, O or A, which have been used largely by the editors of the Rome *Biblia Sacra* to establish their Hieronymian text. But we cannot tell whether this apparent partial independence of Theodore's Genesis was unusual or simply a characteristic complexity in the Italian texts of the time.

use of the Vulgate vocabulary within the Old Latin formula (but without *foras*): *egrediamur in agrum*. This variation is overlooked in the critical apparatus of *Vetus Latina* II, 83–4. Bede's version precisely follows the Vulgate in every other respect in each of the three cola of Gen. IV.8.

13

Theodore's Bible: the gospels

PATRICK McGURK

As a guide to the gospel text used at Canterbury by Archbishop Theodore, the *lemmata* in Milan, Biblioteca Ambrosiana M. 79 sup. are limited in two ways: they are few in number, totalling only 127, and one-third of them are of single words.[1] When set against the number and variety of gospels available in the seventh century, so small a sample makes difficult the identification of particular textual affiliations.

The text is Vulgate and not Old Latin, being supported by Vulgate witnesses in nearly all readings, and the following *lemmata* have little or no Old Latin support. (The numbers on the left are those in *Biblical Commentaries*, ed. Bischoff and Lapidge, and the sigla for textual witnesses are explained in the Appendix, below, pp. 258–9.)

EvII 25　Matth. XII. 1: 'sata', where most Old Latin witnesses have 'segetes', except for Xdl and the mixed text Ea.

EvII 28　Matth. XIII. 33: 'sata', where most Old Latin witnesses give 'mensura', except for Xk ('sata') and Xlo and the mixed Ea (all three have 'satis' here).

EvII 58　Matth. XXVII. 6: 'corbanan', where most Old Latin witnesses have 'loculum', 'corbam' or 'corba', except for Xl ('corbanan') and Xo ('corbanam').

---

[1] The *lemmata* are ptd *Biblical Commentaries*, ed. Bischoff and Lapidge. In the edition of EvII, there are 151 items, but twenty-four are comments apparently not focused on, or accompanied by, a *lemma*. The *lemmata* for each of the four gospels open with a comment on the evangelist in question, which might conceivably have been based on the so-called 'Monarchian' prologues. The reasons for the selection of individual gospel passages for comment, and for particular clusters of text, remain to be discovered. Thus, for example, the comments in EvII 4, 12, 45, 47, 55, 60, 80, 93, 102 and 150 deal with money, tribute and trade; and it would be interesting to know why EvII 101 repeats EvII 59.

EvII 67   Mark III. 21: '(quoniam) in furorem reuersus est', where Old
Latin witnesses give 'quoniam exsentiat eos', except for Xl and the
mixed Ea Jg.

EvII 78   Mark IX. 48: 'omnis enim uictima salietur'. It is the accompanying commentary on this *lemma* which might just indicate use of the
Vulgate. Like the Vulgate, the Canterbury commentator refers to fire
and sacrifice where the Old Latin does not specifically mention fire.
Compare the normal Vulgate 'omnis enim igne sallietur et omnis
uictima sallietur' with the normal Old Latin 'omnis uictima sale
salietur'.

EvII 82   Mark XIV. 21: 'bonum est ei si non esset natus', where no Old
Latin witness has 'est'.

EvII 94   Luke III. 13: 'non amplius quam constitutum est', against the
Old Latin 'nihil amplius quam quod constitutum est', though note that
the normal Vulgate has 'nihil' for 'non'.

EvII 99   Luke V. 7: 'factum est in sabbato secundoprimo', where the
only Old Latin witnesses with 'secundoprimo' are Xad and the mixed
Ea.

EvII 104   Luke X. 34: 'duxit in stabulum', against Old Latin 'duxit ad
stabulum', though Xalk and the mixed Ea have 'in'.

EvII 105   Luke XI. 28: 'quippini' against Old Latin, which either omits
or gives 'immo' or 'etiam', though the mixed Ea has 'quippini'.

EvII 113   Luke XVI. 6: 'cautionem' against the Old Latin 'litteras' or
'chirographum', though Xa and the mixed Ea Jg have 'cautionem'.

EvII 144   John XV. 3: 'et uos mundi estis propter sermonem', where no
Old Latin witness has 'et'.

It is more difficult to pinpoint particular Vulgate allegiances. Readings
which have relatively narrow support include:

EvII 94   Luke III. 13: '*quam* constitutum est' with 'quam' found in Jfo
Nay Ge Hq.

EvII 105   Luke XI. 28: '*quippini*' supported by Jmopx Nay.

EvII 18   Matth. X. 29: 'asse *ueneunt*' with Jfox.

EvII 109   Luke XV. 7: 'iust*os*' with Jx Hdq, though Old Latin Xacr and
the mixed Jg also have 'iustos'.

EvII 118   Luke XXIII. 34: 'sort*em*' with Jox.

EvII 72   Mark VII. 34: '*aperire*' against 'adaperire' with Ge Hdq.

EvII 91   Luke I. 80: '*ad* diem ostensionis' with Hqr.

EvII 133   John VIII. 9: 'remansit *Iesus* solus' with Hdr.

Insofar as these mostly trivial variants allow any conclusions to be drawn, the *lemmata* disagree least often with Jox, which could well have been in England at the time of Theodore, though it must be asked whether teachers did not use more utilitarian gospelbooks than these prestigious cousins. In any case, the following readings with little or no Vulgate support show that the *lemmata* of the Canterbury biblical commentaries can differ (sometimes significantly) from Jox.

EvII 21 Matth. X. 39: 'qui *amat* animam suam perdet illam'. All Vulgate and Old Latin witnesses have 'qui *inuenit* animam. . .', except for the Old Latin Corbeiensis (Xo). It is also possible that the parallel John XII. 25 ('qui amat animam suam perdet eam') is being echoed here.

EvII 40 Matth. XVII. 1: 'adsumsit *secum* Petrum', against the usual reading 'adsumsit Iesus Petrum'. Mark XIV. 33 reads 'adsumit Petrum. . . secum', and could just possibly explain this *lemma*.

EvII 51 Matth. XXIII. 24: 'excolentes' against the usual 'excolantes'. This could easily be due to scribal confusion.

EvII 67 Mark III. 21: 'in furorem *reuersus*', against the usual 'in furorem *uersus*'. This reading is shared by some later gospels.[2]

EvII 74 Mark VIII. 24: 'uideo homines *quasi* arbores', against all Vulgate and Old Latin witnesses, which have 'uelut arbores', except for the 'Bobbiensis' (Hk). The rendering of the Greek ὡς by *quasi* in the African Old Latin text is discussed by von Soden.[3]

EvII 77 Mark XI. 13: 'non enim *uenit* tempus ficcorum', against the more usual 'non enim *erat* tempus ficcorum'. The reading *uenit* appears earlier in the same verse, and the sense of 'erat' in the *lemma* approximates to 'uenit'.

EvII 94 Luke III. 13: '*non* amplius' against '*nihil* amplius'. Professor Frede kindly draws my attention to the reading in St Gallen, Stiftsbibliothek, 48: 'n ł [= *uel*] nl amplius'. Confusion between 'non' and 'nihil' could easily have arisen when the two negatives were placed side by side in this way.

EvII 95 Luke IV. 5: 'et ostendit illi omnia regna *mundi*', where the more usual reading gives 'omnia regna *orbis terrae*', except for the Graeco-

---

[2] See Fischer, *Die lateinischen Evangelien bis zum 10. Jahrhundert. II. Varianten zu Markus*, p. 145 (variant 2137c).

[3] See H. von Soden, *Das lateinische Neue Testament in Afrika zur Zeit Cyprians*, Texte und Untersuchungen 33 (Leipzig, 1909), 82.

Latin 'Codex Bezae' (Xd), the sixth-century 'Brixianus' (Jg) and the
Irish 'Book of Mulling' (Hm). The parallel Matth. IV. 8 gives 'mundi',
and Professor Frede points out to me that the rendering of the Greek
κόσμου (in the Graeco-Latin 'Codex Bezae') is also found in Jerome's
translation of Origen's *Homiliae*.[4]

EvII 103   Luke XIX.9: '*iste* est filius Abrahae' for '*ipse* filius sit/est
Abrahae'. Professor Frede suggests to me that the Greek word αὐτός
could be used demonstratively.

EvII 137   John X. 27: 'et uocem *meam audient*' against 'et oues uocem *eius
audiunt*'.

EvII 143   John XIV. 27: 'non quomodo *hic* mundus'. The reading *hic* is
not otherwise attested here.

One or two of the above readings could have arisen in the transmission of
the text either before or after Theodore's teaching. The transfer of a word
from parallel texts in other gospels or from a neighbouring verse or line
could have led to other variants, thus in Matth. X. 39 (EvII 21, discussed
above), 'amat' could have been transferred from the parallel John XII. 25,
and in Mark XI. 13 (EvII 77, discussed above), 'uenit' could have been
taken from earlier in the verse. But in at least two of the above *lemmata*
(EvII 51 and 103), the reading is supported by the commentary, and
might therefore represent a genuine variant in Theodore's text. And the
possible Greek background for readings in *lemmata* in EvII 74, 95 and 103
is of interest.[5]

APPENDIX

Sigla used in reference to manuscripts of the gospels

The following sigla are used in Bonifatius Fischer, *Die lateinischen Evangelien bis
zum 10. Jahrhundert*, 4 vols., Aus der Geschichte der lateinischen Bibel 13, 15, 17

---

4   Jerome, *Translatio Homiliarum .XXXIX. Origenis in Evangelium Lucae*, ed. M. Rauer,
    *Origenes Werke IX. Die Homilien zu Lukas in der Übersetzung des Hieronymus und die
    griechischen Reste der Homilien und des Lukas-Kommentars*, GCS 49 (Berlin, 1959), 170.14,
    182.20 and 173.1.

5   I must record my thanks to Professor H. J. Frede for giving his views on the *lemmata* with
    little or no Vulgate support. The quality of the comments on these *lemmata* has thereby
    been greatly improved, though he is in no way responsible, however, for any errors in
    their interpretation.

and 19 (Freiburg, 1988–92). I also give (in square brackets) the sigla used in *Novum Testamentum Latine I. Quattuor Evangelia*, ed. J. Wordsworth and H. J. White, 1 vol. in 5 pts (Oxford, 1889–98).

Xk   [k] 'Codex Bobiensis': Turin, Biblioteca Nazionale, G. VII. 15 (Africa, s. iv)

Xa   [a] 'Codex Vercellensis': Vercelli, Biblioteca Capitolare, s.n. (? Vercelli, s. iv^2)

Xr   [r^1] 'Codex Usserianus I': Dublin, Trinity College 55 (Ireland, s. vii^1)

Xl   [l] 'Codex Rehdigeranus': Berlin, Stiftung Preussischer Kulturbesitz, Staatsbibliothek, Depot Breslau 5 (N. Italy, s. viii^1)

Xo   [ff^1] 'Codex Corbeiensis': St Petersburg, Public Library, O. v. I. 3 (France, s. viii^1)

Xd   [d] 'Codex Bezae': Cambridge, University Library, Nn. 2. 41 (s. v)

Jf   [F] 'Codex Fuldensis': Fulda, Landesbibliothek, Bonifatianus 1 (Capua, AD 547)

Jg   [f] 'Codex Brixianus': Brescia, Biblioteca Queriniana, s.n. (? Ravenna, s. vi)

Jm   [M] 'Codex Mediolanensis': Milan, Biblioteca Ambrosiana, C. 39 inf. (N. Italy, s. vi^2)

Jo   [O] Oxford, Bodleian Library, Auct. D. 2. 14 (Italy, s. vi/vii)

Jy   [P] Split, Bibl. Capituli, s.n. (Italy, s. vi/vii)

Jx   [X] 'Gospels of St Augustine': Cambridge, Corpus Christi College 286 (Italy, s. vi)

Na   [A] 'Codex Amiatinus': Florence, Biblioteca Medicea-Laurenziana, Amiatino 1 (Wearmouth–Jarrow, s. viii^{in})

Ny   [Y] 'Lindisfarne Gospels': London, British Library, Cotton Nero D. iv (Lindisfarne, AD 698–721)

Ge   [∓P] 'Echternach Gospels': Paris, Bibliothèque Nationale, lat. 9389 (s. viii^{in})

Hd   [D] 'Book of Armagh': Dublin, Trinity College 52 (Armagh, *c.* AD 807)

Hq   [Q] 'Book of Kells': Dublin, Trinity College 58 (? Iona, s. viii/ix)

Hr   [R] 'MacRegol Gospels': Oxford, Bodleian Library, Auct. D. 2. 19 (? Birr, *c.* AD 822)

Ea   [aur] 'Codex Aureus': Stockholm, Royal Library, A. 135 (S. England [?Canterbury], s. viii^2)

14

Theodore and Anglo-Latin octosyllabic verse

MICHAEL LAPIDGE

What is probably the earliest surviving piece of Latin verse written in Anglo-Saxon England (certainly the earliest which is securely datable) is a poem of six lines' length addressed by Archbishop Theodore to his colleague Hæddi, bishop of Winchester:

> Te nunc, sancte speculator,
> Verbi Dei digne dator,
> Hæddi, pie praesul, precor,
> Pontificum ditum decor,
> Pro me tuo peregrino
> Preces funde Theodoro.

There need be no doubt that the Theodore of the poem is Theodore, archbishop of Canterbury (668–90): the poem is transmitted with a copy of Theodore's *Iudicia* in Cambridge, Corpus Christi College 320 (a St Augustine's, Canterbury, manuscript of late tenth-century date), where it serves as a sort of rubric (p. 71) to various regulations on penitence;[1] and the poet describes himself as a *peregrinus*, which would be an appropriate

---

[1] The poem, in its setting in Cambridge, Corpus Christi College 320, is illustrated in *The Making of England: Anglo-Saxon Art and Culture AD 600–900*, ed. L. Webster and J. Backhouse (London, 1991), p. 74 (no. 58). The poem has been printed on a number of occasions, beginning with F. Liebermann, 'Reim neben Alliteration im Anglolatein um 680', *ASNSL* 141 (1921), 234, and most recently by M. Lapidge, 'The School of Theodore and Hadrian', *ASE* 15 (1986), 45–72, at 46. It is listed *ICL*, no. 16100. For discussion, see M. Deansley and P. Grosjean, 'The Canterbury Edition of the Answers of Pope Gregory I to St Augustine', *Journal of Ecclesiastical History* 10 (1959), 1–49, at 19–20, and A. Orchard, *The Poetic Art of Aldhelm*, CSASE 8 (Cambridge, 1994), 29–31. An edition and translation of the poem are given below, p. 275.

description of our archbishop of Canterbury. Hæddi was bishop of Winchester from 676 to 705: the poem was therefore composed between 676 and Theodore's death on 19 September 690.

The most striking feature of this (otherwise perhaps unremarkable) little poem is its rhythm, for it seems to be constructed with attention to the natural stress of Latin words. (All Latin words were naturally stressed on the penultimate syllable, except in the case of polysyllabic words whose penultimate syllable was short, in which case the accent was thrown forward on to the antepenultimate syllable.) If we read the poem with this rule in mind, we find that it has a consistently trochaic rhythm (that is, alternating strong and weak stresses: / x), with only one word (*pontificum*, assuming classical vowel length) falling outside this trochaic rhythm:

> Te nunc sáncte speculátor
> Vérbi Déi dígne dátor
> Hǽddi píe práesul précor
> Pontifícum dítum décor
> Pro me túo peregríno
> préces fúnde Theodóro.

What was Theodore's model for this sort of trochaic rhythmic verse?[2] The answer to so apparently simple a question is far more complex than might be suspected, for, to my knowledge, there are virtually no antecedents in Latin verse earlier than the seventh century.[3] It may be helpful to begin by eliminating one possible model: that is to say, the model was *not* the Latin iambic dimeter hymns which were composed from the late fourth century onwards by poets such as Ambrose, Prudentius, Caelius Sedulius and Venantius Fortunatus.[4] It was Ambrose who pioneered the

---

[2] I previously mooted the possibility that a model for Theodore's trochaic octosyllables might be found in Greek rhythmical verse of the sixth and seventh centuries ('The School', p. 47, n. 16), but left the matter open, pending the further research which is the subject of the present essay.

[3] Cf. the remarks of M. Lapidge, 'A Seventh-Century Insular Latin Debate Poem on Divorce', *CMCS* 10 (Winter 1985), 1–23, at 11; M. Herren, 'The Stress Systems in Insular Latin Octosyllabic Verse', *CMCS* 15 (Summer 1988), 63–84, at 82–3; and Orchard, *The Poetic Art of Aldhelm*, pp. 29–31.

[4] These Late Latin hymns are conveniently collected by A. S. Walpole and A. J. Mason, *Early Latin Hymns* (Cambridge, 1922), and by W. Bulst, *Hymni Latini Antiquissimi LXXV* (Heidelberg, 1956).

iambic dimeter form, whence it has always been conventional to speak of 'Ambrosian' hymns.[5] Consider the following example:

> Splendor paternae gloriae
> de luce lucem proferens
> lux lucis et fons luminis
> dies dierum inluminans.[6]

Ambrosian hymns were metrical: that is, their metrical structure was based on the length of syllables, not on natural stress. In an Ambrosian hymn, each line consists of four feet, of which the second and fourth must be iambs (that is, a short followed by a long syllable), with the first and third being either iambs or spondees (or very occasionally anapests).[7] Four such lines – normally consisting of eight syllables – were then combined to make up a stanza. The quoted stanza is scanned as follows (note that in the fourth line, the last syllable of *dierum* elides with the first syllable of *inluminans* to constitute one long syllable):

> Splēndōr | pătēr- | -nāē glō- | -rǐāē
> dē lū- | -cě lū- | -cēm prō- | -fěrēns
> lūx lū- | -cǐs ēt | fōns lū- | -mǐnīs
> dǐēs | dǐēr- | -ū(m in)lū- | -mǐnāns.

At some time in late antiquity (the precise chronology is uncertain) distinctions based on quantity disappeared in Latin pronunciation, to be replaced by distinctions based on stress. Various verse-forms, modelled on quantitative metrical forms such as the iambic dimeter, now arose, in which stress replaced metre as the structuring principle. For example, rhythmic octosyllables, based on (metrical) iambic dimeters, seem to have originated in Ireland, probably in the late sixth century.[8] If we take the stanza of Ambrose quoted above, and think of it in terms of natural stress rather than quantity, one structural principle quickly emerges: in the final

---

[5] As for example in the *Regula S. Benedicti*, where a hymn appointed for the Office is referred to as an 'Ambrosianum' (chs. 9, 12, 13 and 17).

[6] *Ambrogio: Inni*, ed. M. Simonetti (Florence, 1988), p. 26; also ed. Walpole and Mason, *Early Latin Hymns*, pp. 35–6, and Bulst, *Hymni Latini Antiquissimi*, p. 40: 'O the brilliance of our Father's glory, bringing forth light from light, the light of light and the fountain of light, the day illuminating all days.'

[7] See P. Klopsch, *Einführung in die mittellateinische Verslehre* (Darmstadt, 1972), pp. 8–16.

[8] On this point, see the valuable discussion by Herren, 'The Stress Systems', esp. pp. 66–74.

position of each line we frequently find a trisyllabic word. The reason is that a short syllable was required in the penultimate position of the iambic dimeter, and bisyllabic Latin words rarely have a short first syllable (an exception is *pater*, and this word is indeed found in the final position of a line of Ambrose: *et totus in Verbo pater*;[9] but such examples are rare). Now according to the Latin rule of natural stress, trisyllabic words with short penultimate syllables are stressed on the antepenultimate syllable. Thus the final words in the stanza of Ambrose quoted above are stressed as follows: *glóriae, próferens, lúminis* and *inlúminans*. It thus became a structural principle for the composers of rhythmic Latin octosyllables, beginning with the Irish in the sixth century and continuing with their seventh-century English imitators, to place a trisyllabic word carrying stress on its antepenultimate syllable, in the final position of each line. Consider an example from the *Carmen rhythmicum* of Aldhelm:

> His tantis tempestátibus
> Ac terrorum turbínibus
> Nostra pavent precórdia,
> Tot monstrorum prodígia
> Quando cernebant lúmina:
> Tectorum laqueária
> Horrisonis fragóribus
> Concuti ac crepóribus.[10]

All the lines in this excerpt (and indeed all two hundred lines of Aldhelm's poem) have stress like this on the antepenultimate or proparoxytone, though there is lack of regular stress earlier in the line; hence they are designated (in the system of notation elaborated by Dag Norberg for describing rhythmical verse)[11] as '8 pp', where the numeral '8' refers to the number of syllables in the line, and 'pp' signifies that the stress falls on the proparoxytonic (that is, antepenultimate) syllable. In the entire length of

---

9 The last line of the hymn 'Splendor paternae gloriae'. ed. Simonetti, *Ambrogio: Inni*, p. 28.

10 *Aldhelmi Opera*, ed. R. Ehwald, MGH, Auct. Antiq. 15 (Berlin, 1919), 527 (lines 137–44); trans. M. Lapidge and J. L. Rosier, *Aldhelm: the Poetic Works* (Cambridge, 1985), p. 178: 'Amidst these mighty gales and tempests of terror our hearts trembled when our eyes beheld such horrendous events: the vault of the roof was creaking with terrifying moans and groans.'

11 D. Norberg, *Introduction à l'étude de la versification latine médiévale* (Stockholm, 1958), esp. pp. 6 and 7–37.

Aldhelm's poem there is not a single line ending with a bisyllabic word; nor is such a line to be found in the entire corpus of octosyllabic verse by Aldhelm's disciple, Æthilwald.[12]

Although Aldhelm studied at some point of his career with Theodore, he certainly did not learn the rhythmical structure of his octosyllables from Theodore, if the poem 'Te nunc sancte speculator' is anything to go by. In the compass of a six-line poem, three of Theodore's lines end with bisyllabic words; all lines carry stress on the penultimate syllable, not – as in Aldhelm's verse – on the antepenultimate. The rhythmical form of Theodore's verse cannot, therefore, be explained in terms of the development of rhythmical verse from iambic dimeter hymns. In this respect, Theodore's verse stands utterly outside the Latin tradition.

Where, then, did Theodore learn this unusual verse-form? I stated earlier that there were 'virtually' no antecedents; but there is in fact one hypothetically possible antecedent which requires discussion, if only to be rejected. Early in the second century AD the emperor Hadrian had a brief and witty poetic exchange with a poet named Florus. Florus had apparently written that he would not want to be Caesar [= Hadrian], wandering all over the world – to Britain, to the realm of Scythian frosts:

> Ego nolo Caesar esse
> ambulare per Britannos
> < . . . . >
> Scythicas pati pruinas.[13]

To this the emperor replied that he would not want to be Florus, wandering aimlessly from pub to pub, inhabiting greasy-spoon cook-houses:

> Ego nolo Florus esse
> ambulare per tabernas
> latitare per popinas
> culices pati rotundos.[14]

---

[12] *Aldhelmi Opera*, ed. Ehwald, pp. 528–37 (nos. II-V); cf. also discussion by Orchard, *The Poetic Art of Aldhelm*, pp. 33–7.

[13] Ptd *Minor Latin Poets*, ed. J. W. and A. M. Duff, rev. ed. (Cambridge, MA, and London, 1982), p. 426: 'I don't want to be Caesar, travelling among the Britons <. . .>, suffering the frosts of Scythia.'

[14] *Ibid.*, p. 444: 'I don't want to be Florus, frequenting taverns, lurking in cook-houses, the prey of fat mosquitoes.'

However, this charming verse-exchange between poet and emperor did not apparently circulate separately in manuscript; it is known solely from the *Vita Hadriani* transmitted as part of the *Scriptores Historiae Augustae*, and although this compilation is preserved in a ninth-century manuscript from Fulda written in Anglo-Saxon minuscule,[15] and was known to Sedulius Scottus,[16] there is no evidence, as far as I am aware, that it was ever known in England.[17] In any event, it would be a long shot to argue that seven lines of verse buried in any enormous compilation like the *Historia Augusta* served as a model for Theodore's verse. An explanation closer at hand is required.

In fact the verses of the emperor Hadrian and the poet Florus are not rhythmical trochaic octosyllables (though they can be read that way if the metre is disregarded and emphasis is laid on the natural stress of the words). Rather, they are Latin imitations of a Greek verse-form known as the 'anaclastic' ionic dimeter.[18] Because this form of verse was practised by the Greek poet Anacreon, who flourished in the sixth century BC, it is customarily referred to as 'anacreontics'. The metrical structure may be illustrated by a fragment of Anacreon:

> Πολιοὶ μὲν ἡμῖν ἤδη
> κρόταφοι κάρη τε λευκόν
> χαρίεσσα δ' οὐκέτ' ἤβη
> πάρα, γηράλέοι δ' ὀδόντες
> γλυκεροῦ δ' οὐκέτι πολλός
> βιότου χρόνος λέλειπται.[19]

Each verse consists of two ionic feet (each of which is scanned ˘˘‾‾); but because the scansion of the fourth and fifth syllables is reversed (this is the 'anaclasis' (ἀνάκλασις) or 'bending back'), what would originally be

[15] Bamberg, Stadtliche Bibliothek, Class. 54 (E. III. 19) (Fulda, s. ix$^{2/4}$); on which see B. Boyer, 'Insular Contributions to Medieval Literary Tradition', *Classical Philology* 43 (1948), 31–9, at 33–9.

[16] See *Sedulii Scotti Collectaneum Miscellaneum*, ed. D. Simpson, CCSL 67 (Turnhout, 1988), pp. xx, xxv and 305–13; the poetic exchange between Florus and Hadrian is at p. 313.

[17] See *Texts and Transmission: a Survey of the Latin Classics*, ed. L.D. Reynolds (Oxford, 1983), pp. 354–6.

[18] See, for sake of convenience, J. W. Halporn, M. Ostwald and T. G. Rosenmeyer, *The Meters of Greek and Latin Poetry* (New York, 1963), pp. 24 and 92.

[19] *Anacreon*, ed. B. Gentili (Rome, 1968), p. 28 (no. 36); also ed. D. A. Campbell, *Greek Lyric*, 4 vols. (Cambridge, MA, and London, 1982–92) II, 78–9 (no. 395): 'My temples

scanned as ˘ ˘ ‾ ‾ | ˘ ˘ ‾ ‾ is in fact scanned as ˘ ˘ ‾ ˘ | ‾ ˘ ‾ ‾. The Latin verses of the emperor Hadrian and Florus are to be scanned in the same way: *ĕgŏ nōlŏ Flōrŭs ēssē*.

The anacreontic form proved to be very popular with later Greek poets as a vehicle for light and witty poems, usually – like those of Anacreon himself – on lighthearted themes to do with the pleasures of life. There survive some sixty *carmina anacreontea*, all pagan and classicizing in sentiment and dating from late antiquity, which are preserved as a collection in a tenth-century manuscript now in Paris (BN, grec suppl. 384, fols. 675–90).[20] But it was in late antiquity that the form was first adapted for Christian purposes.[21] For example, Gregory of Nazianzus (d. 390), one of the great Greek fathers of the church, adopted the anacreontic form for two of his poems, one of them a hymn-like prayer in honour of Christ and the creation:

> Σέ, τον ἄφθιτον μονάρχην,
> δός ἀνυμνεῖν, δὸς ἀείδειν,
> τὸν ἄνακτα, τὸν δεσπότην·
> δι᾽ ὅν ὕμνος, δι᾽ ὅν αἶνος·
> δι᾽ ὅν ἀγγέλων χορεία,
> δι᾽ ὅν ἥλιος προλάμπει,
> δι᾽ ὅν ὁ δρόμος σελήνης
> δι᾽ ὅν ἄστρων μέγα κάλλος,
> δι᾽ ὅν ἄνθρωπος ὁ σεμνὸς
> ἔλαχεν νοεῖν τὸ θεῖον,
> λογικὸν ζῷον ὑπάρχων . . .[22]

Shortly after Gregory's experiment in Christian anacreontics, the urbane African landowner Synesius (d. *c.* 412), who was born to a pagan family but was persuaded late in his life to become bishop of Cyrene in Libya,

are already grey and my head is white; graceful youth is no more with me, my teeth are old and no long span of sweet life remains now.'

[20] *Carmina Anacreontea*, ed. M. L. West (Leipzig, 1984); see discussion by Campbell, *Greek Lyric* II, 4–18, esp. 14–15 on the problems of dating the *anacreontea*.

[21] See the still valuable discussion by F. Petit, in *DACL* I.2 (1924), 1863–72, s.v. 'Anacréontiques'.

[22] PG 37, 508–10: also ed. R. Cantarella, *Poeti bizantini*, ed. F. Conca, 2 vols. (Milan, 1992) I, 132: 'Grant that I may praise, that I may sing You, O immortal Monarch, our Lord and Ruler, through Whom the hymn, through Whom the praise, through Whom the choir of angels, through Whom the infinite aeons, through Whom the sun shines forth, through Whom the course of the moon, through Whom the great beauty of the

composed two hymns in anacreontics;[23] as Gregory before him, Synesius used the anacreontic form for a hymn of praise to the Creator and His creation:

> Ὅλος οὗτος εἷς τε πάντῃ,
> ὅλος εἰς ὅλον δεδυκώς,
> κύτος οὐρανῶν ἑλίσσει·
> τὸ δ' ὅλον τοῦτο φυλάσσων
> νενεμημέναισι μορφαῖς
> μεμερισμένος παρέστη,
> ὁ μὲν ἀστέρων διφρείαις,
> ὁ δ' ἐς ἀγγέλων χορείας.[24]

Here as elsewhere in Synesius the metaphorical language is Neoplatonic in origin; the point is simply that Synesius was using anacreontics for a very serious Christian purpose. In this respect Gregory and Synesius had many followers.

It was particularly in the schools of Palestine and Syria that anacreontics were cultivated for Christian purposes.[25] A large collection of such anacreontics is preserved in a manuscript now Vatican City, Biblioteca Apostolica Vaticana, Barberini gr. 310, written in the late tenth century at

stars, through Whom divine mankind is able to comprehend the divine, being a thinking creature.'

[23] The anacreontics of Synesius are Hymns I and II in the earlier numbering: ed. PG 66, 1588–92 (no. I) and 1592–3 (no. II). Since the edition of Nicola Terzaghi (1939), however, scholars have cited the hymns according to a different numbered sequence which more closely reflects the order in which they were composed. Accordingly, the former Hymn no. I is now cited as no. IX, and the former no. II is now no. V. The hymns of Synesius are conveniently edited by C. Lacombrade, *Synésios de Cyrène, I. Hymnes* (Paris, 1978), from which I quote. On Hymn no. IX (the former no. I), see discussion by M. M. Hawkins, *Der erste Hymnus des Synesius von Kyrene. Text und Kommentar* (Munich, 1939), as well as R. Keydell, 'Zu den Hymnen des Synesios', *Hermes* 84 (1956), 151–62, esp. 152–62.

[24] Hymn no. IX, lines 85–92 (ed. Lacombrade, p. 103): 'This one mighty being, entire in every respect, a whole having descended to become a whole, causes the vault of the heavens to rotate; protecting that entire entity in the forms over which it has control, it is manifest in all its parts, one of which impels the chariot of the stars, while another drives the choirs of angels.'

[25] See discussion by Cavallo, above, p. 62. The principal study of Byzantine anacreontics is that by T. Nissen, *Die byzantinischen Anakreonteen*, Sitzungsberichte der Bayerischen Akademie der Wissenschaften, phil.-hist. Abteilung (Munich, 1940); see also H. Hunger, *Die hochsprachliche profane Literatur der Byzantiner*, 2 vols. (Munich, 1978) II, 93–5, and (briefly) *ODB* I, 83.

Constantinople, but compiled from earlier materials of Syro-Palestinian origin.[26] The collection includes anacreontics ranging in date from the sixth century to the ninth, from those by John of Gaza and George the Grammarian, both of whom were active during the reign of Justinian (527–65), to those of Elias Syncellus and Michael Syncellus (d. 846), both of Jerusalem and of ninth-century date. However, the Christian poet whose anacreontics are best represented in Barberini gr. 310, and who is most relevant to the present discussion, is Sophronius, patriarch of Jerusalem (634–8).[27] Little is known of Sophronius's life, save that he received early training in rhetoric at Damascus, that he entered the monastery of Theodosius (Deir Dosi) near Bethlehem in 580,[28] that, in company with his friend John Moschus, he travelled to Alexandria where the two of them studied with the great polymath Stephen of Alexandria, that he and John travelled from there to Constantinople, where he spent a period of time in the 620s, and that he was, with his follower Maximus the Confessor, one of the principal opponents of the imperial doctrine of monotheletism.[29] He was appointed patriarch of Jerusalem in 634, and died in 638, soon after the city fell to the Arabs. Sophronius is known for various works in Greek,[30] among them a number of homilies, accounts of the miracles of SS Cyrus and John,[31] and (in collaboration with John Moschus) a *vita* of John

---

[26] See C. Gallavotti, 'Note su testi e scrittori di codici greci, VII. Il codice Barb. gr. 310', *Rivista di studi bizantini e neoellenici* ns 24 (1987), 29–83; a detailed catalogue of the contents of the manuscript is given on pp. 35–42.

[27] See Nissen, *Die byzantinischen Anakreonteen*, pp. 13–26. Nissen presents evidence (p. 19) to suggest that George the Grammarian was from Egypt rather than Gaza.

[28] On this monastery, see Y. Hirschfield, *The Judean Desert Monasteries in the Byzantine Period* (New Haven, CT, and London, 1992), pp. 15, 102 and 248–9.

[29] The best monograph on Sophronius is C. von Schönborn, *Sophrone de Jérusalem. Vie monastique et confession dogmatique*, Théologie historique 20 (Paris, 1972); see also the indispensable studies by H. Chadwick, 'John Moschus and his Friend Sophronius the Sophist', *JTS* ns 25 (1974), 41–74, and E. Follieri, 'Dove e quando morì Giovanni Mosco?', *Rivista di studi bizantini e neoellenici* ns 25 (1988), 3–39. This last article contains the important demonstration that John Moschus died in Constantinople (rather than in Rome) in 634.

[30] Listed *CPG* III, nos. 7635–53.

[31] Listed *BHG*, nos. 475–6 (*Laudes*) and 477–9 (*Narratio miraculorum*); ed. PG 87, 3380–421 and 3424–676 respectively. The latter text is also ed. N. Fernández Marcos, *Los 'Thaumata' de Sofronio. Contribución al estudio de la 'Incubatio cristiana'* (Madrid, 1975); and see J. Duffy, 'Observations on Sophronius' "Miracles of Cyrus and John"', *JTS* ns 35 (1984), 71–90.

the Almoner, now unfortunately lost. Sophronius is also known as the author of various poems, including a number of epigrams preserved in the 'Palatine Anthology'[32] and a collection of some twenty-three anacreontics preserved principally in the aforementioned Barberini manuscript.[33] Like his Christian predecessors, Sophronius used the anacreontic form for hymns in praise of God the Creator:

Γενέτης Θεὸς τὰ ὄντα
σοφίῃ τέτευχε πάντα,
ἀγαθῶν ὅπως τε θείων
ἐσαεὶ κτίσις μετάσχοι.
Διὸ δὴ χερῶν κρατίστων
ἀπὸ γῆς κόνιν κομίσσας
μερόπων ἔτευξε φύτλην
μεγάλα βροτοῖς ὀπάζων.[34]

It is widely recognized that Sophronius brought a new rhetorical sophistication to the anacreontic form;[35] he also introduced many formal innovations. For example, many of his anacreontics are of a substantial length (one hundred or more lines), and most are in acrostic form, with each stanza or group of stanzas beginning with a successive letter of the alphabet; sometimes a stanza consisting of four octosyllabic lines (called an οἶκος) will be punctuated by a refrain or κουκούλιον, consisting of two twelve-syllable lines.[36] In any event, the anacreontics of Sophronius were

---

32 See Alan Cameron, 'The Epigrams of Sophronius', *Classical Quarterly* 33 (1984), 284–92.
33 Ed. PG 87, 3725–840 (repr. from Pietro Matranga's edition of 1840, with accompanying Latin translation by Marranga); and more recently by M. Gigante, *Sophronii Anacreontica* (Rome, 1957). For discussion, see Nissen, *Die byzantinischen Anakreonteen*, pp. 27–46, and H. Donner, *Die anakreontischen Gedichte Nr. 19 und Nr. 20 des Patriarchen Sophronius von Jerusalem* (Heidelberg, 1981).
34 PG 87, 3733: 'God the Creator in His wisdom fashioned all things so that His creation should eternally participate in divine goodness. Accordingly, having gathered up dust from the earth, He fashioned the human race with His mighty hands, bestowing great gifts on men.'
35 Cf. Donner, *Die anakreontischen Gedichte*, p. 7: 'Aber niemand hat sich der Form der Ode im anakreontischen Maß so souverän und rhetorisch versiert bedient wie Sophronius von Jerusalem; keiner vermochte wie er den christlichen Hymnenstil in das Prokrustesbett dieses heidnischen Metrums zu zwingen.'
36 See Nissen, *Die byzantinischen Anakreonteen*, p. 27, who suggests that the alphabetical acrostic form – which Sophronius was the first to employ in Greek anacreontics – may

immensely influential, not only on later poets in Palestine and Syria, such as Elias Syncellus and Michael Syncellus, but on Greek poets as far afield as Syracuse in Sicily, where in the ninth century a monk named Theodosius modelled anacreontic verses closely on those of Sophronius (his verses are even referred to in manuscript as ᾽Ανακρεόντεια κατὰ Σωφρόνιον).[37] The later history of anacreontics need not concern us;[38] what is important to note is that Sophronius was an older contemporary of Theodore, and that there is some reason to believe that their lives may have intersected at some point. We know that Theodore spent some time in Constantinople, since in the Canterbury biblical commentaries he is reported as having seen with his own eyes the Dodekathronon, or the relics of the Twelve Baskets (in which the fragments of bread and fish were collected after Christ had miraculously fed the 5,000), which we know to have been housed in a shrine at the base of the famous 'Porphyry Column' in Constantinople, still standing – in a much dilapidated state – in present-day Istanbul.[39] Furthermore, it has recently been demonstrated beyond reasonable doubt that Sophronius (in company with John Moschus) spent some time in Constantinople, before Sophronius's election to the patriarchate of Jerusalem in 634.[40] Could Theodore have met Sophronius there? At one point in the Canterbury biblical commentaries, Sophronius is cited as the source of an opinion concerning the Hebrew etymology of the name Emmaus;[41] and since no such etymology can be found in the surviving writings of Sophronius, there is reason to suspect that Theodore may have derived the information by word of mouth. Given personal contact of this sort, Theodore may also have known of Sophronius's poetic endeavours in the field of anacreontic hymnody. In any case there is no difficulty in assuming that he was familiar with Christian anacreontic verse.

have been influenced by Syriac hymns; on the form of the οἶκος and κουκούλιον, see Donner, *Die anakreontischen Gedichte*, pp. 8–10.

[37] See the important studies by B. Lavagnini, 'Anacreonte in Sicilia e a Bisanzio', *Atti dell'Accademia di scienze, lettere e arti di Palermo* 4th ser. 38 (Palermo, 1980), 471–84, and *idem, Alle origini del verso politico*, Istituto siciliano di studi bizantini e neoellenici: Quaderni 11 (Palermo, 1983), esp. 14–29.

[38] It is treated by Nissen, *Die byzantinischen Anakreonteen*, pp. 46–81.

[39] See *Biblical Commentaries*, ed. Bischoff and Lapidge, pp. 550–2, and above, pp. 11–12. On the 'Porphyry Column', see the indispensable articles by C. Mango, *Studies on Constantinople* (Aldershot, 1993), nos. II (pp. 306–13), III and IV.

[40] See Follieri, 'Dove e quando morì Giovanni Mosco?', esp. pp. 19–23 and 38–9.

[41] PentI 35 (*Biblical Commentaries*, ed. Bischoff and Lapidge, p. 310).

With this hypothesis in mind, let us return to the metrical form of Greek anacreontic verse. All the poets mentioned in the previous paragraph wrote metrical, that is quantitative, anacreontics: their concern was with the length, not the stress, of syllables. However, like Latin, the Greek language changed during the course of centuries, and from the second century AD onwards there ceased to be a distinction between long and short /o/ (ω/o) and /e/ (η/ε), and all the Greek diphthongs were monophthongized (these changes in pronunciation are clearly reflected in the orthography of papyri from this period).[42] As Herbert Hunger has noted, this tendency to (what is called) isochrony, where all vowels have equal weight, meant that the quantity of syllables became less important as a principle of verse composition; the substitution (say) of two short for one long vowel lost its point, and in lieu of syllable 'measuring' or 'scanning' (*Silbenmessung*), syllable counting became the structuring principle.[43] And so in Greek, as also in Latin, accentual verse came to be written in which word accent took the place of long syllables in metrical verse forms. Such changes inevitably affected the structure of anacreontic verse.

Such a transformation did not take place over night, however, and with verse of the earlier Byzantine period (fifth to seventh centuries) it is often difficult to estimate the role of accent in the structure of the verse. Nevertheless, certain tendencies emerge. In terms of syllable counting, it will be clear that each anacreontic line is an octosyllable. Within each verse, the penultimate or paroxytonic syllable was stressed, and eventually the first, third and seventh syllables came to be stressed as well. In other words, the accentual form of a Greek anacreontic verse came to be nothing

---

[42] See, in general, R. Browning, *Medieval and Modern Greek*, 2nd ed. (Cambridge, 1983), pp. 25–6, as well as the more detailed studies by F. T. Gignac, *A Grammar of the Greek Papyri of the Roman and Byzantine Periods, I. Phonology* (Milan, 1976), pp. 183–294, and esp. 325–7 (on quantity) and S.-T. Theodorsson, *The Phonology of Ptolemaic Koine*, Studia Graeca et Latina Gothoburgensia 36 (Göteborg, 1977), with the evidence from papyri given at 62–208 and analysis relevant to the present discussion at 214–38 (with conclusions stated briefly at 238).

[43] Hunger, *Die hochsprachliche profane Literatur* II, 89; cf. also A. Dihle, 'Die Anfänge der griechischen akzentuirenden Verskunst', *Hermes* 82 (1954), 182–99, who rejects earlier theories that the emergence of *Isosyllabie* in Greek Christian hymns can be satisfactorily explained in terms of influence from Syriac hymnody (pp. 191–5), and sees the development as a reflex of the practice of singing hymns, a process which began in the late fourth century (pp. 195–7).

271

other than a trochaic octosyllable. Michael Jeffreys has recently put this point succinctly: 'Later Byzantine Anacreontics (which might better be called trochaic octosyllables) had a rather monotonous tendency to include a stress on odd-numbered syllables and a central caesura after the fourth syllable.'[44] This monotonous tendency can be seen in the following verses by the late Byzantine poet Markos Angelos (the lines describe the cosmic force of Eros, as this is revealed in the workings of a magnet):

> Τὴν γὰρ δὴ μαγνῆτιν λίθον
> τίς οὐκ ἄν ἰδὼν θαυμάσῃ
> καὶ τὸν ἄξονα τῆς σφαίρας
> πῶς τοσοῦτον ἀφεστῶτα
> καὶ μηδὲν ἀλλήλοις ὄντα
> κατὰ γένος, κατὰ φύσιν,
> κατὰ πάντα λόγον ἄλλον,
> φίλτρον τρέφουσιν ἀλλήλοις;[45]

In each of these octosyllabic verses, the stress falls on the first, third, fifth and seventh syllables. The rhythmical structure, in other words, is precisely the same as in the octosyllabic verses of Theodore beginning 'Te nunc sancte speculator'. The most reasonable explanation of the form of Theodore's octosyllables is that he was imitating in Latin a rhythmical verse-form with which he was familiar in Greek.

There are various ways in which this hypothesis requires qualification, however. The anacreontics of Markos Angelos were composed in the fourteenth century, and are not therefore a reliable index to the treatment of stress by seventh-century Byzantine poets; they reflect the culmination of a tendency which had certainly begun as early as the seventh century, but had not by then achieved the rhythmical regularity seen in the verses of Markos. Nevertheless certain characteristic features in the treatment of accented syllables had begun to emerge. In the anacreontic verse of the early Byzantine period, for example, there is an unmistakable tendency to

---

[44] *ODB* I, 83, s.v. 'Anacreontics'; cf. Hunger, *Die hochsprachliche profane Literatur* II, 95: 'Der anakreontische Vers had sich damit weitgehend dem trochäischen Achtsilber angenähert: ⁻ˇ⁻ˇ | | ⁻ˇ⁻ˇ.'

[45] Ed. Nissen, *Die byzantinischen Anakreonteen*, p. 77; also ed. Cantarella, *Poeti bizantini* II, 960: 'Who would not marvel at seeing the magnet and the axis of the (earth's) sphere, since, through being so very different and having nothing in common, neither by origin nor by nature, nor by any other reason, they nevertheless nurture a deep attraction for each other?'

end the line with stress on the paroxytonic (that is, the penultimate syllable). Thus in the two anacreontic hymns of Gregory of Nazianzus, 79 per cent of verses are so accented.[46] By the sixth century, the proportion of stressed syllables in the paroxytone had risen to 93 per cent in John of Gaza and to 97.5 per cent in George the Grammarian.[47] In the octosyllables of Sophronius, a similarly high proportion of paroxytonic stress is found (93 per cent),[48] so that it is appropriate to speak of a 'mixture of quantitative and accentual composition' in Sophronius.[49] The structure of Sophronius's octosyllables can thus be represented as follows:[50]

$$\cup\cup - \cup - \mid \cup - \cup$$

Sophronius has not yet achieved the monotonous, trochaic regularity which will later characterize the anacreontics of Markos Angelos, but with stress on the third, fifth and seventh syllables, his verse is clearly moving in that direction.

We have seen that the Anglo-Latin octosyllables composed by Aldhelm and his followers, which were based ultimately on the iambic dimeter hymns of late antiquity, invariably had stress on the proparoxytone or antepenultimate syllable, and were thus utterly distinct in structure from the octosyllables of Theodore. No model for Theodore's octosyllables, which are invariably trochaic and have stress on the paroxytone or penultimate syllable, could be found in the Latin tradition. Given that Theodore was Greek by birth and training, it seemed legitimate to seek such a model in Greek tradition. In fact the octosyllabic anacreontics composed by Greek poets such as Gregory of Nazianzus and especially Sophronius of Jerusalem provide an exact model for Theodore's Latin octosyllables. The simplest hypothesis is that Theodore was attempting to recreate in Latin a form of verse with which he was familiar in Greek.

This demonstration has several important consequences. If it can be

---

[46] Nissen, *Die byzantinischen Anakreonteen*, p. 7; Hunger, *Die hochsprachliche profane Literatur* II, 93. The high proportion of *Paroxytonierung*, or stress on the penultimate syllable, in the two octosyllabic hymns of Gregory of Nazianzus, caused Dihle to doubt their authenticity ('Die Anfänge', p. 196).

[47] Nissen, *Die byzantinischen Anakreonteen*, p. 21; Hunger, *Die hochsprachliche profane Literatur* II, 94.

[48] Nissen, *Die byzantinischen Anakreonteen*, p. 34.

[49] Hunger, *Die hochsprachliche profane Literatur* II, 93–4: 'bei Sophronios von Jerusalem (7. Jh.) mischten sich quantierende und akzentuierende Auffassung.'

[50] Donner, *Die anakreontischen Gedichte*, p. 9.

accepted that Theodore's Latin octosyllables were composed in imitation of a Greek verse-form which he had inherited from his Greek background and education, it follows that they were for him an individual (and idiosyncratic) creation. Their individuality is worth stressing in view of the fact that three other Latin octosyllabic poems having precisely this rhythmical structure have been preserved anonymously in an English manuscript of the early ninth century, the so-called 'Book of Cerne' (Cambridge, University Library, Ll. 1. 10): those beginning 'Sancte sator suffragator', 'Christum peto, Christum preco' and 'Heloi heloi Domine mi'.[51] All three poems have paroxytonic stress, with the trochaic rhythm created by the natural stress falling on the first syllable of bisyllabic words, as in Theodore's verses to Hæddi. Given the distinctive nature of the verse-form, the likelihood is that these three poems were composed by Theodore himself, and this attribution may be confirmed by various other considerations. All three poems contain a striking amount of Greek vocabulary, as one might expect from a native speaker of Greek. Most importantly, all three poems take the form of prayers to Christ the Creator. As we have seen, the anacreontic poems of Gregory of Nazianzus, Synesius of Cyrene and Sophronius were all conceived as hymns to Christ. The three Anglo-Latin poems thus owe not only their metrical form, but also their function, to Greek anacreontic tradition.

Close analysis of the metrical form of an apparently insignificant six-line Anglo-Latin poem thus opens for us a whole new vista on the intellectual links between the Byzantine East and Anglo-Saxon England. As in other domains of knowledge, it was the remarkable career of Archbishop Theodore which forged these links. His career provides a clear demonstration that, in the pursuit of greater understanding of early Anglo-Saxon culture, it will henceforth be necessary always to have firmly in mind the achievements of seventh-century Byzantium.[52]

[51] The attribution of these three poems to Theodore was first suggested by Lapidge, 'The School of Theodore and Hadrian', p. 47; they are ptd below, pp. 276–80 (nos. II-IV).

[52] I am grateful to Andy Orchard for constructive criticism of a number of points in this article.

APPENDIX

Theodore's trochaic octosyllables

The four poems printed here share a number of unusual characteristics, which suggests that they were very likely composed by the one author – Archbishop Theodore, on our reasoning – or were at least composed under his supervision, since it is clear that their metrical form is modelled on that of the Greek anacreontic hymns of late antiquity. All four poems have a pronounced trochaic rhythm, based on the natural accentuation of Latin words; all have a medial caesura in each octosyllabic line; all have bisyllabic rhyme – a feature not found in their Greek antecedents – although there are minor differences between them, such that whole octosyllabic lines in no. I are linked by bisyllabic rhyme, whereas nos. II-IV have internal bisyllabic rhyme, with the syllables before the medial caesura rhyming with those at the end of the line. Poems I, III and IV are preserved uniquely in Anglo-Saxon manuscripts; only no. II enjoyed a wide continental distribution.

I Theodore's Greeting to Bishop Hæddi

Te nunc, sancte speculator,		You, now, holy bishop,
uerbi Dei digne dator,		worthy giver of the Word of God,
Hæddi, pie praesul, precor		Hæddi, holy prelate, I beseech you,
pontificum ditum decor:		the glory of powerful pontiffs:
pro me tuo peregrino	5	for me, your foreign visitor,
preces funde Theodoro.		pour out prayers for Theodore.

This poem (*ICL*, no. 16100) is preserved uniquely in Cambridge, Corpus Christi College 320 (St Augustine's, Canterbury, s. x^{ex}), p. 71, where it is associated with the *Iudicia* of Theodore.

I.1 *speculator*. The Latin word *speculator* here corresponds to Greek ἐπισκόπος; see H. Goelzer and A. Mey, *Le Latin de Saint Avit* (Paris, 1909), pp. 428–9, and esp. P. Grosjean, 'Notes d'hagiographie celtique. 41. Speculator, superspeculator, superinspector', *AB* 76 (1958), 379–87, who discusses the present poem, and draws attention to a number of patristic sources where *speculator* is used for *episcopus*, including Isidore, *Etym.* VII.xii.12.

275

II A Hymn to Christ

Sancte sator, suffragator,		Holy creator, sustainer,
legum lator, largus dator,		lawgiver, bountiful provider,
iure pollens es qui potens		You Who are mighty in Your laws,
nunc in ethra firma petra;		are now a firm rock in heaven;
a quo creta cuncta freta	5	by Whom were created all the seas
quae aplustra ferunt, flustra		which bear ships – the calm seas
quando celox currit uelox;		when the swift keel runs;
cuius numen creuit lumen		Whose power, beyond the heavens,
simul solum supra polum.		created light and earth as well.
Prece posco prout nosco	10	I ask You in prayer, as I know my (sins),
caeli arce, Christe, parce		from the summit of heaven, Christ, spare (me)
et piacla dira iacla		and my foul sins, those dire darts,
trude tetra tua scethra:		thrust them aside with Your shield:
quae capesso et facesso		(sins) which I often commit and perpetrate
in hoc sexu sarci nexu.	15	in my sexual organs, the bond of the flesh.
Christi umbo meo lumbo		May the shield of Christ be on my loins,
sit, ut atro cedat latro		so that the Thief with his black,
mox sugmento fraudulento.		deceptive growth may straightway yield.
Pater, parme, procul arma		O Father, O shield, drive afar
arce hostis ut e costis	20	the Enemy's weapons, as from my ribs,
imo corde sine sorde;		from the depth of my heart, free from filth;
tum deinceps trux et anceps		then straightway may the very cruel
catapulta cadat multa.		and dangerous missile collapse.
Alma tutrix atque nutrix		Kindly Hand, protectress and nurse,
fulce, manus, me, ut sanus	25	sustain me, so that, purified
corde reo prout queo		in my guilty heart I may say as best I can,
Christo theo qui est leo		to Christ the God, Who is the lion,
dicam, 'Deo gratis geo',		'I give [pour out?] thanks to God',
sicque beo me ab eo.		and thus am gladdened by Him.

Uniquely among the four octosyllabic poems edited here, 'Sancte sator' (*ICL*, no. 14640) enjoyed a wide manuscript circulation, both in England and on the Continent. The earliest English manuscript in question is Cambridge, UL, Ll. 1. 10 (the 'Book of Cerne'), 66r-v, a manuscript written probably in Mercia in the early ninth century (see M. P. Brown, 'Paris, Bibliothèque Nationale, lat. 10861 and the Scriptorium of Christ Church, Canterbury', *ASE* 15 (1986), 119–37, at 135, n. 67; it is ed. from this manuscript by A. B. Kuypers, *The Prayer Book of Aedeluald the Bishop, commonly called the Book of Cerne* (Cambridge, 1902), pp. 131–2 (no. 31)). The poem had been transmitted to the Continent by Anglo-Saxon missionaries no later than the second half of the eighth century, for it was seemingly quoted by the English nun of Heidenheim, Hygeburg, in her *vita* of her two brothers, Wynnebald and Willibald (MGH, SS 15, 117; see E. Gottschaller, *Hugeburc von Heidenheim* (Munich, 1973), pp. 14–15); another reflex of this route of transmission is the presence of the poem in Munich, Staatsbibliothek, Clm. 19410 (Tegernsee, s. ix^med^), on which see G. Baesecke, *Das lateinischalthochdeutsche Reimgebet (Carmen ad Deum) und das Rätsel vom Vogel federlos* (Berlin, 1948), pp. 9–24, who rightly ascertained the English origin of the poem, as well as B. Bischoff, *Mittelalterliche Studien*, 3 vols. (Stuttgart, 1966–81) III, 102. Another agent of transmission to the Continent was Alcuin, who paraphrases several of its verses in one of his rhythmical poems (MGH, PLAC 4, 903–7). In a letter addressed by Alcuin to his colleague Arno of Salzburg, dated 802 (MGH, Ep. 4, 417 (no. 259)), Alcuin explained that he was sending to Arno a 'handbook' (*manualem libellum*) which contained Alcuin's commentaries on the seven penitential psalms and the fifteen gradual psalms, as well as that on Ps. CXVIII; he also included in this handbook some hymns (by Bede, *inter alia*), and among the hymns, apparently, was a copy of 'Sancte sator'. The original copy of Alcuin's handbook does not survive, but there are at least three later copies of it in continental libraries: (1) Cologne, Dombibliothek, 106 (Werden, s. ix^in^), 59v, on which see L. W. Jones, 'Cologne MS 106: a Book of Hildebold', *Speculum* 4 (1931), 27–61, at 29–36, together with Bischoff, *Mittelalterliche Studien* III, 7, n. 8; (2) Munich, Bayerische Staatsbibliothek, Clm. 14447 (Salzburg, s. ix^2/4^), 141r, on which see B. Bischoff, *Die südostdeutschen Schreibschulen und Bibliotheken in der Karolingerzeit*, 2nd ed., 2 vols. (Wiesbaden, 1960–80) II, 140–1; and (3) Karlsruhe, Badische Landesbibliothek, Aug. perg. 135, pt III (fols. 134–60) (Reichenau, s. x), 159v. The poem also occurs in Cambridge, UL, Gg. 5. 35 (St Augustine's, Canterbury, s. xi^med^), 388v, where it presumably derives (directly or indirectly) from a continental copy of the poem; certainly it is not a copy of that in the 'Book of Cerne'. The present edition is based solely on the copy in the 'Book of Cerne' as being the earliest English witness to the text (variant readings in later continental manuscripts can almost always be understood as emendations by scribes who did not understand the difficult text they were copying); an edition based on the continental manuscripts is found in *AH* 51, 299–301 (no. 229).

II.5 *creta*: for *creata*. The spelling *creta* for *creata* is found in early Anglo-Saxon glossaries (such as the Second Erfurt Glossary: *CGL* 5, 282.10); see B. Löfstedt, *Der hibernolateinische Grammatiker Malsachanus* (Uppsala, 1965), p. 138, n. 2.

II.6 *aplustra*: a rare archaic word, frequent in glossaries (cf. discussion by Pheifer, below, p. 330, n. 78), originally from Greek ἄφλαστον, meaning the ornamentation of a ship, hence by synecdoche 'a ship'; see *Thesaurus Linguae Latinae* II (1900–6), col. 241.

II.8 *creuit*: probably for *creauit* (as above, n. to II.5), but might also be the preterite of *cerno*, hence 'whose power discerned the light and earth'.

II.10 MS *preci*.

II.13 *scethra*: for *caetra*; cf. the similar spellings in Aldhelm, *Carmen de virginitate* 2631 (ed. Ehwald, p. 459), where the MS spelling variants *scetra* and *scedra* are recorded.

II.15 *sarci*: a grecism from σαρκός (gen. sg. of σάρξ), 'of the flesh'; cf. Aldhelm, *Carmina ecclesiastica* IV.x.19: 'salvator nostrae ... sarcis' (but note that Aldhelm gives the genitive as *sarcis*, not *sarci*).

II.18 *sugmento*: a form attested in the early Anglo-Saxon glossaries as a (mistaken) spelling of *augmentum*: ErfI (*CGL* 5, 390.31) and Corpus (S637). Löfstedt points out that this spelling is characteristically Insular (*Malsachanus*, p. 139).

II.20 *ut e*. Some continental manuscripts have *uti*; cf. Blume (*AH* 51, 300), who comments: 'wahrscheinlich ist das durch alle Quellen verbürgte *uti* ein Infinitivus graecus = "zum Gebrauchen, damit ich gebrauche"'. But Cerne's *ut e* makes adequate sense, so there is no need to posit a Greek infinitive construction.

II.23 *multa*: used adverbially here, as sometimes in verse (cf. Vergil, *Aen.* III.226; IV.301; V.869; etc.).

II.25 *fulce* MS, a spelling for *fulci*.

II.27 *theo*: for Greek θεῷ.

II.27 *leo*. The association of Christ and the lion derives almost certainly from ch. 1 of the *Physiologus*, a text originally composed in Greek (*CPG* II, no. 3766), no later than the end of the fourth century, and attributed falsely in manuscript to Epiphanius. The text circulated in many recensions; various Latin translations were made, the earliest of which may be dated between the fourth and sixth centuries. Given Theodore's background, he may have been familiar with the *Physiologus* in either a Greek or Latin version. The Greek text is ed. PG 43, 517–34, and (critically) by F. Sbordone, *Physiologi Graeci singul{ae} variarum aetatum recensiones* (Milan, 1936); the various Greek recensions are ptd in parallel by D. Kaimakis, *Der Physiologus nach der ersten Redaktion*, Beiträge zur klassischen Philologie 36 (Meisenheim, 1974). One Latin version is ed. F. Carmody, *Physiologus Latinus. Editions préliminaires. Versio B* (Paris, 1939); a convenient translation is M. J. Curley, *Physiologus* (Austin, TX, 1979). On the text itself, see F. Sbordone, *Ricerche sulle fonti e sulla composizione del Physiologus greco* (Naples, 1936); on its medieval circulation, see (conveniently) N. Henkel, *Studien zum Physiologus im Mittelalter* (Tübingen, 1976), esp. pp. 12–20 (on the Greek versions) and 21–58 (on the Latin versions).

II.28 *gratis* MS, a spelling for *grates*.

II.28 *geo*. Löfstedt (*Malsachanus*, pp. 138–9), has advanced interesting arguments in favour of taking *geo* – a form attested three times in Malsachanus – as a simplex of *degeo*, hence as a synonym for *ago* in the phrase *grates ago*; cf. also Gottschaller, *Hugeburc von Heidenheim*, pp. 14–15. It may be better, however, to adopt Blume's emendation to *cheo*, a grecism from χέω, 'to pour'.

III A Prayer to Christ

Christum peto, Christum preco		I beseech Christ, I pray to Christ,
Christo reddo corde laeto		I give thanks to Christ with joyous heart,
gratis, homo, imo fono,		I, a man, from the depth of my voice (?),
uti latro tetro metro		just as the thief at his foul limit
pendens ligno petit regno	5	hanging from the cross seeks to be
fore, uiso paradiso		in the Kingdom, having seen Paradise,
in †clalisso† in abysso		in †clalisso†, in the abyss, the Enemy
hoste truso ac deluso.		having been expelled and deceived.
Sic et ego quantum queo		Thus I, as far as I am able,
manus Deo leuo meo,	10	raise my hands up to my God,
quo cum †reuo† fruar eo.		so that, with †reuo†, I may enjoy Him.
†Gignans† chio patri pio		†Gignans† I pour out to Our Holy Father
fletus riuo quando uiuo.		a river of tears as long as I live.
†Sarcem turno pauli culmo		†..........
uti uideo stirpem limeo†	15	...........†

This poem (*ICL*, no. 2283) is preserved uniquely in the 'Book of Cerne' (Cambridge, UL, Ll. 1. 10, 66v), from which it is printed; it is also ed. Kuypers, *The Prayer Book of Aedeluald*, p. 132 (no. 32), and *AH*, 51, 301 (no. 230).

III.1 *preco*: apparently the very rare active form of *precor*, used here for sake of the rhyme.

III.3 *gratis* MS, a spelling for *grates* (see above, n. to II.28).

III.3 *fono*. Apparently a grecism; Blume (*AH* 51, 301) suggests φωνῶ ('with a sound, cry'), whence *imo fono* would mean 'with a profound sound'. But this is not wholly satisfactory, since φωνή is fem., not masc. It is also possible that *fono* is from Greek φόνος, 'murder, homicide', in view of the mention of the thief on the cross in lines 4–5. *Imo* could also be a spelling of *immo*. But in general this poem is too corrupt to be sure of any emendation.

III.4 *metro*: from Greek μέτρῳ ('measure, limit').

III.5 As Blume observes (*AH* 51, 301), it is necessary to understand *in* with *regno*.

III.7 *clalisso*: evidently corrupt; perhaps a grecism in origin.

III.8 MS *deliso*; but bisyllabic rhyme with *truso* confirms the correction to *deluso*.

III.11 *reuo*: a meaningless form in either Greek or Latin.

III.12 *gignans* is also meaningless; perhaps it is a corruption of *gemens* ('sighing, I pour out my heart').

III.12 *chio*: probably from the Greek χέω, 'to pour'; cf. above, n. to II.28.

III.13 *fletus*: *flatus* MS.

III.14–15: These lines are corrupt and beyond emendation or translation. Possibly *sarcem* is from Greek σάρξ once again (cf. II.15); but *turno* is meaningless in either Greek or Latin. In line 15 both *uideo* and *limeo* (a meaningless form) destroy the trochaic metre. Note that in the manuscript the words *altum caelum qui creauit terras atque aequora* follow the corrupt *limeo*; but since these are not trochaic octosyllables, I have removed them from the text. The words 'qui creauit terras atque aequora' form a rhythmical line of 4p + 7pp.

IV A Prayer to Christ

Heloi Heloi Domine me		O God, O God, my Lord,	
adiuro te custodi me		I beseech You: protect me,	
diligam te instrue me.		teach me that I may love You.	
Dei agne Iesu magne,		O Lamb of God, mighty Jesus,	
tu dignare me saluare.	5	please deign to save me.	
Deus uere miserere		True God, have mercy,	
adiuuare, conseruare.		support me, preserve me.	
Rex sanctorum angelorum		O King of the holy angels	
custodi me amantem te.		protect me who loves You.	
In te credo Deo uero	10	I believe in You the true God	
permanente nunc et ante,		existing now and before,	
sine fine, sancte trine		without end, Holy Trinity,	
Deus unus et non solus.		One God and not only One.	

This poem (*ICL*, no. 6189) is preserved uniquely in the 'Book of Cerne' (Cambridge, UL, Ll. 1. 10, 62v). It has been edited by Blume, *AH* 51, 301 (no. 231).

IV.1 *Heloi Heloi*: Mark XV.34 (the Crucified Christ cries out at the ninth hour): 'Heloi Heloi lama sabacthani quod est interpretatum Deus meus Deus meus ut quid dereliquisti me.' Cf. also the Greek NT: Ἐλωῒ Ἐλωῒ.

IV.12 *sancte trine*: *sanctae trinae* MS

IV.13 Following this line in the manuscript are six verses in a wholly different metre ('Vnitas triplex te deprecor per merita / ne imputes mihi peccata praeterita') which apparently did not form part of the original octosyllabic poem.

15

The Canterbury Bible glosses: facts and problems

J. D. PHEIFER

The 'Leiden Glossary', preserved in a late eighth- or early ninth-century manuscript from St Gallen (now Leiden, Bibliotheek der Rijksuniversiteit, Voss. lat. Q. 69, fols. 7–46, at 20ra-37ra, referred to hereafter as Ld.),[1] is a primary source for the history of Anglo-Saxon education, since its chapters or lists of *glossae collectae*,[2] many with Old English interpretations, give a conspectus of the books read in the school of Theodore and Hadrian at Canterbury, as Michael Lapidge pointed out in his pioneering article on that school.[3] The linch-pin that connects the 'Leiden Glossary' with the school of Canterbury is the reference to Theodore in Ld. xii.40 ('Cyneris: nablis idest citharis longiores quam psalterium nam psalterium triangulum fit theodorus dixit'), a gloss on the word *cinyris* in Ecclus. XXXIX.20.[4] As one might expect from the nature of early medieval

---

[1] On the manuscript, see J. H. Hessels, *A Late Eighth-Century Latin-Anglo-Saxon Glossary preserved in the Library of the Leiden University* (Cambridge, 1906), pp. ix-xxxv; *CLA* X, no. 1585; and N. R. Ker, *A Catalogue of Manuscripts containing Anglo-Saxon* (Oxford, 1957), App. no. 17. The 'Leiden Glossary' is hereafter abbreviated 'Ld.'; all references are to the edition of Hessels.

[2] Henry Bradshaw borrowed the term *glossae collectae* from a rubric in Cambridge, Corpus Christi College 153 to describe collections of interlinear or marginal glosses extracted from the text to which they referred (*Collected Papers of Henry Bradshaw* (Cambridge, 1889), p. 462).

[3] M. Lapidge, 'The School of Theodore and Hadrian', *ASE* 15 (1986), 45–72, at 54–8.

[4] All references to the Latin Vulgate Bible are to *Biblia sacra iuxta vulgatam Versionem*, ed. R. Weber, 3rd ed., 2 vols. (Stuttgart, 1985). Hessels's note (*A Late Eighth-Century Glossary*, p. 90), hesitates between Theodore of Heraclea, Theodore of Mopsuestia and Theodore of Tarsus; however, further references in the Canterbury biblical commentaries and glosses to both Theodore and Hadrian establish beyond doubt their connection with the last. The orthography of their Old English interpretations also points to a late seventh-century origin.

education, nearly half of Ld.'s forty-eight chapters are devoted to books of the Bible: chs. vii–xxv (23vb–27va) extend from Paralipomenon (Chronicles) through the rest of the Old Testament (including Jerome's prologues and most of the apocryphal books, but not Psalms and Maccabees) to the gospels, and ch. xxix (28vb–29rb) glosses Jerome's commentary on Matthew.[5]

Although Ld. chs. vii–xxv begin and end without any gaps in the manuscript, it is a reasonable hypothesis that they are an incomplete copy of what earlier was a full set of Bible glosses. This hypothesis is supported by related sets of biblical glosses in several other manuscripts. The principal manuscripts in question are the following three: Cambridge, University Library, Kk. 4. 6 (Worcester, s. xii[1]), 41ra–44vb (hereafter 'Cam.');[6] Paris, Bibliothèque Nationale, lat. 2685 (NE Francia, s. ix[2]), 48vb–57vb (hereafter 'Paris');[7] and Milan, Biblioteca Ambrosiana, M. 79 sup. (Piacenza, s. xi[2]), 59v–89r (hereafter 'Milan').[8] Also relevant to our understanding of the transmission of these Canterbury biblical glosses are the so-called 'Reichenau Bible Glosses', preserved in Karlsruhe, Badische Landesbibliothek, Aug. perg. 99, 37r–52v,[9] Aug. perg. 135, 96r–105v,[10] and Aug. perg. 248, 102r–154v,[11] as well as Fulda, Hessische Landesbibliothek, Aa. 2, 38r–117v,[12] Vatican City, Biblioteca Apostolica Vaticana, lat. 1469, 83va–155va,[13] and many others.[14] All of these begin with

---

[5] *Commentarii in euangelium Matthaei*, ed. D. Hurst and M. Adriaen, CCSL 77 (Turnhout, 1969).

[6] Cf. Hessels, *A Late Eighth-Century Glossary*, p. xliii. Cam. is unpublished.

[7] On the manuscript, see Ker, *Catalogue*, App. no. 23; the Old English glosses are ptd H. D. Meritt, *Old English Glosses* (New York, 1945), nos. 33–5, 40–2, 48 and 53. The glossary has been the subject of an important but unprinted doctoral dissertation: H. Schreiber, *Die Glossen des Codex Parisinus 2685 und ihre Verwandten* (unpubl. PhD dissertation, Jena Univ., 1961); see pp. 69–117 on the relationship of Paris to other Leiden-Family glossaries, and the text of Paris at pp. 119–46.

[8] See Lapidge, 'The School of Theodore', p. 70, and *Biblical Commentaries*, ed. Bischoff and Lapidge, which contains edition, translation and commentary on the first series of Pentateuch glosses (PentI) in 'Milan'.

[9] See *CLA* VIII, no. 1078; Ker, *Catalogue*, App. no. 14; and below, n. 14.

[10] See Ker, *Catalogue*, App. no. 15.

[11] See below, n. 14.   [12] See Ker, *Catalogue*, App. no. 11.

[13] Excerpts ptd *CGL* V, 520–8; cf. discussion *ibid.* IV, xvii–xviii and V, xxx.

[14] On the Reichenau Bible glosses, see E. Steinmeyer and E. Sievers, *Die althochdeutschen Glossen*, 5 vols. (Berlin, 1888–1922) V, 108–407. Steinmeyer prints the marginal glosses on Exodus–Judges in Fulda Aa. 2 (also incorporated into the text of Aug. perg.

Jerome's Prologue to the Pentateuch, followed by glosses to Genesis – Kings and further sections, some of which correspond to Ld. We may begin our analysis by considering the glosses in the first of these witnesses, namely the Cambridge manuscript.

CAMBRIDGE, UL, KK. 4. 6

Hessels pointed out the close relationship between the biblical glosses in the Cambridge manuscript (Cam.), which end abruptly at the bottom of 44vb in the middle of the Job section, and Ld. vii-xix.38.[15] Almost all the entries in the corresponding sections of Cam. (188 out of 199) have counterparts in Ld.; for example, thirty-two of thirty-three Cam. glosses to Ecclesiasticus correspond closely to those in Ld. xii ('DE ECCLESIAS-TICO'), as may be seen from the following list (all taken from Cam. 44rb):

'Euergetis. Boni operantis'; cf. Ld. xii.1: 'Euergitis boni operis uel factoris' (Ecclus prol. 33: 'Ptolomei Euergetis').

'Obductionis. Dilectionis idest mortis'; cf. Ld. xii.3: 'Obductionis dilectiones idest mortis' (Ecclus II.2: 'dilectionis').

'Implanauit. Seduxit'; cf. Ld. xii.4: 'Inplanauit seduxit inmisit' (Ecclus XV.12: 'implanauit').

'Placorem. Placationem' = Ld. xii.7 (Ecclus IV.13).

'Rusticatio. Cultura terre' = Ld. xii.8 (Ecclus VII.16: 'rusticationem').

'Caccabus. Testa est duas manubrias habens aliquando de eramento sicut et olla'; cf. Ld. xii.9: 'Cacabus de testa... eremento ... olla' (Ecclus XIII.3: 'caccabus').

'Ceruicatus. Superbus' = Ld. xii.10 (Ecclus XVI.11).

'Inpendis est Rebus'; cf. Ld. xii.11: 'Inpendiis rebus' (Ecclus XXI.9: 'inpendiis').

'Calculus arene. Ipse minute petre'; cf. Ld. xii.12: 'Calculus minutissima petra arene' (Ecclus XVIII.8: 'calculus harenae')

'Echariter. Sine gratia idest amariter'; cf. Ld. xii.13: 'Alacriter sine gratia amariter' (Ecclus XVIII.18: 'achariter').

'Loramentum. Ligamentum' = Ld. xii.14 (Ecclus XXII.19).

'Cementa. Petre molliores' = Ld. xii.15 (Ecclus XXII.21: 'cementa').

248), and the glosses on Jerome's Prologue to the Pentateuch and Genesis–II Kings in Aug. perg. 99, Aug. perg. 248 and Fulda Aa. 2 (*ibid.* pp. 115–27 and 135–225). He lists fifty-five manuscripts of the Reichenau Bible glosses (*ibid.*, pp. 108–11), and sixteen more are added by J. J. Contreni, 'The Biblical Glosses of Haimo of Auxerre and John Scottus Eriugena', *Speculum* 51 (1976), 411–34, at 418, n. 36.

[15] *A Late Eighth-Century Glossary*, p. xliii.

'Infruntæ. Effrenate'; cf. Ld. xii.16: 'Infrunite infrenate' (Ecclus XXIII.6: 'infrunitae').

'Platanus. Arbor boni odoris'; cf. Ld. xii.17: 'Platanus arbor est boni odoris' (Ecclus XXIV.19).

'Affaltum. Squalor'; cf. Ld. xii.18: 'Aspaltum **spaldur**' (Ecclus XXIV.20: 'aspaltum').

'Aromatizans. Redolens' = Ld. xii.20 (Ecclus XXIV.20).

'Galbanum. Pigmentum album'; cf. Ld. xii.19: 'Calbanus pigmentum album' (Ecclus XXIV.21: 'galbanus').

'Vngula et gutta. Pigmenta de arboribus'; cf. Ld. xii.21: 'Ungula... pigmentum de arboribus' (Ecclus XXIV.21).

'Storax. Incensum' = Ld. xii.22 (Ecclus XXIV.21).

'Dorix. Proprium nomen fluminis'; cf. Ld. xii.24: 'Dorix idest proprium nomen fluminis' (Ecclus XXIV.41: 'Doryx').

'In ormentum. In ornamentum' = Ld. xii.25 (Ecclus XXIV.21: 'in ornamentum').

'Aporia. Abhominatio'; Ld. xii.26: 'Apporia abominatio subitania' (Ecclus XXVII.5).

'Tortura' [no *interpretamentum*]; cf. Ld. xii.27: 'Tortura torquemina' (Ecclus XXXI.23).

'Lingua tercia. Discordans lingua uel rixosa'; Ld. xii.29: 'Lingua tertia discordians lingua uel rixosa' (Ecclus XXVII.16: 'lingua tertia').

'Colera nausia idest Gutta pessima'; Ld. xii.30: 'Colera nausia *only* (Ecclus XXXI.23: 'cholera').

'Frugi. Parcus'; cf. Ld. xii.32: 'Frugis parcus' (Ecclus XXXI.19: 'frugi').

'Infrunita sine freno uel moderatione' = Ld. xii.34 (Ecclus XXXI.23: 'infrunito').

'Sophistice. Conclusione'; cf. Ld. xii.38: 'Sophistice conclusione uel reprehensione' (Ecclus XXXVII.23: 'sofistice').

'Plestia. Habundantia siue indigeries'; cf. Ld. xii.39: 'Plestia abundantia uel indegeries' (Ecclus XXXVII.33: 'aplestia').

'Cineris. Nablis'; cf. Ld. xii.40: 'Cyneris nablis idest citharis longiores quam psalterium nam psalterium triangulum fit theodorus dixit' (Ecclus XXXIX.20: 'cinyris').

'Lino crudo. Viride necdum cocta ueste'; cf. Ld. xii.41: 'Lino crudo idest uiride ... ueste' (Ecclus XL.4).

'Vasa castrorum Arma exercituum. Militie celi dicuntur quod bella futura possint prouideri in sole et luna'; cf. Ld. xii.42: 'Vasa... exercitum milicie celi dicitur enim quod ... preuideri ... luna' (Ecclus XLIII.9: 'uas castrorum').

The thirty-third and last Cambridge entry, 'Pediles. Caliges', is an intruder from glosses to the *Regula S. Benedicti*,[16] and corresponds to an

---

[16] Ed. R. Hanslik, 2nd ed., CSEL 75 (Vienna, 1977), ch. 55: 'pedules caligas'; cf. Lapidge, 'The School of Theodore', pp. 62–4, and below, p. 286.

entry in Ld. ii.40 (from the chapter 'DE REGULIS'), where the *lemma* 'Pedules' alone is given.

From this evidence, it will be seen that the Ecclesiasticus section in Cam. includes two-thirds (32 : 48) of the glosses in Ld. xii. These proportions roughly pertain throughout. More than half the entries in Ld. vii-xix.38 correspond to glosses in Cam. (188 out of 349), excluding the second series of Ezechiel glosses, headed 'ITEM ALIA' in Ld. xv, the glosses 'IN HIEZECHIEL' (37–48) and the twenty-five entries in Ld. xvii ('DE IOHEL VEL DE PROPHETIS MINORIBVS') and xviii ('DE OSE SPECIALITER'), which have no counterparts in Cam. and were presumably not available to its compiler. Cam. omits the reference to Theodore found in Ld. xii.40; the interpretation of 'Affaltum. Squalor', which corresponds to Ld. xii.18 ('Aspaltum **spaldur**'), presumably survived only because it was corrupt, since Cam. normally either dropped the vernacular interpretations in Ld., or replaced them with Latin ones, as may be seen from the following examples:

[43vb] 'Lapides onichinos. Gemma admirabilis'; cf. Ld. vii.4: 'Lapides onichinos **dunne**' (I Par. XXIX.2: 'lapides onychinos').

[44va] 'Pilosi. Incubi Monstra'; cf. Ld. xiii.24: 'incubi monstri idest **menae**' (Is. XIII.21).

'Viciam. Pisas agrestes'; cf. Ld. xiii.35: 'Uiciam pisas agrestes idest **fugles beane**' (Is. XXVIII.25).

'Perpendiculum dicitur modica petra de plumbo quam ligant in filo quando edificant parietes'; cf. Ld. xiii.40: 'Perpendiculum...plumbo qua licant... parietes **pundar**' (Is. XXXIV.11).

'Paliurus. Herba que crescit in tectis domorum folia grossa habens'; cf. Ld. xiii.41: 'Paliurus erba ... domorum grossa folia habens **fullae**' (Is. XXXIV.13).

[44vb] 'Paxillus. Qui in stantem parietem mittitur'; cf. Ld. xv.5: 'Paxillus fusticellus qui in stantem mittitur **negil**' (Ezek. XV.3).

'Carectum. Arundo'; cf. Ld. xix.16. 'Carectum **hreod**' (Job VIII.11)

'Oriona. Multe stelle cuiusdam signi in celo'; cf. Ld. xix.17: 'Oriona **ebirdhring**' (Job IX.9).

'Capito. Summitas tunice'; cf. Ld. xix.26: 'Capitio **haubitloh**' (Job XXX.18: 'capitio tunicae').

'Ibix. Capra montuosa': cf. Ld. xix.29: 'Hibicum **firgingata**' (Job XXXIX.1: 'hibicum').

'Herodion. Genus accipitris'; cf. Ld. xix.35: 'Herodion **ualchefuc**' (Job XXXIX.13: 'herodii').

'Gurgustium. Vbi pisces mittuntur capti'; cf. Ld. xix.38: 'Gurgustium **chelor**' (Job XL.26: 'gurgustium piscium').[17]

On the other hand, Cam. contains eleven entries, mostly on Jerome's prologues, not found anywhere in Ld. vii-xix:

[43vb] 'DABRELAMIN. Idest uerba dierum' (Par. Prol. 36: 'Dabreiamin id est Verba dierum').
[44ra] 'Basileus. Custos populi' (cf. LXX I Par. XVII.16: ὁ βασιλεὺς Δαυίδ, etc.).
'MASLOTH. Idest hebraice parabolas uel uulgaris editio prouerbia' (Prol. in libris Salomonis 10–11: 'Masloth, quas Hebraei Parabolas, vulgata editio Proverbia vocat').
'COELETH. Idest Ecclesiasten grece contionatorem Latine' (Prol. in libris Salomonis 11–12: 'Coeleth, quam graece Ecclesiasten, latine contionatorem possum dicere').
'Syrasim Cantica canticorum' (Prol. in libris Salomonis 12: 'Sirassirim, quod in nostram linguam vertitur Canticum Canticorum')
[44rb] 'Pediles. Caliges' (*Regula S. Benedicti* lv.19: 'pedules caligas').[18]
[44va] 'Samis. Argilla unde faciunt testas' (Is. XLV.9: 'de samiis terrae').
'ANATHOTHITES. a loco Anathot est uiculus tribus a Ierusalem distans milibus' (Jer. Prol. 4–5: 'Fuit enim Anathothites, qui est usque hodie viculus tribus ab Ierosolymis distans millibus').
'Notarii. Exceptoris. Ab ore enim loquentis notarius uerba excipiebat' (Jer. Prol. 13: 'Baruch, notarii eius').
'Emulis. Inuidis uel imitatoribus' (Jer. Prol. 14: 'ab aemulis').
[44vb] 'Fagolydoros hoc est manducans senecias' (Ezech. Prol. 55: φαγολοίδοροι (+ *v.l.*: 'quod est manducantes senecias')).

There are various similar cases where Cam. contains a fuller entry than that found in Ld. For example, the entry in Cam., 'Fornacula. In quibus faciunt focum ad coquendum' (44vb), which corresponds in position to Ld. xv.28 ('Fornacula' only), completes the interpretation of the duplicate entry in the 'ITEM ALIA' section of Ld. xv.42 ('Culine fornacula', from Ezek. XLVI. 23: 'culinae'). In all, seven Cam. glosses offer significantly fuller interpretations than their counterparts in Ld.:

17 The rest of the entries with vernacular interpretations in the corresponding sections of Leiden were omitted altogether (namely Ld. viii.15, 34, 50, 52 and 53; xv.4 and 36; xvi.28; xvii.11; xviii.2; and xix.19, 29 and 36).
18 Cf. above, n. 16.

[44ra] 'Paranetos. Sapientia uel parabole filii Sirach Pseudograph<os> Sapientia Salomonis'; cf. Ld. viii.1: 'Panarethos sapientia' *only* (Prol. in libris Salomonis 13: 'πανάρετος Iesu filii Sirach liber et alius Ψευδεπίγραφος qui Sapientia Salomonis inscribitur').

'Myrra et aloe. Herbe sunt aromatice'; cf. Ld. x.18: 'Murra et aloe herbe sunt' *only* (Cant. IV.14: 'murra et aloe').

[44rab] 'Lanugo uel lanuginatio pene idem sunt idest squalor lanuge in carce lanuginatio in uellere'; cf. Ld. xi.3: 'Lanugo et aluginatio pene idem est squalor lanugo in carne' *only* (Sap. V.15: 'lanugo').

[44rb] 'Colera nausia idest Gutta pessima'; cf. Ld. xii.30: 'Colera nausia' *only* (Ecclus XXXI.23: 'colera'; and cf. above, p. 284).

'Vermiculus. Tinctura ad similitudinem uermis'; cf. Ld. xiii.3: 'Uermiculus a similitudine uermis' (Is. I.18).

'Murenulas. Catenas de auro mirifice factas'; cf. Ld. xiii.10: 'Murenulas catenulas' *only* (Is. III.20).

[44vb] 'Syncronon. Vnius temporis uel contemporaneus'; cf. Ld. xv.32: 'Sinchronon unius temporis' *only* (Prol. .XII. Prophetarum 7: 'σύγχρονον Osee Isaiae').

Apart from the Latin/vernacular alternatives in entries such as Cam. 'Lapides onichinos. Gemma admirabilis' (43vb; cf. Ld. vii.4 'Lapides onichinos **dunne**'), only one headword common to both glossaries has an entirely different interpretation in each: Cam. 'Commissuras. Idest iuncturas' (43vb) and Ld. vii.3: 'Commisuras ligaturas uel composituras' (I Par. XXII.3). The sum of this evidence therefore suggests that the Cambridge and Leiden Bible glosses derive independently from the 'original English collection' compiled at Canterbury in the time of Theodore and Hadrian.

PARIS, BIBLIOTHEQUE NATIONALE, LAT. 2685

A similar situation obtains with respect to the Bible glosses in Paris, BN, lat. 2685, as Michael Lapidge noted,[19] although here the material is scrappier and at first glance the connection looks more remote. The Paris Bible glosses (48vb-57vb)[20] form two series that may conveniently be labelled I and II. Series I (48vb-56rb) consists of glosses, with some vernacular interpretations, on Jerome's Prologue to the Pentateuch,

[19] 'The School of Theodore', p. 56 and nn. 60–1.
[20] See above, n. 7. These Bible glosses are preceded by sections entitled 'DE CANONIBVS' and 'DE REGVLA' (47ra-48va) which include some entries found in Leiden chs. i and ii, as pointed out by Lapidge, 'The School of Theodore', p. 70.

Genesis, Exodus, Leviticus, Numbers, Deuteronomy, Joshua, Judges, Ruth, Kings, Chronicles, Proverbs, Ecclesiastes, Canticles, Wisdom, Isaiah, Jeremiah, Ezechiel, Daniel, Hosea, Joel, Job, Judith, Esther, Esdras, Jerome's commentary on Matthew, and Mark, most of which are found in the corresponding sections of Ld., including eleven with vernacular interpretations:

[54va] 'Uitia piscis agrestes idest **flugles bene**'; cf. Ld. xiii.35: 'Uiciam pisas agrestes idest **fugles beane**' (Is. XXVIII.25: 'viciam').

'Perpendiculum dicitur de plumbo modica petra quam ligant in filo quando edificant idest **pundur**'; cf. Ld. xiii.40: 'Perpendiculum modica petra de plumbo qua licant . . . edificant parietes **pundar**' (Is. XXXIV.11).

[54vb] 'Circino ferrum duplex **gabilrunt**'; cf. Ld. xiii.53: 'Circino ferrum duplex unde pictores faciunt circulos idest **gaborind**' (Is. XLIV.13).

[55ra] 'Litura inpensa **liim** uel **claum**'; cf. Ld. xv.4: 'Litura inpensa **lim** uel **clam**' (Ezek. XIII.2).

[55va] 'Lagunculas ex lasna diminutione idest **crooc**'; cf. Ld. xix.60: 'Lagungulas ex lagina dimin **croog**' (Job XXXII.19).

'Erodion **uualeauuc**'; cf. Ld. xix.35: 'Herodion **ualchefuc**' (Job XXXIX.13: 'herodii').

'Gurgustium **caelor**'; cf. Ld. xix.38: 'Gurgustium **chelor**' (Job XL.26).

'Sternutatio **nere**'; cf. Ld. xix.65: 'Sternutatio **nor**' (Job XLI.9).[21]

'Incus **umueliti**'; cf. Ld. xix.41: 'Incus **osifelti**' (Job XLI.15).

[55vb] 'Lampates insimiles **sculdre** de ligno duas talas fatiunt interponentes ne citius putrescant'; cf. Ld. xxi.20: 'Labastes in similitudine **schuldre** de ligno duas tales faciunt interponentes ficos ne citius putrescant' (Judith X.5: 'palatas' (*v.ll.* 'lapatas', 'lapastas')).

---

[21] OE *__hnor(a)__; cf. the 'First Erfurt Glossary' (Erfurt, Wissenschaftliche Bibliothek, Amplonianus F. 42, 1ra–14va) [hereafter ErfI], ptd *CGL* V, 337–401, S44: 'Sternutatio **huora**', and Hessels, *A Late Eighth-Century Glossary*, p. 197. The interpretation of the parallel entry in the 'Epinal Glossary' (Epinal, Bibliothèque municipale 72 (2), 94ra–107vc [hereafter Ep, collated with ErfI in *CGL* V, 337–401], is **fnora**, the normal OE form, as in the 'Corpus Glossary' (Cambridge, Corpus Christi College 144, 4ra–64vb; hereafter Cp), ed. J. H. Hessels, *An Eighth-Century Latin-Anglo-Saxon Glossary preserved in the Library of Corpus Christi College, Cambridge* (Cambridge, 1890), S521. On the relationship between these various English glossaries, see J. D. Pheifer, *Old English Glosses in the Epinal-Erfurt Glossary* (Oxford, 1974), pp. xxv and xxvii–xxxi; *idem* in *The Epinal, Erfurt, Werden and Corpus Glossaries*, ed. B. Bischoff *et al.*, EEMF 22 (Copenhagen, 1988), 49–54; and *idem*, 'Early Anglo-Saxon Glossaries and the School of Canterbury', *ASE* 16 (1987), 1–44, esp. 17–19 and 34–6. ErfI and Ep are cited by the alphabetical section numbers used in EEMF 22, which contains complete facsimiles of the Epinal, Erfurt and Corpus manuscripts.

[56ra] 'Murico de auro facta tonica idest **gespan**'; cf. Ld. xxix.11: 'Mauria ...
facta in tunica idest **gespan**' (*Comm. in Matth*. VI.28: 'Murice').

Three more Series I glosses with vernacular interpretations correspond to
all-Latin entries in Ld.: [54va] 'Fascinatio laus stulta idest **mascrunc**'; cf.
Ld. xi.1: 'Fascinatio laudatio stulta' *only* (Sap. IV.13); [55ra] 'Aurugo
color sicut pedes accipitris idest **geligelu**'; cf. Ld. xiv.19: 'Arugo ...
accipitris' *only* (Jer. XXX.6: 'auruginem'); and [55vb] 'Ascopa **cilli**'; cf.
Ld. xxi.13: 'Ascopa similis utri' (Judith X.5: 'ascopam').[22] In this respect,
at least, Paris I seems closer to the fountain-head than Leiden itself, and it
has a similar relationship with Cam., whose entries correspond more
closely to those of Ld.

Series II (56rb-57vb) consists of further glosses (all-Latin only) on
Exodus, Leviticus, Numbers, Deuteronomy, Joshua/Judges, Ruth,
Judith, Esther, Kings, Maccabees and Chronicles. Its negligible Judith
and Chronicles sections have no entries in common with Ld., but
Cam.-type glosses predominate in the longer ones, for example in the
Joshua/Judges section, all of whose six entries have counterparts in Cam.

[57ra] 'Raphaim gigantum'; cf. Cam. 43rb: 'Rafium. Gigantum' (Jos. XII.4:
  'Rafaim').
'Filii gemini duo filii ioseph efraim et manasses'; cf. Cam. 43rb: 'Filii Gemini.
  Idest filiorum Ioseph quia duo fuerunt' (Judg. XIII.15: 'filii Iemini').
'Caniculum paruum hostium': cf. Cam. 43rb: 'Postica cuniculum. Idest humile
  ostium' (Judg. III.24: 'posticam').
'Clauum tabernaculi quando tabernaculum tenditur claui ferrei in terra figuntur';
  cf. Cam. 43rb: 'Clauum tabernaculi. Idest quando tenditur tabernaculum claui
  ferrati terre infiguntur' (Judg. IV.21).
'Sibellus blandimenta regum'; cf. Cam. 43rb: 'Sibyiius. Regum blandimenta'
  (Judg. V.16: 'sibilos gregum').
'Pallæntes fugientes'; cf. Cam. 43rb: 'Palantes. Fugientes' (Judg. IX.44:
  'palantes').

The relationship between Paris I and II is problematic. Only three of the
thirteen headwords which they have in common receive corresponding
interpretations, and Paris I has vernacular interpretations instead of Latin
ones in two other cases, as may be seen from the following examples (note

---

[22] Cf. Ep/ErfI A310: 'Ascopa in similitudinem utri' and Cp A852: 'Ascopa kylle', in
corresponding position. The original form of the interpretation may be preserved in
Karlsruhe 135, 100v: 'Ascopam idest in similitudinem utri idest **cylli**'.

that in each case I give the entry from Paris I first, followed by that from Paris II):

[49va] 'Abominationes idest oves quas coloerunt et noluerunt manducare'; [56va] 'Abominationes idest idola' (Ex. VIII.26: 'abominationes enim Aegyptiorum')

'Praetium pudititiæ idest .xii. solidi qui ipsam tradidit marito debet puellæ dare'; [56va] 'Pretium pudicitie id duodecim solidus' *only* (Ex. XXI.10: 'pretium pudicitiae').

'Fibulas hringan'; [57va] 'Fibules ubi unci pendentur' (Ex. XXVI.11: 'fibulas').

'Capitium quod circa collum sit halsetha'; [57va] 'Capicium ubi capud intrat in tunicam' (Ex. XXVIII.32: 'capitium').

'Crustula panis unius coloris est oleo consparsa est in medio cauus et tortus'; [57va] 'Crustula genus panis tenui' (Ex. XXIX.2).[23]

[50ra] 'Quando redeundi anni tempora concluduntur hoc est mense septimo quod egyptii initium anni et finem sic fecerunt'; [56va] 'Quando redeunt tempora anni idest septembrium mense quia eo mense annus egyptorum inchoatur' (Ex. XXXIV.22: 'quando redeunte anni tempore cuncta conduntur').

[50rb] 'Renunculi leuintlegum Lumbulos lembradum'; [56vb] 'Renunculi id duo paria lumbula id super lumbos iacens caro' (Lev. III.4: 'cum renunculis').

[52rb] 'Sibilos regum blandimenta'; [57ra] 'Sibellus blandimenta regum' (Judg. V.16: 'sibilos gregum').

'Palantes fugientes'; [57ra] 'Pallæntes fugientes' (Judg. IX.44: 'palantes')

'Zarcinulas idest in quibus portant cibos'; [57ra] 'Sarcinula pere parua quam uiatores portant' (Ruth II.9: 'sarcinulas').

[52va] 'Reditus quod semper redire solet post circulum dierum idest anni'; [57rb] 'Redi dierum quia de vinea colligitur et terra' (I Reg. VIII.15: 'vinearum reditus').

[54ra] 'Exedra exterior sedes ubi sedet presbiter incausus cum communionem dat populo in lateribus ecclesie Edra dicitur interior sedes ubi papa sedet'; [57rb] 'Exedra locus templi aderens ut sit secretorium' (IV Reg. XXIII.11: 'iuxta exedram').

[55vb] 'Mundum muliebrem debuerunt multo tempore ungueri uariis pigmentis et indui uestis regalibus illud dicitur mundum muliebre'; [57rb] 'Mundum muliebrem genus uestimenti est quo mulieres apico perses uncte pigmentis antequam intrassent ad regem utebantur' (Esther II.3).

Consequently only three of the sixty-three entries in Paris II and the 259 entries in the corresponding sections of Paris I overlap, but there is a more substantial overlap with Cam., which has counterparts for nearly half the

---

[23] These three entries – 'Fibulas', 'Capitium' and 'Crustula' – together with some others were added to the section 'DE LIBRO REGVM' of Paris II.

entries in the corresponding portions of Paris I (157 out of 357) and nearly two-thirds of those in the corresponding portions of Paris II (thirty-five out of fifty-five). The Exodus section in Cam., for example, has entries corresponding to roughly half of the Exodus glosses in Paris I (twenty-three out of forty-seven) and Paris II (five out of nine).

[42rb] 'Tetigit pedes eius idest pueri' = Paris I (49rb) (Ex. IV.25: 'tetigitque pedes eius').

'Sponsus sanguinis tu mihi es idest puer qui de sanguine meo natus est uel circumcisus'; cf. Paris I (49rb): 'Sponsus . . . est circumcisus' (Ex. IV.25).

'Est in monte dei. In monte Synai Chroeb et synai unum sunt'; cf. Paris I (49rb): 'Est in monte dei hoc est in sina' *only* (Ex. IV.27: 'perrexit . . . in montem dei').

'Virga moysi et uirga Aaron una erat quam habuit Moyses quando primum apparuit ei dominus in Madian'; cf. Paris II (56rb): 'Virga aaron et uirga moysi . . . quando apparuit ei moyses primum in madian' (Ex. VII.12: 'virga Aaron' *only*).

'Dracones et colubres pro uno nominauit'; cf. Paris II (56rb): 'Dracones . . . nomin<auit> (Ex. VII.10: 'colubrum'; 12: 'dracones').

'Abominationes. Oues quas coluerunt et noluerunt manducare'; Paris I (49va): 'Abominationes idest oues quas coloerunt . . . manducare' (Ex. VIII.26).

'Columna nubis et columna ignis idem esse creditur ex altera parte ignea et ex altera parte similis nube'; cf. Paris I (49va): 'Columna . . . ignis esse creditur . . . altera similis nube pertigens quia diu ipsi debuerunt mouere in una mansione stare. Stetit et columna quando debuerunt mouere ipsa perambulabat' (Ex. XIII.21: 'columna nubis . . . columna ignis').

'Ad habitaculum sanctum tuum ad terram repromissionis'; cf. Paris I (49va): 'ad habitaculum secundum idest in terram repromissionis' (Ex. XV.13: 'ad habitaculum sanctum tuum').

'Bucine. Lignee sunt et longiores quam tube'; cf. Paris II (56va): 'Bucine de ligne fiunt longiores quam tube' (Ex. XIX.13: 'bucina').

'Pretium pudicitie. Duodecim solidos qui ipsam tradidit marito debuit puellam dare'; cf. Paris I (49va): 'Praetium pudicitiæ idest .xii. solidi qui . . . puellæ dare', Paris II (56va): 'Pretium pudicitie id duodecim solidus' *only* (Ex. XXI.10: 'pretium pudicitiae').

'Pelles arietum. Sine lana quasi particula'; cf. Paris I (49vab): 'Pelles arietum idest sine lana quasi parcica idest **rochloschi**' (Ex. XXV.5).

'Pelles iacincthinas sine lana'; cf. Paris I (49va): 'Pelles iacincinas idest sine lana arco ad tegendum non est in britannia' (Ex. XXV.5: 'pellesque ianthinas').[24]

---

[24] For the significance of the expression 'non est in britannia', see Pheifer, 'Anglo-Saxon Glossaries', pp. 25–6.

'A summo usque ad summum a fine usque ad finem'; cf. Paris I (49va) 'A sommo ... finem' (Ex. XXVI.28: 'a summo usque ad summum').

[42va] 'Portabid iniquitates intercedet pro iniquitatibus'; cf. Paris I (49vb): 'portabit iniquitatem idest intercedat pro iniquitate' (Ex. XXVIII.38: 'portabitque Aaron iniquitates').

'Arietes immaculatos. Vnius coloris non morbidos non lesos non scabrosos'; cf. Paris I (49vb): 'Arietes immaculatos idest unius coloris et non morbidos non scabiosos non lesos aliqua parte' (Ex. XXIX.1: 'arietes duos immaculatos').

'Crustula. Panis est oleo compressus in medio cauus et tortus'; cf. Paris I (49vb): 'Crustula panis unius coloris est oleo consparsa est in ... tortus' (Ex. XXIX.2: 'crustula ... quae conspersa sint oleo').

'Lagana similiter panis est in prima plasma longus postea curuatus finis ad finem. Coquitur in aqua primitus postea in sartagine et oleo frigatur'; cf. Paris I (49vb): 'Lagana ... longus propterea curuatus... aqua prius postea ... fricatur' (Ex. XXIX.2).

'Decimam partem idest modii subauditur quod est .iiii.ta pars hin'; Paris I (50ra): 'Decimam partem subauditur modii quod est .iiii.' *only* (Ex. XXIX.40: 'decimam partem ... quod habeat mensuram quartam partem hin').

'Labrum. Vas eneum est quadrangulum'; cf. Paris I (50ra): 'Labrum uasem quadrangulum' (Ex. XXX.18: 'labium aeneum').

'Smirna. Calami cassia in arboribus nascuntur ad pigmenta'; cf. Paris I (50ra): 'Zmirna et calami et cassia ... ex pigmenta' (Ex. XXX.23–4: 'zmyrnae ... calami ... cassiae').

'Cynamomum. Cortex dulcis est'; cf. Paris I (50ra): 'Cinamomum quortex dulcis' *only* (Ex. XXX.23: 'cinnamomi').

'Iesus cum Moyse utrum ieiunasset .xl. diebus an cibum ibi habuisset an in obuiam uenisset incertum habemus quia de tribus tantum dicitur quod ieiunassent hoc dierum numero idest Moyses Helias et dominus'; cf. Paris II (56va): 'Ihesus utrum ieiunauit cum moyse .xl. diebus an cibos ibi habuit an ubiam ei uenit incertum habetur quia tale ieiunium de tribus legitur de moyse et de elia et de christo' (cf. Ex. XXXIV.28: 'fecit ergo ibi cum domino quadraginta dies et quadraginta noctes panem non comedit et aquam non bibit').[25]

'Quando redeunte tempore anni cuncta concludunt idest mense Septembrio quia egyptii initium anni et finem sic fecerunt'; cf. Paris I (50ra): 'quando redeundi anni tempora concluduntur hoc est mense septimo quod ... fecerunt' (Ex. XXXIV.22).

'Dextralia. Ampla erat ante manicam et poterant ibi coniungi uno cla<ui>'; cf. Paris

---

[25] Cf. Milan 75ra: 'Iosue cum moyse utrum ieiunasset .xl. diebus an cibum ibi habuisset an obuiam uenisset incertum habemus quod quia de tribus tantum dicitur quod ieiunassent idest moyses helias et dominus.'

I (50rb): 'Dextralia **armbogus breida** ante manicas et ibi coniunguntur claui' (Ex. XXXV.22).

'Carpentarius. Lignarius tamen a carro dicitur'; Paris I (50rb): 'Opere carpentario idest lignario eccaro tamen dicitur' (Ex. XXXV.33: 'opere carpentario').

'Abietarii. Lignarii de abiete arbore'; cf. Paris I (50rb): 'abietarii idest lignarii uel de abiete arbore' (Ex. XXXV.35: 'opera abietarii').

'Posuit testimonium id est tabernaculi'; cf. Paris I (50rb): 'Posuit testimonium in arca idest duas tabulas; Sub tecto testimonii idest tabernaculi' (Ex. XL.18: 'posuit et testimonium in arca'; 24: 'sub tecto testimonii').

One entry in Cam. (42rb), 'Fibula catenatio cinguli' (glossing Ex. XXVI.11, 'fibulas'), has a headword corresponding to a gloss in Paris I with an Old English interpretation (49ra: 'Fibulas **hringan**'), and a gloss in Paris II with a different Latin interpretation (57va: 'fibules ubi unci pendentur').[26] Typically, the Paris I reference to Britain was dropped in the Cambridge gloss on *pelles iacinc(t)inas*.

THE RELATIONSHIP OF THE LEIDEN, CAMBRIDGE AND PARIS GLOSSES

It is clear that Cambridge and Paris took their Bible glosses independently from the same source as Leiden, and that both reflect the literal, Antiochene mode of interpretation favoured in the school of Canterbury,[27] which verges on the rationalistic in the Cam./Paris II scholion on Ex. XXXIV.28 (cited above). The question remains, however, how to account for the two series in the Paris manuscript. The obvious explanation would be that they represent two originally independent sets of glosses, like the two sets of glosses on Ezechiel in Ld. xv,[28] which the Cambridge compiler or one of his predecessors conflated. But it is also possible that the two collections used by the compiler of the Paris glossary were drawn independently from a single collection of Bible glosses corresponding to those in Cam., as their five common entries might seem to suggest, and that he

---

[26] This is one of the Exodus glosses added to the section 'DE LIBRO REGVM' of Paris II (see above, n. 23).

[27] See B. Bischoff, 'Wendepunkte in der Geschichte der lateinischen Exegese im Frühmittelalter', *Sacris erudiri* 6 (1954), 189–281, at 193–5 (repr. in his *Mittelalterliche Studien*, 3 vols. (Stuttgart, 1966–81) I, 205–73, at 207–9), and *Biblical Commentaries*, ed. Bischoff and Lapidge, pp. 243–9.

[28] See above, pp. 285 and 286.

tried to avoid duplication,[29] which would explain the fact that only one of the twenty-seven Cambridge Exodus glosses (42rb: 'Pretium pudicitie. Duodecim solidos' etc.) appears in both series of Paris. That the Paris compiler should have used two sets of Bible glosses is not in itself surprising, for Leiden, as well as its two sets of Ezechiel glosses, has two sets of Hosea glosses, one following the first sequence of Ezechiel glosses (xv.32–6), as in Cam., and the other in a separate section (Ld. xviii: 'DE OSE spetialiter'), as in Paris. Unlike the Ezechiel glosses, the two sets overlap, and both contain entries corresponding to Leiden's sister glossaries which help to clarify the relationship between them:

Ld. xv

[32] 'Sinchronon unius temporis'; cf. Cam. [44vb] 'Syncronon. Vnius temporis uel contemporaneus' (Prol. .XII. Prophetarum 7: σύνχρονον).

[33] 'Uinacia quod remanet in uuis quando premuntur'; cf. Cam. [44vb]: 'Vinacia. Quod remanet in uuis quando premuntur' (Hos. III.1: 'vinacia uvarum').

[34] 'Foedi foederamni' (Hos. III.2: 'fodi').

[35] 'Teraphin idolum sic nominatur'; cf. Cam. [44vb]: 'Therafin. Idolum sic nominatum' (Hos. III.4: 'teraphim').

[36] 'Lappa clite' (Hos. IX.6].

Ld. xviii

[1] 'CYNXRONON unius temporis'; cf. Paris I [55rb]: 'Cinxronon unius temporis'

[2] 'lappa clate'

[3] 'Uinatia que remansit in uuis quando premuntur'; cf. Paris [55rb]: 'Vinacia quod remansit in uuis quando premuntur'

[4] 'Foedi foederaui'

The entries Ld. xv.32–3 + Cam. 44vb ('Sinchronon...remanet'), when compared with Ld. xviii.1–3 + Paris I ('CYNXRONON...remansit') show that the dichotomy between Ld. xv and xviii was reflected in Cam. and Paris I, and the substantial overlap between the two lists – notwithstanding their brevity (three out of five entries in Ld. xv and four in Ld. xviii) – shows that each pair came from a common source. The relationship of Ld. xv.32–6 and xviii with the corresponding entries in Cam. and Paris I can

---

[29] The compiler of the Corpus Glossary also tried to avoid duplication under similar circumstances: cf. my remarks in *The Epinal, Erfurt, Werden and Corpus Glossaries*, ed. Bischoff *et al.*, pp. 51–2.

therefore be represented by a simple two-branch stemma in which A represents the common ancestor of Ld. xv.32–6 (L^1) and Cam. (C), B the common ancestor of Ld. xviii (L^2) and Paris I (P), and X the common source of A and B:

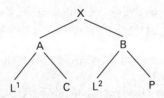

The genetic relationship is less straightforward, however, between entries corresponding to Cam. and Paris I in the apparently homogeneous chapters of Ld., where the overlap is comparatively slight, like that between the entries in Paris I and II, although in both series most of the sections that correspond to Ld. consist almost entirely of entries common to it. In the relevant sections of Cam., 184 of the 199 entries have counterparts in Ld. (not counting Ld. glosses with vernacular interpretations only), as do 110 of the 119 entries in the relevant sections of Paris I; yet only 38 of the 184 Cam. and 72 Paris I glosses that correspond to Ld. vi-xix.38 are common to both, that is, slightly more than one-fifth of those in Cam. and just over half of those in Paris I. These proportions are accurately reflected in Ld. xiii ('IN LIBRO ISAIE PROPHETE'), thirty-five of whose sixty-one entries appear in Cam., and thirteen in Paris I, but only seven in both:

LD. XIII ('IN LIBRO ISAIE PROPHETE')

[1] 'Cucumerarium hortus in quo cucumerus crescit bona erba ad manducandum siue ad medicinam'; cf. Cam. (44rb): 'Cucumerium. Hortum . . . cucumeris . . . medicinam' (Is. I.8: 'cucumerario').

[3] 'Uermiculus a similitudine uermis'; cf. Cam. (44rb): 'Vermiculus. Tinctura ad similitudinem uermis' (Is. I.18)

[5] 'Commolitus exterminatus' = Cam. (44rb) (Is. III.15: 'commolitis').

[6] 'Lunulas quas mulieres in collo habent de auro uel argento a similitudine lune diminutiue dicuntur'; cf. Cam. (44rb): 'Lunulas . . . ad similitudinem lune *only* (Is. III.18).

[7] 'Discriminalia unde discernuntur crines de auro uel argento uel aere'; cf. Cam. (44rb): 'Discriminalia . . . ere' (Is. III.20).

[8] 'Periscelidas armillas de tibiis'; cf. Cam. (44rb): 'Periscelides. Armillas de argento' (Is. III.20: 'periscelidas').

[9] 'Olfactoriola turibula modica de auro uel argento mulieres habent pro odore'; cf. Cam. (44rb): 'Olfactoriola ... argento que mulieres ... odere'; Paris I (54va): 'Olfactoriola ... argento mulis ... odore' (Is. III.20).

[10] 'Murenulas catenulas'; cf. Cam. (44rb): 'Murenulas catenas de auro mirifice factas' (Is. III.30).

[11] 'Mutatoria uestimenta alia meliora et mundiora'; cf. Cam. (44rb): 'Mutatoria ... meliora' *only*; Paris I (54va): 'Mutatoria ... meliora et mundiora' (Is. III.22).

[12] 'Teristra subtilissima curtina'; cf. Cam. (44va): 'Theristra. Subtilissima corona' (Is. III.23: 'theristra').

[13] 'Fascia pectoralis uestis circa pectus uoluitur'; cf. Cam. (44va): 'Fascia pectoralis uestis que circa pectus uoluitur' (Is. III.24: 'fascia pectorali').

[14] 'Lambruscas malas uuas'; cf. Cam. (44va): 'Labruscas malas uuas' (Is. V.2: 'labruscas').

[15] 'Decem iugera uinearum .x. iugeres uel diurnales'; cf. Cam. (44va): 'Decem ... decem ... diurnales' (Is. V.10: 'decem enim iuga vinearum').

[16] 'Tabehel proprium nomen uiri'; cf. Cam. (44va) 'Tabeel ... uiri' (Is. VII.6: 'Tabeel').

[17–18] 'Parum paruum, Sarculum ferrum fossorium duos dentes habens'; cf. Cam. (44va): 'parculum ferrum ... habens' (Is. VII.13: 'parum'; 25: 'sarculo').

[19] 'Sarientur fodientur'; cf. Cam. (44va): 'Sarcuntur. Fodiuntur' (Is. VII.25: 'sarientur').

[21] 'Carcamis nomen loci uel ciuitatis' = Cam. (44va) (Is. X.9: 'Charchamis').

[22] 'Calanan similiter'; cf. Cam. (44va): 'Calanne similiter' (Is. X.9: 'Chalanno').

[23] 'Ganniret quasi cum ira inrideret'; cf. Cam. (44va): 'Ganniret cum ira quasi rideret' (Is. X.14).

[24] 'Pilosi incubi monstri idest **menae**'; cf. Cam. (44va): 'Pilosi. Incubi monstra' *only* (Is. XIII.21).

[25] 'De radice colubri nascitur regulus qui manducat aucellas idest basiliscus secundum historiam dicitur de colubri nasci'; cf. Cam. (44va): 'De colubro... aucellas' *only* (Is. XIV.29: 'de radice enim colubri egredietur regulus').

[27] 'Flaccentia contracta' = Cam. (44va); cf. Paris I (54va): 'Placentia contracta grecum' (Is. XIX.10: 'flaccentia').

[29] 'Mede nomen loci' = Cam. (44va) (Is. XXI.2).

[32] 'Riui aggerum congregatio aquarum' = Cam. (44va) (Is. XIX.6).

[33] 'Bige equitum duorum exercitum'; cf. Cam. (44va): 'Bige ... exercituum' (Is. XXI.9: 'bigae equitum').

[35] 'Uiciam pisas agrestes idest **fugles beane**'; cf. Cam. (44va): 'Viciam pisas agrestes' only; Paris I (54va): 'Uitia piscis agrestes idest **flugles bene**' (Is. XXVIII.25: 'viciam').

[36] 'In serris serra dicitur lignum habens multas dentes quod boues trahunt';
cf. Cam. (44rb): 'Serra. Dicitur . . . dentes quo boues trahunt'; Paris I (54va):
'In serri ferri . . . habens dentes mutas bous trahens' (Is. XXVIII.27: 'in serris').

[37] 'Malus nauis caput in arbore nauis a similitudine milui'; cf. Cam (44rb)
'maius' *only* (Is. XXX.17: 'malus navis').

[39] 'Migma et mixtum idem est'; cf. Cam. (44va): 'Smigmata et Commixtum.
Idem sunt' (Is. XXX.24: 'commixtum migma').

[40] 'Perpendiculum modica petra de plumbo qua licant in filo quando edificant
parietes **pundar**; cf. Cam. (44va): 'Perpendiculum dicitur modica . . . plumbo
quam ligant. . . parietes' *only*; Paris I (54va): 'perpendiculum dicitur de plumbo
modica petra quam ligant . . . parietes idest **pundur**' (Is. XXXIV.11).

[41] 'Paliurus erba que crescit in tectis domorum grossa folia habens **fullae**'; cf.
Cam. (44va): 'Paliurus. Herba . . . habens' *only* (Is. XXXIV.13).

[42] 'Epocentaurus equo Onocentaurus asino mixtum moster'; cf. Cam. (44va):
'Onocentaurus. Aino mixtum monstrum' *only* (Is. XXXIV.14).

[43] 'Lamia dea silue dicitur habens pedes similes caballi caput et manus totum
corpus pulcre mulieris et uiderunt multi aliqui manserunt cum ea'; cf. Cam.
(44va): 'Lamia . . . caput uere et manus et totum corpus pulchrum simile
mulieris' *only* (Is. XXXIV.14).

[45] 'Apotecas cellaria'; cf. Cam. (44va): 'Apothecas. Cellaria'; Paris I (54vb):
'Apoteca cellaria' (Is. XXXIX.2: 'apothecas').

[46] 'Cataplasmarent contritos inponerent' = Paris I (54vb) (Is. XXXVIII.21).

[47] 'Plaustrum in similitudinem arce rotas habens intus et ipse dentes habent
quasi rostra dicitur in quibus frangent spicas'; cf. Cam. (44va): 'Plaustrum. . .
arce . . . habent' *only* (Is. XLI.15).

[49] 'Plastes figulus' = Paris I (54vb) (Is. XLI.25).

[51] 'Calamum pigmentum ex arbore'; cf. Paris I (54vb) 'Calamum pigmentum
de arbore' (Is. XLIII.24).

[53] 'Circino ferrum duplex unde pictores faciunt circulos idest **gaborind**'; cf.
Paris I (54vb): 'Circino ferrum duplex **gabilrunt**' (Is. XLIV.13).

[57] 'Saliuncula erba medicinalis habens spinas miri odoris crescit in montibus';
cf. Cam. (44va): 'Saliunca herba est medicinalis habens spicas . . . crescitque in
montibus'; Paris I (54vb): 'Saliuncula herba est miri odoris' *only* (Is. XLV.23
'saliunca').

[58–9] 'In lecticis a similitudine lecti dicuntur, Feretri in quibus portantur filie
nobilium super .IIII. equis coopertis desuper cortina sicut currus'; cf. Paris I
(54vb): 'In lecticis assimilitudine lecti dicuntur feretri . . . quattuor equos quo
opertis desuper cortine sicut curri' (Is. LXVI.20).

Leiden xiii has counterparts to all the Cam. and Paris I Isaiah glosses, with
one exception (Cam. 44va: 'Samis. Argilla unde faciunt testas', glossing

Is. XLV.9: 'samiis terrae'). The Cam. and Paris I glosses, like those in Paris I and II, could have been taken from a single collection substantially identical with Leiden, but in their case, unlike that of Paris I and II, there was no reason to avoid duplication. On the other hand, the uninterrupted run of Paris I glosses corresponding to Ld. xiii.43–7, 49, 51 and 53 and similar runs of Cam. glosses seem to favour the supposition that Ld. xiii combined entries from two sources which incorporated common material, like Ld. xv and xviii.

THE REICHENAU BIBLE GLOSSES

A wider survey of the Canterbury Bible glosses shows, however, that processes of selection and combination often operated concurrently in their history, as they apparently did to produce the tangled relationship between Leviticus glosses preserved in several manuscripts: St Gallen, Stiftsbibliothek 913, pp. 139–45; Berlin, Bibliothek der Stiftung Preussischer Kulturbesitz, Grimm 132, 2 (the 'Grimm fragment'); Milan, Biblioteca Ambrosiana, M. 79 sup., 75va–77rb; and the Reichenau Bible glosses. The Leviticus glosses in St Gallen 913 and in the so-called 'Grimm fragment' have recently been printed and discussed in detail by Bischoff and Lapidge, who have demonstrated their relationship to the first series of Leviticus glosses (PentI) in the Milan manuscript; I need not repeat their demonstration here.[30] However, several points relevant to the present discussion need to be made. The glosses on bird and animal names in St Gallen 913 consist in fact of two separate series, which were apparently combined by the scribe of the St Gallen manuscript; of the twenty-five entries in the first series, nineteen have counterparts in Cam. or Paris I (seventeen in Cam., with Latin interpretations replacing the vernacular ones of St Gallen 913, and twelve in Paris I). The second series of glosses in St Gallen 913, however, has a counterpart in the 'Grimm fragment', as Bischoff and Lapidge have shown.[31] It would seem, therefore, that there were two collections of Leviticus glosses circulating in the school of Canterbury (though only one was used by the common source of Cam. and Paris I) and this impression is confirmed by the evidence of Milan M. 79 sup. It will be recalled that in this manuscript there are three

[30] *Biblical Commentaries*, ed. Bischoff and Lapidge, pp. 534–45.
[31] *Ibid.*, pp. 534–6.

separate series of Pentateuch glosses, called by Bischoff[32] PentI, PentII and PentIII (it is the first of these series, PentI, which is edited by Bischoff and Lapidge as *Biblical Commentaries*;[33] PentII and PentIII are as yet unprinted). Of these, the first and third series correspond respectively to the second and first series of glosses in St Gallen 913.

The Milan II Pentateuch glosses (= Bischoff's PentII), on the other hand, which were hardly used, if at all, by the compilers of the Cam./Paris I Pentateuch glosses, were the major source of the corresponding section in the Leiden family's most prolific branch, the Reichenau Bible glosses, a single sequence of glosses covering both Testaments which crossed Europe in the Carolingian period and reached Rome itself by the year 908, when Vatican lat. 1469 was copied there.[34] Among the seventy-odd manuscripts containing these glosses,[35] two stand out, Karlsruhe 99 and Fulda Aa. 2. Karlsruhe, Badische Landesbibliothek, Aug. perg. 99, the earliest manuscript of the Reichenau Bible glosses which (like Ld.) dates from the late eighth century and originated at Reichenau itself, is a hybrid that combines a variant version of the Reichenau Genesis-II Kings gloss and an unidentified English-style commentary on III-IV Kings with a series of glosses cognate with Ld. vii-xxxiii; like Cam., it includes entries corres-

---

32 'Wendepunkte', pp. 191–2 (repr. in *Mittelalterliche Studien* I, 207–8); cf. also discussion by Bischoff and Lapidge, *Biblical Commentaries*, pp. 285–7.

33 *Ibid.*, pp. 298–385.

34 The manuscript is dated precisely by the interpretation (in the 'Asbestos' Glossary which it contains) of the word *era* (23rb): 'Era domina uel capitulum item era in calculi supputatione ponitur ut era .dcccc.viii.' There is an identical entry dated to the following year in Monte Cassino, Archivio della Badia 218, 27rb (see E. A. Lowe, *Scriptura Beneventana*, 2 vols. (Oxford, 1929) II, xxxiii and pl. LIII), probably copied from the same exemplar. Another copy of the Reichenau Bible glosses is found in Monte Cassino, Archivio della Badia 205, pp. 1–126. Vatican 1469 and Monte Cassino 205 (or their exemplar) were presumably the source of the Canterbury glosses which are found in the eleventh-century Vatican and Monte Cassino glossaries, for example, the glosses on Jerome's prologue to the Pentateuch in Vatican City, Biblioteca Apostolica Vaticana, lat. 1468 and Monte Cassino, Archivio della Badia 90, which are not recorded elsewhere in alphabetical Latin glossaries. The Vatican 1469 glosses are ptd W. M. Lindsay (who did not recognize their source) in 'Glossae collectae in Vat. Lat. 1469. CATOMVM. NAVMACHIA', *Classical Quarterly* 15 (1921), 38–40. He got the relationship of Vatican 1469 to the later Vatican and Monte Cassino glossaries right, however, in 'The Festus Glosses in a Monte Cassino MS. (No. 90)', *Classical Review* 31 (1917), 130–2.

35 See above, n. 14.

ponding to Ld. xv.32–6 (47v) but lacks entries corresponding to Ld. xv.37–48 and Ld. xviii; unlike Cam., it also has a (somewhat shorter) chapter 'DE IOHEL' corresponding to Ld. xvii (48r). Fulda Aa. 2, a tenth-century manuscript from Konstanz, offers the standard version of the Reichenau *textus receptus* with a marginal gloss which includes further material from the same sources.[36] Each in its way sheds light on the history of the Canterbury glosses, but Fulda is more useful for purposes of comparison.[37]

Since the Reichenau glosses were intended for a wider, continental audience, vernacular (that is, Old English) interpretations are mostly eliminated (except in Karlsruhe 99, which was copied from an Anglo-Saxon exemplar),[38] and references to Theodore and Hadrian are generally suppressed, as in Fulda 79r ('Cynaris nablis citharas longiores fiunt quam psalterium. Nam psalterium triangulum fit'), which omits the reference to Theodore found in Ld. xii.40 (cited above, p. 281). Enough attributions survive, however, to show beyond doubt the origin of the collection.[39] We may now examine the content of the Reichenau Bible glosses, beginning with glosses to Jerome's prologue to the Pentateuch, then proceeding through the various books of the Pentateuch – Genesis and Exodus, Leviticus, Numbers and Deuteronomy – and concluding with a survey of the remaining books of the Bible.

Jerome's prologue to the Pentateuch

Most of the Reichenau Bible glosses on Jerome's prologue to the Pentateuch and on Genesis and Exodus (Fulda 38r-42v) have counterparts in

---

[36] See below, pp. 310–18.

[37] The internal relations of the Reichenau Bible glosses are beyond the scope of this paper, but the idiosyncracies of Karlsruhe 99 (some but not all of which are also found in St Gallen, Stiftsbibliothek 9 and 295: Ker, *Catalogue*, App. nos. 4 and 7; the glosses are cited from Steinmeyer and Sievers, *Die althochdeutschen Glossen*) will be clear to anyone who studies Steinmeyer's parallel text of Genesis-II Kings (see above, n. 14), while the representative character of Fulda is confirmed by its regular agreement with Vatican 1469. Steinmeyer's account of these manuscripts is still valuable, but needs revision in light of our knowledge of the commentaries in Milan M. 79 sup. *Die Reichenauer Glossen*, ed. H.-W. Klein and M. Raupach, 2 vols. (Munich, 1968–72) is concerned exclusively with the Bible glosses and alphabetical glossary in Karlsruhe 248 (I), which are only tangentially related to the glosses described below.

[38] *CLA* VIII, no. 1078.

[39] These are ptd and discussed in *Biblical Commentaries*, ed. Bischoff and Lapidge, pp. 177–8.

Milan II, for example twenty-three of the twenty-six Fulda glosses on the prologue:

[38r] 'PROLOGUS ID EST PREFATIO et dicta prefacio quasi prelocutio premium est initium dicentibus Si enim premia principia librorum que ante cause narrationem ad instruendas audientium aures coaptantur'; cf. Milan II (67va): 'Prologus ... prefatio quasi prelocutio Proemium est initium dicendi Sunt enim proemia ... coaptantur' (*title*).[40]

[38v] 'Presagium idest prescientia uel signum futurorum; presagus idest prescius futurorum'; cf. Milan II (67va): 'presagium idest prescientia idest signum futurorum; Presagus prescius futurorum' (Prol. 1: 'praesagio').

'Pentatheucum .v. librorum'; cf. Milan II (67va): 'Pentatheucum grece latine quinque uolumina' (Prol. 3: 'Pentateuchum').

'Obtrectatorum detrahentium'; cf. Milan II (67va): 'Obtrectatorum idest detrahentium' (Prol. 4).

'Sugillatione idest suffocatorem uel reprehensorem'; cf. Milan II (67va): 'Suggila-tonem idest suffocationem' *only* (Prol. 5: 'suggillationem').

'Cudere idest condere uel scribere'; cf. Milan II (67va): 'Cudere ... uel fabricare' (Prol. 5).

'Fedare sordidare'; cf. Milan II (67va): 'Fedare sordidare' (Prol. 7 'foedari').

'Asterisco idest stella; Obelo idest ueru uel uirga'; cf. Milan II (67va): 'Asterisco idest stella uel stelle similitudo; Obelu ueru uel uirga' (Prol. 9: 'asterisco et obelo id est stella et veru').

'Iugulat condemnat'; cf. Milan II (67va): 'Suggilat condemnat' (Prol. 10: 'iugulat').

'Sintagma idest compositio uel documentum idest proprium sensum uel proprium intellectum'; cf. Milan II (67va): 'Sintagina compositio' *only* (Prol. 16: σύνταγμα).

'Aeque similiter' = Milan II (67va) (Prol. 19).

'Apocriforum dubiorum' = Milan II (67va) (Prol. 19).

'Hiberas idest nomen gentis hispaniae'; cf. Milan II (67va) 'Hiberas nomen gentis est' *only* (Prol. 20).

'Nenias uanitates uel mendatia uel carmina sepulcri idest res superuacuas'; cf. Milan II (67va) 'Nenias uanitates uel mendatia' *only* (Prol. 20).

'Autenticis auctoritate plenos uel antiquos uel ueteribus'; cf. Milan II (67va): 'Autenticos ... anticos' *only* (Prol. 20: 'authenticis').

'Vatem prophetam uel sacerdotem' = Milan II (67va) (Prol. 29).

'Oeconomicon dispensatorem uel archanum uel secretum'; cf. Milan II (67va): 'Oemonicon ... secretum' (Prol. 31: 'Oeconomicum').

---

[40] Cf. Isidore, *Etym.* VI.viii.9: 'Proeemia est initium dicendi. Sunt enim prooemia princi-pia librorum, quae ante causae narrationem ad instruendas audientium aures coaptantur.'

'Pro xenofontis proprium nomen auctoris'; cf. Milan II (67vb): 'Prothe[. . .]ris' (Prol. 31: 'Xenofontis . . . Pro Ctesifonte').[41]

'Emulus inuidus'; cf. Milan II (67vb): 'Emulus inui[. . .]' (Prol. 39: 'aemule').

'Charismata dona'; cf. Milan II (67vb): '[. . .] dona spiritualia' (Prol. 41: 'spiritualia charismata').

'Liuore uulnere'; cf. Milan II (67vb): 'Libore uuln[. . .] inuidia' (Prol. 42: 'livore').

One Fulda gloss also appears in Milan I (60ra = PentI 4): 'Fedare sordidare', and five more also appear in Milan III.[42] Only three Fulda glosses are not found in any of the Milan series, and another Milan II gloss (67va: 'Dogma idest doctrina', on Prol. 23) not found in Fulda itself is nevertheless found in a closely related manuscript of the Reichenau Bible glosses, namely Karlsruhe 248 (102va: 'Docma doctrina').

Genesis and Exodus

The same pattern repeats itself on a larger scale in the Genesis and Exodus sections of the Reichenau Bible glosses (Fulda 38r-42v), where an even higher proportion of entries – 234 out of 247 – have counterparts in Milan II. Of these, only one overlaps with Milan I (39v: 'In articulo diei in initio diei' = PentI 78, glossing Gen. VII.13), whereas twenty-four overlap with Milan III, and may be listed as follows:

[39v] 'Euilath proprium nomen terre'; cf. Milan II (68rb): 'Euilath hoc proprium nomen est terre'; Milan III (69rb): 'Euilath proprium nomen terre' (Gen. II.11: 'Evilat').[43]

'Perizomata femoralia'; cf. Milan II (68rb): 'Perizomata idest femoralia'; Milan III (69va): 'Perizomata femoralia' (Gen. III.7).

'Tristega idest Tricamarata'; cf. Milan II (68rb): 'Tristega tricamerata'; Milan III (68va): 'Tristega tria camera de tabula de tabulis' (Gen. VI.16: 'tristega').

---

[41] Here and in the following entries the top of Milan fol. 67 has been torn away, with some loss of text.

[42] These are as follows (all from 38v of Fulda): 'Sintagma idest compositio uel . . . intellectum'; cf. Milan III (69ra): 'Sintagit idest conpositionem' *only*; 'Hiberas idest nomen gentis hispaniae'; cf. Milan III (69ra): 'Hibera nomen gentis' *only*; 'Nenias uanitates uel . . . superuacuas'; cf. Milan III (69ra): 'Nenias uanitates' *only*; 'Oeconomicon dispensatorem uel . . . secretum'; cf. Milan III (69ra): 'Economicum dispensatorem' *only*; and 'Xenofontis proprium nomen auctoris'; cf. Milan III (69ra): 'Xenofontis nomen proprium auctoris libri'.

[43] Cf. Karlsruhe 99, 37r: 'Euilat hoc est proprium nomen terre', and the interpretations of *mandragora* quoted below, p. 304, n. 46.

'Trimam idest triennem'; cf. Milan II (68rb): 'trimam triennem'; Milan III (69vb): 'Trimam idest capram triennem' (Gen. XV.9: 'uaccam triennem et capram trimam').

[40v] 'Opilio pastor ouium' = Milan II (68vb); cf. Milan III (70rb): '[O]pilio pastor' (Gen. XXXVIII.12).[44]

'Heliopolis ciuitas solis' = Milan II (68vb) = Milan III (70rb) (Gen. XLI.45: 'Heliopoleos').

'Lacinia ora uestimenti' = Milan II (68vb); cf. Milan III (70rb): 'Lacinia ora uel finis uestimenti' (Gen. XXXIX.12).

'Nutu prouidentia uel potestate' = Milan II (68vb); cf. Milan III (70rb): 'Nutum prouidentiam' *only* (Gen. XLII.6: 'nutum').[45]

'In genibus ioseph in potestate eius' = Milan II (68vb); cf. Milan III (70va): 'In genibus ioseph idest sub potestate eius' (Gen. L.22).

'Cerastes serpens habens cornua multum nocens per flatum'; cf. Milan II (68vb-69ra): 'Cerastes serpentem habens cornua multum nocentia per flatum'; Milan III (70va): 'Cerastes serpens cornutus multum nocens de flatu' (Gen. XLIX.17).

'In papirione in scirpeo uasculo' = Milan II (72vb) = Milan III (73vb) (Ex. II.5: 'in papyrione').

'Ab heri et nudius tercius Totum tempus preteritum significat'; cf. Milan II (72vb): 'Ab ... tertius ... significat'; Milan III (73vb): 'Ab ... tercius ... significat' (Ex. IV.10: 'ab heri et nudius tertius').

[41r] 'Sponsus sanguinis tu mihi es idest quod de sanguine meo natus es aut quia circumcisus'; cf. Milan II (72vb): 'Sponsus sanguinum ... idest quia de ... circumcisus'; Milan III (73vb): 'Sponsus ... idest puer quia quod de ... es uel circumcisus Adonai exercituum' (Ex. IV.25: 'sponsus sanguinum').

'Abominationes egiptiorum oues quas coluerunt et noluerunt manducare'; cf. Milan II (72vb-73ra): 'Abominationes egyptiorum ... manducare oues quippe egyptii non comedebant eo quod ammon in ariete adorabant'; Milan III (74ra): 'Abhominationes idest oues ... manducare' *only* (Ex. VIII.26: 'Abominationes enim Aegyptiorum').

'In montem dei in montem sinai Coreb et synai unum sunt'; cf. Milan II (72vb): 'In montem domini in montem synai Choreb ... sunt'; Milan III (73vb): 'In monte dei idest sinai Choreb et sinae unum sunt' (Ex. IV. 27: 'in monte dei').

[41v] 'Virga aaron et moysi una erat' = Milan II (73ra); cf. Milan III (73vb-74ra): 'Virga aaron et uirga moysi una erat quam habuit moyses quando primo apparuit ei dominus in madian' (Ex. VII.12: 'virga Aaron').

'Columna ignis et columna nubis una ex una parte ignea ex altera parte similis nube'; cf. Milan II (73ra): 'Columna ... una erat Nam ex ... ignea et ex altera

---

44 The top of Milan fol. 70 has been torn away with some loss of text.

45 Cf. Karlsruhe 99, 38v: 'Nutum prouidentiam uel potestatem; In genibus ioseph idest sub potestate eius.'

similis erat nube'; Milan III (74ra): 'Columna nubis et columna ignis idem esse creditur Ex ... ignea ex ... nubi' (Ex. XIII.21: 'columna nubis... columna ignis').

[42r] 'Crustula panis est oleo conspersus in medio concauus et tortus' = Milan II (73va); cf. Milan III (74vb): 'Crustula ... consparsus ... tortus' (Ex. XXIX.2: 'crustulam').

'Lagana de farina est primum in aqua postea in oleo frigitur' = Milan II (73va); cf. Milan III (74vb): 'Lagana similiter panis est in prima plasma longus postea curuatus finis ad finem quoquitur in aqua prius postea in sartagine et oleo frigitur' (Ex. XXIX.3).

[42v] 'Suppellectile diuerse res mobiles'; cf. Milan II (73va): 'Suppillectile diuerse res mobiles'; Milan III (75ra): 'Suppellectiles res diuerse mobiles' (Ex. XXX.28: 'suppellectilem').

'Armilla rotunde sunt'; cf. Milan II (73vb): 'Armille rotunde sunt'; Milan III (75rb): 'Armillas rotundas' (Ex. XXXV.22: 'armillas').

'Dextralia ampla et ante manicam portantur'; cf. Milan II (73vb): 'Dextralia ampla sunt et ante manicas portantur'; Milan III (75rb): 'Dextralia ampla erant ante manicas et ibi coniungitur uno claui' (Ex. XXXV.22).

'Abietarii lignarii ab abiete arbore'; cf. Milan II (73vb): 'Abietarii lignarii Abietes arbores sunt'; Milan III (75rb): 'Abietarii lignarii uel de abiete arbore' (Ex. XXXV.35).

'Bratteas idest laminas aureas subtilissimas' = Milan II (73vb); cf. Milan III (75rb): 'Bratteas laminas subtilissimas' (Ex. XXXIX.3).

There is a small number of cases where there is closer agreement between Milan II and other manuscripts of the Reichenau Bible glosses (esp. Karlsruhe 99), than there is between Milan II and Fulda.[46]

---

[46] Thus Karlsruhe 99 (37v) 'Inclitus nobilis', glossing Gen. XXXI.1 = Milan II (68vb), while Fulda (40r) 'Inclitus locupletatus' = Karlsruhe 248 (103va). In the entries for mandrake (Gen. XXX.14: 'mandragoras'), however, Karlsruhe 99 agrees with Milan III, while Fulda and Karlsruhe 248 agree with Milan II: cf. Karlsruhe 99, 37r: 'Mandragoras fructus similis pomi in illa herba nascuntur et habet duorum sexuum masculini et feminini et in radicibus ostendit similitudinem femine et est fertilis et dicitur qui eam eradicat non posse uiuere'; Milan III (70ra); '... in herba nascuntur et dicitur herba duorum sexuum et feminini et masculini et in radicibus similiter ostendit uirum et ipsa femina fertilis et dicitur quicunque eradicauit non posse uiuere'; Fulda (39v-40r): 'Mandragora dicta eo quod habeat mala siue olentia quam latini malum terre uocant Hanc erbam poete antrophimoleas appellant eo quod habeat radicem formam hominis similantem huius species sunt due Femina foliis lactuce similibus Mala generans in similitudinem pruinarum Masculus uero foliis bete similibus'; Karlsruhe 248, 103vb: 'Mandragora ... mala sua uiolentia quam ... terrae ... poetae antropi-

Leviticus

The Leviticus glosses (Fulda 43r-44r), on the other hand, combine entries corresponding to Milan II and III more evenly. The nature of this combination may be seen, for example, in glosses to the bird and animal names found in Leviticus XI.[47]

[43r] 'Cyrogrillus bestia spinosa maior erinatio'; cf. Milan III (77ra): 'Chærogilius illius animal spinosum maior quam ericius' (Lev. XI.5: 'chyrogryllius').
'Alietum auis similis aquile sed maior tamen minor uultore'; cf. Milan III (77ra): 'Alietum similis . . . uulture' (Lev. XI.13: 'alietum').
'Noctua coruus nocturnus uel cauannus'; cf. Milan II (76rb): 'Noctua . . . cauanagnus' (Lev. XI.16: 'noctuam')
'Larus auis maritima habens ungulas quasi accipiter' = Milan II (76rb) (Lev. XI.16: 'larum').
'Bubo auis nocturna idest buuo haec cum in urbe uisa fuerit solitudinem significare dicunt de qua ouidius foedaque fit uolucris uenturi nuncia luctus ignauus bubo durum mortalibus nomen';[48] cf. Milan II (76rb-va): 'Bubo auis nocturna Hec . . . significari . . . ouidius Versus Foedaque . . . nomen' (Lev. XI.17: 'bubonem').
'Onocratallum auis que delectetur in stagnis Onocratolon greci uocant longum rostrum';[49] cf. Milan II (76va): 'Onocrotalum auis que delectatur . . . Onogrotalum . . . rostrum' (Lev. XI.18: 'onocrotalum').
'Herodion forma fulice similis sed maior idest capiet quasi falco quod dicitur **uualuhchabuhc**';[50] cf. Milan II (76va): 'Herodion . . . maior' *only* (Lev. XI.19: 'erodionem').
'Porphyrionem quidam auem albam similem cigno dicunt et omnem cibum in

nioleos quod . . . duae fena foliis . . . similitudine prunarum . . . bete similibus'; Milan II (68rb-va): 'Mandragora . . . mala suaueolentia . . . terre . . . poete antropomeneos quod . . . similantem Cuius cortex mixta uino ad bibendum datur his quorum corpus propter curam secandum est ut soporati dolorem non sentiant Huius species . . . lactuce . . . bete similis'. The Milan II interpretation derives from Isidore, *Etym.* XVII.ix.30.

47 Cf. these Leviticus entries with those in Milan I = PentI 354–61 (*Biblical Commentaries*, ed. Bischoff and Lapidge, pp. 364–7) and in St Gallen 913 (*ibid.*, pp. 534–5).
48 Ovid, *Met.* V.549–50: 'foedaque . . . dirum mortalibus omen'; also quoted by Isidore, *Etym.* XII.vii.39.
49 Cf. *Etym.* XII.vii.32: 'Onocrotalon Graeci uocant rostro longo'.
50 Cf. St Gallen 460, 21: 'erodion **uualuchaebuc**' and Paris I (50va): 'herodianum **uualuchabuch**'. For the confusion between ἐρωδιός, 'heron', and **uualuhchabuch**, 'falcon', see Pheifer, *Old English Glosses*, p. 92.

aquam tingi Postea cum pede ad rostrum ferens';[51] cf. Milan II (76va): 'Porphirionem . . . dicunt' *only* (Lev. XI.18: 'porphirionem').

'Caradrion ignota'; cf. Milan III (77ra): 'Charadrion ignota auis' (Lev. XI.19: 'charadrion').

'Attacus ignota'; cf. Milan III (77ra): 'Atiacus ignota auis' (Lev. XI.22: 'attacus'). 'Opimachus ignota' = Milan II (76va) (Lev. XI.22: 'ophiomachus'). 'Bruchus similis locuste sed maior' = Milan III (77ra) (Lev. XI.22: 'brucus'). 'Migale similis cameleon'; cf. Milan III (77ra): 'Migale ignota dicitur tamen similis esse cameleoni' (Lev. XI.30).

[43rv] 'Corcodrillus bestia in flumina simillis lacerte sed maior et est quadrupes pariter terre et flumine unum hoc animal Terreste lingue usu caret et unum superi mobili maxilia inprimit morsum alias terribile pectina instipante se dentium syrie magnitudine excedit plerumque duodeuiginti cubita parit oua quanta anseres unguinibus autem armatus est contra ictus cute inuicta dies in terra noctes in aqua temporis agit';[52] cf. Milan III (77rab): 'Corcodrillus . . . flumine similis lacerte sed maior ita ut homines manducerit'[53] (Lev. XI.29: 'corcodillus').

[43v] 'Cameleon similis lacerte sub aspectu enim mutat colores uarius ut pardus dictus autem ita ad colores cameleontis quod uidet facillima conuersione uariatur quia aliorum animalium non est ita facilis corpulenta ad conuersionem';[54] cf. Milan III (77rb): 'Cameleon similis est lacerte tamen sub aspectu mutat colores' *only* (Lev. XI.30).

'Si super eum fusa aqua fuerit idest in qua lauantur hec uasa'; cf. Milan III (77rb): 'Si fusa fuerit super eum aqua lauabuntur uasa' (Lev. XI.34: 'si fusa fuerit super eum aqua').

---

51 Pliny, *Historia naturalis* X.129: 'porphyrio . . . est proprio genere, omnem cibum aqua subinde tinguens, deinde pede ad rostrum ueluti manu adferens'.

52 Pliny, *Historia naturalis* VIII.89: 'Corcodrilum habet Nilus, quadripes malum et terra pariter ac flumine infestum, unum hoc animal terrestre linguae usu caret, unum superiore mobili maxilla inprimit morsum, alias terribile pectinatim stipante se dentium serie, magnitudine excedit plerumque duodeviginti cubitos. Parit ova quanta anseres . . . unguinibus autem armatus est, contra omnes ictus cute invicta, dies in terra agit, noctes in aqua, teporis utrumque ratione.'

53 Cf. St Gallen 295 (ptd Steinmeyer, *Die althochdeutschen Glossen* V, 161, 15–16): 'Corcodrillus bestia in flumine similis lacerte sed maior ita ut homines manducet', and Cam. (42vb): 'Corcodryllus . . . manducet'.

54 Isidore, *Etym.* XII.ii.18: 'Chamaeleon non habet unum colorem, sed diversa est varietate consparsus, ut pardus . . . Huius chamaeleontis corpusculum ad colores quos vicet facillima conversione variatur, quod aliorum animalium non est ita ad conversionem facilis corpulentia.' The quotations from Pliny and Isidore also appear in the

'Stelio genus serpentis similis lacerte'; cf. Milan II (76va): 'Stellius genus est serpentis similis lacerte sed maior de colore inditum nomen habet Est enim tergore pictus fulcitur fulgentibus guttis in modum stellarum Ideoque dictus stellius quod stellatum habet corpus'[55] (Lev. XI.30: 'stelio').

In all, twenty-nine of the fifty-three Fulda Leviticus glosses have counterparts in Milan II, and twenty-one have counterparts in Milan III. Two such glosses are common to both: Fulda 43v ('Effloruerit apperuerit', glossing Lev. XIII.12) = Milan II (76va) = Milan III (77rb); and Fulda 44r ('Siclus .xx. obolus habet') = Milan II (76va) = Milan III (77va), with minor spelling variants only. In one case a gloss in Fulda (44r) having a precise equivalent in Milan II (76va: 'Inquilinus colonus uel uernaculus', glossing Lev. XXII.10) represents a combination of a gloss in Milan I (PentI 390: 'Inquilinus idest rusticus colonus') with one in Milan III (77va: 'Inquilinus uernaculus'); on another occasion, a gloss in Fulda (44r: 'Spatulas fructus palme antequam aperiantur idest in similitudinem spade inde spatula dicitur', glossing Lev. XXIII.40) having a nearly verbatim equivalent in Milan III (77va) corresponds to a gloss in Milan I (PentI 395: 'Spatulas fructus palme dicitur pro similitudine spade' *only*).

Numbers and Deuteronomy

In the last two books of the Pentateuch, entries in Fulda (45r–46v) that correspond to Milan II are found once again to predominate: forty-nine of the sixty-two Fulda Numbers glosses and thirty-seven of the fifty Fulda

Hrabanus Maurus/Walahfrid Strabo commentary on Leviticus (ptd PL 114, 795–846, at 815–16), which Steinmeyer assumed to be Fulda's immediate source, but the commentary itself drew heavily on the Reichenau glosses, as his appendix shows (*Die althochdeutschen Glossen* V, 483–5). It seems that Haymo of Auxerre and John Scottus Eriugena also used Canterbury glosses in their commentaries. For example, the gloss in Cam. (41ra), 'NENIAS Vanitates Nenie sunt carmina que in tumbis id est In memoriis mortuorum scribuntur que EPITHAPHIA primum HIBERI inuenerunt', glossing Jerome's Prol. in Pentateuchum 20, is attributed to John Scottus Eriugena in the ninth-century Bible glosses in Vatican City, Biblioteca Apostolica Vaticana, Reg. lat. 215 and Bern, Burgerbibliothek, 258: see Contreni, 'The Biblical Glosses', p. 422.

55 Isidore, *Etym.* XII.iv.38: 'Stellio de colore inditum nomen habet; est enim tegore pictus lucentibus guttis in modum stellarum. De quo Ovidius: aptumque colori Nomen habet, variis stellatus corpore guttis.' The reference to Ovid is to *Met.* V.461–2.

Deuteronomy glosses have correspondences in Milan II. The main alternative source in Numbers is still Milan III, which has thirteen entries corresponding to it, one each of which overlaps with Milan I and II respectively, as shown below:

[44v] 'Sanctificauit capud radit'; cf. Milan III (79rb): 'Sanctificabit idest radet caput' (Num. VI.11: 'sanctificavitque caput').

'Plaustra tecta corio cooperta'; cf. Milan III (79rb): 'Plaustra tecta idest corio cooperta' (Num. VII.3: 'plaustra tecta').

'Corus .xxx. modios capit'; cf. Milan II (78vb): 'Chorus mensura est capiens modios .xxx.'; Milan III (79va): 'Corus unus .xxx. modios' (Num. XI.32: 'choros').

'Vatilla pala ferea ad focum similis uasis cum quibus aqua proicitur de naui'; cf. Milan III (79rb): 'Vatilla pala ad focum similis uasis quibus aqua de nauibus proicitur' (Num. IV.14).

'Puteus super quo locutus est dominus petra quam iussit dominus moysen percutere'; cf. Milan III (79va): 'Puteus ... dominus idest petra quam iussit dominus moysi percutere' (Num. XXI.16).

'Querimonia planctus uel frequens querela'; cf. Milan III (79va): 'Querimonias querelas' (Num. XVII.5: 'querimonias').

'Sceptro regia potestate' = Milan III (79va) (Num. XVIII.2: 'sceptrum').

'Cyneum nomen gentis'; cf. Milan III (79va): 'Cineum nomen gentis' (Num. XXIV.21: 'Cineum').

'Pugione gladio' = Milan III (79vb) (Num. XXV.7).

'In libro bellorum domini idest bellorum israel'; cf. Milan III (79va): 'In ... idest ipsius gentis israel; Bella domini bella israel' (Num. XXI.14).

[45r] 'Murenulas catenas latas et spissas quae ad ornandum collum aptantur'; cf. Milan III (79vb): 'Murenulas ... spissas' *only* (Num. XXXI.50).

'Mare salsissimum mare mortuum'; cf. Milan I (78vb = PentI 458): 'Mare salsissimum idest mare mortuum'; Milan III (79vb): 'Salsissimo mare idest mare mortuo' (Num. XXXIV.3: 'mare Salsissimum').

'Ascensum scorpionis proprium nomen loci' = Milan III (79vb) (Num. XXXIV.4).

One Numbers gloss has a counterpart in Milan I *only* (Fulda 44v: 'Nausia uomitus', on Num. XI.20: 'nausiam'; cf. PentI 417: 'Nausia grece latine uomitus') and another has counterparts in both Milan I and II (Fulda 44v: 'In trieribus in nauibus exercitus', on Num. XXIV.24; cf. PentI 446: 'In ... nauibus tres ordines remorum habentibus Romanos significat', and Milan II (79ra): 'In... nauibus maioribus').

The same pattern of relationships is found in the Deuteronomy glosses from the 'Reichenau Bible glosses' as represented in the Fulda manuscript: twelve of the fifteen entries without counterparts in Milan II have counterparts in Milan III,[56] as may be seen below:

[45v-46r] 'Dipsas genus serpentis [*bis*] et pede semis longus Et duarum palmarum grossus caudam curuam habens et uenenatam cum qua pungit et interpretatur situla et sitis quia homo ab ea percussus siti moritur'; cf. Milan III (79rb-80ra): 'Dipsas genus serpentis est Quando percussit hominem siti moritur ipse homo Vnde ipse serpens dipsas dicitur idest sitis. Habet longitudine pedem et semis grossitudine sicut due palme ambiunt et de cauda percutit idest quia quod curua et uenenata est'[57] (Deut. VIII.15).

[46r] 'Concio conuentus populi'; cf. Milan III (80ra): 'Contio populi idest conuentus conuentio uel tumultus' (Deut. IX.10: 'contio').

'Filii belial filii pestilentie' = Milan III (80ra) (Deut. XIII.13).

'Pirargon et orgen et camelo et pardalus ignote bestie'; cf. Milan III (80ra): 'Pirargon et orien et Cameleon pardalum ignote bestie sunt' (Deut. XIV.5: 'pyrargum orygem camelopardalum').

'Ixion auis de genere uulturis alba et minor quam uultur'; cf. Milan II (80r): 'Yxon ... alba sed minor quam uultur' (Deut. XIV.13: 'ixon').

'Caradrium ignota auis' = Milan III (80ra) (Deut. XIV.18: 'charadrium').

'Sicera omne potum absque uino in quo inebriari potest'; cf. Milan III (80ra): 'Sicera dicitur omne quod inebriari potest excepto uino quod faciunt in asia de panibus et aqua et melle' (Deut. XIV.26: 'siceram').

[56] Note that at this point in the Milan manuscript, for the Deuteronomy glosses only, it appears that the scribe absent-mindedly reversed the order in which he copied glosses from his source-manuscripts, so that here Milan III precedes Milan II, which in turn is followed by Milan I (= PentI); see *Biblical Commentaries*, ed. Bischoff and Lapidge, p. 285. The proportions of Reichenau Deuteronomy glosses corresponding to Milan I and III are consistent with this supposition.

[57] Cf. Isidore, *Etym.* XII.iv.13: 'Dipsas genus aspidis, qui latine situla dicitur, quia quem memorderit siti perit.' See also the Corpus Glossary, ed. Hessels, *An Eighth-Century Latin-Anglo-Saxon Glossary preserved in the Library of Corpus Christi College, Cambridge*, D292: 'Dipsas genus serpentis est intollerabilis quando percusserit hominem siti moritur ipse homo unde ipsa serpens dipsas id est sitio dicitur habet longas pedes et semes grossitum sicut duae palmae ambiunt et de cauda percutit quia uenenata et curba est.' The Corpus Glossary, which is now dated to the second quarter of the ninth century (by Malcolm Parkes, in *The Epinal, Erfurt, Werden, and Corpus Glossaries*, ed. Bischoff *et al.*, pp. 24–5), incorporates most of Ep/ErfI and adds more material from the same sources: see Pheifer, *Old English Glosses*, pp. xxviii-xxxix, and 'Anglo-Saxon Glossaries', pp. 17–19 and 34–6.

'Lucus nomen arboris cuius folia non cadit sicut therebinthi et ilicis'; cf. Milan III (80ra): 'Lucus dicitur arbor frondosa ut est therebintus et ilicus et multe que folia non abiciunt sicut iste' (Deut. XVI.21).

[46v] 'Adsumet ebria sicientem idest que iam ebria fuit in idolis sicientem in dei cultura ducunt merorem'; cf. Milan III (80rb): 'Adsumat ebria sitientem ... ydolis sitientem ... culturam ducet in errorem' (Deut. XXIX.19: 'absumat ebria sitientem').

'Meracissimum purissimum' = Milan III (80rb) (Deut. XXXII.14).

'Recens in presenti dicitur nouum in futuro'; cf. Milan III (80rb): 'Recens ... Nouus in futuro' (Deut. XXXII.17: 'novi recentesque').

'Thesaurus arenarum terrena sapientia'; cf. Milan III (80rb): 'Thesaurus arenarum idest sapientia terrena' (Deut. XXXIII.19: 'thesauros absconditos harenarum').

One Deuteronomy gloss is common to Milan II and III: Fulda (46r: 'Mancer filius scorti', glossing Deut. XXIII.2) is found with slightly variant orthography in Milan II (80vb) and III (80rb); another entry in Fulda (45v: 'Sequester susceptor pugnarum uel minister', glossing Deut. V.5) was evidently confected from Milan II (80va: 'Sequester susceptor pignorum') and Milan III (79vb: 'Susceptor minister'). In general the 'Reichenau Bible glosses' to Numbers and Deuteronomy, as represented in the Fulda manuscript, follow the same pattern of allegiances as in the preceding books of the Pentateuch.

THE MARGINAL GLOSSES IN FULDA AA. 2 AND IN KARLSRUHE 248

In addition to the Pentateuch glosses in Fulda Aa. 2 which we have been considering hitherto, however, there is a second series pertaining to Exodus, Leviticus, Numbers and Deuteronomy which were copied in one or both margins of Fulda 40r-45r and 46v (on Fulda 45rv this second series was copied into the main text). From their location in the margins of Fulda Aa. 2, these additional Bible glosses are often referred to as the 'Randglossar'. Another copy of these same glosses is found in Karlsruhe 248 (104va-105rb, 106va-108ra, 108va-109ra and 109vb-110va). Of these second series glosses, those to Exodus and Leviticus are only tangentially related to the Canterbury glosses we have been discussing. For example, only five of the fifty-seven Exodus glosses have parallels in Milan III,[58] and only one of the fifty-one Leviticus glosses incorporates a Milan III explanation: cf. Fulda (42vb), 'Dicit iosepus hibis est animal serpentibus inimicum et est mitis sed tamen serpentem deuorat et sunt in affrica longum rostrum habentia',[59] and Milan III (77ra), 'Ibin auis in affrica habens longum rostrum', both glossing Lev. XI.17. Two other entries with vernacular interpretations are paralleled in Paris I: Fulda (41rb), 'Fibule **ringa**'; cf. Paris I (49vb), 'Fibulas **hringan**', glossing Ex. XXVI.11; and Fulda (43rb), 'Graculus **ruohc**'; cf. Paris I (50va), 'Garula **rouca**', added to the Leviticus bird-name glosses. The Numbers and Deuteronomy glosses, however, are a very different matter. Of the forty-two second series (that is, marginal) glosses to Numbers in Fulda Aa. 2, thirty-eight have counterparts in the Milan III Numbers section:

[45r] 'Sursaddi idest unum nomen'; cf. Milan III (79rb): 'Surisaddi unum est nomen' (Num. I.6: 'Surisaddai').

'Replete manus idest unctionis oleo' = Milan III (79rb) (Num. III.3: 'repletae et consecratae manus').

'Coram domino ad ostium tabernaculi'; cf. Milan III (79rb): 'Coram domino idest ad ostium tabernaculi' (Num. V.16).

[45v] 'Amarissimas propter maledictiones'; cf. Milan III (79rb): 'Amarissimas idest propter maledictiones' (Num. V.18).

---

[58] These are as follows: Fulda (40ra): 'Columna nubis et columna ignis unum est altera parte ignea et altera parte nubis pertingens ad terram quamdiu ipsi debuerunt in una mansione manere stetit columna quando debuerunt ire ipsa elevans preibit'; cf. Milan III (74ra): 'Columna nubis et columna ignis idem esse creditur ex altera parte ignea ex altera similis nubi Quandiu ipsi debuerunt in una mansione stare stetit et columna Quando debuerunt mouere ipsa perambulabat (glossing Ex. XIII.21); Fulda (40va): 'Tetigit pedes idest pueri' = Milan III (74ra) (glossing Ex. IV.25); Fulda (40vb): 'Digitus dei idest potestas in moyse'; cf. Milan III (74ra): 'Digitus dei spiritus dei in moyse' (glossing Ex. VIII.19); Fulda (41rb): Precium pudicicie idest .xii. solidi debet dare puelle qui tradet eam'; cf. Milan (74rb): 'Precium pudicitie idest duodecim solidos qui ipsam tradit marito debet puelle dari' (glossing Ex. XXI.10); and Fulda (41rb): 'Bu[..] lignea est et he[.] longiores quam tube'; cf. Milan III (74rb)· 'Bucine lignee sunt longiores quam tube' (glossing Ex. XIX.13).

[59] The reference to Josephus is presumably to Rufinus's translation of *Antiq.* II.x.2: 'Hoc autem animal [*sc.* ibides] serpentibus inimicum est, fugiunt enim eas aduenientes: et cum se celare uoluerint, flatu uelut ceruorum arreptae deuorantur. Ibides autem sunt ualde mansuetae, et generi tantum serpentino feroces' (quoted from the Paris edition of 1528). On the use of Josephus in the Canterbury biblical commentaries, see discussion by Bischoff and Lapidge, *Biblical Commentaries*, pp. 216–17.

'Votum idest aliqua abstinentia'; cf. Milan III (79rb): 'Votum abstinentiam aliquam uel ieiunium' (Num. VI.2).

'Vua passa idest sicca oleo peruncta' = Milan III (79rb) (Num. VI.4).

'Acinum unum granum de botro'; cf. Milan III (79rb): 'Acinum uno grano de botro' (Num. VI.4).

'Nouacula idest ferrum subtile quadrangulum latum in superiori parte'; cf. Milan III (79rb): 'Nouacula ferrum . . . latum' *only* (Num. VI.5).

'Aqua lustrationis idest purgationis' = Milan III (79rb) (Num. VIII.7).

'Concisius idest longius uel intercepto silenti'; cf. Milan III (79rb): 'Concisius longius uel incisa uoce' (Num. X.5: 'prolixior atque concisus').

'Ad locum directionis id ubi nubes stabat'; cf. Milan III (79rb): 'Ad directionis locum idest ubi nubes stabat ibi directi fuerat' (Num. X.21: 'ad erectionis locum').

'Ignis deuorabit idest subito apparuit et deuorauit'; cf. Milan III (79rb): 'Ignis deuorauit extremam castrorum partem idest subito apparuit et incendit eos' (Num. XI.1: 'ignis Domini devoravit extremam castrorum partem').

'Vulgus promiscuus qui de egipto ascendit'; cf. Milan III (79rb): 'Vulgus promiscuus idest qui de egypto ascendebant' (Num. XI.4: 'vulgus quippe promiscuum quod ascenderat cum eis').

[44ra] 'Augeram de spiritu tuo idest non diminuo sed eundem eis gratiam dabo'; cf. Milan III (79rb-va): 'Augeram . . . tuo non diminutione sed de eadem gratia' (Num. XI.17).

'Bdelli uel bogelli herba est albi coloris'; cf. Milan III (79rb): 'Boelli herba . . . coloris' (Num. XI. 17: 'bdellii').

'Iosue filius nun idest post mortem moysi iesu naue dicitur'; cf. Milan III (79va): 'Iosue filius nun dicitur uiuente moyse post mortem eius ihesus filius naue' (Num. XI.28).

'Quantum una die confici potest idest ambulare potes idest .xxx. milia'; cf. Milan III (79va): 'Quantum . . . ambulare potest . . . milia' (Num. XI.31).

'Plaga magna idest pestilentia' = Milan III (79va) (Num. XI.33).

'Si pater eum spuisset idest iratus ei fuisset'; cf. Milan III (79va): 'Si . . . iratus fuisset ei' (Num. XII.14).

'Monstra signum ipsos gigantes'; cf. Milan III (79va): 'Monstra ipsos gigantes' (Num. XIII.34).

'Ephi quatuor modios habet'; cf. Milan III (79va): 'Ephi tres modios de pulmenti de cibis omnibus' (Num. XV.4: 'oephi').

'In domo leui idest in tabernaculo testimonii'; cf. Milan III (79va): 'In . . . testimonii quod ipsi custodiebant' (Num. XVII.8).

[44rb] 'Portabit iniquitatem idest offerat pro iniquitatibus'; cf. Milan III (79va): 'Portabitis iniquitatem sanctuarii idest offeratis pro iniquitatibus israhel et uritis in sanctuario' (Num. XV.31).

'Cananeus a prouincia aran dicitur proprium nomen uiri'; cf. Milan III (79va): 'Arad proprium nomen uiri' (Num. XXI.1: 'Chananeus rex Arad').

'Etatis integre idest triennem' = Milan III (79va) (Num. XIX. 2: 'aetatis integrae').

'Ultro se obligunt idest anathematizare omnia que fuerunt gentis illius'; cf. Milan III (79va): 'Voto se . . . fuerant gentis illius' (Num. XXI.2: 'Voto se Domino obligans').

'Pro signo idest altiorem locum'; cf. Milan III (79va): 'Pro signo idest in altiorem locum' (Num. XVI. 38).

'Ignotos idest pro nimia ferocitate' = Milan III (79va) (Num. XXI.6: 'ignitos').

'Puteus super quo locutus est dominus idest petra quam iussit percutere'; cf. Milan III (79va) 'Puteus . . . quam dominus iussit moysi percutere' (Num. XXI.16).

'Dixit homo cuius obscuratus est oculus idest de se ipso dixit forsitan luscus fuit uel oculus mentis propter auaritiam'; cf. Milan III (79va): 'Dixit homo cuius obturatus . . . de ipso dixit' *only* (Num. XXIV.3: 'dixit . . . obturatus est oculus').

'Rex eius idest amorreorum uel saul propter agag regem quem samuhel occidit' = Milan III (79va) (Num. XXIV.7: 'propter Agag rex eius').

'Principium gentium idest qui inter gentes significant que in christo crediderunt'; cf. Milan III (79vab): 'Principium gentium idest quia gentes in te significantur que in christo crediture sunt' (Num. XXIV.20).

[44rb-45va] 'Si fueris electus de stirpe cain idest qui fuistis homicide sicut cain. Comparat enim peccatores stirpi cain ex quo scelus homidicie descendit. Iustos autem ad set simulat'; cf. Milan III (79vb): 'Si . . . idest quia fuistis homicide sicut cain' *only* (Num. XXIV.22: 'et fueris electus sicut Cain').

[45va] 'Partem glorie idest non totam quia eleazar debuit consulere pro eo non ipse'; cf. Milan III (79vb): 'Partem . . . totam quod eleazar . . . ipse' (Num. XXVII.20).

'Portabit iniquitatem eius idest tollet a mulier'; cf. Milan III (79vb): 'Portabit . . . muliere (Num. XXX.16: 'portabit ipse iniquitatem eius').

'Claui in oculis idest conpunctiones' — Milan III (79vb) (Num. XXXIII.55).

'Asce[..] scorpionis idest nomen loci'; cf. Milan III (79vb): 'Ascensum scorpionis proprium nomen loci' (Num. XXXIV.4: 'ascensum Scorpionis').

'Montem altum idest libanum uel olympum'; cf. Milan III (79vb): 'Montem altissimum olimpum puto' (Num. XXXIV.7: 'montem Altissimum').

In spite of the large Milan III presence in the first series (see above, pp. 307–8), only two entries are duplicated in the Fulda marginal glosses ('Puteus . . . percutere' and 'Ascensum . . . loci'). The entry 'Concisius . . . silenti' also has a first-series counterpart in Karlsruhe 99, 39r and Karlsruhe 248, 108rb ('Concisius longius' *only*). A third series of eight Numbers glosses without parallels in Milan follows in Fulda (44vb) and Karlsruhe 248 (109ra), to which Karlsruhe 248 adds three entries with counterparts in Milan II.[60]

The sixty-seven Deuteronomy marginal glosses in Fulda likewise fall into three mini-series, the first of which contains one entry with a counterpart in Milan III (Fulda (45ra): 'Syrus persequebatur patrem meum idest laban iacob uel abraham in ur caleorum'; cf. Milan III (80rb): 'Syrus persequebatur patrem meum idest abraham quando eduxerit eum dominus de hur idest de igne chaldeorum', glossing Deut. XXVI.5). Similarly to the Numbers glosses, the second and third mini-series of Deuteronomy glosses contain sequences of eleven and five entries respectively that also correspond to Milan III.

[45va]   'Epulaueris tu idest deci[. . .] quas in ciuitate dereliquisti'; cf. Milan III (80ra): 'Et epulaberis tu et domus tua idest decimis quas reliquisti in ciuitate tua' (Deut. XIV.26: 'et epulaberis tu et domus tua').

'In pascha ceperunt falcem mittere in segetem idest primo mense .xv.^ma die primi mensis'; cf. Milan III (80ra): 'In pasca . . . mense' *only* (Deut. XVI.9: 'septem hebdomadas numerabis tibi ab ea die qua falcem in segetem miseris').

'Sollicitans idest suadens secum ambulare ut uendant eum'; cf. Milan III (80rb): 'Sollicitans eum ut ambulet secum quocunque et postea in itinere uenderit eum' (Deut. XXIV.7).

'Transfert terminos idest inuadet alienam terram' = Milan III (80rb) (Deut. XXVII.17).

'Descendit cinis super te idest illa plaga quam egiptii habuerunt'; cf. Milan III (80rb): 'Descendat . . . idest plaga aliqua sicut in egyptios' (Deut. XXVIII.26: 'descendat super te cinis').

'Deficientes oculi idest propter famem'; cf. Milan III (80rb): 'Deficientes oculos propter famem' (Deut. XXVIII.65: 'deficientes oculos').

[45vb]   'Medulla tritici idest simila' = Milan III (80rb) (Deut. XXXII.14).

'Recens in presenti dicitur nouus in futuro' = Milan III (80rb) (Deut. XXXII.17: 'novi recentesque')

'In exitu id inceptu tuo'; cf. Milan III (80rb): 'In exitu tuo inceptu tuo' (Deut. XXXIII.18: 'in exitu tuo').

'Undatio maris idest nationis ad Christum'; cf. Milan III (80rb): 'Inun-

---

60 These are: 'Coaceriassent idest congregassent'; cf. Milan II (79ra): 'Coacerbassent congregassent' (glossing Num XVI.19); 'Coierunt conuenerunt' = Milan II (79ra) (glossing Num. XX.2); and 'Quin pocius multo magis' = Milan II (79ra) (glossing Num. XXI.23).

dationem... nationes ad Christum' (Deut. XXXIII.19: 'inundationem maris').

'Thesauros arenarum idest terrena sapientia'; cf. Milan III (80rb): 'Thesauros ... sapienta terrena' (Deut. XXXIII.19: 'thesauros absconditos arenarum').

'Inuisit idest uisitauit'; cf. Milan III (80ra): 'Inuisit uisitat uel considerat' (Deut. XI.12).

[45vb-46ra] 'Tempora idest initio uerni (bis) aestatis uel diei idest autumni'; cf. Milan III (80ra): 'Tempore quo temperies uenit idest ut uerno initio estatis uel diei' (Deut. XI.14: 'temporaneam').

[46ra] 'Serotinam idest in finem diei uel estatis'; cf. Milan III (80ra): 'Serotinam ... fine ... estatis uel autunni' (Deut. XI.14).

'Pones benedictionem et maledictionem super duos montes idest non titulos sed condicere et iurare'; cf. Milan III (80ra): 'Pones ... montes non quia titulos ponere debuisset sed ... iurare' (Deut. XI.29: 'pones benedictionem super montem Garizim maledictionem super montem Hebal').

'Non facies ibi que nos hic facimus idest malum quod frequenter fecisti'; cf. Milan III (80ra): 'Non facietis ... fecistis' (Deut. XII.8: 'non facietis ibi quae nos hic facimus').

One main-gloss entry is duplicated ('Thesauros ... terrenam'). A single gloss appended to the third mini-series, Fulda 46ra, 'Porfirio idest **pheluphur**' (glossing Deut. XIV.17: 'porphirionem'), corresponds to Paris I (51vb): 'porfilio **philfor**'. In general, however, the Fulda marginal glosses draw principally on the glosses in Milan III.

GLOSSES TO THE REMAINING BOOKS OF THE BIBLE

The Reichenau Pentateuch gloss elaborated the pattern of source relations established by the prologue in ways that recall the interlaced ornament which contemporary artists delighted in. The extra series of glosses to Exodus-Deuteronomy in the margins of Fulda Aa. 2 and in Karlsruhe 248 show that the Milan glosses, especially Milan II and Milan III, continued to be available to continental students of the Bible. After Deuteronomy there are two uninterrupted series of glosses in the Milan manuscript.[61] The first (Milan 81ra-91rb) comprises the remaining books of the Old Testament except Psalms and Maccabees, Jerome's Commentary on

---

[61] Note that, from this point onwards, the Milan I glosses no longer correspond to PentI (ptd *Biblical Commentaries*, ed. Bischoff and Lapidge), but are a collection of as yet unprinted explanations pertaining to the remaining books of the Bible.

Matthew, and two sets of glosses on the gospels. The second series (Milan 91va-123ra), headed *Apostrofa glosarum per precedentes libros a ihesu naue et deinceps in prologo iosue*, covers the whole of the Vulgate from Joshua onward. The Reichenau gloss consists mainly of entries that correspond to one Milan series or the other. Thus thirty-four of the forty-two Joshua glosses in Fulda, the last twelve of which form a new sequence also found in Karlsruhe 135 (104r) and Karlsruhe 248 (111ra), have counterparts in Milan: eighteen in Milan I and seventeen in Milan II (one entry combines interpretations that correspond to Milan I and II and another collapses two Milan I glosses, while one Milan gloss is split into two Fulda entries):

[46va] 'Tandem postremum uel postmodum'; cf. Milan II (91va): 'Tandem postremo uel postmodum' (Jos. Prol. 1).

'ΕΖΑΠΛΟΙΣ idest exemplaribus'; cf. Milan II (91va): 'ΕΖΑΠΛΟΙΣ exemplaribus' (Jos. Prol. 9: ἐξαπλοῖς).

'Arcuato uulnere quia cauda scorpionis curuata est unde fert'; cf. Milan I (81ra): 'Arcuato uulnere idest curuo uulnere quia ... unde nocet' (Jos. Prol. 13).

'Ediciones translationes'; cf. Milan II (91va): 'Editiones translationes' (Jos. Prol. 25: 'editiones').

'Postliminem post mortem patris et matris'; cf. Milan I (81ra): 'Postliminio idest post mortem patris uel matris' (Jos. Prol. 31: 'postliminio').

'Sirenarum meretricum per magicas artes uel undarum crispantium'; cf. Milan I (81ra): 'Sirenarum cantus dixit sicut fecit ulixis in insula meretricum maicas'; and Milan II (91va): 'Syrenarum undarum crispantium' (Jos. Prol. 33: 'sirenarum cantus').

'Quippe certe Nimirum sine dubio' = Milan II (91va) (Jos. II.3).

'Fateor confiteor' = Milan II (91va) (Jos. II.4).

'Funiculus iste quo se cinxit a renibus usque ad pectus; Coccinus rubeus'; cf. Milan I (81ra): 'Funiculus coccineus idest fascia rubeus uel similis purpura qua se cingerat pectus' (Jos. II.18: 'funiculus iste coccineus').

'Mole magnitudine' = Milan II (91va) (Jos. III.13).

'Polenta farina subtilissima'; cf. Milan I (81ra): 'polenta subtilissima farina' (Jos. V.11: 'polentam').

'Per prona per preceps per inclinata' = Milan II (91va) (Jos. VII.5).

'Conglobanta in unum collecta'; cf. Milan II (91va): 'Conglobata ... collecta' (Jos. VII.9).

'Degesserat descripserat ordinauerat'; cf. Milan II (91va): 'Digesserat descripserat ordinauerat' (Jos. VIII.32: 'digesserat').

'Pittaciis modicis coriolis uel palastris'; cf. Milan I (81ra): 'Pittacis palastris idest modica coriola' (Jos. IX.5: 'pittaciis').

'In libro iustorum in annalibus israhelitarum'; cf. Milan I (81ra): 'In ... in israhelitarum annalibus uel in aliis' (Jos. X.13).

'Decreuit constituit' = Milan II (91va) (Jos. IX.27: 'decreuitque').

'Presidia firmitates' = Milan II (91va) (Jos. X.19: 'praesidia').

'Subneruabis subiugabis uel deficere facies' = Milan II (91va) (Jos. XI.6).

'Vnam tantum asur flamma conbussit quia ipsam solam totam conbussit'; cf. Milan I (81ra): 'Absortam idest ipsam solam flamma consumsit' (Jos. XI.13: 'unam tantum Asor munitissimam flamma consumpsit').

'Raphaim idest gigantum'; cf. Milan I (81ra): 'Raphaim gigantum' (Jos. XII.4: 'Rafaim').

'A lingua maris idest a sonitu maris'; cf. Milan I (81ra): 'A ... sonitu maris uel a sinu maris' (Jos. XV.5).

'Ciuitas litterarum quia in ea litterati fuerunt uel littere custodiebantur'; cf. Milan I (81ra): 'Ciuitas litterarum quia in ea littere fuerunt ... custodiebantur' (Jos. XV.15).

'Marcetis languetis' = Milan II (91va) (Jos. XVIII.3).

'Ignauia inbecillitate'; cf. Milan II (91va): 'Ignauia inbecillitate uel pigritia' (Jos. XVIII.3).

'Carmelum maris proprium nomen loci' = Milan I (81rb) (Jos. XIX.26).

'Conubia coniugia' = Milan II (91va) (Jos. XXIII.12).

'Sudes stipites' = Milan II (91va) (Jos. XXIII.13).

'Nouellis ouibus unius anni qui necdum generarunt'; cf. Milan I (81rb): 'Nouellis ouibus idest iuuenibus que nec nondum generant' (Jos. XXIV.32).

[47r] 'In domum dei in superiori parte Vallis autem inferior est'; cf. Milan I (81ra): 'In domum dei ad tabernaculum (Jos. IX.23); Conuallius dicitur in late montis in superiori parte uallis inferior' (Jos. XIII.19: 'in monte conuallis').

'Adam maximus idest primus'; cf. Milan I (81ra): 'Adam ... primus homo' (Jos. XIV.15)

'Funiculi manasses idest fortes uel herditas'; cf. Milan I (81ra): 'Funiculi manasse fortes uel hereditas' (Jos. XVII.5: 'funiculi Manasse').

'Ferreis curribus armati idest currus et equi'; cf. Milan I (81rab): 'Ferreis curribus idest armati equi et currus' (Jos. XVII.16).

The last four entries in Fulda, which belong to the new sequence, take their counterparts from the minority supplier in the first series, as do the marginal glosses to Numbers and Deuteronomy. A Milan II gloss (91va: 'Vallatus circumdatus', to Jos. VIII.10), which precedes the entry 'Digesserat descripserat ordinauit' in Karlsruhe 99 (39v), is appended to the second series in Karlsruhe 248 (111ra). The Karlsruhe 135 gloss corresponding to Fulda 47r ('Regulam aureum idest uirga Iosephus dicit illam clamidem esse rigiam totam auro textam habentem auri massam hoc est ciclos pondo .cc.',[62] glossing Jos. VII.21), a marginal entry not found in Milan, substitutes an Old English interpretation also found in Paris I for *uirga*: cf. Karlsruhe 135, 104r ('Regulam auream idest **hyingan gyrdisles** iosephus ... regiam ... contextam ... hoc est solidorum pondo .cc.') and Paris I, 52ra ('Regulam auream **ringan gurdiles**').

THE RELATIONSHIP OF THE MILAN GLOSSES TO THOSE IN CAMBRIDGE, PARIS, LEIDEN AND KARLSRUHE 99

Between them the Milan and Reichenau glosses answer many, if not all, of the questions raised by the glosses in the Cambridge and Paris manuscripts. Except for the earlier part of the long Genesis section in Cam. (41ra–42rb), which consists largely of geographical and other *scholia* from Isidore,[63] most Cambridge and Paris glosses are paralleled in one or other of the series of Milan glosses. Consider, for example, the sixteen Genesis glosses common to both:

Cam. 41ra: 'Sintagmata Compos'; Paris I (48vb): 'Sintisma compositio'; cf. Milan I (60ra): 'Sintagma idest compositio uel subnumeratio meliusque sic dicitur'; Milan II (67va): 'Sintagma compositio'; and Milan III (69ra): 'Sintangit compositionem' (Prol. in Pentateuchum 16: σύνταγμα).

Cam. 41rb: 'Signum cain Tremor'; Paris I (48vb): 'Posuitque deus signum idest tremorem'; and cf. Milan III (69rb): 'Posuitque ... tremorem' (Gen. IV.15: 'posuitque dominus Cain signum').

Cam. 41rb: 'In articulo diei in initio'; Paris I (48vb): 'in ... initio diei'; cf. Milan I (62va): 'In articulo idest in initio diei'; and Milan II (68rb): 'In articulo diei in initio diei' (Gen. VII.13: 'in articulo diei').

Cam. 41vb: 'Placito Condicto'; Paris I (49ra): 'Placido conducto'; and cf. Milan III (69vb): 'placido conducto' (Gen. XXIX.28: 'placito').

Cam. 42ra: 'Terebinthus sub qua abscondit Iacob idola Est autem in Sicimis iuxta

---

[62] The reference is to Rufinus's translation of Josephus, *Antiq.* V.i.10: 'Achar vero quidam Zebedaei filius ex tribu Iuda, dum invenisset clamydem regiam totam auro contextam habentem auri maxam, hoc est siclorum pondo ducenta'; cf. above, n. 59.

[63] Cf., for example, Cam. (41ra): 'PHYSON Ipse est et GANGES Ganges autem dictus est a Gangaro rege Indie Physon uero dictus est a caterua quod decem fluminibus sibi adiunctis impletus efficitur unus' with Isidore, *Etym.* XIII.xxi.8; and Cam. (41ra): 'ONICHINVS lapis dictus quod habeat permixtum in se candorem in similitudinem unguis humane Graeci enim unguen ONYCHON dicunt Hunc India et Arabia gignit Sed indicus igniculos habet albos cum ingentibus zonis Arabicus uero niger est cum candidis zonis genera eius sunt quinque' with *Etym.* XVI.viii.3.

Neapolim Terebinthus et quercus idem sunt Terebinthus enim Grecum nomen est et est arbor generans resinam omnium resinarum prestantiorem[64] et habet fructus modicos qui manducari possunt'; Paris I (49ra): 'Terebintus et quercuus idem sunt et habet fructus modicos et mandi possunt dicitur quercus mambre permansisse a conditione mundi usque ad tempus constantini'; and cf. Milan III (70ra): 'Terrebintus genus arboris habens fructus modicos et manducari possunt Terrebintus et quercus idem sunt Dicitur quercus mambre... constantini' (Gen. XXXV.4: 'terebinthum').

Cam. 42ra: 'Filii Seir horrei de genere horreorum'; cf. Paris I (49ra): 'Filii seir orrei ... orreorum' = Milan I (64va) (Gen. XXXVI.20).

Cam. 42ra: 'Crimini pessimo Extra naturam'; Paris I (49ra): 'Crimine pessimo idest extra naturam'; and cf. Milan I (64rb): 'Accusauitque fratres crimine pessimo idest contra naturam' (Gen. XXXVII.2: 'accusauitque fratres ... crimine pessimo').

Cam. 42ra: 'Nutus prouidentia' = Paris I (49ra); cf. Milan II (68vb): 'nutu prouidentia'; and Milan III (70rb): 'nutum prouidentiam' (Gen. XLII.6: 'nutum').

Cam. 42ra: 'De manu Amorrei Idest emor' = Paris I (49ra) = Milan III (70rb) (Gen. XLVIII.22).

Cam. 42ra: 'In gladio et arcu meo Quia filii eius eum occiderunt'; Paris I (49ra): 'In ... arcu eo quia filii eius occiderunt eum'; and cf. Milan III (70rb): 'In ... arcu meo quia filii eius occiderunt eum' (Gen. XLVIII.22: 'in gladio et arcu meo').

Cam. 42ra: 'Effusus es sicut aqua Quia lapsus fuisti in adulterio Concubine'; cf. Paris I (49rb): 'Effusus ... quia labiis ... concubine mee'; and Milan III (70rb-va): 'Effusus ... quia labilis ... concubine mee' (Gen. XLIX.4).

Cam. 42ra: 'Ad predam quia predam tulisti occisus Emor et Sychem'; Paris I (49rb): 'Ad predam tulisti enim predam occisis ... sichem'; and cf. Milan III (70va): 'Ad predam Tulisti enim occisis ... sichem' (Gen. XLIX.9: 'a praeda').

Cam. 42ra: 'Ceruus emissus Emissus dicitur quando ceruam sequitur Et equus emissarius quando equam sequitur'; Paris I (49rb): 'Ceruus emissus dicitur ... emissus quando equas sequitur'; cf. Milan II (69ra): 'Emissus dicitur ceruus quando ceruam sequitur' *only*; and Milan III (70va): 'Ceruus emissus dicitur quando ceruam sequitur Et equus emissus quando equam sequitur' (Gen. XLIX.21: 'ceruus emissus').

Cam. 42ra: 'Filie discurrerunt Anime fratrum'; Paris I (49rb): 'Filie discurrunt idest anime fratrum' = Milan III (70va) (Gen. XLIX.22: 'filiae discurrerunt').

Cam. 42rb: 'Currus aliquando duas rotas habet aliquando .iiii.'; cf. Paris I (49rb):

---

[64] Cf. Isidore, *Etym.* XVII.vii.52: 'Terebinthus arbor, Graecum nomen, generans resinam omnium resinarum praestantiorem.'

'Currus aliquando duas rotas aliquando quattuor habet'; and cf. Milan III
(70va): 'Currus aliquando duas rotas aliquando .iiii.' *only* (Gen. L.9).
Cam. 42rb: 'In genibus Ioseph Sub potestate eius'; Paris I (49rb): 'In ... sup
postestate eius'; cf. Milan II (68vb): 'In ... in potestate eius'; and Milan III
(70va): 'In genibus ioseph idest sub potestate eius' (Gen. L.22).

The relationship of Cambridge and Paris I with the Milan Genesis glosses
is weakest in Milan I; their relationship with Milan II and III is complicated by the overlap between the latter, but their common source seems to
have been very closely related to Milan III. The 134 Cambridge glosses on
Jerome's Prologue to the Pentateuch and on the text of Genesis itself
include seven entries with parallels in Milan I, twenty-eight with parallels
in Milan II, and fifty-two with parallels in Milan III (one entry combines
Milan I and II, two combine Milan I, II and III, and eleven combine Milan
II and III). The thirty-nine Paris I glosses on the Prologue and Genesis
include four entries with parallels in Milan I, five with parallels in Milan
II, and thirty-five with parallels in Milan III (one entry combines Milan I
and II, one combines Milan I, II and III, and three combine Milan II and
III). A glossary substantially identical with Milan III was obviously the
chief – if not the only – source of the Paris I Genesis glosses, and both
glossaries maintain the same pattern in the remaining books of the
Pentateuch. Seventy-five of the seventy-nine Cambridge Exodus glosses
have counterparts in Milan III and twenty-four in Milan II, twenty-one of
which overlap with Milan III; fifty-five of the fifty-eight Cambridge
Leviticus glosses have counterparts in Milan III and four in Milan II, two
of which overlap with Milan III; thirty-two of the thirty-three Cambridge
Numbers glosses have counterparts in Milan III, two of which overlap
with Milan I, and one has a counterpart in Milan II; and nineteen of the
twenty-one Cambridge Deuteronomy glosses have counterparts in Milan
III, one of which overlaps with Milan II. Forty-one of the forty-seven Paris
I Exodus glosses have counterparts in Milan III, nine of which overlap with
Milan II; twenty-nine of the thirty-nine Paris I Leviticus glosses (not
counting entries with vernacular interpretations only) have counterparts in
Milan III, one of which overlaps with Milan II; twenty-two of the
twenty-three Paris I Numbers glosses have counterparts in Milan III; and
seventeen of the twenty Paris I Deuteronomy glosses (not counting those
with wholly vernacular interpretations) have counterparts in Milan III. Six
of the nine Paris II Exodus glosses have counterparts in Milan III, one of
which overlaps with Milan II; four of the five Paris II Leviticus glosses have

counterparts in Milan III; six of the seven Paris II Numbers glosses have counterparts in Milan III, one of which overlaps with Milan I; and two of the three Paris II Deuteronomy glosses have counterparts in Milan III, one of which also overlaps with Milan II. Taken together, this evidence demonstrates that the great majority of Cambridge and Paris glosses on the Pentateuch derive from a source substantially identical with Milan III.

The Cambridge and Paris glosses maintain a close relationship with the first of the two series of Milan glosses from Joshua onwards as far as the first of its two sets of gospel glosses (81ra-89ra).[65] Consider, for example, their Joshua glosses:

Cam. 43ra: 'De libro Iosue ben nun id est filii NUN'; cf. Milan I (81ra): 'In libro iosue benun siue ihesu naue filius nun Huius libri scriptor secundum hebreos ipse iosue extitit' (Vulgate *titulus*: 'INCIPIT LIBER IOSVE BENNVN ID EST IESV NAVE').

Cam. 43rb: 'Arcuato uulnere quia cauda scorpionis curuata est unde nocet homines'; Paris I (52ra): 'Arecuato uulnere idest incuruato uulnere quia ... nocet' *only*; cf. Milan I (81ra): 'Arcuato uulnere idest curuo uulnere quia ... nocet' *only* (Prol. 13: 'arcuato uulnere').

Cam. 43rb: 'Post liminio Post mortem patris uel matris'; Paris I (52ra): 'Post-limenio idest post mortem patris' *only*; cf. Milan I (81ra): 'Postliminio idest post mortem patris uel matris' (Prol. 31: 'postliminio').

Cam. 43rb: 'Sirenarum cantus Meretricum magicas sicut Vlixes in insula'; Paris I (52ra): 'Sirenarum cantus dixerunt sicut fecit Ulexes in insula idest metricum magicas'; cf. Milan I (81ra): 'Sirenarum cantus dixit sicut fecit ulixis in insula meretricum maicas' (Prol. 33).

Cam. 43rb: 'Funiculus cocci Roseus uel rubeus quo se cingit a renibus usque ad pectus'; cf. Milan I (81ra): 'Funiculus coccineus idest fascia rubeus uel similis purpura qua se cingerat a ... pectus' (Jos. II.18: 'funiculus iste coccineus').

Cam. 43rb: 'Spitatis modica coriola'; Paris I (52ra): 'Paticis idest palistris idest modica coriola'; cf. Milan I (81ra): 'Pittacis palustris idest modica coriola' (Jos. IX.5: 'pittacis').

Cam. 43rb: 'In libro iustorum In annalibus israhelitarum'; cf. Milan I (81ra): 'In ... in israhelitarum annalibus uel in aliis' (Jos. X.13).

Cam. 43rb: 'Assur tantum flamma conbussit Ipsam totam solam combussit'; Paris I (52ra): 'assartum idest ipsum solum flamma consumsit'; cf. Milan I (81ra): 'Absortam idest ipsam solam flamma consumsit' (Jos. XI.13: 'unam tantum Asor munitissimam flamma consumpsit').

[65] See above, pp. 315–16.

Cam. 43rb: 'Rafium Gigantum'; Paris II (57ra): 'Rafaim gigantum'; cf. Milan I (81ra): 'Raphaim gigantum' (Jos. XII.4: 'Rafaim').

Cam. 43rb: 'A lingua maris a sonitu maris'; Paris I (52ra): 'A linguam maris idest a sinu maris'; cf. Milan I (81ra): 'A lingua maris idest a sonitu maris uel a sinu maris' (Jos. XV.5: 'a lingua maris').

Cam. 43rb: 'Ciuitas litterarum Quia ibi litteratales homines fuerunt uel fecerunt uel ibi custodiunt'; Paris I (52ra): 'Ciuitas litterarum propter litteratos qui ibidem custodiuntur'; cf. Milan I (81ra): 'Ciuitas litterarum quia in ea littere fuerunt uel littere custodiebantur; Ciuitas litterarum propter litteratos qui ibi custodiuntur' (Jos. XV.15).

Paris I 52ra: 'Ferreis curribus idest armenti equi et curris'; cf. Milan I (81rab): 'Ferreis curribus idest armati equi et currus' (Jos. XVII.16).

Cam. 43rb: 'Carmellum maris Proprium nomen loci'; Paris I (52ra): 'Carmelum maris propter nomen loci'; cf. Milan I (81rb): 'Carmelum maris proprium nomen loci' (Jos. XIX.26).

Cam. 43rb: 'Nouellis ouibus Iuuenibus qui necdum generant'; cf. Milan I (81rb): 'Nouellis ouibus idest iuuenibus que nec nondum generant' (Jos. XXIV.32).

Only one entry in Cambridge and Paris lacks a counterpart in Milan I, namely Cam. 43rb: 'Regulam auream fibula' (glossing Jos. VII.21: 'regulamque auream'); cf. Paris I (52ra): 'Regulam auream **ringam gurdiles**'.[66] This series of Milan glosses has all-Latin entries corresponding to Cambridge instead of vernacular interpretations like Paris, as in this example: Milan I (82vb): 'Camis lignum sine ferro quod cantum dicitur, Modioli lignum in quo radii mittuntur'; cf. Cam. (43vb): 'Camis . . . que Cantum dicitur, Modioli . . . mittuntur'; and Paris I (53ra): 'Canis **felgunt** modioli **nap**' (III Reg. VII.33: 'canti et modioli').

From Chronicles onward Milan I is also cognate with the 'Leiden Glossary' chs. vii–xxv and xxix (recall that the 'Leiden Glossary' has no entries for the Pentateuch or for Joshua, Judges and the four books of Kings), as well as with the corresponding sections of Karlsruhe 99, 46r–48v and 49v–50r. This relationship may be illustrated by the Milan I Isaiah glosses corresponding to Leiden and Karlsruhe 99:

[85rb]   'Tugurium domuncula' = Ld. xiii.2 (Is. I.8).

'Cucumerium hortum in quo cucumeres crescunt cucumeres crescunt Herba bona ad esum et medicinam'; cf. Ld. xiii.1: 'Cucumerarium hortus in quo cucumerus crescit bona erba ad manducandum siue ad medicinam' = Karlsruhe 99, 47r (Is. I.8: 'cucumerio').

---

[66] See above, pp. 317–18.

'Vermiculus tinctura ad similitudinem uermis'; cf. Ld. xiii.3: 'Vermiculus a similitudine uermis' = Karlsruhe 99, 47r (Is. I.18).

'Fissura scissura diuisura' = Ld. xiii.4 = Karlsruhe 99, 47r (Is. II.21: 'fissuras').

'Lunulas quas mulieres in collo habent de auro uel argento ad similitudinem lune diminutiue dicuntur'; cf. Leiden xiii.6: 'Lunulas . . . argento a similitudine lune diminutiue dicuntur'; and Karlsruhe 99, 47r: 'Lunulas quasi mulieres . . . argento' *only* (Is. III.18).

'Discriminalia unde discernuntur crines de auro uel ere'; cf. Ld. xiii.7: 'Discriminalia . . . aere'; and Karlsruhe 99, 47r: 'Discriminalia . . . aerre' (Is. III.20).

'Murenulas catenas de auro et argento mirifice factas'; cf. Ld. xiii.10: 'Murenulas catenulas' *only* = Karlsruhe 99, 47r (Is. III.20).

'Olfatoriola uascula muliebria uel turibula modica de auro uel argento quibus odoromenta gestantur mulieres habent pro odore'; cf. Ld. xiii.9: 'Olfactoriola turibula modica de auro uel argento mulieres habent pro odore'; and Karlsruhe 99, 47r: 'Olfacturiole turibula . . . odore' (Is. III.20).

'Mutatoria uestimenta alia meliora et mundiora' = Ld. xiii.11; cf. Karlsruhe 99, 47r: 'Mutatoria . . . meliora' *only* (Is. III.22).

'Theristra subtilissima curtina'; cf. Ld. xiii.12: 'Teristra subtilissima curtina'; and Karlsruhe 99, 47r: 'Terestra subtilissima curtina' (Is. III.23: 'theristra').

'Fascia pectoralis uestis que circa pectus uoluitur'; cf. Ld. xiii.13: 'Fascia pectoralis uestis circa pectus uoluitur'; and Karlsruhe 99, 47r: 'Fascia pectoralis uest [*sic*] circa pectus uoluitur' (Is. III.24: 'fascia pectorali').

'Lambruscas malas uuas' = Ld. xiii.14 = Karlsruhe 99, 47r (Is. V.2: 'labruscas').

'Decem iugata uinearum decem iugera uel diurnales'; cf. Ld. xiii.15: 'Decem iugera uinearum .x. iugeres uel diurnales'; and Karlsruhe 99, 47r: 'Decem . . . uel iurnales' (Is. V.10: 'decem enim iuga uinearum').

'Tarbeel proprium nomen uiri'; cf. Ld. xiii.16: 'Tarbehel . . . uiri' = Karlsruhe 99, 47r (Is. VII.6: 'Tarbeel').

'Parum paruum' = Ld. xiii.17 = Karlsruhe 99, 48r (Is. VII.13).

'Sarculum ferrum fossorium duos dentes habens'; cf. Ld. xiii.18: 'Sarculum ferrum fossorium habens duos dentes' = Karlsruhe 99, 47r (Is. VII.25: 'sarculo').

'Sarientur fodientur' = Ld. xiii.19; cf. Karlsruhe 99, 47r: 'Sarcientur fodientur' (Is. VII.25: 'sarientur').

'Carcamis nomen loci uel ciuitatis' = Ld. xiii.21 = Karlsruhe 99, 47r (Is. X.9: 'Charchamis').

Calanon similiter'; cf. Ld. xiii.22: 'Calanan similiter'; and Karlsruhe 99, 47r: 'Calcanan similiter' (Is. X.9: 'Chalanno').

'Inniti confisi confidentes' = Ld. xiii.20; cf. Karlsruhe 99, 47r: 'Inniti confidentes' *only* (Is. X.20).

'Ganniret cum ira quasi rideret'; cf. Ld. xiii. 23: 'Ganniret quasi cum ira inrideret' = Karlsruhe 99, 47r (Is. X.14).

'Gabaa ciuitas saulis' = Ld. xii.26 (Is. X.29).

'Pilosi incubi monstri'; cf. Ld. xiii.24: 'Pilosi incubi monstri idest **menae**'; *and Karlsruhe 99, 47r: 'Pilosi incubi monstri* **miere**' (Is. XIII.21).

[85rb-va] 'Syrene mulieres marine que per maicas incantant'; cf. Ld. xiii.28: 'Sirene mulieres marine' *only* (Is. XIII.22: 'sirenae').

[85va] 'De radice colubri egredietur regulus qui manducat aues idest aucellas uel basiliscus secundum historiam dicitur de colubre nasci'; cf. Ld. xiii.25: 'De radice colubri nascitur regulus qui manducat aucellas idest basiliscus . . . nasci'; and Karlsruhe 99, 47r: 'De colubri nascitur . . . aucellas' *only* (Is. XIV.29: 'de radice enim colubri egredietur regulus et semen eius absorbens uolucrem').

'In triuiis in tribus uiis' = Ld. xiii.30 (Is. XV.3).

'Papiri unde faciunt cartas' = Ld. xiii.31 (Is. XVIII.2: 'papyri').

'Flaccentia contracta' = Ld. xiii.27 = Karlsruhe 99, 47r (Is. XIX.10).

'Riui aggerum congregatio aquarum' = Ld. xiii.32 = Karlsruhe 99, 47r (Is. XIX.6).

'Bige equitum idest due rote duorum exercitus'; cf. Ld. xiii.33: 'Bige equitum duorum exercitum'; and Karlsruhe 99, 47r: 'Bige aequitum duorum exercituum' (Is. XXI.9: 'bigae equitum').

'Vitiam pisas agrestes'; cf. Ld. xiii.35: 'Uiciam pisas agrestes idest **fugles beane**' = Karlsruhe 99, 47r (Is. XXVIII.25: 'uiciam').

'In sertis Serra dicitur lignum habens dentes multas qa [*sic*] boues trahunt'; cf. Ld. xiii.36: 'In serris . . . habens multas dentes quod boues trahent'; and Karlsruhe 99, 47r: 'Serris . . . trahunt' (Is. XXVIII.27: 'in serris').

'Malus nauis capud in arbore nauis ad similitudinem milui que uela sustinet et dictus malus ad similitudinem mali'; cf. Ld. xiii.37: 'Malus nauis caput in arbore nauis a similitudine milui' *only* = Karlsruhe 99, 47r (Is. XXX.17).

'Argum angustum' = Ld. xiii.38 = Karlsruhe 99, 47r (Is. XXX.20).

'Migma et mixtum idem est' = Ld. xiii.39; cf. Karlsruhe 99, 47r: 'Migma et conmixtum idem sunt' (Is. XXX.24: 'commixtum migma').

'Perpendiculum dicitur de plumbo modica petra quam ligant in filo quando edificant parietes'; cf. Ld. xiii.40: 'Perpendiculum modica petra de plumbo qua licant . . . parietes **pundar**'; and Karlsruhe 99, 47r: 'perpendiculum . . . quod ligant quando edificant parietes pondus' (Is. XXIV.11).

'Paliurus herba que crescit in tecto domus grandia folia habens'; cf. Ld. xiii.41: 'Paliurus erba . . . tectis domorum grossa folia habens **fullae**'; and Karlsruhe 99, 47r: 'paliurus . . . **fulie**' (Is. XXXIV.13).

'Onocentaurus asino mixtum monstrum epocentaurus equo'; cf. Ld. xiii.42: 'Epocentaurus equo Onocentaurus asino mixtum moster'; and Karlsruhe 99, 47r: 'Onocentaurus asino mixtum monster' *only* (Is. XXXIV.14: 'onocentauris').

'Lamia dea silue dicitur habens pedes similes caballi caput et manus et totum corpus pulchre mulieris Et uiderunt multi ut quidam dicunt aliqui manserunt cum ea'; cf. Ld. xiii.43: 'Lamia ... manus totum corpus ... multi aliqui manserunt cum ea'; and Karlsruhe 99, 47r: 'Lamia ... caput manus ex totum corpus pulchrum simile mulieris' *only* (Is. XXXIV.14).

'Fouit cubat idest calefaciendo producit'; cf. Ld. xiii.44: 'Fouit cubat calefaciendo' *only* = Karlsruhe 99, 47r (Is. XXXIV.15).

'Cataplasmarent contritos imponerent'; cf. Ld. xiii.46: 'Cataplasmarent ... inponerent' = Karlsruhe 99, 47r (Is. XXXVIII.21).

'Apothecas cellaria'; cf. Ld. xiii.45: 'Apotecas cellaria' = Karlsruhe 99, 47r (Is. XXXIX.2: 'apothecas').

'Plaustrum in similitudine arce habens rotas intus et ipse dentes habent qui rostra serrantia dicuntur in quibus frangent spinas'; cf. Ld. xiii.47: 'Plaustrum in similitudinem arce rotas habens intus ... habent quasi rostra dicitur ... spicas' = Karlsruhe 99, 47r (Is. XLI.15).

'Mirtus modica arbor boni odoris semperque uiride'; cf. Ld. xiii.48: 'Myrtus modicus ... semper uiride'; and Karlsruhe 99, 47r: 'Myrtus modicus arboni odoris semper uiride' (Is. XLI.19: 'myrtum').

'Plastes figulus' = Ld. xiii.49; cf. Karlsruhe 99, 47r: 'plastes figuli' (Is. XLI.25).

'Calamum pigmentum de arbore'; cf. Ld. xiii.51: 'Calamum pigmentum ex arbore' = Karlsruhe 99, 47r (Is. XLIII.24).

'Bel et nabo ydola sunt'; cf. Ld. xiii.54: 'Del et hnabot' *only*; and Karlsruhe 99, 47r: 'Del et hnaboth idola' *only* (Is. XLVI.1: 'Bel ... Nabo').

'Uellentibus tollentibus pilos de genis' = Ld. xiii.56 (Is. L.6: 'genas meas uellentibus').

'Runcina bidugio'; cf. Ld. xiii.50: 'Runtina pidugio **uitubil**' (Is. XLIV.13: 'runcina').

'Circino ferrum duplex unde pictores faciunt circulos'; cf. Ld. xiii.53: 'Circino ... circulos idest **gaborind**'; and Karlsruhe 99, 47r: 'Circino ... **gabolrind**' (Is. XLIV.13).

[85vab] 'Samis argillum unde faciunt testa'; cf. Karlsruhe 99, 47r: 'Samis ... testas idest **thore**'[67] (Is. XLIV.5: 'testa de samiis terrae').

[85vb] 'Adcola et accola idem sunt'; cf. Ld. xiii.55: 'Adcola et acola idem sunt'; and Karlsruhe 99, 47r: 'Adcola et accola idem sunt' (Is. XLIV.15).

'Salincula herba est medicinalis habens spinas miri odoris crescit in montibus'; cf. Ld. xiii.57: 'Saliuncula erba medicinalis ... montibus'; and Karlsruhe 99, 47v: 'Saliuncula erba est medicinalis ... montibus' (Is. LV.13: 'saliuncula').

'Dromedarii castrati cameli dromedarius unus'; cf. Ld. xiii.60: 'Dromedarie ... unus' (Is. LX.6: 'dromedariae').

'Muricem soricem'; cf. Ld. xiii.61: 'Murem soricem' (Is. LXVI.17: 'murem').

'In lecticis ad similitudinem lecti dicuntur feretri in quibus portantur filie

---

[67] Primitive OE *þohæ, 'clay'; cf. Ep/ErfI A8: 'Argillus thohae/thoe', and Pheifer, *Old English Glosses*, pp. lxxxii-lxxxiii and 59.

nobilium super .iiii. equos cooperti desuper curtina sicut curri; Lectica uehiculum est quod trahitur a mulis siue equis'; cf. Ld. xiii.58: 'In lecticis a similitudine lecti dicuntur' and xiii.59: 'Feretri ... .iiii. equis coopertis desuper cortina sicut currus'; and Karlsruhe 99, 47v: 'In ... dicuntur; Feretri ... currus' (Is. LXVI.20).

Milan I lacks entries corresponding to Ld. xiii.5 ('Commolitus exterminatus'), 8 ('Periscelidas armillas de tibiis'), 29 ('Mede nomen loci'), 34 ('Telam orditus **inuuerpan uuep**') and 52 ('Lima qua limatur ferrum **fiil**'); it adds *tinctura*, the correct interpretation of *vermiculus* (Is. I.18) to Ld. xiii.3 and *Samis ... testa*, to which Karlsruhe 99 appends an Old English interpretation, after Ld. xiii.53. Both these Milan I additions are found in the Cambridge Isaiah glosses, which also exclude vernacular interpretations and agree with Milan I against Leiden and Karlsruhe 99 in the entries corresponding to Ld. xiii.3, 10, 13 and 23. On the other hand, Cambridge agrees with Karlsruhe 99 against Leiden and Milan I in the entries corresponding to Ld. xiii.11, 25, 33, 39 and 43, and Karlsruhe 99 combines the Cambridge and Leiden interpretations of *periscelidas* in 47r ('Priscelidas armillas de tibia aut arg[ento]').

Milan I glosses often clarify anomalies in the other glossaries, for example, the entry 'Culine fornacula in quibus faciunt focum ad coquendum' (86rb), to Ex. XLVI.23, supplies the headword missing from Ld. xv.28: 'Fornacula' (cf. Cam. 44vb, 'Fornacula in quibus faciunt focum ad coquendum' and Ld. xv.42). Milan I, like Cambridge, has Latin interpretations corresponding to vernacular ones in Leiden (cf. 83rb 'Lapides onichinos gemma admirabilis' and Ld. vii. 4, 'Lapides onichinos **dunne**'). It also has the references to Theodore and Hadrian in the gloss on IV Reg. XVIII.16–17, in which they apparently disagreed on the interpretation of *ualuas*: Hadrian defined them as *muros in circuitu templi*, while Theodore is said to have identified them with the *aque ductus idest ipse fistule per quas aqua ducitur* referred to in the next verse.[68] Milan I (84rb) likewise has the reference to Hadrian in the Canticles gloss (not found in Leiden), namely 'Stipite stringite Adrianus dicit idest remissionem peccatorum per baptismum' (Cant. II.5),[69] showing that the Milan I glosses added to Leiden vii-xxv and xxix also derive from the school of Canterbury. The only

---

[68] Ptd and discussed *Biblical Commentaries*, ed. Bischoff and Lapidge, p. 178; see also Steinmeyer and Sievers, *Die althochdeutschen Glossen* V, 276.

[69] *Ibid.*, p. 177; also found in Grimm 132, 2, fol. 1.

Cambridge gloss with a different interpretation from the corresponding entry in Leiden – apart from vernacular ones – namely 'Commissuras idest iuncturas' (Cam. 43vb; cf. Ld. vii.3: 'Commissuras ligaturas uel composituras', on I Par. XXII.3) agrees with Milan I (83rb), 'Commissuras iuncturas'.

Cambridge has three other Milan I entries not found in Leiden chs. vii-xxv or xxix.[70] Paris I, however, has fourteen, nine of them in the section headed 'VERBA OBSCVRATA TRACTA HIERONIMI', that is, from Jerome's Commentary on Matthew, a section which corresponds to Leiden ch. xxix ('INCIPIT VERBORVM INTERPRETATIO'):[71]

[53vb] 'Mungitur emulgetur'; cf. Milan I (83vb): 'Emungitur emulgitur' (Prov. XXX.33: 'emungit').

[55va] 'Famelicus paciendo famem dicitur'; cf. Milan I (87ra): 'Famelicus a paciendo famem dicitur' (Job V.5).

[55vb] 'Per crepidinem per ascensum' = Milan I (87rb) (Judith VII.3).

[56ra] 'Fornorum nomen proprium idest genitiues'; cf. Milan I (88ra): 'Fornorum Alias edicit thanuorim nomen ... gentiles' (II Esdr. III.11: 'turrim furnorum').

'Elogium testimonium'; cf. Milan I (88ra): 'Elogium testimonium' (*In Matth.* XXVI.19: 'eloquia').[72]

'Veneunt uenduntur' = Milan I (88ra) (*In Matth.* X.29).

'Ephenditen scapulare' = Milan I (88rb) (*In Matth.* XIV.28: 'ependite').

'Commentariensis artifex lapidum'; cf. Milan I (88rb): 'Cementarius artifex lapidum' (*In Matth.* XXI.42: 'caementarios').

'In loculis in bursis'; cf. Milan I (88rb) 'In ... bursis' (*In Matth.* XVII.27).

'Silogismum ineuitabilis uel conclusio'; cf. Milan I (88rb): 'Silogimum ineuitabile uel conclusio'[73] (*In Matth.* XII.33: 'syllogismo quem Graeci uocant ἄφυκτον nos ineuitabilem possumus appellare').

'Cenos inanes uel uaculus'; cf. Milan I (88rb): 'Cenos ... uacuus' (*In Matth.* V.22: 'id est inanis aut uaculus').

---

70 These are: Cam. (44ra): 'COELETH idest Ecclesiasten grece contionatorem latine' and 'Syrasirim Cantica canticorum' (Prol. in lib. Sal. 11–12), which correspond to section headings in Milan I (83rb), 'In libro Syrasirim idest cantica canticorum' and (83vb) 'In libro qui ebraice dicitur coeleth Grece ecclesiasten uel concionator hoc est multitudinis allocutor'; and Cam. (44va): 'Samis Argilla unde faciunt testas'; cf. Milan I (85vab): 'Samis argillum ... testas'.

71 See above, p. 282 and n. 5.   72 Quoting Ps. XI.7: 'eloquia domini eloquia casta'.

73 Cf. Ep/ErfI S32, 'Syllogismus conclusio', in a miscellaneous group before a Bible batch, and Cp S713, 'Syllogismus conclusio ineuitabile', which corresponds to it in position.

'Apocinu excommunicationis'; cf. Milan I (88rb): 'Apocynu excommunicationis' (LXX Lam. I.7: ἀπωσμῶν).[74]

'Ausisin crescentem'; cf. Milan I (88va): 'Auxisin crescentem' (*In Matth.* XI.19: αὔξησιν).

[56rb] 'Pugillaris tabula que in pugillo **rung**'; cf. Milan I (88rb) 'Pugillarem tabule que in pugillo continentur' (Luke I.63: 'pugillarem').

Only one of these Milan I entries is found in Karlsruhe 99 (48v: 'Foruor proprium nomen' *only*).

The most striking feature of the relationship between Cambridge, Paris, Milan and Leiden is its complexity, which must go back to a very early stage in the history of the Canterbury Bible glosses, for the three series of Milan Pentateuch glosses share a number of common entries and the Milan Canticles glosses in their present form are associated with other components of the Leiden-family glossaries in the mid-eighth-century Grimm Fragments. Since Milan I, II and III each include entries corresponding to the other two and the Reichenau Leviticus–Deuteronomy sections combine their stock of Milan II glosses with further entries corresponding to Milan III, and since Cambridge and Paris follow a similar pattern in their Pentateuch sections and thereafter adhere now to Milan, now to Leiden when the latter differ, it therefore seems clear that they too represent an independent branch of the tradition. Whether or not the missing Genesis–Kings section of the Leiden Bible glosses ever existed must remain an open question. The closely related Chronicles–New Testament glosses in Karlsruhe 99 show that their common ancestor circulated independently in the eighth century, and the fact that the common ancestor of Leiden, Cambridge, Paris and Karlsruhe 99, unlike that of Fulda and other members of the Reichenau group, apparently did not include entries corresponding to the second Milan Joshua-New Testa-

---

[74] Not found in Jerome's *Comm. in Matth.* Lam. I.7 may have been quoted in a scholion on Jerome, commenting on Matth. XXIII.37, where Jerusalem is also personified: 'Hierusalem (non saxa et aedificia ciuitatis sed habitatores uocat) quam patris plangit affectu' (CCSL 77, 221); cf. Origen, *In Lamentationes Hieremiae*, ἡ Ἰερουσαλήμ τουτέστιν οἱ κατοικοῦντες αὐτήν (*Origenes Werke III: Jeremiahomilien, Klageliederkommentar, Erklärung der Samuel- und Königsbücher*, ed. E. Klostermann, GCS 6, 243). Hurst and Adriaen's edition of Jerome shows that Origen's commentary on Matthew was used by Jerome, while his commentary on Lamentations was quoted by Maximus the Confessor (GCS 6, xxxvii-xxxix), so it was presumably available to Theodore. On the possible use of Origen in the Canterbury biblical commentaries, see Bischoff and Lapidge, *Biblical Commentaries*, pp. 219–20.

ment series isolates them to some degree from the mainstream tradition of the Milan/Reichenau Bible glosses.

THE 'ORIGINAL ENGLISH COLLECTION' AND THE EPINAL/ERFURT GLOSSARY

The question therefore arises whether the second Milan gloss from Joshua onward and the corresponding Reichenau glosses really belonged to the 'original English collection' associated with the school of Theodore and Hadrian. Some evidence that they did is afforded by the only contemporary witness to its curriculum, namely the Epinal/Erfurt I Glossary (Ep/ErfI), the older manuscript of which (Epinal, Bibliothèque municipale, 72 (2)) has been dated by Malcolm Parkes to the end of the seventh century.[75] Epinal/Erfurt I is an alphabetical glossary compiled from various sources that include 'batches' of entries corresponding, sometimes very closely, to Leiden and the Grimm Fragments.[76] Indeed one series of batches contains a heterogeneous collection of 135 Bible glosses (interspersed with other material),[77] thirty-two of which have counterparts in Milan and/or Fulda:

[A45] 'Anudus quartana die quarta'; cf. Milan II (116rb): 'Anudus quartana die Alia editio a quarta die usque in hanc horam' (Act. X.10: 'a nudius quartana die usque in hanc horam').

[A174] 'Agiographa sancta scriptura'; cf. Milan I (86rb): 'Agiographa sancta scripta'; Milan II (111vb): 'Agiographa sancta scriptura'; and Fulda (95v): 'Aiographa sancta scriptura' (Dan. Prol. 46: 'Agiographa').

[A176] 'Abra ancilla' = Milan I (87rb); cf. Fulda (85r): 'Abram ancillam' (Judith X.2: 'abram'; X.10: 'abra').

---

[75] In *The Epinal, Erfurt, Werden and Corpus Glossaries*, ed. Bischoff *et al.*, p. 16; this dating is consistent with the archaic orthography of the Old English interpretations (Pheifer, *Old English Glosses*, pp. lvii–xci, esp. lxxxix–xc). The origin of the Epinal manuscript is unknown, but its early date makes a continental origin unlikely.

[76] Cf. Pheifer, 'Early Anglo-Saxon Glossaries', pp. 19–26. The batches and their significance were pointed out by W. M. Lindsay, *The Corpus, Epinal, Erfurt and Leyden Glossaries* (London, 1921), pp. 1–43.

[77] Cf. Lindsay, *ibid.*, pp. 14–15, and Pheifer, *Old English Glosses*, pp. xlix–li. Lindsay's 'Bible batches' (*ibid.*, pp. 32–5) contain 184 entries in all, to which should be added Ep/ErfI N38 ('Nardus arbor'), a gloss on Jerome *Comm. in Matth.* also found in Ld. xxix.34 which immediately precedes his N-batch.

[C316] 'Colaphus pugnus'; cf. Milan II (114va): 'Colaphis pugnis' (Matth. XXVI.67: 'colaphis').

[E19] 'Emissarii ministri'; cf. Milan I (82ra): 'Emissariis idest nuntiis uel regis ministris a mittendo' (I Reg. XXII.17: 'emissariis').

[E20] 'Effeminati molles'; cf. Milan II (96rb): 'Effeminati molles id sordidi uel osceni' (III Reg. XIV.24).

[F63] 'Falcatis curribus armatis'; cf. Fulda (47r): 'Falcatis currunt idest ornatis cum ferro'[78] (Judg. I.19: 'falcatis curribus').

[F64] 'Flaccentia contracta' = Milan I (85va) = Fulda (90r) (Is. XIX.10).

[H47] 'Herodius **uualhhebuc**'; cf. Fulda (43r): 'Herodion forma fulice similis sed maior idest capiet quasi falcho quod dicitur **uualuhchabuhc**'[79] (Lev. XI.19: 'erodionem').

[I10] 'Idioma proprietas' = Milan I (87ra); cf. Milan II (105va): 'Idioma proprietas sermonis'; and Fulda (79v): 'Idioma proprietas sermonum' (Job Prol. 28).

[I63] 'In triuiis in tribus uiis' = Milan I (85va) (Is. XV.3).

[N38] 'Nardus arbor'; cf. Milan I (88rb): 'Nardum arbor' (Jerome, *In Matth.* XXVI.7: 'nardum').[80]

[N39] 'Napta genus fomenti idest **tyndir**'; cf. Milan I (86va): 'Napta genus fomitis' *only*; Milan II (112ra): 'Napta genus fomitis apud persas quo uel maxime nutriantur incendia Alii ossa oliuarum que proitiuntur cum amurca arefacta napta appellari putant'; and Fulda (97r): 'Napta genus fomitis aput persas quo ... proiciuntur ... naptam appellari putant'[81] (Dan. III.46: 'naptha').

[P145] 'Pinnaculum quicquid preminet' = Milan I (89ra) (Matth. IV.5).

[P146] 'Per crepidinem per ascensum' = Milan I (89ra) (Judith VII.3).

[P147] 'Polenta farina subtilis'; cf. Fulda 85ra 'Polenta subtilis farina'[82] (Judith X.5: 'pulenta').

[P150] 'Praeteriola domuncula micina in naue'; cf. Milan I (86rb): 'Preteriola

---

[78] Cf. the 'Abolita Glossary' (Vatican City, Biblioteca Apostolica Vaticana, lat. 3321; ptd *Glossaria Latina*, ed. W. M. Lindsay *et al.*, 5 vols. (Paris, 1926–31) III, 97–183): AP5 'Aplustria ornamenta [*v.l.* armamenta] navis'.

[79] Cf. Milan II (76va): 'Herodion forma fulice similis sed maior' *only*.

[80] Citing Mark XIV.3 ('alabastrum unguenti nardi spicati pretiosi'; cf. Ld. xxix.34 ('nardum arbor') and Milan II (90va): 'Nardi spicati Nardus est arbor cuius est fructus ut lauri bac Et in caldarium mittitur et coquitur usque ad pinguedinem et cocleario desuper tollitur oleum Deinde commiscitur cum oleo supradicte arboris et inde odorem sumit et fit unguentus plusquam .iii. centis denariis.'

[81] Jerome, *Commentarii in Danielem* I (ed. F. Glorie, CCSL 75A, 805): 'Et Sallustius scribit in Historiis [= frag. 61] quod "napta" sit genus fomitis apud Persas quo uel maxime nutriantur incendia; alii "ossa oliuarum" quae proiciuntur cum amurca arefacta, "naptam" appellare putant.'

[82] Cf. Milan I (82ra): 'Polenta subtilis farina' (I Reg. XVII.17).

... naue unius cubiti in quibus abscondunt cybos suos' (Ezech. XXVI.6: 'praetoriola').

[P153] 'Panis collyri panis quadrangulus'; cf. Milan I (82rb): 'Colirida panis modicus triangulus' (II Reg. VI.19: 'collyridam panis').[83]

[P174] 'Pistilia capitella'; cf. Milan II (96ra): 'Pistilia capitella que super columnas ponuntur et est grecum' = Fulda (57v)[84] (III Reg. VII.6: 'epistylia').

[P254] 'Plumario in similitudine plumae'; cf. Milan III (74va): 'Plumario ... plume facto'; and Fulda (42v): 'Plumario ... plum factum' (Ex. XXVI.1).

[R19] 'Rithmus dulcis sermo'; cf. Milan I (87ra): 'Rithmus dulcis sermo sine pedibus' (Job Prol. 30: 'rithmus ipse dulcis').

[R23] 'Repticius demoniosus'; cf. Milan I (86ra): 'Arepticium demoniosum' (Jer. XXIX.26: 'arrepticium').

[R28] 'Rinoceres unicornis';[85] cf. Fulda (83rv): 'Rinocerus unicornis et est indomite omnino nature ita ut si quando captus fuerit teneri nullatenus possit inpaciens quippe ut fertur illico moritur' (Job. XXXIX.9: 'rinoceros').

[S12] 'Spatulas rami a spati similitudine'; cf. Milan I (76rb): 'Spatulas fructus palme dicitur pro similitudine spade'; and Fulda (44r): 'Spatulas fructus palme antequam aperiantur idest ni similitudinem spade inde spatula dicitur' (Lev. XXIII.40: 'spatulasque palmarum et ramos ligni').

[S15] 'Serotinum tardentium'; cf. Milan II (116vb): 'Serotinum tardum' = Fulda (105r) (Jas. V.7).

[S19] 'Sarculum ferrum id **uueadhoc**'; cf. Milan I (85rb): 'Sarculum ferrum fossorium habens duos dentes'; and Fulda (89v): 'Sarculum ferrum fossorium' *only* (Is. VII.25: 'sarculo').

[S184] 'Saraballa apud caldeos crura hominum dicuntur'; cf. Milan I (86va): 'Saraballa ... hominum uocantur'; Milan II (112ra): 'Pro bracis aquila et theodotion sarabaeta dixerunt Lingua autem caldeorum sarabara cura hominum

---

[83] Cf. Milan II (76rb): 'Colliridas cibus quem nos nebulam dicimus; Collirida modicus panis triangulus quem nos nebulam uocamus' (Lev. VII.12). The discrepancy between Ep/ErfI P153 'quadrangulus' and Milan I (82rb) 'triangulus', neither of which is attested outside the circle of these glossaries, may be due to scribal confusion of '.iii.' and '.iiii.'.

[84] Isidore, *Etym.* XV.viii.15: 'Epistolia sunt quae super capitella columnarum ponuntur; et est Graecum' (the same definition is repeated at XIX.x.24); cf. Ld. i.49: 'Epistilia grece quae super capitella columnarum ponuntur'; Milan I (83vb): 'Epistilia capita columnarum' (glossing III Reg. VII.6); and Cam. (43vb): 'Epystilia columnarum'.

[85] Cf. Milan I (87ra): 'Rinocerus bestia que in nares cornua habet. Monoceros unicornis'; Ld. xix.31–2: 'Rinocerus naricornu in nare namque cornu habet, Monoceros unicornis'; and Jerome, *Commentarii in librum Iob* xxxix (PL 26, 619–902, at 770): 'Ex diversa editione transferentium advertimus, quod ipsum sit rhinocerus quod et monoceros, et Latine intellegatur unicornis, sive super nares cornu habens.'

uocantur et tibie quasi crurales et tibiales appellate sunt';[86] and Fulda (96r):
'Pro theodicio sarabillas sarabilla crura cruralis sunt' (Dan. III.21: 'bracis' and
94: 'sarabara' [*v.l.* 'sarabal(l)a']).

[S185]   'Sandalia calciamenta quae non habent desuper corium' = Milan I (87rb)
(Judith X.3).

[S226]   'Sparatistes defensor'; cf. Milan I (60rb): 'Yperaspistis idest defensor'
(Prol. in Pent. 27: ὑπερασπιστής).

[U26]   'Urido urens uentus'; cf. Fulda (40v) 'Vridine uento urente'; and Milan I
(64va): 'Vridine idest flaru uenti urentis Vrio enim uentus dicitur grece quia
supra modum siccat omne quod tangit' (Gen. XLI.6: 'uredine').

[U90]   'Uehemoth animal'; cf. Milan II (107rb): 'Beemoth ex hebrea uoce in
latina lingua animal sonat [Isidore, *Etym.* VIII.xi.27] et quadrupedia ostendi-
tur Et significat hostem antiquum idest diabolum'; and Fulda (83v): 'Veemoth
... quadrupes ... diabolum' (Job. XL.10: 'Behemoth').

[U92]   'Uiri cordati bono corde' = Milan I (87ra) (Job XXXIV.10).

The Epinal/Erfurt I Bible batches, in addition to glosses common to Milan
and/or Fulda which have counterparts in Leiden, Cambridge or Paris,[87]
also contain glosses (mostly with vernacular interpretations) common to
Leiden, Cambridge and/or Paris not found in Milan or Fulda:

[A320]   'Carectum **hreod**' = Ld. xix.16 (Job VIII.11).

---

86   Jerome, *Commentarii in Danielem* I (CCSL 77, 802–3): 'Pro "bracis", quas Symmachus
ἀναξυρίδας interpretatus est, Aquila et Theodotio "saraballa" dixerunt, et non ut
corrupte legitur "sarabara"; lingua autem Chaldaeorum "saraballa" crura hominum
uocantur et tibiae, et ὁμωνύμως etiam "bracae" eorum, quibus crura teguntur et tibiae,
quasi "crurales" et "tibiales" appellatae sunt.'
87   Cf. Ep/ErfI A174 = Ld. xvi.23: 'Agiografa sancta scriptura' and Cam. (44vb):
'Agiographa idest sancta scriptura'; Ep/ErfI A 176 = Ld. xxi.6 = Paris I (55vb): 'Abra
ancilla'; Ep/ErfI E29 = Paris I (52vb): 'Amissariis nuntiis uel ministris A mittendo';
Ep/ErfI F64 = Ld. xiii.27 = Cam. (44va): 'Flaccentia contracta' and Paris I (65va):
'Placentia contracta grecum'; Ep/ErfI H 47 = Paris I (50va): 'Herodianum **uualuchæ-
fuc**'; Ep/ErfI I10 = Ld. xix.7: 'Idioma proprietas' and Cam. (44vb): 'Idioma Proprietas
uniuscuiusque lingue'; Ep/ErfI I63 = Ld. xiii.30: 'In triuiis in tribus uiis'; Ep/ErfI N38
= Ld. xxix.34 = Paris I (56rb): 'Nardum arbor'; Ep/ErfI N39 = Ld. xvi.10: 'Nappa
genus fomitis'; Ep/ErfI P146 = Paris I (55vb): 'Per crepidinem per ascensum'; Ep/ErfI
P147 = Ld. xxi.15: 'Polenta farina subtilissima'; Ep/ErfI P150 = Ld. xv.11 = Cam.
(44vb): 'Preteriola domuncula micina in naue unius cubiti in quibus abscondunt cibos
suos'; Ep/ErfI P 153 = Cam. (43va): 'Collirida Panis modicus triangulus'; Ep/ErfI P254
= Cam. (42rb): 'Plumario in similitudinem plumis factum'; Ep/ErfI R19 = Ld. xix.10:
'Ridhmus dulcis sermo sine pedibus'; Ep/ErfI R23 = Ld. xiv.17: 'Arreptitium demoni-
osum' and Cam. (44va) 'Arrepticium demoniosum'; Ep/ErfI S12 = Paris I (50vb):
'Spatule habent similitudinem spade inde spadule dicuntur'; Ep/ErfI S19 = Ld. xiii.18:
'Sarculum ferrum fossorium duos dentes habens'; Ep/ErfI S184 = Ld. xvi.11: 'Saraballa

[A322]   'Canti **felge**'; cf. Paris I (53va): 'canti ferrum circa rotas, Camites quoque cant dicunt, Canis **felgunt**'[88] (III Reg. VII.33).

[A323]   'Circinno **gabelrend**'; cf. Ld. xiii.53: 'Circino ferrum duplex unde pictores faciunt circulos idest **gaborind**';[89] and Paris I (54vb): 'Circino ferrum duplex **gabilrunt**' (Is. XLIV.13: 'circino').

[F65]   'Fagalidori manducantes'; cf. Cam. (44vb): 'Fagolydoros hoc est manducans senecias' (Ezech. Prol. 15: φαγολοίδοροι glossed 'hoc est manducantes [*v.l.* manducans] senecias').

[H47]   'Herodius **uualchefuc**'; cf. Ld. xix.35: 'Herodion **ualchefuc**'; and Paris I (55va): 'Erodion **uualeauuc**' (Lev. XI.19: 'erodionem').

[L117]   'Laris **meu**'; cf. Paris I (50va): 'Larum **meu**' (Lev. XI.16: 'larum').

[L121]   'Lappa **cliþae**'; cf. Ld. xv.36: 'Lappa **clite**' and xviii.2: 'Lappa **clate**' (Osee IX.6).

[M45]   'Modioli **nabae**'; cf. Paris I (53va): 'Modioli **nap**' (III Reg. VII.33).

[S44]   'Sternutatio **fnora**'; cf. Ld. xix.65: 'Sternutatio **nor**'; and Paris I (55va): 'Sternutio **nere**' (Job XLI.9: 'sternutatio').

[S183]   'Simila farina subtilis'; cf. Cam. (41vb): 'Simila subtilissima farina' (Gen. XVIII.6: 'similae').

Scanty though they are, the Epinal/Erfurt I Bible batches suggest that the whole spectrum of Milan-Fulda and Leiden-Cambridge-Paris glosses was available to their compiler in the late seventh century. This does not mean, of course, that every single item in those glossaries emanated from Theodore and Hadrian's immediate circle: in the Milan Glossary and its derivatives, as in other medieval *scholia*, scholarly annotation rubs shoulders with elementary or otiose comments, the sources of which may be impossible to identify. Yet the variety of these collections and their complex interrelations are an impressive testimony to the intense educational activity that took place in early Anglo-Saxon England and its outposts abroad.

crura hominum uocant apud caldeos' and Cam. (44vb): 'Saraballa Crura hominum chaldaice uocantur'; Ep/ErfI S185 = Ld. xivi 10: 'Sandalia calciamenta que non habent desuper corium'; Ep/ErfI U26 = Cam. (42va): 'Vredo ueiituo urens et flans'; Ep/ErfI U92 = Paris I (55va): 'Viri recordati bono corde'.

88   For the Latin interpretations, cf. Milan I (82vb): 'Canti conti ferrum circa rotas. Camites quoque canti dicuntur. Camis lignum sine ferro quod cantum dicitur'; Fulda (38r): 'Canti ferrum circa rotas. Camis lignum sine ferro quod cantum dicitur'; Cam. (43vb): 'Canti Ferrum circa rotas et simul ferrum et camites canti dicuntur; Camis lignum sine ferro que cantum dicitur'; and Cp C92: 'Canti ferrum circa rotas' and C135: 'Canti **faelge**'. On the Corpus Glossary (Cp), see above, nn. 14 and 57. See also above, p. 322.

89   For the Latin interpretations, cf. Milan I (85va): 'Circino ferrum duplex unde pictores faciunt circulos' *only*.

Index

Acacian schism, 89
Acca, bishop of Hexham, 103–4
Adam (OT), 213
Adomnán of Iona, 145, 160–1; *see also Canones Adamnani*
Ælberht, archbishop of York, 104
Ælfflæd, abbess of Whitby, 27
Æthelred, king of Mercia, 27
Æthilwald (poet), 105, 264
Aetius of Amida, 15
Afra, St, 185n
Africa, North, 50, 67, 68, 72, 77, 85, 91; church of, 124
Agatho, pope (678–81), 23, 24, 27, 65, 79n, 85, 89, 92–3, 94–5, 128–9, 212
ages of the world, 212–13
Agilbert, bishop of Winchester and Paris, 228
Albinus, abbot in Canterbury, 183n, 207
Alcuin, 104, 277; revision of Vulgate, 242, 243n, 245, 246, 247, 248; penitential handbook of, 277
Aldfrith, king of Northumbria, 27
Aldhelm, 17, 18, 26, 105, 162, 207, 209, 210, 211, 264; *Carmen rhythmicum* of, 263–4, 273; *De virginitate* of, 183, 185, 187, 278; and the *Passio SS Victoriae et Anatholiae*, 183–91
Aldred of Chester-le-Street, 220
Alexander of Tralles, 15
Alexandria, 13, 14, 16, 17, 90; philosophical school of, 15–16, 18, 46, 55, 58–60, 268
Alexandrine biblical exegesis, 4, 31; *see also* Origen
Alexius, St, 42
Ambrose, St, 185; Latin hymns of, 261–2
Ammianus Marcellinus, 4
Ammonius of Alexandria, 46
Amphilochius, bishop of *Iconium* (Konya), 158
Anacreon (Greek poet), 265–6

anacreontic verse, 24, 29, 61–2, 64, 265–74
Ananias of Shirak, 59, 66
Anastasia, St, 185n
Anastasius II, pope (496–8), 131, 138
Anastasius (Magundat), St, 14, 20, 42, 175–7, 185n, 218; cult of, at Constantinople, 180, 181; cult of, at Rome, 175, 177–81, 218, 219; Greek *acta* of, 175, 176–7, 180, 181n, 182, 192–9; *see also Passio S. Anastasii*
Anastasius Sinaita, 60, 91n
Anatholia, St, 185n, 186–7
Ancyra, Council of (314), 127n, 134n, 136, 144, 145, 146n, 172
Andrew, St, of Tarsus (Cilician martyr), 229
Annals of Tigernach, 147n
Annals of Ulster, 146
Annegray, 211n
Antioch-on-the-Orontes (Antakya), 3–4, 6, 7, 13, 41n, 60, 205, 223, 230, 231n; patriarchate of, 3, 6, 91, 94, 231n, 233; Persian conquest of, 8; Arab conquest of, 10
Antioch, Council of (341), 135
Antiochene biblical exegesis, 4, 5, 6, 8, 31, 34, 46, 51, 127n, 205, 208, 293; in *Laterculus Malalianus*, 214–15, 221
Antony, St, 39
Aphrahat, 32
Apostolic Constitutions, 121
Arabic, translations of Greek philosophical writings into, 45
Arator, *Historia apostolica* of, 99n, 104n, 111
Aratus Latinus, 197
Aristotle, study of, 16, 18, 43–4, 46, 47n, 48, 49, 59–60
Arles, 83, 123; 'Second Council' of, 123
Armagh, 160, 161
Armenia, 176; schools of, 59

Index

Armenian, translations of Greek writings into, 224

Arno, archbishop of Salzburg, 277

astrology, 16, 17, 18

astronomy, 14, 16, 17, 18, 48, 59

Athanasius, 38; cult of, 229

Athanasius II, patriarch of Balad, 45, 46

Athens, 54, 55, 58, 230

Athos, Mount, liturgy of, 232

Augustine of Canterbury, 88, 96, 97; liturgical practices of, 222n

Augustine of Hippo, 88, 94, 113, 117, 208n, 209, 216

Babai the Great, 51n

Babylas, St, of Antioch, 230

Bardaisan, 32

Barnabas, 229

Basil of Caesarea, 38, 121, 136n, 152, 155, 158–9, 161, 162–4, 165, 169, 170, 215n, 230, 253

Bede, 52, 66, 89, 92–3, 96, 100, 103, 105, 120–1, 124, 129, 205, 207, 212, 215, 220n; *Historia abbatum* of, 107, 182n; *Historia ecclesiastica* of, 1, 18, 19, 88, 182, 203, 207; and the Canterbury school, 18, 203, 207, 208; and the council of Hatfield, 88–9, 125; and the council of Hertford, 125–6; and the life of Archbishop Theodore, 1, 19, 20, 25, 26, 27, 29, 120–1, 203; *Passio S. Anastasii* of, 20, 182, 202, 219, 221; *Chronica Maiora* of, 179n, 203, 210n; *Comm. in Proverbia* of, 109–10; *Martyrologium* of, 185, 186, 223, 224, 225, 228–30

Beirut, 13

Benedict II, pope (684–5), 79

Benedict, St, of Nursia, 222; *Regula* of, 284–5

Benedict Biscop, 89, 99, 103, 104, 107–10, 129, 182n, 183, 207, 209, 245

Bertila, abbess of Chelles, 105

Bible, 28, 214, 236–59, 281–333; Hebrew (Massoretic) text of, 254; Latin Vulgate text of, 5, 202, 215–17, 220, 236, 237, 238, 239, 240, 242, 246, 255; *Vetus Latina* version of, 216, 217, 252–3, 255; *see also* Peshitta; Septuagint; Syrohexapla
Old Testament: Pentateuch, 236–54, 283, 287, 298–9, 300, 320, 322, 328; Genesis, 18, 35, 236, 237, 238, 239, 241, 244, 245, 246, 247, 248, 249, 250, 251, 252, 253, 254, 288, 299, 300, 302–4, 318–20, 332, 333; Exodus, 9, 202n, 216, 236, 238, 239, 241, 246, 247, 248, 249, 250, 251, 288, 289,

290–3, 294, 300, 302–4, 310, 311, 320, 331; Leviticus, 236n, 238, 244, 245, 247, 248, 251, 288, 289, 290, 298, 300, 305–7, 310, 311, 320, 330, 331, 333; Numbers, 7, 236n, 237, 238, 239, 244, 248, 249, 288, 289, 300, 307–10, 311, 312–13, 317, 320, 321; Deuteronomy, 236n, 238, 244, 250, 288, 289, 300, 307–10, 311, 314–15, 317, 320, 321; Joshua, 288, 289, 316–17, 321–2; Judges, 240, 288, 289, 290, 322, 330; Ruth, 240, 241, 288, 289, 290; Kings, 241, 288, 289, 290, 299, 322, 330, 331, 333; Paralipomenon (Chronicles), 282, 285, 286, 288, 289, 322, 327; Ezra, 288; Esther, 288, 289, 290; Job, 240, 285, 286, 288, 330, 331, 332, 333; Psalms, 216, 282, 315; Proverbs, 288; Ecclesiastes, 241, 288; Song of Songs, 35, 287, 288, 326, 328; Wisdom, 288, 289; Ecclesiasticus, 281, 283–4; Jeremiah, 288, 289, 331; Ezechiel, 285, 288, 293, 294, 331, 333; Daniel, 288, 329, 330, 331–2; Minor Prophets, 285, 288, 294, 300, 333; Maccabees, 282, 289, 315
New Testament: gospels, 255–9; Matthew, 255, 256, 257, 328, 330; Mark, 178, 256, 257, 288; Luke, 202n, 256, 257; John, 13, 256; Acts, 329

Biblical exegesis: *see* Alexandrine biblical exegesis; Antiochene biblical exegesis

Bili, *Vita S. Machuti* of, 225

Bobbio, 184, 211n

Boethius, 94n; as translator of Aristotle, 45

Boniface, St, 116, 210n

Book of the Cave of Treasures, 8

Bordeaux, 83

Breviarium Alarici, 116

Brittany, 144, 145, 146, 209

Cædwalla, king of Wessex, 209

Caelestius, 211n

Caelius Sedulius, *Carmen paschale* of, 104n, 111, 190n, 209, 215, 216, 261

Caesarea (Palestine), 176, 177, 179

Caesarius of Arles, 167

'Calendar of St Willibrord', 223, 227, 228, 230

Canones Adamnani, 144–6, 160

Canones apostolorum, 126, 127n

Canterbury, school of, 1, 17–19, 26, 28–9, 67, 100, 105, 183, 185, 191, 203, 206, 235, 237, 250, 252, 253; biblical glosses from, 281–333; monastery of SS Peter and Paul (St Augustine's) at, 207, 212, 228

Index

Index

Hertford, synod of (673), 26, 28, 120, 125–8, 136, 159
Hild, abbess of Whitby, 210n
Hippo Diarrhytus, 50
Hippocrates, 15, 16, 18, 19
Hippolytus, 37, 214
Hiridanum (monastery near Naples), 54
Historia monachorum, 39
Honorius I, pope (625–38), 75, 79, 80, 91, 94n
Honorius, archbishop of Canterbury, 97, 100
Honorius Augustodunensis, 110
Hormisdas, pope (514–23), 132
horoscopy, 16, 17, 18
Hrabanus Maurus, 143n, 224, 306n
Hunayn ibn Ishaq, 44
Hwætberht (Eusebius) of Monkwearmouth-Jarrow, 250
Hygeburg of Heidenheim, 277

Ignatius of Antioch, 37
India, 4, 48, 50n
Innocent I, pope (402–17), 138
Iona, 102, 142n, 146, 160, 161–2
Ireland, 28, 52, 102, 143, 144, 145, 146, 160, 161, 167, 168, 209, 211; Irish scholarship, 205, 210; Irish script, 102, 206; Irish missionaries in Northumbria, 99, 102; Irish students at Canterbury, 100, 206; Irish *peregrini* on the Continent, 143, 206, 210–11; influence of Theodore's penitential in, 147; Hiberno-Latin hymns of, 262–3
Irenaeus, 37, 214
Isaac of Nineveh, 47, 230
Isaiah, Abba, 40, 48
Isidore, 130n, 131, 133–4, 135, 206, 275, 305n, 309n, 318, 319n
Israel the Grammarian, 233
Iudicia Theodori: *see Capitula Dacheriana*

Jacob Baradaeus, 30
Jacob Intercisus, St, 42
Jacob of Edessa, 7, 35–6, 37, 40n, 44, 49, 50n, 52
Jacob of Serugh, 32, 41, 214
Jacobites (Syrian Orthodox), 30–1, 32, 34, 38, 45, 47, 50, 230
Jarrow: *see* Monkwearmouth-Jarrow
Jeremiah (OT prophet), cult of, 229
Jerome, 40, 48, 115, 220, 236, 242, 251, 258, 282, 283, 286, 300–2, 320; *Comm. in Matthaeum* of, 282, 288, 289, 315–16, 327–8, 329, 330
Jerusalem, 9, 10, 20, 21, 61, 176, 177, 178,

180, 181, 213, 232, 238, 240; relic of 'True Cross' at, 176; conquest of, by Arabs, 268
John, precentor of St Peter's, Rome, 89, 93, 105, 128–9
John the Almoner, St, 42n, 268–9
John the Baptist, St, 42; feast of Invention of the Head of, 229
John Chrysostom, 4, 5, 38, 208, 214, 215, 230
John Damascene, 60
John Lydus, 56
John Malalas, 4, 6; *Chronographia* of, 6, 14, 29, 200, 204, 205, 206, 212–13
John Moschus, 16, 17, 60–1, 62, 66, 85, 268, 270
John Philoponus, 58, 59
John Scholasticus, 127n, 152n
John Scottus Eriugena, 307n
John of Antioch, 6
John of Gaza, 62, 268, 273
John the Syrian, 197, 220–1
Josephus, Flavius, 208, 215, 311n, 318n
Julian, patriarch of Qenneshrin, 45–6
Junilius, *Instituta regularia* of, 46–7
jurisprudence, study of, 14, 15, 17
Justin Martyr, 37
Justinian, emperor (527–65), 3, 11, 31n, 55, 71, 89, 203n, 268; *Corpus iuris ciuilis* of, 17

Kirkuk (*Bethsaloe*), Iraq, site of martyrdom of St Anastasius, 176

Lateran Council (649), 21–3, 25, 68, 80, 85, 88, 89, 91, 128–9, 178; *acta* of, 64–5, 88n, 128, 179n, 218
Laterculus Malalianus, 29, 183, 193n, 194n, 201, 202, 203, 204–21; contents of, 212–14; Bible-text of, 216–18
law, canon, 26, 28, 49, 120–40
law, Roman civil, 17, 136
Leo I, pope (440–61), 89, 126, 138, 139, 206
Leontius of Neapolis, 42
Libanius, 4
Liber pontificalis, 68, 78, 79, 94n, 179n
litany of the saints, 233
liturgy, 28, 49, 82, 222–35; Byzantine liturgy, 231–2; Georgian liturgy, 232; Antiochene rite, 231n; Neapolitan rite, 107, 226–8; Roman rite, 232; liturgical music, 233–5; *see also*: litany of the saints; sacramentaries
Livy, *Histories* of, 111, 112, 117
Lombards, 69, 71, 78, 92, 179

338

Index

340

Index

Index